PUBLIC PRAYER
and the
CONSTITUTION

PUBLIC PRAYER

and the

CONSTITUTION

A Case Study in Constitutional Interpretation

By RODNEY K. SMITH

SR *Scholarly Resources Inc.*
Wilmington, Delaware

The paper used in this publication meets the minimum requirements of the American National Standard for permanence of paper for printed library materials, Z39.48, 1984.

Portions of Chapters 2 through 6 of the book first appeared in article form in 20 *Wake Forest Law Review* 569 (1984) and portions of Chapters 9 and 12 appeared in article form in 37 *Alabama Law Review* 345 (1985). They are published in this book with the permission of those publications.

Scholarly Resources Inc.
104 Greenhill Avenue
Wilmington, Delaware 19805

Library of Congress Cataloging-in-Publication Data

Smith, Rodney K.
    Public prayer and the Constitution.

    Includes index.
    1. Prayer in the public schools—Law and legislation—United States.
I. Title
KF4162.S63 1987   344.73'0796   86-28020
ISBN 0-8420-2260-0   347.304796

To my father and mother,
Willis and GeorgiAna Smith

Contents

Acknowledgments

While in law school one of my professors, Jim Sabine, shared a bit of wisdom with me that I have remembered always. He taught that, at the beginning of each day, we should reflect upon something new for which we are grateful. I have tried to follow that advice, thinking each day about something new that has blessed my life. In writing a book, one incurs new debts of gratitude on almost a daily basis. In this brief acknowledgment, I would like to thank those who have helped and supported me in this endeavor.

I am particularly grateful to my wife Danielle whose unfailing support has been a great blessing in my life and has been a source of constant encouragement. I am also grateful to Professor Carl S. Hawkins at the J. Reuben Clark Law School of Brigham Young University, for the help and support he offered in making my dream of one day becoming a teacher a reality. Similarly, my gratitude is extended to Judge Arlin Adams of the Third Circuit Court of Appeals. In his First Amendment course at the University of Pennsylvania, Judge Adams literally taught me to love the First Amendment. Additionally, I would like to thank my colleagues, Marcia O'Kelly, Tom Lockney, and Robert Lipkin, whose friendship and support has been appreciated greatly. Finally, as a general matter, I would like to thank my students who have always been a source of inspiration to me.

On a more specific note, I would like to thank Dean W. Jeremy Davis of the University of North Dakota Law School and Dean Anthony J. Santoro of the Delaware Law School of Widener University for their friendship, encouragement, and financial support. I am also indebted to my research assistants. While at the University of North Dakota, I was assigned a number of Burtness Fellows, who helped with various aspects of this project. In particular, I would like to thank David Probst, Reagan Pufall, Dale Hanke, Laura Wetsch, Juli Point, Dennis Tighe, Scott Corbett, and Scott Jensen. While I have taught at the Delaware Law School, Glenn Blackwell has helped put the refining touches on the manuscript and also provided extensive assistance in preparing the index.

I would like to thank especially my secretaries for their support. Susan St. Aubyn and Jane Clement were particularly helpful while I served on the faculty at North Dakota, and Bernice Mullins has served ever so ably in that same capacity at the Delaware Law School. I would also like to thank Philip Johnson at Scholarly Resources Inc. for his friendship and support. He has taken a genuine interest in the book and has offered many helpful suggestions.

Of course, the problem with any set of acknowledgments is that it simply cannot be comprehensive enough. Those who may have been omitted inadvertently from these pages know how absentminded I can be, and I trust they will forgive me for my oversight.

Finally, I am grateful for my faith that has helped to remind me of the great importance of religious liberty in our contemporary world. While I willingly accept responsibility for all the errors that may appear in this book, I nevertheless acknowledge the inspiration I have felt, from so many worthy sources, during the writing of it.

Introduction

As the title indicates, this is a book about public prayer and the Constitution. However, I believe that it is more than just another book about a hot constitutional issue. It is a book about how the principles embodied in our Constitution, a document about to enjoy its bicentennial, remain viable in resolving difficult contemporary issues—issues related to matters of individual conscience in a world characterized by an ever-expanding public sector. This is not just a book about how best to resolve the public-prayer issues that have vexed the courts for the better part of a generation; it is also a book about constitutional interpretation. With their recent debate, Attorney General Edwin Meese III, who believes that the original intent of the framers can be discovered and applied to resolve constitutional issues, and Justice William Brennan, who finds the Meese view to be nothing more than arrogance cloaked as humility and who believes that original-intent analysis is unworkable, have given the public a taste of a controversy that has troubled legal commentators for the past decade. Commentators have disagreed over the role and relevance of historical data relating to the framing and ratification of the Constitution in resolving contemporary constitutional issues.

In this book, I apply the pertinent history and, in doing so, refute, at least in some measure, the objection that original-intent analysis is unhelpful in resolving twentieth-century public-prayer issues. However, I also differ with Attorney General Meese to some degree, because I am convinced that the history is often incomplete and, when carefully examined, yields only general principles and not specific solutions. Additionally, I believe that Mr. Meese has, on occasion, either misread or misapplied the historical data in his effort to support a certain ideological position. This, therefore, is directed to two separate but related controversies: the controversy over substantive public-prayer issues and the controversy over how the Constitution should be interpreted.

Almost daily we are harangued by pundits from the Left and from the Right who are engaged continually in arguments related to the proper role of religion and morality in contemporary society and who display little or no tolerance for the views of those who disagree with their political agenda or who are considered to be anathema to their religious dogma. In this volatile setting, issues related to the right of conscience will be raised and decided under the aegis of the First Amendment. The First Amendment cannot dispose of differences in doctrine and ideology, but it must serve to establish the ground rules for public discourse and religious exercise.

Four decades ago, Justice Robert Jackson referred to the First Amendment as the "fixed star in our constitutional constellation." I heartily agree. The religion clauses of the First Amendment provide that "Congress shall make no law respecting an establishment of religion or prohibiting the free exercise thereof." Among my aspirations for this book is my hope that it will serve as a reminder that these sixteen words deserve more than an idle, perfunctory gaze; they deserve study. They are also worthy, I believe, of a certain reverential awe—awe of the sort displayed by one of my professors in law school when he closed the final meeting of a First Amendment seminar by simply and tearfully expressing his appreciation for the ideas embodied by those sixteen words. That moment stands out to this day as the high point in my legal education.

The Establishment Clause is contained in the phrase, "Congress shall make no law respecting an establishment of religion...," and the Free Exercise Clause is set forth in the following phrase, "[Congress shall make no law]...prohibiting the free exercise thereof." These seemingly straightforward clauses have been the source of considerable confusion and controversy during the past forty years. The Supreme Court and commentators continue to wrestle with the pressing religious-liberty issues of our day, but, if anything, the confusion and controversy seem to have expanded with little hope for abatement.

This confusion is generally attributable to an apparent conflict between the purposes of the Establishment and Free Exercise clauses. A doctrinaire reading of either clause would seem to render the other clause ineffectual. For example, if one reads the Establishment Clause as providing for a strict separation of church and state, there is no room for the free exercise of one's religion in an increasingly pervasive public sector. On the other hand, if one reads the Free Exercise Clause as being paramount, the strictures of the Establishment Clause often seem to be rendered meaningless. Nowhere is this conflict more evident than in the case of public prayer and religious exercise. If the Establishment Clause mandates a strict separation of church and state, as some believe, individuals must be prohibited from exercising freely their religion in a public place. Conversely, if there is no limit to the right of free exercise, the threat of religious dominance by the majority or the powerful would hardly be idle.

James Madison, who is considered generally to be the author of the First Amendment, recognized the potential for conflict when he noted that "it may not be easy, in every possible case, to trace the line of separation, between the rights of the religious and the civil authority, with such distinctness, as to avoid all collisions and doubts on unessential points."[1] Madison, nevertheless, was conscientious in his desire to dispel the confusion and to confirm that it only created "doubt on *unessential* points." This book demonstrates that Madison succeeded and that we can still enjoy the fruits of his success.

Today, members of the Supreme Court have recognized repeatedly the perplexing nature of the apparent Free Exercise/Establishment conflict. Even Justice Hugo L. Black, the author of the Court's majority opinion in *Everson v. Board of Education,*[2] the first Supreme Court opinion of the twentieth century dealing expressly with the Establishment Clause, and *Engel v. Vitale,*[3] the first prayer decision of the Supreme Court, recognized that "these two [religion] clauses may in certain instances overlap."[4] In the summer of 1985, in *Wallace v. Jaffree,*[5] a case dealing with Alabama's meditation-or-voluntary-prayer statute, Justice Sandra D. O'Connor acknowledged the conflict when she stated that:

> On the one hand, a rigid application of the *Lemon* test [the test that the Court has developed to deal with Establishment issues but which has recently been seriously questioned as a dispositive standard] would invalidate legislation exempting religious observers from generally applicable government obligations. By definition, such legislation has a religious purpose and effect in promoting the free exercise of religion. On the other hand, judicial deference to all legislation that purports to facilitate the free exercise of religion would completely vitiate the Establishment Clause.[6]

It is clear that this apparent conflict is reflected in the issues raised in the public-prayer cases. May school districts permit students to recite voluntarily a prayer composed by state personnel or do such activities violate the Establishment Clause? May a state permit its school personnel to provide for a moment of silent meditation, or prayer, in the public classroom? Must a school district permit students desirous of forming a

---

1. From Madison's letter in 1833 to the Rev. Jasper Adams, then president of the College of Charleston, as cited in Koch, MADISON'S ADVICE TO MY COUNTRY, at 43 (1966).
2. 330 U.S. 1 (1947).
3. 370 U.S. 421 (1962).
4. *Id.* at 430 (1962).
5. Wallace v. Jaffree, 105 S. Ct. 2479 (1985).
6. *Id.* at 2504 (Justice O'Connor concurring).

student religious club the same rights that the school affords to other student organizations of a secular nature? May state legislatures and other governmental entities hire chaplains or otherwise permit prayers to be offered at public gatherings? These and other difficult issues cut to the very core of the seeming conflict between the purposes of the Establishment and Free Exercise clauses.

Given the tenor of these disputes, and the public sentiment they seem to engender, it is imperative, in the words of Justice O'Connor, that the Court's "goal should be to frame a principle for constitutional adjudication that is not only grounded in the history and language of the First Amendment, but one that is also capable of consistent application to the relevant problems."[7]

I have come to the conclusion that a close look at the applicable constitutional history has a liberating effect, freeing the Court from the confusion engendered by the apparent conflict between the Establishment and Free Exercise clauses. It is my position that the history performs two functions: (1) it provides the Court with viable and just principles capable of resolving difficult cases and has the effect of extricating the Court from the apparent conflict between the Establishment and Free Exercise clauses; and (2) since these principles are based on the intent of the framers and ratifiers of the First Amendment, they carry a legitimacy that the Court has not been able to muster in support of its prior decisions in the church-and-state area.

Furthermore, I will show how the Court has, in effect, maintained a sort of instinctive fidelity to the framers' intentions. In the process, I will also explain how the Court can uphold Nebraska's practice of permitting the legislature to pay a chaplain, while refusing to permit New York to compose a prayer for voluntary recitation by students in its public schools. These and other similar issues have confounded commentators, who have bemoaned the Court's inconsistency. Just as the history offers solace in face of the apparent conflict between the purposes of the Establishment and Free Exercise clauses, it also offers a principled explanation for the Court's decisions, which heretofore seem to have been based more on intuition than on principled insight.

Admittedly, this book is presumptuous in its purported ends. It must be conceded that if it succeeds in even a minor degree in achieving its ends, its importance cannot be gainsaid.

However, while as the author my aspirations for the book are significant, I must emphasize two points. First, I trust that the reader will not confuse my auspicious aims of the book with arrogance on the part

---

7. *Id.* at 2497.

of the author. I will confess that were James Madison's or even Justice Joseph Story's ideas my own, I would have substantial cause for arrogance. However, they are not my ideas; I have merely taken this occasion to collate and apply them to the prayer issue. Second, I hope that in some small measure the reader will be struck by the relevance of the historical ideas presented in this book and that she will, therefore, become more conscious of the role of the framers in the development of contemporary constitutional law. In a related sense, I trust that the reader will be more apt to revel a bit in the upcoming bicentennials of the Constitution, in 1987, and the Bill of Rights, in 1991, for having read this book.

CHAPTER

1

The Originalist Approach:
Some Comments on Methodology

Currently in legal circles there is a debate raging over the issue of what constitutes legitimate constitutional decision making. The debate has recently occupied many pages in the best law reviews and, in all likelihood, will continue to do so. In the words of Prof. Michael Perry, the debate "seems interminable."[1] Therefore, it would no doubt be foolish for me to presume to dispose of the controversy in a single, short chapter in this book. Nevertheless, since my analytical approach is based on an originalist theory, one of the schools engaged in the controversy, a few comments are in order before I commence my analysis of the history and the cases.

Essentially, the disputants divide into two camps, although it must be acknowledged that there are many differing positions on each side of the debate. For the purposes of this chapter, I will ignore the divergence of opinion within the two camps and will concentrate on the core views held by each side.

---

1. Professor Perry notes that, "It is not surprising that debate in constitutional theory seems interminable. As I have explained, any argument for or against a particular conception of judicial note—any such conception, including the originalist one—is, in the nature of things, contingent, speculative, and provisional, and therefore revisable. That is why reasonable people (among others) have disagreed and will continue to disagree about the problem of judicial role." Perry, *The Authority of Text, Tradition and Reason: A Theory of Constitutional Interpretation,* 58 So. CAL. L. REV. 551, 588–89 (1985), hereinafter cited as "Perry."

1

Those who hold to the interpretivist or originalist viewpoint maintain that in exercising judicial review, judges must refer to the text of the Constitution and to the intent of the framers and ratifiers of the provision or provisions at issue in a given case. Interpretivists or originalists rely on the authors' original intent to give a constitutional provision its legal meaning or force. On the other hand, the noninterpretivists or nonoriginalists in varying degrees refuse to accept the proposition that the contemporary judiciary is bound by the original understanding of the framers and ratifiers of a given constitutional provision. The proponents of nonoriginalist review typically seek to legitimate judicial activity by a means other than examining the framers' and ratifiers' intended meaning.

In this book, I apply the originalist or interpretivist mode of analysis, because I am convinced that it is preferable to the nonoriginalist viewpoint and because I am convinced that it is mandated by the Constitution itself.[2] As to the second point, that the interpretivist mode is

---

2. In an intriguing recent article Prof. H. Jefferson Powell has asserted that while it is "commonly assumed that the 'interpretive intention' of the Constitution's framers was that the Constitution would be construed in accordance with what future interpreters could gather of the framers' own purposes, expectations, and intentions. Inquiry shows that assumption to be incorrect." Powell, *The Original Understanding of Original Intent*, 98 HARV. L. REV. 885, 948 (1985). He added that the term intentions used by the framers "referred to the 'intentions' of the sovereign parties to the constitutional compact, as evidenced in the Constitution's language and discerned through structural methods of interpretation; it did not refer to the personal intentions of the framers or of anyone else." *Id.* In part, Professor Powell is correct; the framers certainly did intend that the focus would be on the language and structure of the Constitution and the meaning attributed to that language by the people in their ratification conventions. However, public as opposed to private statements by the framers in support of the Constitution and explaining the meaning attributable to its provisions and the structure of government created thereby are certainly sound evidence of what the people in all likelihood believed the language to mean, absent evidence to the contrary. Powell may be correct in his assertion that the framers may have intended that the Court would use methods of construction other than or supplementary to originalism. However, he is clearly incorrect in my view in asserting that the intention of the framers and their views were to be disregarded and, moreover, that originalist methodology, as we know it today, is of later origin.

While I am presently preparing a lengthy paper responding to Professor Powell's article, and challenging his thesis that early judicial interpretation did not focus on original intent, at this juncture it will suffice to cite a few cases supporting my position that originalist analysis was used from the inception of our constitutional government, both at the federal and the state levels. *See e.g.,* Stuart v. Laird, 5 U.S. (Cranch) 298 (1803), in which counsel for the petitioner in error relied on a contemporaneous exposition of the Constitution based on references to *The Federalist* and on contemporaneous statements made by Mad-

mandated by the Constitution, I acknowledge that such an argument is in a sense tautological. Such an argument relies on the the history or the meaning attributed by the framers and and ratifiers of the Constitution to the role of the judiciary to establish the historical or originalist approach

---

ison, Nicholas, and Marshall at the time of the ratification of the Constitution. In Stuart, the Court noted that "it is sufficient to observe, that the practice [of permitting Supreme Court justices to sit in the capacity of circuit judges], and acquiescence under it, for a period of several years, commencing with the organization of the judicial system, affords an irresistible answer, and has indeed fixed the construction. It is a contemporary interpretation of the most forcible nature." *Id.* at 308; Terrett v. Taylor, 13 U.S. 43 (1815), in which Justice Story wrote the opinion of the Court rejecting the Virginia legislature's interpretation of its state constitution, and stressing, "Whatever weight such a declaration might properly have, as the opinion of wise and learned men, as a declaration of what the law has been or is, it can have no decisive authority. It is, however, encountered by the opinion successively given by former legislatures, from the earliest existence of the Constitution itself, which were composed of men of the very first rank for talents and learning. And this opinion, too, is not only a contemporaneous exposition of the Constitution, but has the additional weight, that it was promulgated or acquiesced in by a great majority, if not the whole, of the very framers of the Constitution." *Id.* at 50.; Martin v. Hunter's Lessee, 14 U.S. 304 (1816), in which the Court opined that "it is plain that the framers of the Constitution did contemplate that cases within the judicial cognizance of the United States, not only might, but would, arise in the state courts, in the exercise of their ordinary jurisdiction." *Id.* at 339.; and, Dartmouth College v. Woodward, 17 U.S. 518 (1819), in which Chief Justice Marshall, in writing for the Court, noted that "The general correctness of these observations cannot be controverted. That the framers of the Constitution did not intend to retrain [sic] the states in the regulation of their civil institutions adopted for internal government, and that the instrument they have given us, is not to be so construed, may be admitted." *Id.* at 629. Similarly, state courts engaged in originalist analysis from the beginning in construing their state constitutions. *See e.g.,* Stoddart v. Smith, 5 Pa. (Binney) 354 (1812), in which the court stated that it could not help supposing that "light might be thrown on [the constitutional issue involved in the case] by the testimony of persons who have not yet been examined, persons who assisted in framing the constitution of Maryland, and know the construction put upon it, and the practice of the legislature from the beginning." *Id.* at 364; and, Kamper v. Hawkins, 1 Va. Cas. 20, 24 (1792), in which the Court discussed the significance of a written constitution as a limitation on legislative action and in which it emphasized, "A constitution is that by which the powers of government are limited. It is to the governors, or rather to the departments of government, what a law is to individuals—nay, it is not only a rule of action to the branches of government, but it is that from which their existence flows, and by which the powers, (or portions of the right to govern) which may have been committed to them are prescribed—it is their commission—nay, it is their creator. The calling this instrument the constitution or form of government, shews that the framers intended it to have this effect."

as applied to other issues. In other words, one uses the originalist approach in evaluating the historical data to conclude that the intended and, therefore, legitimate judicial role is itself originalist. In this sense, espousal of the originalist view becomes an act of faith. I would also concede that originalist analysis has certain inherent limitations. It must be understood that to utilize the originalist mode of analysis is not to claim that such analysis yields "perfection or certainty."[3] As Prof. G. Edward White noted in a recent article, interpreting history is somewhat more than indulging in ideological speculation[4] and somewhat less than objective reconstruction of true historical fact.[5] The inherent limitations in historical analysis, however, do not render the examination of historical data worthless. Rather, to recognize that there are inherent limits on such historical analyses compels one to admit that the same data base

---

3. Professor Maltz has noted that, "interpretive theory demands neither perfection nor certainty—any more than certainty is a prerequisite for reliance on perceived legislative intent in cases of statutory interpretation." Maltz, *Some New Thoughts on an Old Problem—The Role of the Intent of the Framers in Constitutional Theory,* 63 B.U. L. REV. 811, 813 (1983). In a related sense, it is often impossible to glean the intent of the parties with regard to the meaning of a provision in a contract, but courts do not use this practical limitation in the usefulness of history as a justification for ignoring evidence indicative of that intent. If it is viable in contract law, it certainly is no less viable in constitutional law.

4. As to history being more than mere ideological speculation, Professor White concluded that

However one defines the function of a historian, it is not synonymous with the function of an ideologue. Even if one rejects the criteria for "successful" historical scholarship that I have set forth in this Essay, I suspect that one would have to substitute criteria that sharply distinguish the art of historical interpretation and the art of ideological oratory.

White, *Truth and Interpretation in Legal History,* 79 MICH. L. REV. 594, 614 (1981).

5. *Id.* Professor White places some reliance upon the detachment of the truth-in-history approach, but he also acknowledges that "'current common sense' determines the success of historical interpretations." *Id.* at 613–14. Professor White acknowledges that such moderation in his approach to legal history renders his approach vulnerable to attack from the ideologue as well as the historical purist. However, he asserts that to recognize limits to the historical approach, while simultaneously noting the impact of the views of the historian on the record itself, does not condemn the approach. Such candid recognition of the limitations on any historical exegesis are, I believe, more indicative of a sincere desire to understand the actual "relationship between truth and interpretation in history."

may yield differing, albeit often equally legitimate, interpretations, while nevertheless demanding that "the judge make her best effort to divine the framers' intent and then apply that intent in the case before her as accurately and faithfully as possible."[6]

Examining the history rarely, if ever, yields clear-cut answers. Rather, it provides one with parameters within which legitimate judicial decision making should take place. It relieves some of the anxiety that necessarily accompanies the rendering of a decision by giving the court a more objective basis upon which to decide, while simultaneously necessitating that the court wrestle with what is left, the historical limits within which a legitimate decision can fall but within which differing directions and emphases are commonly disclosed.

Historical or intent analysis serves as an appropriate beginning for constitutional decision making, but it rarely serves as a panacea, or as a substitute for additional analysis. Prof. William Van Alstyne states that:

> Ordinary judicial conscientiousness in respect to interpretations of our Constitution cuts both ways. It certainly does mean that the boundaries are to be respected, but there is no reason to take this as counsel of despair. The words of the Constitution are instructive. They do impose constraints, equally upon courts as upon other agencies of the government. Yet one's own reading ought not to be close-minded nor premature. History, moreover, is germane in a more confining way. Quite frequently, what it yields is heavily dependent upon the premises of its users—which may be far too narrow or wizened, rather than too wishful. More often than one might suppose, one may be surprised that what was first thought doubtful in respect to the manner in which a given clause or combination of clauses might be applicable to a particular case, is not such a puzzle after all. One may be surprised that an imperfect, brief, and aged document, even absent those amendments one thinks would significantly improve it, can still speak usefully to our condition, without need to strain its provisions; yet I think it still does.[7]

Constitutional interpretation, with its reliance on the language of the document and the contemporaneous history of its framing, adoption, ratification, and application, is at once confining, as a matter of degree, and often flexible in terms of potential outcomes within those confines.

---

6. Maltz, *supra* note 3, at 813.

7. Van Alstyne, *Interpreting This Constitution: The Unhelpful Contributions of Special Theories of Judicial Review*, 35 U. FLA. L. REV. 209, 234 (1983).

Furthermore, the framers and ratifiers of the Constitution often used open-textured language to embody broad principles, principles that rarely are self-executing and that, therefore, are themselves subject to some interpretive license. Of course, the breadth of the interpretive limits, and the principles delineating those limits, provide the Court with expansive discretion. As such, an important issue of constitutional interpretation remains: How is the Court to exercise the broad discretion that often results as a matter of originalist analysis? In this regard, for example, it can be argued that the Court should simply defer to the decisions of Congress and the executive so long as those decisions by the other more democratic branches of the government fall within the principled limits provided by originalist review, or it might be argued that the Court should be free to hold acts by Congress or the executive unconstitutional even if those acts fall within the parameters provided by originalist review. If the Court takes the latter course, giving itself the final say within the applicable confines, it would seem to need to justify its doing so on some theoretical or principled basis. Thus originalist review leaves open many methodological as well as substantive issues; often it provides little more than the legitimate, analytical starting point.

This is certainly true in the case of interpreting the religious clauses of the First Amendment. A study of the intent of the framers in using the language that they included in the religion clauses of the First Amendment reveals that there are principled confines within which decisions should properly fall. It also reveals that there is substantial room for discretion within those limits, thereby potentially providing the Court with both the flexibility and the legitimacy it needs to resolve contemporary cases.

In many ways, my views are not too different than those held by many nonoriginalists, who acknowledge that there is some role in constitutional analysis for the normative values articulated by the framers and ratifiers. They generally are willing to admit that the original understanding of particular textual provisions is more than a self-protective formality in which an insecure Court indulges. The intent may not be dispositive, in their view, but it is often helpful.

Nevertheless, while my differences with nonoriginalists like Professor Perry are not extensive, they are of some significance. At a minimum, our differences are a matter of emphasis.[8] For me, where dispositive,

---

8. Specifically, Professor Perry, a nonoriginalist, has pointed out that
   Given the nonauthoritative status of the original (the ratifiers') understanding of particular textual provisions, is the Court's frequent reference to the original understanding merely a self-protective

originalist analysis is pre-eminent; for them, it is but a factor to be weighed in the balance with other equally significant factors such as precedent, tradition, access to the democratic process, contemporary conceptions of fundamental rights, or human dignity.

Nevertheless, I agree with Professor Perry and others when they assert that it is not enough for originalists to merely invoke the intent of the framers; they must also indicate why that intent is critical. I would point out that the historical data from which the intent of the framers and ratifiers can be deduced is significant even for the nonoriginalist in at least two senses: (1) the Court relies on and uses historical data in its decision making, although the extent of that reliance is itself open to dispute;[9] and more importantly (2) even if one disregards the independent force of the historical data, as a guide in discerning the intended meaning and appropriate application of the religion clauses, it must nevertheless be conceded that if such an historical or originalist analysis produces certain values or certain principles, then those values ought to be analyzed in terms of their contemporary utility. Perhaps, even some nonoriginalists would be willing to give presumptive weight to those principles, acknowledging that they should be controlling absent a persuasive argument to the contrary.

In this sense, it is a central thesis of this book that such an historical exegesis does yield the very treasure the Court and commentators have long been searching for in the context of the religion clauses, a viable and just means of reconciling the purposes or values of the Free Exercise and Establishment clauses. For the nonoriginalist who argues that originalist review is either no real option at all or that it will, at

---

formality?

Of course not. The ratifiers and their polity were participants in the tradition. The ways in which they shaped and responded to the aspirations of the tradition may very well shed light on how we should shape and respond to those aspirations. Why assume we have nothing to learn from our past? The Court is right to consult the ratifiers' normative judgments.

Perry, *supra* note 1, at 569.

9. As will be obvious as we look at the Court's opinions in the area of public prayer, the Court respectfully genuflects to the history. Nevertheless, it is not clear whether the Court examines the history to ascertain what the meaning or application of a provision should be (the appropriate use of history, in my view) or merely decides a case and then seeks to support that decision after the fact with historical evidence (this is inappropriate and has been labeled as "law office history" or, in Professor Perry's terms, it constitutes using history as a "self-protective formality"). I suspect that the use of history varies from justice to justice. It is unfortunate, if not unexpected, however, for those who find virtue in candor, that the justices who occasionally use history as a self-protective formality are not more honest in revealing their motives.

best, bear fruit in the form of antiquated values, values pertinent two hundred years ago but hardly helpful today, this work should be of substantial interest. It should be interesting because it purports to strike at both those propositions which are central to nonoriginalist theory. For my part, I assert that the values obtained in my originalist analysis, particularly those attributed to James Madison, are preferable to all contemporary substitutes in terms of their appeal and fairness.

Nevertheless, in support of my originalist analysis, I would argue that for judges to ignore the framers' and ratifiers' intentions, whether by flippantly casting aside constitutional history as irrelevant or outmoded,[10] or by substituting their own preferred meaning of a provision of the Constitution for that of its authors,[11] is to arrogate power that does not properly belong to the judicial branch. Such an assumption of policymaking authority in constitutional analysis places the judicial role in jeopardy. When the Court is enticed to ignore the intent of the framers

---

10. In its crassest form, this argument proceeds along the line that the intent of the framers is of little or no significance because it is founded in archaic thought that has little relevance in our modern society. Such a view is really little more than a guise to permit its proponents to substitute their views for the views of the framers. In a slightly more sophisticated form, the adherent of such a view argues that the society in which she now lives is so different from the milieu of the framers that to take the view of the framers as guidance, let alone as dispositive, in deciding contemporary issues would be foolhardy. Again, this is a thinly veiled justification that permits her to substitute her views for views with which she does not agree. In either event, dispensing with the historical record in such a flippant manner is born of an arrogance to history that at best disregards, without justification, that which may be of value in the historical record, and is at worst an invitation to have history repeat itself in a less than pleasant manner.

11. *See, e.g.,* Michael J. Perry, THE CONSTITUTION, THE COURTS, AND HUMAN RIGHTS (1982). Professor Perry argues that the judiciary should be activist in pursuing human rights. He defines a court as being activist "if, and to the extent that, it exercises noninterpretive review (supplanting policy choices made by electorally accountable governmental officials with policy choices of its own) and *passivist* if, and to the extent that, it confines itself to interpretive review (making no policy choices of its own, but simply safeguarding policy choices constitutionalized by the framers)." *Id.* at 7. Put simply, Perry feels that his and other enlightened contemporary views regarding human rights are more apt to vindicate individual rights than are the positions of the framers. In fact, he concludes his book by noting that

The lesson for us, then, is this: If in the past constitutional policy-making by the judiciary has been an essential matrix of human rights, in the future, as government's regulatory powers extend even more widely and deeply into the fabric of our society, it will certainly be no less essential. Noninterpretive review will surely be a crucial safeguard

and to substitute its own judgment for that intent, it risks being unmasked. If the electorate discovers that the Court is exercising essentially unbridled discretion, as judges effectively do under most wide-ranging theories of nonoriginalist view, the people might act, through their elected representatives, to cut back on the Court's power, leaving the Court powerless to act to secure liberties available under interpretivist legal analysis. Thus, many judicially secured liberties, liberties secured by originalist analysis, could be lost in a single act of public vengeance in response to the unmasking of the Court. As discussed in Chapter 12 of this book, one need look no further than recent efforts in Congress to limit the jurisdiction of the Court over prayer, busing, and other constitutional issues to see that this threat is genuine.[12]

Additionally, courts generally recognize that such historical analysis adds a sense of legitimacy or mystique to its decisions. Such legitimacy, which plays a significant ritualistic role in judicial decision making, is necessary to placate a sometimes restive public, even though some contemporary commentators, who effectively advocate *ex parte* amendment of the Constitution by the Judiciary, are reluctant to acknowledge this role for the history. Most members of the Court who are repeatedly placed in the agonizing position of having to decide, as opposed to simply discuss, difficult constitutional issues are inclined, at a minimum, to give a vote to the past by examining the pertinent history, in the form of intent analysis, and by weighing precedent in light of that intent.

Actually, some nonoriginalists have argued in a similar vein when they have asserted that *stare decisis,* the finding force of precedent or case law, has the effect of limiting or objectifying the power of the Court in exercising its jurisdiction. However, there are at least two reasons why

---

for the individual caught in the grip of the bureaucratic state—the individual intent on maintaining, or regaining, his or her autonomy. *Id.* at 165. One must wonder, however, what nonoriginalists will do when, like the impetuous Richard Rich in Robert Bolt's play, *A Man for All Seasons,* having apparently destroyed all vestiges of evil that stand between them and the devil of our constitutional play (the tyrannical majority), that majority turns its fury on them and their preferred rights.

12. *See, Oversight Hearings to Define the Scope of the Senate's Authority Under Article III of the Constitution to Regulate the Jurisdiction of the Federal Courts,* 97th Cong., 1st Sess. (1981). *See also, Washington Post,* September 24, 1982, at 1, for an article indicating how close Sen. Jesse Helms came in his effort to strip the federal courts of their jurisdiction on the prayer issue. In the crucial vote to break the filibuster, the supporters of the court-stripping legislation came within seven votes of the sixty votes necessary for cloture. A majority of the Senate supported their effort.

precedent alone, without reference to applicable history as to intent, is insufficient as a control on judicial review. First, and obviously, even though they are reluctant to do so, courts can disregard or overrule precedent. Second, precedent itself can become incoherent. In this regard, as courts extrapolate from one precedent to the next, logic is strained and the decision-making process becomes attenuated. Indeed, in analogizing from one opinion or precedent to the next, syllogisms break down and doctrines lose their coherence.[13] However, when one looks first to the principles derived from the history and then (but only then) to case law, intent analysis can minimize the nontransitivity problem to some extent by requiring that each successive decision conforms to the underlying principles derived from the originalist analysis. As such, originalist analysis, which demands conformity to the principles derived from an analysis of the pertinent history, serves to anchor the law and to minimize extensive drifting in the course of constitutional decision making.

With its power of judicial review, the Court in effect becomes the final arbiter of constitutional issues, but it also remains, by its very nature, essentially nondemocratic or antimajoritarian. Federal judges are appointed for life and are not subject to election, although they are subject to impeachment, a tool rarely used since the early nineteenth century. It is often argued, therefore, that by virtue of its nondemocratic status, the Judiciary ought to engage in self-restraint of the type minimally afforded by originalist review.[14]

---

13. Dean Bennett has voiced a similar argument against originalist review:
[O]riginalism falls victim to one or both of two features of analogical reasoning: the accommodation of nontrivial value judgments by analogizing, and the nontransitivity of the analogy relationship. Once those two features of analogical reasoning are acknowledged, originalist reference points can start an organic decisional process but can never dominate the course of its development unless that development is to lead nowhere at all. In a viable constitutional law, originalist reference points can act only as an ever-diminishing drag on decisions made under the impetus of a requirement in legal reasoning that (analogically) like cases be decided alike.
Bennett, *The Mission of Moral Reasoning in Constitutional Law,* 58 S. CAL. L. REV. 647, 649 (1985). *See also* Bennett, *Objectivity in Constitutional Law,* 132 U. PA. L. REV. 445 (1984). Dean Bennett offers what for him must be a telling

14. *See e.g.,* Bork, *Neutral Principles and Some First Amendment Problems,* 47 IND. L. J. 1 (1970); Rehnquist, *The Notion of a Living Constitution,* 54 TEX. L. REV. 693 (1976); and, Monaghan, *Our Perfect Constitution,* 56 N. Y. U. L. REV. 353 (1981), for support of the originalist position regarding the nondemocratic nature of the Court and the need for judicial self-restraint; but *see also,* Perry, *supra* note 1, at 575–83, for an argument supporting the notion that nonoriginalist review is supportable in terms of democratic theory.

Of course, nonoriginalists argue that it is not necessary to invoke originalist analysis to legitimize the Court's role in an otherwise democratic society. They assert that a host of limitations exist that objectify and legitimize judicial review. The process-based theorists, such as John Hart Ely, argue that the Court can and must intervene to assure success to the democratic process. Rights-based theorists, such as Michael Perry, argue that the Court should intervene in instances in which human rights and dignity are being abridged by the actions of the other branches of government. Pragmatists like Dean Bennett, on the other hand, seem inclined only to describe and justify what the Court does by arguing "that the judiciary is engaged in projecting the past of the institution it serves into the future, that that role brings constraint with it, and that the primary mechanisms of constraint are just what judicial opinions suggest: deference to precedent, to original intentions, and to judgments of politically responsible agencies."[15] Finally, deconstructionists argue that judicial review is necessarily and overwhelmingly or totally a political venture and should be recognized as such, with judicial formalisms being little more than cloaks to cover and obscure judicial politicking.[16] Unfortunately, the only thing on which these nonoriginalists seem to agree is the inappropriateness of originalism as a primary theory of constitutional interpretation.

Aside from the fact that there is little coherence among nonoriginalist theories of judicial review, I remain skeptical of any such theories for a number of reasons. First, they all seem more prone to drift away from the realm of judging or interpreting into the domain of politics and personal preference. Indeed, the very incoherence of many such theories makes it difficult to present them in a manner that would persuade a restive public that they offer something more than judicial politics as usual. Thus, when Justice Brennan recently asserted that the Court's job was to interpret the Constitution to protect human dignity, it is not surprising that he was scored not only for arrogating fundamental value choices to himself and other justices, giving the Court the power to

---

objection when he notes that, "any theory of the substance of constitutional law that pretends to authoritativeness will readily overwhelm prior decisions it can brand as 'wrong.'" *Id.* at 454. Since for Bennett precedent is pre-eminent, such a conclusion dooms originalism's claim to authoritativeness to failure. However, it is precisely this point that strengthens originalism from the vagaries of ever-changing precedent—reliance on the intent of the framers does demand that precedent be brought into conformity with the principles derivable from such a historical analysis.

15. Bennett, *Mission of Moral Reasoning, supra* n. 13, at 656.
16. *See e.g.,* Tushnet, *Anti-Formalism in Recent Constitutional Theory,* 83 MICH. L. REV. 1502 (1985).

overrule value choices made by the democratic organs of government, but also for transcending the Constitution, because one looks in vain for the term human dignity in the four corners of the Constitution. Second, unable to agree among themselves, nonoriginalists threaten to fragment constitutional decision making to the point that those who are inclined to balance away individual rights in pursuit of their personal ideologies will easily divide and conquer, leaving the Constitution in disarray and rights unrecognized. Third, and finally, while I might not be adverse to being judged according to Justice Brennan's nonoriginalist sense of human dignity, I am less certain that I would like to be judged by his successor's set of values. For my part, I am content to cast my lot with the framers and ratifiers, rather than with a dubious and uncertain future. The framers thought in terms of values, values that would enshrine personal freedom for the most part, while many today believe that values are relative and, in the process, seem to want to exalt economic and utilitarian efficiency or their personal political agenda.

The very fact that a provision for amending the Constitution was added to the document tends to strengthen this argument. When constitutional principles cease to endure or are no longer viable, the Constitution can be amended, not by the Court but by following prescribed procedures. Similarly, when the Court creates new rights or principles, principles outside the bounds of the Constitution, it exceeds its authority.

The nonoriginalist would, of course, disagree. However, in my view the burden is on the nonoriginalists because (1) as has been discussed, their theory is less defensible in terms of democratic theory; and (2) since their theory is not self-limiting, as is originalist theory, which is limited by its own methodology, they must articulate a viable, principled limit or admit that their theory provides for unbounded judicial discretion. This burden requires a justification of the nonoriginalist position, as well as requiring that its proponents provide a coherent theory that would not subject future generations to the whim and fancy of self-exalting judges. This they have failed to do to my satisfaction. In order to extend the Constitution to fit their political agenda, these advocates of essentially unbounded judicial review threaten the very core of rights and the institutional fabric provided for in the Constitution and the Bill of Rights.

My analysis of the prayer issue will serve to illustrate my abiding discomfort with nonoriginalist review, while depicting the strengths and weaknesses of originalist review. The principles articulated by the framers and ratifiers of the religion clauses of the First Amendment are appealing because they can extricate us from the dilemma presented by the issues raised in the Introduction, the apparent conflict between the purposes of the Establishment and Free Exercise clauses. It provides principled answers in an area already plagued by too much nonoriginalist and non-interpretivist review. The nonoriginalists on the Court and in academia simply have failed to come up with a better prescription for what ails us in the area of judicial review, in general, or in the area of religious liberty, in specific, than the prescription offered some two hundred years ago by the authors of the First Amendment.

2

The Colonial Antecedents

Professor Paul Brest recently noted that, "an interpreter [of the Consti-
tution] must read [the] text in light of its social as well as linguistic
context."[1] It is not enough just to examine the words of the Constitution,
even if one endeavors to read them in their linguistic context. Since, in
interpreting a constitution, the intent of the ratifiers is critical, it becomes
necessary to look at the social, philosophical, and historical context as
well. One can only understand what the ratifiers intended with regard to
a given provision of the Constitution, by immersing one's self in the
social, philosophical, and political culture of the era. Such a feat can
never be performed perfectly; we are all bound by our own biases and
by the biases and assumptions of our own era.

In an effort to place the debate over the ratification of the Constitution in its proper context, I will need to look briefly at its colonial
antecedents. For those readers interested in a more detailed discussion
of the issues in the colonial period, I would recommend the introductory
materials in Stokes and Pfeffer's *Church and State in the United States,*
which offers a more in-depth analysis of English and European philosophical, political, and, to some extent, theological antecedents to the
First Amendment, and particularly Curry's *The First Freedoms: Church
and State in America to the Passage of the First Amendment,* for a
recent, thorough treatment of colonial and revolutionary antecedents to
the religion clauses of the First Amendment. I would also strongly recommend Berman's *Law and Revolution: The Formation of the Western*

---

1. Brest, *The Misconceived Quest for the Original Understanding,* 60 B.U.
L. REV. 204 (1980).

Legal Tradition for an enlightening view of the interplay of law and religion generally in the formation of our western legal tradition.

The thought of John Locke, Voltaire, and others, coupled with theological and political developments in England and Europe, clearly influenced the framers and ratifiers of the religion clauses of the First Amendment. Nevertheless, actual colonial experience with regard to issues of religious liberty is even more helpful in understanding the context of the ratification era. It was largely this colonial experience that provided the impetus for and content of the Bill of Rights.

The colonies generally followed the lead of Great Britain in gradually increasing religious toleration in the seventeenth and eighteenth centuries. There were other forces at work in the colonies as well that contributed to the development of colonial attitudes toward toleration and to the eventual development of an antipathy toward governmentally established religions. Among the factors that contributed to this were (1) the desire for religious freedom on the part of many of the migrants to the colonies, who were fleeing intolerance or persecution elsewhere; (2) the independent nature of many of the religious sects in the colonies and the increased emphasis on individual conversion that resulted from the growth of the evangelical movement and the Great Awakening in the eighteenth century; (3) the growth of the Enlightenment as a philosophical movement during the same time; and (4) the fact that, with the growing economic independence of the colonies and geographic separation from Britain, the colonists felt less dependent upon English legal and theological tradition, particularly as manifested in the established Anglican Church. The New England colonies with their puritanical congregationalism, and the Middle Colonies, with their many and generally tolerated sects, began to interact for mutually beneficial economic as well as political reasons. Forces contributing to religious and economic pluralism in the colonies also began to stimulate the drive for ever-increasing religious toleration. Indeed, to understand best the forces at work in the colonies, it is instructive to look first at developments in each colonial area.[2]

---

2. In his excellent book, Thomas J. Curry divides his analysis of colonial developments in a different, although not necessarily contradictory, manner. He looks just at New England, then at Virginia and Maryland and finally at the Restoration Colonies (the Carolinas, New York, New Jersey, and Pennsylvania), all of which were formed during the Restoration era. *See* Curry, THE FIRST FREEDOMS: CHURCH AND STATE IN AMERICA TO THE PASSAGE OF THE FIRST AMENDMENT (1986). Certainly, it might be more accurate, as a geographical matter, to include Rhode Island with New England, and to separate the Restoration Colonies. For analytical purposes, I have discussed the colonies less in their geographic and more in their developmental sense.

New England

In 1620, the *Mayflower* landed in Plymouth Bay, bringing a small group of religious independents or Puritans, who had previously fled England and briefly sojourned in Holland, to the shores of North America. On 11 November 1620, the colonists drafted the famous Mayflower Compact, which provided, in part, that they had undertaken their voyage for "the advancement of the Christian faith, and the honor of [their] King and Country."[3] As the very act of the drafting and adoption of the compact indicates, these colonists were imbued with a certain democratic, albeit heavily theological, spirit. Initially, the democratic spirit was limited. It only extended in the colony to those who adhered to the same doctrine as the Puritans. Nevertheless, this limited democratic sentiment helped to set in motion forces that would ultimately contribute to increased religious and political liberty in New England.[4]

Another parallel colonial experience was also soon under way in New England at Massachusetts Bay. Referring to the Massachusetts Bay Colony, Professor Stokes has stated that

> religion of an intolerant Calvinistic type, and government were to be closely associated in accordance with English tradition; a Puritan state church, especially closely related to town government gradually developed from nonconformity to take the place of the old Anglican state church to which the Puritans had been accustomed in England.... The church...expected the state to support public worship and suppress heresy. They did not wish it to interfere in strictly religious questions, but recognized that in matters of church government and ecclesiastical affairs state and church should work together.[5]

---

3. As cited in Cornelison, THE RELATION OF RELIGION TO CIVIL GOVERNMENT IN THE UNITED STATES OF AMERICA (1895), hereinafter "Cornelison."

4. *See e.g.*, Stokes and Pfeffer, CHURCH AND STATE IN THE UNITED STATES, at 5, for a short discussion of the "democratic spirit prevailing in Plymouth." *But, see* Curry, *supra* note 2, at 1–10, and Haskins, LAW AND AUTHORITY IN EARLY MASSACHUSETTS (1960). Professor Haskins concludes that, "these ideas and practices can hardly be described as democratic in a modern sense, but Puritan doctrine, like that of the medieval Church from which it ultimately derived, was little concerned about the equality of men.... In the eyes of the Massachusetts leaders, not only was the right to share in the government restricted to those few 'visible saints' who were proven elect, but the supreme power in the government belonged only to the magistrates. The latter accordingly objected to the concessions wrung from them by the 'people,' for they viewed them as evidence of an unfortunate 'democratical spirit.'" *Id.* at 45.

5. Stokes and Pfeffer, *supra* note 4, at 5.

It is clear that these Puritans, who had themselves been driven from their homes for religious reasons, nevertheless "believed in religious liberty for Puritans alone."[6] For his part, Curry noted that during the seventeenth century, "Puritans believed that accomplishment of their goal, the achievement of truth according to the Word of God, would render discussion of toleration redundant.... When New England ministers did write about freedom of religion, they were less concerned with debating a substantive issue than with trying to keep an irrelevant one from interrupting their lives and work."[7]

While much has also been made of the fact that in New England the "Church-State rested on a social compact confined to the relatively few elect,"[8] this point should not be overemphasized. Other matters must also be examined to get an accurate picture of colonial developments in terms of religious liberty. For example, even in early Puritan New England, the church elder was not eligible to serve as a civil magistrate; the civil and ecclesiastical functions were separated to some extent.[9] The willingness of the Puritans to begin to distinguish between the role of the state and the role of the church was ultimately to have a significant effect on developments in terms of religious liberty and toleration in the colonies. Thus, while the influence of the clergy and religious doctrine in the early colonial period in New England was substantial, the seeds of some independence of the religious sphere from the civil authority had gained a foothold.

These developments were, however, at an embryonic stage. Thomas Curry believes that historians have read too much into the inclination of the Puritans to separate the functions of church and state:

> In commenting on the Puritan colonies, historians have ranged from portraying them as theocracies ruled by dour Protestant clergy to describing them as practicing a separation of church and state. The terms "theocracy" and "separation of church and state" are of little use in attempting to understand seventeenth-century New England. Theocracy, now a word of opprobrium, expressed for Puritans the optimum form of government, "to make the Lord our governor." Separation of

---

6. W. Marnell, THE FIRST AMENDMENT, at 55 (1972).

7. Curry, *supra* note 2, at 16; Marnell, *supra* note 6, at 60.

8. Marnell, after generally explaining the civil electoral process in these colonies, concludes that, "what is of major consequence is that New England Puritanism resulted in a church-state ruled by a small and highly select aristocracy of the elect, with grades of citizenship and non-citizenship, even as Plymouth. Church and state were one and inseparable, and the church completely dominated the state."

9. Stokes and Pfeffer, *supra* note 4, at 5.

church and state, now considered laudable, would for them have represented an unthinkable arrangement.[10]

Thus, while there was some movement toward religious independence from civil authority in early Massachusetts, that civil authority certainly supported the church financially and even doctrinally. The Puritan churches in New England came in some respects to resemble their vilified English counterpart, the Church of England.

Much has been written about the existence of severe religious intolerance in Puritan New England. Stokes and Pfeffer, for example, see the trial and ultimate banishment of Anne Hutchinson as strong evidence of a highly tolerant attitude on the part of the colonists. They point out that Anne Hutchinson was banished in 1638 because "she stubbornly persisted in teaching the heretical and immoral doctrine of Antinomianism, which denied the need of good works and held that a believer whose heart was right toward God was fulfilling the law irrespective of his conduct."[11] Professor Haskins, an authority on the Massachusetts Bay Colony, disagrees, at least as a matter of emphasis, with those who persist in emphasizing the extent of religious intolerance, without placing that intolerance in its historical context. He views the trials of Anne Hutchinson in their historical context and concludes that both the religious and civil authorities in the colony were at least as tolerant as their English counterparts. In this regard, Haskins notes the extensive efforts of the clergy and finally of the civil officials to redeem Hutchinson and avoid banishment.[12] Banishment after lengthy efforts to redeem Hutchinson was, when placed in its historical perspective, a relatively tolerant or benign act on the part of the colonial leaders. Particularly when viewed in light of the severe penalties for heresy extant in England during the reign of Henry VIII, and the English demand for strict conformity to the articles of faith and modes of worship of the Anglican Church, Professor Haskins is no doubt correct in concluding that Hutchinson received more tolerant treatment in Massachusetts than she would no doubt have received in Britain. Under any circumstances, the worst that

---

10. Curry, *supra* note 2, at 4. *See also,* Haskins, LAW AND AUTHORITY IN EARLY MASSACHUSETTS at 88 (1968).

11. Stokes and Pfeffer, *supra* note 4, at 9.

12. Haskins, *supra* note 10, at 47–53. Curry seems to agree with Haskins, in noting that "the authorities could not allow such a radical [as Anne Hutchinson] to undermine the infant colony, but neither would they suppress her out of hand without discussion. Only when she overreached herself in claiming an immediate revelation from God could the General Court find a clear basis on which to condemn her." Curry, *supra* note 2, at 11.

can be said is that Massachusetts and New England followed the English example to some extent, in the area of church-state relations. While the New England colonists may not have been more tolerant toward religious dissenters than their English counterparts, they certainly were no less tolerant.[13]

The Haskins view is also supported somewhat by the adoption in 1657 of the Halfway Covenant in the colony, which admitted children of members into church membership and, perhaps more importantly, into citizenship in Massachusetts, without placing stringent religious requirements on the children. Perhaps, unintentionally, that covenant encouraged further movement toward increased political and religious toleration in New England.[14] In 1708, Connecticut went a step further, passing the Saybrook Platform recognizing the full citizenship and freedom of worship of dissenting Protestant sects. By 1721, the Puritan leaders Increase Mather and his son Cotton were found participating in a Baptist ordination in Boston and preaching on the need for harmony between differing sects.[15]

Thus, while in a limited sense, it can be asserted that toleration and a somewhat democratic spirit enjoyed some growth throughout the second half of the seventeenth century and early eighteenth century in New England, it would be inaccurate to read too much into these early de-

13. In this regard, Curry notes that:
Magistrates and ministers agreed on the need for religious conformity; yet in the absence of a central church government to define and enforce orthodoxy, the semi-independent congregations were undoubtedly apt to degenerate rapidly into religious pluralism, a condition Puritans considered synonymous with anarchy. Consequently, in their efforts to maintain and promote uniform religious practice, Puritan governments gradually began to assume roles reminiscent of those of English ecclesiastical authorities.
Id. at 6.

14. *See* Morgan, THE SUPREME COURT AND RELIGION, at 13 (1972). Curry notes that, "The persistence of dissension in America and the lamentable penchant of Congregationalists in England for accommodating heterodoxy exemplified and led to the crisis of the New England way that resulted in the Halfway Covenant, the name given to a religious compromise by which those unable to recount an experience of conversion, and thus ineligible for church membership, could have their children baptized nevertheless. It represented a downward adjustment to the actuality that New Englanders did not flock to their churches." Curry, *supra* note 2, at 26–7.

15. *See* Morgan, *supra* note 14, at 13.

velopments.[16] Similarly, too much emphasis on the trial and banishment of dissenters in New England can obscure other significant early developments toward religious toleration and the independence of the church from the state in New England.[17] Indeed, it should be added that the very act of banishing leaders of other sects or proponents of other beliefs from New England, such as Roger Williams and John Clarke, ultimately, if unintentionally, contributed to an increase in religious liberty in other areas.[18] Dissenters took their theology and their views regarding religious toleration to other areas in the New England and the Middle Colonies and ultimately influenced ideas regarding religious liberty throughout colonial and revolutionary America.

By 1750, another factor contributing to increased religious freedom in New England was well under way; the evangelical movement, or Great

---

16. Curry captures the limited nature of these early developments in seventeenth-century New England when he concludes that:

In the 1670's, the complicated process of adjusting Puritan ideas to the existing reality gave rise to some ministerial unrest, but the availability of a common language, whose traditional terms the Fathers had not rendered impractical for the future by precise definitions, eased the storms. As a result, opposing groups did not polarize. Instead, they temporarily diverged in their estimation of the restrictions that traditional phrases implied. Thus, all Puritans could head into the future believing the oft-repeated assertion that New England originated as a plantation for religion, not trade.... All further concurred that civil and religious liberty were inextricably mixed. Finally, as if in anticipation of the Act of Toleration of 1689, New England divines agreed to oppose not toleration but a "boundless toleration."

Curry, *supra* note 2, at 27.

17. Actually, while Anne Hutchinson died at the hands of Indians a short time after her banishment, most dissenters were able, given the abundance of available land in colonial America, to make a new life for themselves. As such, they were ultimately able to contribute to a trend toward more religious toleration and liberty in other geographical areas.

18. For example, John Clarke, a banished New England dissenter, whose role as a proponent of religious liberty was influential, if somewhat overshadowed by that of Roger Williams, wrote a tract (III News from New England), which Stokes and Pfeffer, *supra* note 4, at 17, summarize as follows:

After an account of persecutions, due mainly to his preaching without the necessary licenses and his denying the lawfulness of infant baptism, the author gives quotations from the intolerant laws of Massachusetts. He is specifically concerned about the one which calls for the banishment of those who oppose the baptizing of infants.... He sees clearly that any attempt to force worship "is the ready way to make dissemblers and hypocrites before God." "This outward forcing of men in matters

Awakening, was led by religionists like Jonathan Edwards who, perhaps beyond all men of his time, "smote the staggering blow which made ecclesiastical establishments impossible to America," with his emphasis "on the importance of individual conversion [and his insistence] that the Church and State were very different and that the Church should be exalted as a spiritual and not a political institution."[19] Above all else, Edwards "effectively proclaimed that each individual is answerable to God alone"[20] in religious matters. He, and other ministers during the evangelical era, emphasized individual conscience and a privatization of religious experience and a diversification of churches. Edwards and others[21] taught that the establishment of any particular worship, articles of faith, or religious doctrine by the state tended to denigrate an individual's right to choose in religious matters and was, therefore, antithetical to the individual nature of religious conversion and to his notion of religious freedom.

For his part, Professor Morgan summarizes the influence of this evangelical movement, which spread so rapidly throughout New England in the mid-eighteenth century, by stressing that, "it reemphasized the individual and private character of the Protestant religious experience, and it contributed to the fragmentation of existing churches and sects

---

of conscience towards God to believe as others believe and practice worship as others do, cannot stand with Peace, Liberty, Prosperity, and safety of a Place, Commonwealth, or Nation."
Clarke and his fellow dissenters were not only able to contribute to greater toleration and liberty in other colonies, to which they were banished, thereby taking the cause of religious liberty a long step forward, but their writing also had a substantial influence on thinking both in other colonies and in England. Clarke's early reference to "matters of conscience," for example, was to become a recurrent theme of the late eighteenth century and was espoused by the framers, albeit in a modified sense.

19. Morgan, *supra* note 14, at 15, states that, "the widespread evangelical movement had the effect of stimulating toleration and separationism among American Protestants. It had its beginnings in the Middle Colonies in 1734, but quickly spread to New England, where it found its most influential preacher, Jonathan Edwards." Curry adds that, "The Great Awakening increased an already growing diversity of sects within the colonies.... In its wake, no church or religious group could ever hope to achieve a dominance in doctrine or numbers," Curry, *supra* note 2, at 103.

20. Stokes and Pfeffer, *supra* note 4, at 25–6.

21. Of particular note is Elisha Williams's pamphlet based on Lockean contract notions and advocating a liberty of conscience, which was written in response to the Connecticut Assembly's effort to restrain the forces and effects of the Great Awakening in Connecticut. *See,* Curry, *supra* note 2, at 97–104, for a discussion regarding Williams's pamphlet and the effect of the Great Awakening.

into numerous new bodies."[22] Limited movement in the direction of toleration and democratization in seventeenth-century New England was complemented by the pluralism of the eighteenth century. As religious groups proliferated, the demand for additional toleration and for a developing right of conscience was beyond abatement, even in New England. In a related sense, after concluding that New Englanders were the most republican of all Americans in the latter part of the eighteenth century, Forrest McDonald concludes that "quite possibly, as Philip Greven has suggested, there was a psychological affinity between republicanism and 'the evangelical temperament,' which was inherent in both seventeenth-century puritanism and eighteenth-century revivalism."[23]

Thus, by the time of the Revolution, as a result of practical or economic necessity and increasing philosophical, and in some quarters theological, conviction, New England was becoming increasingly tolerant and pluralistic in religious matters, despite the fact that its historical, Congregationalist religious establishment remained more entrenched in many ways than even the Anglican establishment in the Southern Colonies. One might err in reading too much into these forces of toleration. Most New Englanders remained solidly supportive of their established Congregational religion, and it was not until well after the ratification

---

22. Morgan, *supra* note 14, at 15. Morgan, however, also accurately notes that even the groups derived from the evangelical movement were not overly tolerant of other sects, believing their own form of conversion to be the right one; but their very existence and the rising plural nature of religious sects, other than the established Congregationalism in New England, stimulated the necessity of demand for religious toleration in New England and the colonies prior to the Revolution.

23. McDonald, Novus Ordo Seclorum: The Intellectual Origins Of The Constitution at 73 (1985). Professor McDonald notes that there were various versions of republican thought extant in colonial and revolutionary America, but they held in common the view that "public virtue" was necessary to enable a republic, particularly a democratic republic, to survive. McDonald added that "public virtue entailed firmness, courage, endurance, industry, frugal living, strength, and above all, unremitting devotion to the weal of the public's corporate self, the community of virtuous men. It was at once individualistic and communal: individualistic in that no member of the public could be dependent upon any other and still be reckoned a member of the public; communal in that every man gave himself totally to the good of the public as a whole. If public virtue declined, the republic declined, and if it declined too far, the republic died. Philosophical historians had worked out a regular life cycle, or more properly death cycle of republics. Manhood gave way to effeminacy, republican liberty to licentiousness. Licentiousness, in turn, degenerated into anarchy, and anarchy inevitably led to tyranny." *Id.* at 70–1.

of the First Amendment that the Congregational Church was fully dis-
established in New England. Nevertheless, attitudes toward religious liberty prevailing in New England at the founding of the Republic were at
least the equivalent of the increasingly tolerant British views, which accepted an established church, while increasing toleration for other Christian sects. Such toleration was only ever so slowly extended to Catholics,
Quakers, and Jews. In fact, even at the time of the Revolution, those
groups were often vilified and were seldom extended more than a modicum of toleration.

Indeed, by the close of the eighteenth century, it was not uncommon
for New Englanders to assert that they did not have a religious establishment like England, despite the fact that the state continued for the
most part to support the Congregationalist Church financially and otherwise. Thus, Curry notes that:

> New England authorities believed that their establishments
> amounted to the provision of public worship and support for clergy,
> the teachers of religion and morality. They dismissed out of hand the
> assertions of Baptists and Separatists that Massachusetts and Connec-
> ticut imposed Articles of faith and modes of worship. Their mild and
> tolerant systems had nothing in common with the tyrannizing English
> establishment, the one Adams identified with "creeds, tests, ceremonies,
> and tithes."[24]

The New England aversion to state-imposed tests, modes of worship,
and articles of faith, as the essence of the pernicious English establishment, was to be influential in the course of the debates regarding the
meaning of the First Amendment.

THE MIDDLE COLONIES

The Middle Colonies in which, for my purposes of analysis, I include
Rhode Island, Pennsylvania, New Jersey, Delaware, Maryland, and New
York were the most tolerant of all the colonies throughout the colonial
era. The cause of religious toleration was championed in varying degrees
by such men as William Penn in Pennsylvania, Roger Williams in Rhode
Island, and George Calvert, Baron Baltimore in Maryland.

In 1638, Roger Williams of Rhode Island, himself a banished dissenter from Massachusetts, was the first to establish a community that
recognized the principle that, "an enforced uniformity of religion
throughout a nation or civil state confounds the civil and religious, denies

---

24. Curry, *supra* note 2, at 133.

the principles of Christianity and civility, and that Jesus Christ is come in the flesh."[25]

Williams formed a community based on a recognition that state-enforced or established conformity in religious matters denied not only an individual's rights but also, in his view, denied the essence of Christianity. Williams was no doubt the leading proponent of religious tolerance in the colonial era.[26] His views regarding tolerance were themselves, however, religiously motivated. Williams elaborated his theory of religious liberty in the oft-quoted and ultimately influential analogy of a ship and society:

> There goes many a ship to sea, with many hundreds of souls in one ship, whose weal and woe is common, and is a true picture of a commonwealth or a human combination of society. It hath fallen out sometimes that both Papists and Protestants, Jews and Turks, may be embarked in one ship; upon which supposal I affirm that all liberty of conscience that ever I pleaded for turns upon these two hinges—that none of the Papists, Protestants, Jews or Turks be forced to come to the ship's prayers or worship, if they practice any. I further add that I never denied that, notwithstanding this liberty, the commander of the ship ought to command the ship's course, yea, and also command that

---

25. As cited in Goddard, *The Law and Its Relation to Religion*, 10 MICH. L. REV. 161 at 165 (1912).

26. Thomas Curry notes that "Williams composed most of his works on religious freedom during visits to England in the 1640s and 1650s, nearly all of them written as part of an extended debate with John Cotton." Curry, *supra* note 2, at 15. Curry adds that Rhode Island's example was not taken seriously in other colonies, "with the result that what was an extraordinary experiment in religious freedom turned out to be, apart from Rhode Island itself, an idea too advanced to achieve general acceptance. Ideas of freedom of religion that would later prosper and grow in colonial America would not be derived from the example of Rhode Island." *Id.* at 21. Finally, Curry asserts that:
> Completing the matrix of church-state relations in colonial America, Rhode Island's radical pluralistic traditions bore little significance for contemporaries, who largely ignored them. During the eighteenth century, however, the colony itself came to accept some of the prevailing conventional thinking and practice of the time. Thus, John Callendar, a Baptist minister who wrote a history of the colony in 1739, casually assumed that it was a Christian, i.e. Protestant, commonwealth, and in 1719 Rhode Island excluded Catholics from office, though not from toleration.

Id. at 90. Curry is no doubt correct in asserting that Rhode Island and the thought of Roger Williams were of but minimal significance in colonial America. However, the Rhode Island experience and the thought of Roger Williams did ultimately have a profound effect on the framers, particularly James Madison, who often referred favorably to Williams and the Rhode Island example.

justice, peace and sobriety be kept and practiced among the seamen and all the passengers.[27]

Professors Stokes and Pfeffer, authorities on religious liberty in America and proponents of a very strict separationist viewpoint, extract three principles from the ship analogy: (1) there is a difference between the sacred (the ship's prayer and worship) and the secular (command of the ship's course and enforcement of justice, peace, and sobriety); (2) compulsion may be exercised by officials of the state (the ship's captain) in the area of the secular but not of the sacred; and (3) where the safety and security of the commonwealth are concerned, religious conscience is not a valid excuse for refusal to obey the lawful commands of the state.[28] From this, Stokes and Pfeffer rather presumptuously conclude that "these three principles were later to become the First Amendment declaration against any establishment of religion or prohibiting the free exercise thereof and the basis of the United States Supreme Court's interpretation of that amendment."[29]

While I largely agree with Professors Stokes and Pfeffer that Williams's ship analogy and philosophy regarding religious liberty had a significant influence on the framers of the First Amendment, particularly James Madison, who often referred to the Rhode Island experience, I differ with Stokes and Pfeffer on two points: (1) I believe that their summary of the principles contained in the analogy is too superficial and selective; and (2) while I feel the framers were inclined to agree with the principles included in the ship analogy, I am convinced that neither they nor Williams espoused the brand of strict separation advocated by Professors Stokes and Pfeffer and other twentieth-century commentators.

I discuss the error of this twentieth-century strict separationist position both as a logical and an historical matter throughout this book. However, at this juncture it should suffice merely to point out the nature of the error committed by Stokes and Pfeffer in their interpretation of the ship analogy. Insofar as their conclusions are concerned, Stokes and Pfeffer are generally correct, but they have in a sense left too much meat on the bones. Williams advocated a form of basic separation of the

---

27. Cited in W. O. Douglas, THE BIBLE AND THE SCHOOLS, at 20 (1966). Justice Douglas interestingly concludes that, "many have doubted if we of the twentieth century have reached so advanced a position as the one held by Roger Williams in the seventeenth century." *Id.* at 21.

28. Stokes and Pfeffer, *supra* note 4, at 19.

29. *Id.* at 16.

religious and secular worlds, for the avowed purpose of enhancing the
religious liberty of all sects. Williams did not, however, for example,
argue that the state could not facilitate or even aid religious exercise.[30]

With specific regard to prayers in the ship or society, Williams explained that there are the two hinges upon which the "liberty of conscience" turns: (1) "that none of the Papists, Protestants, Jews or Turks
be forced to come to the ship's prayers or worship, if they practice any";
and (2) that he "never denied that, notwithstanding this liberty, the
commander of the ship ought to command the ship's course...and
...command that justice, peace and sobriety be [maintained]." It is critical
to note, with regard to religious liberty, as evidenced by the existence of
both public and private prayers on the ship, that Williams would permit
ship's prayers (i.e., public prayers or worship) so long as no one: (1) was
compelled to participate in those public prayers; nor (2) was coerced by
the civil authority with regard to their individual prayers or worship. He
would, in other words, permit the ship to have voluntary and noncoercive public prayers or devotional activity. More importantly, the ship's
captain could not legitimately use his power to force individuals to refrain from engaging in their own prayers, even in the ship, which may,
if the analogy can be extended a bit, be said to represent the public
sector or at least the domain of civil authority. These observations should
be viewed, as well, in light of Williams's concern that there be no enforced uniformity of religion. It might be reading too much into the
analogy to say that Roger Williams would require that the ship's prayers
not be supportive of any single religion, but it certainly would not be
too expansive to conclude that he would have *required* that the state do
nothing, by commission or omission, to prevent one from exercising
one's religion, unless there was a strong countervailing state interest mit-
igating against such an exercise. Rhode Island was a virtual paragon of
toleration in the colonial context, but it should be noted that, while all
groups of religions were tolerated, Jews and Catholics were not always
treated with the same equanimity as Protestants.[31]

---

30. *See,* Curry, *supra* note 2, at 89. Curry points out that arguments in
Rhode Island against tax-supported religion did not come until later when they
were more closely tied to the Baptist tradition of voluntary support.

31. Curry points out that:

    Rhode Island's treatment of Jews, the other religious group af-
fected by the law restricting political rights and the holding of office to
Christians, affords a clue to what might have happened to Catholics
had they come to represent any significant portion of the population.
From the middle of the seventeenth century on—though not
continuously—Jewish merchants inhabited the colony. Between 1750

His second hinge also would permit the state to act in its civil sphere of commanding the course of the ship in the interest of maintaining justice, peace, and sobriety. While the state was to have such power, it is presumptively clear that Williams's emphasis was, in his own words, on "the liberty of conscience," thereby precluding the state from intervening except in instances where justice, peace, and sobriety clearly mandated such intervention. The terms justice, peace, and sobriety are never defined. Nevertheless, these terms were, in a sense, destined to develop into a fuller theory as to the proper role of government in regulating matters of conscience, and, as cries for freedom of conscience were renewed with added zeal in revolutionary America, Williams's support of an individual's freedom to exercise her religion, free at a minimum from compulsion on the part of the state, ultimately had a pronounced effect on religious liberty in revolutionary America, although during the colonial period the Rhode Island experience was disparaged in the other colonies. Opposition to state promotion of particular religious groups is in no small measure rooted in the thought and theology of Roger Williams and the Rhode Island experience relative to religious toleration, even though Rhode Island's influence was fairly minimal elsewhere during Williams's life. Indeed, just as prophets are seldom welcome in their own community, they are often rejected by their own contemporaries, although their ideas live on to be given new vitality in a more receptive era. This was certainly true of the thought of Roger Williams. By the time of the Revolution, the framers often referred positively to the Rhode Island experience as a model of religious liberty and toleration.

Pennsylvania was not far behind Rhode Island in terms of affording its residents the fruits of religious toleration. Indeed, in terms of Pennsylvania's influence on contemporary colonial America, it has been argued that, "Pennsylvania from its beginnings...established perhaps the broadest religious liberty in colonial America, and its government provoked no serious charges of persecutions."[32] William Penn, the proprietor

---

and 1756, a Jewish community varying from roughly 60 to 200 persons existed at Newport, a town whose population increased over the same period from 6,000 to 9,000. These Jews built a synagogue and worshipped freely, but they exercised no right to vote and held no office. On one occasion, petitions of two Jews for naturalization were denied by both the legislature and the Supreme Court of Rhode Island, but the reasons for their rejection have not survived. Thus, although Jews in the colony were free to practice their religion, they did so as second-class citizens.

Id. at 90-1. Of course, the second-class citizenship of Jews in Rhode Island was far preferable to the treatment they would have received in less tolerant colonies during that same period of time.

of Pennsylvania, was a strong advocate of increased religious toleration. In 1682, under *The Body of the Laws of Pennsylvania,* he provided

> That no person now or at any time hereafter, living in this province, who shall confess and acknowledge one Almighty God to be the Creator, Upholder and Ruler of the World, and who professes, him or herself obliged in conscience to live peaceably and quietly under the civil government, shall in any case be molested or prejudiced for his, or her conscientious persuasion or practice. Nor shall hee or shee at any time be compelled to frequent or maintain anie religious worship, place or ministry whatever, contrary to his, or her mind, but shall freely and fully enjoy his, or her, Christian liberty in that respect, without any interruption or reflection. And if any person shall abuse or deride any other, for his, or her, different persuasion and practice in matters of religion, such person shall be lookt upon as a disturber of the peace, and be punished accordingly.[33]

While a close reading of this provision of *The Body of the Laws* reveals a substantial stride in the direction of religious toleration, Professor Cornelison is undoubtedly correct in his early assessment that, "in the frame of the government of Pennsylvania, prepared by the proprietor, William Penn, while the principle of toleration was most firmly established, the Christian character of the government was at the same time most positively asserted, and most rigid provisions were made for its establishment."[34] Thus, although having a strong Quaker influence, in Pennsylvania most forms of Christianity were generally tolerated; it might be said that a generalized Protestant brand of Christianity had been established as the government-sanctioned religion for the colony. The extension of liberty or toleration to other non-Christian and even to Catholic groups in Pennsylvania was limited.

By the close of the eighteenth century, Pennsylvania was fairly evenly divided religiously among Quakers, German Lutherans (Pennsylvania Dutch), and Scotch-Irish Presbyterians.[35] Those groups enjoyed a high level of tolerant coexistence, although they tended to oppose toleration for Roman Catholicism, as well as for non-Christian sects. Since non-Christian religious groups were limited in number, the ramifications of this intolerance were minimal. Some intolerance and persecution, however, was directed to Catholics, who constituted a significant minority in Pennsylvania, although Curry has concluded that by the early eighteenth century "the ironic spirit of the Friends prevailed and made

---

32. *Id.* at 75.
33. Cited in Stokes and Pfeffer, *supra* note 4, at 19.
34. Cornelison, *supra* note 3, at 85.
35. *See* Bishop, THE BIRTH OF THE UNITED STATES, at 33 (1976).

Pennsylvania the only English colony where Catholics worshipped in public."[36] Despite its policy toward Catholics, Pennsylvania was certainly ahead of its time in terms of extending religious liberty to its residents.

In Maryland, Cecil Calvert, the second Lord Baltimore, implemented the Act of Toleration of 1649, which was designed to tolerate all Christian religions adhering to the doctrine of the Holy Trinity. Thus, Stokes and Pfeffer conclude that the Act of Toleration and the early influence of Lord Baltimore "gave Maryland a more liberal policy in matters of religion than any other colony...excepting Rhode Island and Pennsylvania."[37] However, Curry concludes that, "representing no rising consensus or felt need within either contemporary Catholicism or Protestantism, Maryland's seventeenth-century toleration proved quixotic and inevitably failed to survive.... Instead of practicing their different religions with equal liberty and maintaining their churches voluntarily, all Marylanders wound up supporting the Church of England. Catholics there worshipped unobtrusively, as the Baltimores planned, but not in freedom."[38]

In all the Middle Colonies, there was a general and growing religious toleration, particularly among Protestant Christian sects. This toleration had its roots in the theology of the region. Professor Marnell has stated, in this regard, that

> It may well be questioned if any contribution of the Middle Colonies to the infant nation was quite so important as the tradition of religious toleration and the separation of Church and State. But even as the question is asked, it should be reiterated that religious toleration in New York and Pennsylvania arose out of religious conviction and not religious indifference.[39]

The Middle Colonies during much of the seventeenth and eighteenth centuries were at the forefront of the colonial movement toward religious liberty. Attitudes toward religious liberty in the Middle Colonies, in turn, were rooted in theological views regarding Christian tolerance and the role of the church and state, which often could be traced back to the views of Martin Luther and John Calvin. It is clear that matters of

---

36. Curry, *supra* note 2, at 76. However, Catholics were precluded, by virtue of the test or oath of abjuration, from participating in public life in the colony. *Id.* at 80.

37. Stokes and Pfeffer, *supra* note 4, at 13. Similarly, Curry notes that, "Maryland's experience in Church and State constituted an extraordinary experiment, although it contributed even less than Rhode Island's to the development of religious freedom in the American Colonies." Curry, *supra* note 2, at 30–1.

38. *Id.* at 52.

39. Marnell, *supra* note 6, at 84.

religious conscience were beginning to transcend the prerogatives of the state. Indeed, this movement in many ways paralleled the decline of the royal prerogative. The state was not to be, and for the colonists in the Middle Colonies it could not be, irreligious; it was at most tolerant of increasing religious pluralism in the colonies.[40]

VIRGINIA AND THE SOUTHERN COLONIES

While Virginia did not fall geographically between the Middle Colonies, with their general religious toleration, and the New England colonies, with their established Congregationalism and slowly growing version of toleration, which essentially followed the English model, it did fall between them in terms of the extension of religious liberty to its residents by the time of the Revolution. This was not the case when the Virginia Colony was formed. At its inception, the Virginia Colony was, in terms of toleration, or the lack thereof, very much like Puritan New England and quite unlike the Middle Colonies.

Among the initial laws enacted in the first Assembly of Virginia in 1619 were statutes that provided for uniformity of the colonial church with the Church of England.[41] Graham has summarized these early statutes as follows:

> During the embryonic days of the Virginia Colony, a statute was enacted for compulsory taxation to support the established church. Other early statutes barred Catholics from holding office, and Quakers from the Colony.... [T]here were [also] statutes enacted to regulate the ministry and proprietary operations of the established church, and even the manner by which subjects were to keep the sabbath. All of these laws were amplified and continued up to the outbreak of the American Revolution.... There was also a general reenactment of the Statute of

---

40. Summarizing developments in what he terms the Restoration colonies, Curry concludes that:

> The Restoration colonies set some of the most important themes for Church-State relations in colonial America. In some of them, English civil and church authorities were able to establish Anglicanism, but unable to make the Church of England really take root. Thus, they set a structure for continuing conflict between an unpopular established church and popular causes and forces in those colonies. On the other hand, as Maryland Quakers were pointing out by the end of the seventeenth century, not only New Jersey but especially Pennsylvania offered a different example of a relationship between religion and government, one wherein churches were prospering on the basis of voluntary support and without benefit of any established religion, thus proving the workability of a system of broad religious liberty.

Id. at 76–7.

41. *See, e.g.,* Cornelison, *supra* note 3, at 6–7.

9 and 10, William III, which punished certain forms of heresy and apostacy.[42]

Like its New England and English counterparts, the Virginia Assembly initially sought to prevent diversity in religious groups on the ground that such diversity was inimical to the civil order.[43] The government, which was run largely by members of the Anglican establishment, simply sought to eliminate other religious groups in Virginia on the ground that their religious practices were offensive and, therefore, inimical to the "public peace." As Curry pointed out, "because the Virginia model of the Church of England continued over the course of its first century to make only relatively moderate demands in the area of worship, it provided the colony with a high degree of social uniformity. This very homogeneity served to make life difficult for such outspoken dissenters as did exist there.[44]

With time, however, a major development began to take hold in Virginia and the Southern Colonies. The clergy in the Southern Colonies, both by tradition and as a practical matter, were originally dependent upon supervision from the Church of England. However, just as the civil governments of the colonies gradually but increasingly separated from their English roots due to their geographical separation and as a result of administrative problems attendant with such separation,[45] the church found itself divorced from the Church of England. The Anglican Church in Virginia was plagued with administrative difficulties, which were often

---

42. Cited in Graham, *A Restatement of the Intended Meaning of the Establishment Clause in Relation to Education and Religion,* 1981 B.Y.U. L. Rev. 333 at 343.

43. One such law, *An Act for the Suppressing of the Quakers,* passed by the Virginia Assembly in 1659–60, is cited in Cornelison, *supra* note 3, at 13:

Whereas, there is an unreasonable and turbulent sort of people, commonly called Quakers, who, contrary to the laws, do daily gather unto them unlawful assemblies and congregations of people, teaching and publishing lies, miracles, false visions, prophecies and doctrines, which have influence upon the community of men, both ecclesiastical and civil, endeavoring and attempting thereby to destroy religions, laws, communities, and all bonds of civil society, leaving it arbitrary to every vain and vicious person whether man shall be safe, laws established, offenders punished, and governors rule; hereby disturbing the public peace and just interest: to prevent and restrain which mischief. . . . It is enacted that no master or commander of any ship or other vessel, do bring into this colony any person or persons called Quakers, under penalty of one hundred pounds sterling.

44. Curry, *supra* note 2, at 30.

45. *See, e.g.,* Bishop, *supra* note 35, at 42–48.

exacerbated by distance. These administrative difficulties ultimately, and perhaps of necessity, engendered a certain religious independence among colonists in the Southern Colonies, because they simply could not wait for decisions to make their way to Virginia from the other side of the Atlantic before acting in all matters.[46]

With the evangelical movement or Great Awakening, this growing independence from the English church was intensified by the presence, in the Southern Colonies, of other dissenting religious groups, including the Baptists and Presbyterians.[47] These groups were themselves strongly independent and began to demand at least minimal toleration of their religious practices. For example, Samuel Davies, an early Presbyterian minister whose ministrations were disturbed in Hanover, Virginia, sought and secured action which implied that the English Act of Toleration extended to the Virginia Colony.[48] The weakly administered Anglican Church in Virginia, despite its claim to a generally strong and influential membership, simply found itself unable to curb the growing demand for religious toleration raised by the plural religious forces in the colony. Curry summarizes the developments or factors that eventually gave rise to efforts to legalize or formalize religious liberty in Virginia and the Southern Colonies as follows:

> Thus, the Anglican Church, in its desire to carry its victory at home to the colonies, contended with the realities that America lacked not only bishops, but to a great extent even lower clergy; that the need to settle profitable colonies took precedence over a strict uniformity of religion; that 3,000 miles separated the Anglican Church in England from its colonial counterpart; and that in the new settlements, the majority of inhabitants belonged to what in England were Dissenting churches. All these conditions shaped the pattern of Church-State relations in the Restoration Colonies.[49]

Each of these factors or developments cited by Curry did indeed contribute to a sentiment favoring increased religious liberty in Virginia, particularly, and in the Southern Colonies, generally.

---

46. Stokes and Pfeffer, *supra* note 4, at 7 state that:

[T]he clergy in the Southern Colonies, being by church tradition dependent on Episcopal supervision, but having none except that of the distant Bishop of London, were frequently disloyal to their trust as spiritual and moral leaders, thereby helping to bring about disestablishment in Virginia about half a century before it took place in Connecticut and Massachusetts.

47. *See* Marnell, *supra* note 6, at 104, for a discussion of the influence of the Baptist dissenters, particularly with regard to the disestablishment issue.

48. Stokes and Pfeffer, *supra* note 4, at 20.

49. Curry, *supra* note 2, at 55.

However, despite this growing pluralism and increasing desire for religious liberty in the Southern Colonies, it would be inaccurate to assume, as some commentators do,[50] that greater strides in the direction of religious liberty had been taken in the Virginia and Southern colonies, at the time of the Revolution or even shortly thereafter, than in the Middle Colonies. This is not to deny the great impact of the laws supporting religious liberty extant in Virginia by 1785, and the influential presence of individuals with a strong commitment to religious liberty in that colony, such as James Madison, Thomas Jefferson, George Mason, and even Patrick Henry. Despite this presence, as a matter of practice, revolutionary Virginia simply did not extend the degree of religious liberty to all or most sects that could be found in some of the Middle Colonies.[51] It would be accurate, however, to say that the movement toward the legalization or formalization of religious liberty was proceeding at a more fervent pace in Virginia than elsewhere, at the time of the Revolution.

At the time of the Revolutionary War, the dedication of many Virginians such as Jefferson, Mason, and Madison to principles of individual freedom included a strong commitment to the protection of the liberty of conscience and the free exercise of religion. Opposition to the established Anglican Church also fueled the effort to formalize religious liberty in Virginia. Certainly, the Tory sentiments of many of the staunchest members of the Anglican Church, and virtually all members of its clergy, also provided a much-needed impetus that pushed many to the Jeffersonian position favoring prompt disestablishment of the Anglican Church in Virginia. This disestablishment sentiment, based at least in part on political factors, was related to the effort to secure the free exercise of religion in Virginia. Thus, while as a practical matter, it is true that Virginia as a colony may not have had the strongest commitment to religious liberty and toleration at the time of the Revolution, it was certainly, by virtue of the quality of its leaders, at the forefront of the movement to enumerate legally such rights. This legal movement, in turn, had a great influence on the development of the First Amendment.

---

50. *See* Malbin, RELIGION AND POLITICS: THE INTENTIONS OF THE AUTHORS OF THE FIRST AMENDMENT, 20, American Enterprise Institute (1978), where he unequivocally concludes that, "no other state—indeed, no other country—went as far toward protecting religious freedom in law as did Virginia in 1785."

51. Thus, when the discussion in the First Congress turned to practical experiences with regard to religious liberty in the colonies, it was the experience of Williams's Rhode Island that was generally cited and not the Virginia experience. *See, e.g., Annals of Congress,* Vol. 1, at 730–31.

SUMMARY OF THE COLONIAL EXPERIENCE

From the early seventeenth to the late eighteenth century, there was a pronounced movement in the direction of increased religious liberty or toleration, albeit in varying degrees, in all of the colonies. This movement was necessitated in significant measure by the pluralistic nature of the religious and economic forces in the colonies and by the positive experience of some of the colonies, most notably the Middle Colonies, in their efforts to provide an environment conducive to unity by extending religious liberty or toleration to diverse sects. Even prior to the Revolutionary War, colonists increasingly sensed the need to set aside religious differences and to tolerate and perhaps even treat with equanimity divergent views in order both to facilitate trade and commerce among the colonies and as a matter of enlightened, republican philosophy. At the time of the Revolution, the demand for unity was acute in light of the audacity of the divided colonies in declaring independence from Britain, the greatest military power in the western world at that time. The threat of war with such a great power mandated at least a momentary setting aside of religious differences in the colonies. After all, as the experience at Valley Forge illustrated, soldiers and patriots of differing religious persuasions had to ignore their differences and cooperate in their efforts against Britain. The isolation of the colonies, economically and otherwise, also contributed to this need for unity. Cooperation, toleration, and coexistence among adherents of various religious beliefs came to be a practical necessity in the colonies, and what may have begun largely as an expedient truce among religionists was soon to find articulation in principles of religious toleration and liberty.

CHAPTER

3

The Revolutionary and Formative Years

MADISON AND THE VIRGINIA REVOLUTIONARY EXPERIENCE: THE FORMALIZATION OF RELIGIOUS LIBERTY

Many influential Virginians during the revolutionary period actively supported, to varying degrees and with differing approaches, the formalization of religious liberty and placing Virginia at the forefront in the legal effort to ensure religious liberty.[1] However, even in the earlier stages of the revolutionary period James Madison played a primary role in the legal debates relative to issues of religious liberty, and his views were clearly influential. By emphasizing Madison's views, I do not intend to depreciate the roles of Thomas Jefferson, George Mason, Patrick Henry, and other Virginia statesmen, but in time Madison's views regarding religious liberty predominated. Given the significance of Madison's role in introducing and crafting the religion clauses of the First Amendment, I am more concerned with the impact the views of other Virginians may have had on Madison, than with the broader impact of the views of other Virginians themselves.

Jefferson was in Philadelphia, in the summer of 1776, preparing for the drafting and signing of the Declaration of Independence. At home in Virginia, in Jefferson's absence, George Mason, an advocate of broad

---

1. Curry, THE FIRST FREEDOMS: CHURCH AND STATE IN AMERICA TO THE PASSAGE OF THE FIRST AMENDMENT at 134 (1986).

religious toleration and colonial independence, introduced the famous Virginia Declaration of Rights.[2]

This Declaration of Rights included a provision regarding religious liberty. As originally introduced, Mason's proposal provided:

> That religion, or the duty which we owe to our Creator, and the manner of discharging it, can be directed only by reason and conviction, not by force or violence; and, therefore, that *all men should enjoy the fullest toleration in the exercise of religion, according to the dictates of conscience, unpunished and unrestrained by the magistrate, unless under color of religion any man disturb the peace, the happiness, or safety of society,* and that it is the mutual *duty of all to practice Christian forbearance,* love and charity toward each other.[3]

While this provision for religious toleration constituted a substantial, if somewhat anticipated, step toward increased legal support for religious liberty in Virginia, it did not satisfy James Madison, then a twenty-six-year-old legislator who had recently completed his education at Princeton, under the tutelage, in part, of President John Witherspoon.

President Witherspoon was "a strong advocate of the tolerant attitude in things ecclesiastical."[4] President Witherspoon's libertarian ideas evidently did not fall upon deaf ears when directed to his student. William Cabell Rives, Madison's classmate, close friend, and biographer, suggested that Madison may have deliberately selected Princeton rather than the seemingly obvious choice of the College of William and Mary for his education on religious grounds, because of the attitude of Wither-

---

2. On 29 June 1776, Virginia formally seceded from the British Empire, having just weeks before met in the Virginia constitutional convention of May 1776 to enact a state constitution. This constitution was to include an expansive declaration of rights, and Mason was responsible for drafting a provision dealing with religious liberty.

3. As cited in M. Malbin, RELIGION AND POLITICS: THE INTENTIONS OF THE AUTHORS OF THE FIRST AMENDMENT 21 (1978) (emphasis added).

4. A. Stokes & L. Pfeffer, CHURCH AND STATE IN THE UNITED STATES at 55 (1964). Stokes and Pfeffer attribute much to the influence of President Witherspoon on Madison's attitudes regarding religious liberty. They also note that "as a young man [Madison] had an experience that profoundly influenced him. He stood outside the jail in Orange, Virginia, and heard an imprisoned Baptist minister preach from the window—the only pulpit legally available to him." *Id.*

spoon, a proponent of disestablishment and broad rights of religious exercise, on the "question of an American Episcopate."[5]

Whatever factors, and there may have been many, that contributed to the early development of Madison's view on the subject of religious liberty, it received its first formal, recorded articulation in Madison's response to Mason's proposed Declaration of Rights. Madison responded to Mason's proposal for dealing with religious liberty with a counterproposal:

> That religion, or the duty which we owe to our Creator, and the manner of discharging it, being under the direction of reason and conviction only, *not of violence, or compulsion,* all men are entitled to the full and *free exercise* of it according to the *dictates of conscience; and therefore no man or class of men ought on account of religion be invested with particular emoluments or privileges, nor subjected to any penalties or disabilities, unless under color of religion the preservation of equal liberty, and the existence of the State be manifestly endangered.*[6]

This written articulation of his position regarding religious liberty differed substantially from Mason's proposal and constituted a step beyond what had been proposed by previous statesmen, including Roger Williams.

This statement by Madison merits examination, not only because he used the words free exercise of religion, terminology that was to reappear in the text of the First Amendment, but also because it is indicative of the general meaning he attributed to that terminology. His addition regarding the investment of "particular emoluments or privileges" is also deserving of consideration, because it seemingly expressed his early view regarding establishments. In fact, it is surprising that Madison's use of this language in conjunction with his use of the familiar free exercise language has received so little attention from the Court or from contemporary commentators.

Before discussing Madison's proposed changes to Mason's draft, it should be pointed out that Madison retained, in substance, the language "that religion, or duty we owe to our Creator, and the manner of discharging it." The retention of this phrase would seem to indicate a special affinity on the part of Madison and Mason for religious matters, matters of individual conscience between human beings and God.

---

5. 1 W. Rives, History Of The Life And Times Of James Madison 11 (1859).

6. *Cited in* M. Malbin, *supra* note 3, at 21 (emphasis added).

Madison probably viewed Mason's effort as a well-meaning but inadequate elaboration of the then-developing view of religious toleration, which held that Christian religion of a nondenominational Protestant sort could be preferred by the government, so long as individuals espousing other religious views were tolerated in the exercise of their religion. Under Mason's view the state could support or assist Christian establishments and could also deprive an individual of the privilege of the free exercise of his or her religion in the interest of the peace, happiness, and safety of the society. Madison, on the other hand, believed that "the right of every man is to liberty—not toleration."[7]

However, there is much more to be gleaned from Madison's proposed amendment to the religious rights portion of the Declaration of Rights than the simplistic conclusion that he rejected the then-popular view of Christian preference and toleration, with its historical antecedents in the Toleration Acts of Britain and the colonies.[8] In his first substantive change to the Mason proposal, for example, Madison substituted compulsion for Mason's use of the term force. Obviously, for Madison compulsion was much more inclusive than force in limiting the role of the state. Compulsion would seem to include in its prohibition more indirect forms of coercion on the part of the state in religious matters. Madison believed that the state should be severely limited in its ability to restrict matters of religious exercise.

In the next substantive alteration of Mason's proposal, Madison deleted the words "all men should *enjoy* the fullest *toleration* of the exercise of religion," and substituted the words "all men are *entitled* to the full and *free exercise* of [religion]." For Madison, these rights were not a mere privilege, to be granted and enjoyed at the whim and fancy of the government; rather, they were in the nature of inalienable rights which were largely beyond the reach of the state.

Next, Madison substituted the language, "no man or class of men ought on account of religion to be invested with particular emoluments or privileges, nor subjected to any penalties or disabilities" in place of Mason's "unpunished or unrestrained by the Magistrate" terminology. For Madison the government could neither compel individuals in religious matters nor invest the majority or any other class or sect, on account of their religion, with "particular emoluments or privileges," or subject them "to any penalties or disabilities" based on their religious preferences. This, for Madison, was the heart of what was subsequently to become his preferred view of the meaning of the Establishment Clause

---

7. A. Stokes & L. Pfeffer, *supra* note 4, at 55.
8. *Id.* at 93

of the First Amendment and constituted a position that would come to be increasingly accepted in Virginia as Virginians sought to disestablish the Anglican Church. His use of the term particular in conjunction with emoluments or privileges is informative when read together with the subjection to any penalties or disabilities language. This terminology seems to indicate that he was not opposed to some benefits to all religions or accommodations of religious exercise generally, provided no person was given any special privilege thereby. For Madison, a particular privilege might compel or inhibit another in the free and equal exercise of his or her religious conviction, while general or equal and nonpreferential access to such benefits by all religious groups might be permitted as a means of facilitating individual free exercise.

This interpretation receives added support from Madison's addition of the terminology the preservation of equal liberty in his next proposed alteration. He substituted the phrase "unless under color of religion the preservation of equal liberty, and the existence of the State be manifestly endangered" for Mason's more innocuous language "unless under color of religion any man disturb the peace, the happiness, or safety of society." Madison's language indicates that he was particularly concerned that all religions be treated equally and that no religion be given a particular benefit or subjected to a particular burden by the state unless that burden was equally applicable to all other religions. Furthermore, state limitations or burdens on religious exercise could only be justified on the ground that the existence of the state would be manifestly endangered if the state were prohibited from enforcing such burdens. When considered in light of Madison's views regarding pluralism, this conclusion is hardly surprising. For Madison, the evils of faction could only be controlled by permitting all factions to interact and by refraining from placing any individual or group of common believers in a position of privilege over other individuals or groups.[9] Equal treatment, without compulsion of any sort, for all religions, both in terms of benefits and burdens, was a must for Madison.

---

9. *See* THE FEDERALIST No. 10, at 77–9 (J. Madison) (R. Rossiter ed. 1961). *See also* Curry, *James Madison and the Burger Court: Converging Views of Church-State Separation,* 56 IND. L. J. 615 (1981). Professor Curry argues that avoiding the evils of faction was central to Madison's thought, and that applying Madison's desire to control factions in the freedom-of-religion area would require a more stringent application of the political divisiveness test. *Id.* at 636. Curry argues that even aid to every sect increases factions and should be avoided under Madison's theory. *Id.* at 635–36. Without disagreeing with Curry's conclusion that the control of faction was extremely important to Madison, I would dispute Curry's proposition that all other matters are secondary to this interest. Instead, I would argue that even the control of factions would not justify the regulation

In this last language, Madison also abandoned the then-prevailing notion that religious liberty could be limited in the interests of preserving public peace, happiness and safety. Rather, he proposed the then (and, unfortunately, even now) extraordinary concept that government could only intervene in matters impinging upon the free exercise of one's conscience or religious conviction when "under the color of religion the preservation of equal liberty, and the existence of the State be *manifestly endangered.*" Apparently, only something of the magnitude of sedition, or the denial by one religious group of the equal liberty of another, would justify governmental action regarding religious matters. Never had anyone gone so far in limiting the power of the state to regulate religious exercise. On occasion, the present Court has edged closer to such a standard. Today, at least as a matter of terminology, if religious exercise is limited by a governmental action, that action must be justified as being in furtherance of a *compelling* state interest. Furthermore, even when the state's action is taken in furtherance of a compelling state interest, the state must also establish that the governmental interest is being furthered in the case at hand in a manner least restrictive of the religious exercise being limited. However, even given the contemporary Court's apparent sensitivity in protecting religious exercise, it must be concluded that no court has gone as far as Madison would have them go toward protecting the free exercise of religion against state action, although it is clear that the broad language in the First Amendment would permit such an expansive reading of the Free Exercise Clause.

Finally, Madison eliminated Mason's language stating that "it is the mutual duty of all to practice Christian forbearance, love and charity toward each other." There are at least two reasons why Madison may have eliminated this language. First, Madison, like Roger Williams, recognized that other religious sects in addition to Christian sects would be

---

of the right to free exercise for Madison unless the existence of the state was manifestly endangered thereby, because the right to free exercise was inalienable. Furthermore, Madison did not view faction or pluralism in the religious area as an evil. Rather, Madison argued that freedom of religion actually "arises from that multiplicity of sects, which pervades America, and which is the best and only security for religious liberty in any one society. For where there is a variety of sects, there cannot be a majority of any one sect to oppress and persecute the rest." 5 J. Madison, THE WRITINGS OF JAMES MADISON 176 n.3 (Hunt ed. 1901). *See also,* discussion in Smith, *Getting Off on the Wrong Foot and Back on Again: A Reexamination of the History of the Framing of the Religion Clauses of the First Amendment and a Critique of the Reynolds and Everson Decisions,* 20 WAKE FOR. L. REV. 569 at 577−78 (1984).

present in the typical state and believed that no sect or group or combination of Christian sects ought to receive special treatment at the hands of the state. All religions, Christian and non-Christian, were to be treated equally. Second, he undoubtedly felt that the use of that language again implied that religious rights were a matter of privilege, to be extended by loving Christians, rather than inalienable rights, which every legitimate government must respect.

As finally enacted, Virginia chose some of Mason's language rather than that which was proffered by Madison. However, what is surprising is that the legislature also accepted much of Madison's language in preference to Mason's proposed language. Mason was an established legislator, with a good reputation, while Madison, as a young man at the time, had but begun to merit the respect of his fellow legislators. Furthermore, while the action of the Virginia Assembly is of some importance in showing the length to which Virginians were willing to go in 1776, it should not be construed as vitiating the substantive portions of Madison's counterproposal that were not accepted in terms of the First Amendment analysis. To the contrary, the counterproposal gives one a starting point from which to assess the development of Madison's philosophical position as it pertains to the First Amendment. In sum, the final result in Virginia, with regard to the Declaration of Rights' provision dealing with religious liberty, is less significant in many ways than the meaning attributed to certain terms by Madison, who ultimately introduced and provided much of the thought and meaning behind the language of the First Amendment.

The proposal finally adopted in the Virginia Declaration of Rights was a compromise between Madison's position and that of Mason. It provided

> That religion, or the duty which we owe to our Creator, and the manner of discharging it, can be directed only by reason and conviction, not by force or violence, and therefore all men are equally entitled to the free exercise of religion, according to the dictates of conscience; and that it is the duty of all to practice Christian forbearance, love, and charity toward each other.[10]

This adopted version utilized Madison's free exercise language and retained Mason's terminology regarding the duty of all to practice Christian forbearance. Madison's establishment or particular-emoluments-and-privileges language was rejected, although Stokes and Pfeffer argue that the Assembly left the establishment issue of public financial support

---

10. Hunt, *Madison and Religious Liberty,* in AMERICAN HISTORICAL ASSOCIATION ANNUAL REPORT 163, 166 (1901), *cited in* M. Malbin, *supra* note 3, at 22.

for the clergy open for future determination, refusing to lend specific support to such a proposition or to expressly oppose it.[11]

The Assembly also avoided the issue of the proper limit upon governmental regulation of religious exercise by refusing to adopt either the Mason or the Madison version. This, in a sense, might be termed a victory for Madison. Not only did the Assembly reject Mason's language regarding toleration, but it also rejected his language regarding the disturbance of "the public peace, happiness, or safety" as the appropriate standard for state regulation of religious matters. This rejection of Mason's language constituted a movement away from the then conventional view that religious liberty was synonymous with religious toleration, and a movement toward the more expansive Madisonian view of religious liberty as an inalienable right. While the legislature was unwilling to accept Madison's whole package, which constituted a radical departure from past convention regarding the issue of religious liberty, it had taken a vital step in the direction of promoting religious liberty, and Madison's influence was only beginning to be felt.

After the passage of the Declaration of Rights in Virginia in 1776, Virginia continued to move in the direction of furthering religious freedom. By December of 1776, Jefferson had returned to Virginia and had reassumed his position as chairman of the Assembly's Committee on Religion. The committee, in turn, reported out two bills intended to repeal penalties placed upon religious dissenters. These bills were passed. Additionally, due to the anti-British sentiment in the legislature, the Assembly voted to suspend the official collection of tithes that had theretofore been used to pay the Anglican clergy. Jefferson could not find enough support for a complete abolition of the tithes in 1776, but the continuing anti-British sentiment in Virginia during the Revolutionary War made it possible for Jefferson to continue to suspend the collection of tithes for such purposes on a yearly basis until 1779, when the public collection of tithes for the Anglican Church was abolished. One by one, the preferences that had been accorded to the Anglican Church were either abolished or extended to all religious sects in Virginia during the latter part of the eighteenth and the early part of the nineteenth centuries.[12]

Thus, with the coming of the Revolutionary War, the climate in Virginia was such that the pro-British sentiment of the established Anglican Church made it vulnerable to the efforts of those who had long desired its disestablishment. However, by 1784, after the Revolutionary

---

11. A. Stokes & L. Pfeffer, *supra* note 4, at 43.
12. *See, e.g.,* M. Malbin, *supra* note 3, at 22–5.

War, an effort was afoot to salvage and promote some vestiges of the faltering Anglican establishment.

Postwar legislative efforts in the House of Delegates to strengthen the ailing Anglican establishment in Virginia occurred on two fronts. On one, there was an effort toward incorporation of the Episcopal or Anglican Church. Rives, a contemporary and friend of Madison, describes the disestablishment and incorporation movements that were simultaneously under way in Virginia as follows:

> Petitions were also presented from the Baptist, Presbyterian, and Protestant Episcopal churches, the two former asking a removal of all remaining distinctions in favor of the Episcopal church, and *that religious freedom be established upon the broad basis of perfect political equality;* and the last demanding the repeal of certain laws which restrained, as they alleged, their power of self-government, and praying for an act of incorporation to enable them to hold their property securely, and to regulate their own spiritual concerns. The Committee on Religion to whom these petitions were referred, reported the demands of all of them to be reasonable, and particularly that the applications made by the clergies of both the Episcopal and Presbyterian Churches, for incorporation of their respective societies, were so; and that "like corporations ought to be extended to all other religious societies within the Commonwealth, which may apply for the same."[13]

Somewhat ironically for the proponents of the Anglican establishment, the original proposal reported out of the Committee on Religion would have essentially provided for equal access to the rights and power of incorporation by all churches which might seek to incorporate. This step indicated a movement away from particularized religious preference and toward equal treatment of all religions. A governmental benefit was to be conferred, but there was a sentiment afoot that while such benefits to religion were acceptable, equal treatment should be required. Proponents of the Anglican establishment understood that they would have to widen the protective or preferential net provided by the state to include other denominations. However, a substantial question remained as to how far state preference should be extended to religious sects other than the Anglicans.

Additionally, as Rives notes, there was a simultaneous effort on the part of the Baptists and Presbyterians to disestablish the Episcopal Church in Virginia or, in other words, to ensure that "religious freedom

---

13. W. Rives, *supra* note 5, at 561⁻62 (footnotes omitted) (emphasis added).

be established upon the broad basis of political equality."[14] The disestablishment movement in Virginia was, therefore, actuated at least in part by a desire for political equality and was considered coextensive with religious liberty. However, not only did the nonestablished or nonstate-supported Protestant groups fail in their outright disestablishment effort, but ultimately even the committee's proposal that incorporation rights and privileges be extended to all religions received little support. The only bill regarding the incorporation issue that was actively supported by a majority of the legislature was one that favored the Episcopal establishment, to the exclusion of other religious groups.

In December of 1784, the bill incorporating the Episcopal Church, but no other, was passed. However, on the very next day, 23 December 1784, a more ominous event darkened the horizon for proponents of religious equality and liberty in Virginia. Fresh from their victory on the incorporation issue and under the able leadership of Patrick Henry, those who were dismayed at the weakened status of the Episcopal establishment turned their efforts toward enactment of the General Assessment Bill of 1784.

Since the history of this bill has received great attention and has often been mentioned by the courts, I will examine it in substantial detail. Even had the Assessment Bill not been given such great weight by the courts as an articulation of the probable intent of the framers, it would deserve consideration as a further elaboration of both the conventional view regarding the establishment issue and Madison's view regarding that issue and religious liberty in general. The Assessment Bill which was "designed to serve as a replacement for the tithe would have (1) named Christianity as the Established Religion of the Commonwealth; (2) declared the Articles of Faith essential to Christianity; (3) defined the forms of congregations that constituted a Christian Church; and (4) assessed each person a certain amount to support the religious teacher and place of worship of his choice [so long as it was Christian]. If he should fail to name a choice, the amount was to be paid into a public fund to aid seminaries."[15]

Despite Madison's staunch opposition and because of the able and respected leadership of Henry, who was generally considered to be an advocate of religious tolerance and liberty, the Assessment Bill appeared destined to pass. Initially, by a vote of 47 to 32, the House passed a resolution, declaring that "the people of the Commonwealth, according to their respective abilities, ought to pay a moderate tax or contribution

---

14. *Id.* at 562.
15. M. Malbin, *supra* note 3, at 23.

or the support of *the Christian religion,* or of some *Christian* church, denomination, or communion of *Christians,* or of some form of *Christian* worship."[16] With this language, which would have treated all *Christians* alike, the bill initially appealed to Presbyterians as well as to the Episcopalians. It appeared certain to pass with such broad-based support. Rives mused that:

> It is perhaps, not to be wondered at that, among a people accustomed from their earliest times to see religion lean for support on the arm of secular power, an apprehension should have been felt of its decline upon withdrawal of that support; and that, under these circumstances, many enlightened minds did not, at first, perceive the departure from fundamental principles, as well as the dangerous precedent, in the measure now proposed. Besides Mr. Henry, who was the leading advocate and champion of the measure, it is known that General Washington and Richard Henry Lee at first favored it; and in the House of Delegates, several of those rising and distinguished men who were the intimate friends of Mr. Madison, and almost invariably acted with him on public questions—such as Henry Tazewell, John Marshall, and his late colleague in Congress, Mr. Jones—now separated from him on the issue of general assessment.[17]

Although the Assessment Bill received a significant measure of support, Madison led a growing opposition to the bill. Where there are no verbatim reports of what was said during the debates regarding this measure, the outline of a speech by Madison, "written on the back of a letter, in a very condensed hand and with many abbreviations,"[18] has been preserved. Those notes give one a good idea of the points raised orally by Madison.

---

16. 1 W. Rives, *supra* note 5, at 600 (emphasis added).

17. *Id.* at 601⁻02. Rives points out that the Presbyterians, themselves proponents of disestablishment of the Episcopal Church, expressed their opinions in favor of such a bill. In a letter to Mason, George Washington indicated his support for the Assessment Bill:

> Altho no man's sentiments are more opposed to any kind of restraint upon religious principles than mine are, yet I must confess, that I am not amongst the number of those who are so much alarmed at the thought of making people pay towards the support of that which they profess, if of the denomination of Christians or declare themselves Jews, Mahometans or otherwise, and thereby obtain proper relief.

Cited in Curry, *supra* note 1, at 140.

18. *Id.* at 603

Having reproduced Madison's outline in full,[19] Rives summarized the thrust of his friend's remarks, specifically stating that

> We learn from it that Mr. Madison contended, first, that the regulation of religion was not within the province of civil power, and that every attempt of the kind tended necessarily to ultimate projects of compulsory uniformity.[20]

The notes left by Madison also enabled Rives to clarify a number of points raised by Madison with regard to his opposition to the bill:

> He then showed that, as the benefits of the proposed provision were to be limited to *Christian* societies and churches, it would devolve upon the courts of law to determine what constitutes Christianity, and thus, amid the great diversity of creeds and sects, to set up by their *fiat* a standard of orthodoxy on the one hand and of heresy on the other, which would be destructive of the rights of private conscience. He argued, finally that the proposition dishonored Christianity by resting it upon a basis of mercenary support, and concluded with vindicating its holy character from such a reproach, contending that its true and best support was in the principles of universal and perfect liberty established by the Bill of Rights [the Virginia Declaration of Rights], and which was alone in consonance with its own pure and elevated precepts.[21]

This lengthy quotation from Rives, together with Madison's notes, support a number of conclusions regarding Madison's position: (1) that such efforts to regulate religions had the effect of compelling uniformity; (2) that religion needs no such artificial props; (3) that history indicates that religious establishments were detrimental (apparently, according to his notes, Madison looked with approval at the experience of Pennsylvania, New Jersey, Rhode Island, and New York); (4) that Virginia would be injured in its efforts to encourage settlement within its boundaries of those of other faiths by such a religiously discriminatory law; (5) that the decay of public morals was attributable to other factors, and that public morality could best be restored by example and by voluntary religious association; (6) that the benefits were limited to Christian societies and would entangle the state in determining what societies, in fact, met the state's criteria of orthodox Christianity and which societies

---

19. For the outline of Madison's remarks, see *id.* at 605.
20. *Id.* at 603.
21. *Id.* at 604–05 (emphasis in original).

were heretical; (7) that efforts by the state to ascertain which groups were Christian for the purpose of allocating such aid would be "destructive of the rights of private conscience" or free exercise; and finally, (8) that the Assessment Bill was contrary to the provisions of the Virginia Declaration of Rights regarding religious liberty.

Madison's concluding remarks evidently centered around his concern that all religions be treated in an equal or uniform fashion and that the state be prevented from determining matters of orthodoxy. While it might be inaccurate to conclude that Madison was inalterably opposed to state aid in any form to all religions, it is clear that he opposed aid not only to a single establishment but to multiple establishments, at least when that aid failed to include so-called heretical sects as well. Even if the Assessment Bill had provided for aid to all religious groups rather than just Christian sects, it is conceivable that Madison might have opposed the bill on the theoretical ground that in selecting what exercises or expressions of conscience would qualify as religions, the state might offend someone's inalienable right of free exercise. At any rate, it is clear that Madison's opposition to the bill centered on the fact that it would discriminate against rights of conscience and the "universal and perfect religious liberty" he believed to be embodied in the Virginia Declaration of Rights.

On 23 December 1784, after the debates, the bill was passed, by a vote of 44 to 42 on the second reading.[22] It must be noted that this vote constituted a substantial reduction of the 47–32 margin originally supporting the assessment resolution. This changing tide, based in part perhaps on the force of all or part of Madison's arguments, may very well have assisted Madison in persuading the delegates to postpone the third and final reading of the bill until the next general session and to print the bill for dissemination for public comment.[23]

With the last-minute postponement of action on this legislation entitled a "Bill establishing a Provision for Teachers of the Christian Religion," opponents of the bill turned their efforts to persuading the people that such an act should be opposed on the ground that it was violative of religious liberty. By 21 June 1785, Madison was able to write that "a very warm opposition will be made to this innovation [the Assessment Bill] by the middle and back counties."[24] However, growing public opposition had to be packaged in a form that would maximize its effect on

---

22. *Id.* at 608.
23. *Id.* at 610.
24. *Id.* at 631.

the legislators. It was decided that the opposition to the bill should be embodied in the form of a written petition, signed by the citizenry.[25] With this in mind, Rives points out that, "At the instance of Colonel Mason, Mr. George Nicholas, and other distinguished friends of religious liberty, Madison prepared a 'Memorial and Remonstrance' to the legislature against the proposed assessment, to be circulated among the people."[26]

Rives describes Madison's role in the drafting of the *Memorial and Remonstrance* as "the crowning victory in a momentous contest."[27] Since the Supreme Court's decision in *Everson v. Board of Education,*[28] contemporary Courts have also looked to the *Memorial* as the guiding light in resolving issues of religious liberty. The *Memorial* is a critical document in understanding Madison's views and for examining how in all likelihood those views were initially infused into the dialogue relating to issues of religious liberty and ultimately into the language of the First Amendment. It should not be crowned, however, as the ultimate source for deciding all issues of religious liberty under the aegis of the religion clauses of the First Amendment. Rather, it is but a piece, albeit a significant piece, in the puzzle that must be put together to understand the original meaning of the First Amendment.

Given the importance of the *Memorial and Remonstrance,* I will examine its language closely to determine Madison's likely intent with

---

25. Actually there were multiple petitions prepared by various opponents of the bill. Curry, for example, notes that:

> In the centuries since its composition, the *Remonstrance* combining as it does political and religious arguments into a balanced and resounding whole, has gained in stature. Judging by the multitude of other petitions submitted to the legislature, however, it did not in its contemporary setting enjoy the preeminence it would acquire over time. On the contrary, the form of petition most favored by opponents of the assessment appeared roughly twice as often. Although it used much the same arguments as the *Remonstrance,* it bore a heavier religious and evangelical emphasis.

Curry, *supra* note 1, at 143−44. However, as previously noted, the fact that Madison's *Remonstrance* was not preeminent at the time is fairly irrelevant for our purposes, since we are more concerned with ascertaining Madison's view, as the author of the First Amendment, than we are with determining the nature of the view predominating in Virginia in 1785, although understanding that view can also lend some light to the issue of original intent since it was clearly espoused by a large number of Virginians.

26. Rives, *supra* note 5, at 631−32.

27. *Id.* at 633.

28. 330 U.S. 1 (1946).

regard to the Assessment Bill itself and more importantly with regard to his general position on issues of religious liberty.

Madison begins his argument in the *Memorial* by noting that the exercise of one's religious convictions constitutes an inalienable right:

> The religion, then, of every man must be left to the conviction and conscience of every man; and it is the right of every man to exercise it as these may dictate. This right is, in its nature, an inalienable right. It is inalienable, because the opinions of men, depending only on the evidence contemplated by their own minds cannot follow the dictates of other men; it is unalienable also, because what is here a right towards men is a duty towards the Creator.[29]

Madison goes on to explain the significance of the inalienable nature of this right by noting that this individually determined duty of homage to the Creator is superior to contrary claims of civil society:

> It is the duty of every man to render to the Creator such homage, and such only, as he believes to be acceptable to Him. This duty is precedent both in order of time and in degree of obligation, to the claims of Civil Society. Before any man can be considered as a member of Civil Society, he must be considered a subject of the Governor of the Universe; and if a member of Civil Society who enters into any subordinate Association must always do it with a reservation of his duty to the general authority, much more must every man who becomes a member of any particular Civil Society, do it with a saving of his allegiance to the Universal Sovereign. We maintain therefore that, *in matters of religion, no man's right is abridged by the institution of civil society, and that Religion is wholly exempt from its cognizance.*[30]

In stating that the duty of every man to pay homage to his Creator, in the manner he sees fit, is exempt from and precedent to civil authority, Madison makes it clear that he continues to hold the same expansive view of free exercise as he articulated in his proposed revision of the religious-freedom portion of the Virginia Declaration of Rights. Madison believed that religious exercise could not be abridged by the state, except when the state was manifestly endangered or when the exercise

---

29. J. Madison, *Memorial and Remonstrance* (1785), quoted in 1 W. Rives, *supra* note 5, at 635.

30. *Id.* (emphasis added).

of one's religion infringed upon another person's religious liberty.[31] By Madison's use of the word homage to clarify the concept of duty toward the Creator, it is also evident that he intended to include religious practices, such as prayer, within the purview of this broad concept of religious liberty.

Madison next postulated that "if religion be exempt from the authority of society at large, still less can it be subject to the legislative body." The departments of government should not be permitted "to overlap the greater barrier which defends the rights of the people."[32]

After next noting that "it is proper to take alarm at the first experiment on our liberties,"[33] Madison turned to the particular detriment to religious liberty that he envisioned in the establishment of the Christian religion provided for in the Assessment Bill:

> Who does not see that the authority *which can establish Christianity, in exclusion of all other Religions* may establish with the same ease any particular sect of Christians, in exclusion of all other Sects? That same authority which can *force* a citizen to contribute threepence only of his property for the support of any *one establishment, may force him to conform to any other establishment* in all cases whatsoever.[34]

In the very next paragraph, Madison explained that such an establishment of Christianity, in preference to all non-Christian sects, constituted an improper denial of the principle of equal treatment by government of the religious beliefs of all persons:

> Because the bill violates that equality which ought to be the basis of every law, and which is more indispensable, in proportion as the validity or expediency of any law is more liable to be impeached.... Above all are men to be considered as retaining an *"equal* title to the free exercise of Religion according to the dictates of conscience." Whilst we assert for ourselves a freedom to embrace, to profess and to observe

---

31. Madison's view of inalienable rights seems tied in some measure to the contract theorists' (Hobbes, Locke, and Rousseau) view that people enter into a social compact and form a government to fulfill certain collective needs, but that certain rights are inalienable and cannot legitimately be usurped by the government. Madison clearly felt that religious liberty was the type of right that could not be usurped by the government. *See, e.g.,* M. Malbin, *supra* note 3, at 30–36 for a discussion of Locke's influence.

32. J. Madison, *Memorial and Remonstrance* (1785), *quoted in* 1 W. Rives, *supra* note 5, at 635.

33. *Id.*

34. *Id.* at 636 (emphasis added).

the religion which we believe to be of divine origin, we cannot deny an
equal freedom to those whose minds have not yet yielded to the evidence which has convinced us.[35]

Thus, for Madison, what was most objectionable about the bill was not
that it aided or accommodated religion generally but that it aided Christianity to the exclusion of other religions. Madison, himself a Christian,
felt that "to deny an equal freedom to those whose minds have not yet
yielded to the evidence which has convinced us" would constitute a grave
error because all men should be free to choose and act, without unequal
or preferential treatment at the hands of the government, in matters of
conscience. Of course, while the language used by Madison is certainly
susceptible to an interpretation that would permit the government to aid
all sects equally, it is also conceivable that Madison may have believed
that any time the government gave financial aid to religious groups, it
would necessarily become entangled in determining which matters of
conscience were religious.[36] He clearly wanted religious exercise to be
construed broadly, as a right of individual conscience, to assure that the
government did not hinder the exercise of matters of conscience. Although such an interpretation would seem less justified based on the
language used, Madison may have opposed the idea that the government
could decide what was religious for aid purposes. He may also have
believed that, as a practical matter, such aid could not be equally distributed by government, and that, therefore, the only way religious
equality could be assured would be for the government to decline to
give its financial support to any religion. Whichever view Madison may
have preferred, and the language used is susceptible of any of the
preceding interpretations, it must be kept in mind that his goal was to
protect rather than inhibit individual religious exercise.

Madison went on to argue his thesis of equal treatment for all religions throughout the *Memorial*. For example, he stated, "a just
government...will be best supported by treating *every* citizen in the
enjoyment of his Religion *with the same equal hand* which protects his
person and his property; by neither invading the equal rights of any

---

35. *Id.*
36. Curry makes a case for the proposition that Madison and many other
framers opposed the notion of having the government extend financial aid to
religious groups, while simultaneously maintaining that aid or assistance on a
nonpreferential basis, in nonfinancial forms, would be acceptable. *See* Curry,
supra note 1, at 143, where he concludes that Madison believed that "a general
assessment would be a foot in the door leading to despotism. If the State could
demand support for all religions, it could also demand support for a particular
religion."

Sect, nor suffering any Sect to invade those of another."[37] After referring to the assessment as a "proposed establishment," Madison returned to the equality theme, arguing that the bill was coercive in that "it is itself a signal of persecution. It degrades from the equal rank of citizens all those whose opinions in religion do not bend to those of the legislative authority."[38] He concluded further that such a bill would have the tendency to banish citizens of non-Christian or unorthodox faiths who had immigrated to Virginia seeking religious liberty.[39]

Having made his argument for "equal and complete liberty," Madison next battled the strongly held, conventional colonial view that it would be proper to establish generalized, nondenominational Christianity, provided other non-Christian religious views were treated with tolerance. He began by observing that "the first wish of those who enjoy this precious gift [of Christianity] ought to be that it may be imparted to the whole race of mankind."[40] After thus reassuring his fellow Christians that he shared their desire to convert the nonbeliever, he concluded that the policy of the Assessment Bill would lessen the likelihood of such conversion, because the bill "at once discourages those who are strangers to the light of revelation from coming into the region of it [Christianity], and countenances by example the nations who continue in darkness [nonbelief in Christianity], in shutting out those who might convey it [the Christian faith] to them."[41] The extensive recitation of these arguments for equality in the *Memorial* illustrates further that Madison's opposition focused on the fact that the bill failed to treat all religions with equal magnanimity, not on the fact that it failed to adhere to a strict or absolute separation of church and state.

Had Madison intended to propose a strict wall of separation between church and state, he could, and I believe would, have used language that would have expressed more clearly that intention. Instead, he used the language of equal treatment or equal access. The strict separationist, who opposes any and all public aid to or accommodation of religion, might counter by asserting that Madison believed in strict separation but realized that he could not get the necessary public support for such a view because the public might have viewed it as being antireligious. Unfortunately, for the strict separationist, this view, even if correct (which I would assert it is not), carries with it the seeds of its own demise. If Madison was trying to avoid an expansion of the prevailing

---

37. Rives, *supra* note 5, at 637–38 (emphasis added).
38. *Id.* at 638.
39. *Id.*
40. *Id.* at 639.
41. *Id.*

public sentiment favoring governmental promotion or accommodation of religion by using language that appealed to that public sentiment, the strict separationist cannot argue that the language used somehow implicitly supports an undisclosed strict-separationist position. Additionally, in examining language to determine its intended meaning, the belief of those supporting it (in the case of the *Memorial,* the people signing it) would take precedence over even the undisclosed but documented intent of its sponsor. Certainly, absent evidence to the contrary, in construing a document one ought to presume that its author meant or intended the plain meaning of what was said to prevail. Strict separationists, including Justice Wiley B. Rutledge, whose position is set forth in his dissent in *Everson,* must ignore the actual historical data in an effort to build a case in terms of "law office history," selectively using historical data to build a case for their position rather than viewing the history itself to determine what was actually intended. Particularly in light of the wealth of evidence to the contrary regarding Madison's views, strict separationists are left to admit that their position is untenable as a matter of historical fact, but justifiable on some other ground, or to use snippets of history to rationalize an otherwise historically unsupportable position.

Despite the fact that Madison's view in the *Memorial* is susceptible to some variation in interpretation, it is nevertheless possible to draw a couple of helpful conclusions.[42] First, it must be emphasized that

---

42. *See, e.g.,* Curry, *supra* note 1, at 136—48 for a slightly different interpretation of the nature of the debate over the General Assessment. Curry summarizes the arguments of the proponents and opponents as follows:

Proponents of a general assessment accepted the "duty" and proposed that the State see to it that everyone fulfilled it, without forcing anyone to follow a particular way of worship. They believed that religion was absolutely necessary to sustain the moral fiber of society, and that the State should promote it as a means to that end. Evangelical opponents of a general assessment agreed on the indispensability of religion, but they viewed it primarily in terms of "conversion," rather than moral "duty." For them the cause of true religion could be furthered only by the grace of God, and State attempts to advance it would result in the creation of a bureaucratic state religion.

Although the opponents of assessment proclaimed that the State should not help religion at all, many of them simultaneously believed that society should be generally Protestant and that the State should see to it that the Sabbath was observed and the Bible respected. Because the vast majority of the populace concurred in these beliefs, they were not forced to confront the tension in their position.

Id. at 138—39.

Madison's primary concern was with securing religious liberty rather than with assuring that the government prohibit all public expressions of religious faith. Second, it is conceivable that Madison may have had substantial doubts about extending public financial aid to all religions, on the ground that such an effort would involve the government in deciding what beliefs it deemed religious for the purpose of receiving such aid and on the ground that government could not, as a practical matter, assure that such aid would be dispensed in an equal and nondiscriminatory manner. However, I believe it is clear that Madison's repeated reference to the equal-treatment rationale expressed his view and that of the public generally that government could accommodate or facilitate religious exercise, particularly on an individual basis, so long as it did so in an equal or nonpreferential manner.

Madison, along with the other petitioners, was able to persuade vast numbers of citizens that the Assessment Bill, as drafted, would adversely affect religious liberty in Virginia. In addition to highlighting Madison's views, the words of the *Memorial* may be considered indicative of the then prevailing public sentiment or intent regarding religious liberty, at least in Virginia.

During the founding era, there were two major public positions with regard to religious liberty in America: (1) the position of those who adhered to the conventional view that Christianity, usually in a generalized, nondenominational sense, should be established and aided by the government as the religion of the nation, provided only that other religious beliefs must also be tolerated (I shall label this view the "Story view," after a leading proponent, Justice Joseph Story); and (2) the position of those who adhered to the newer, yet growing, Madisonian view that no single religion or group of religions should be aided or established to the exclusion of other less orthodox religions (I will refer to this view as the "Madisonian view"). A dispute as to which of these two views ultimately prevailed in the First Congress continued throughout much of the nineteenth century. The current position on the strict separation of church and state, on the other hand, really did not gain significant acceptance until the second quarter of the twentieth century. While such a strict-separationist view advocating, as Justice Felix Frankfurter said, "irreligion" in the public sector might be supported on the ground that the Constitution is a dynamic instrument, those who would seek to support such an argument by historical reference to Madison's *Memorial and Remonstrance* pervert that history. Perhaps the strongest argument that could be raised, as an historical matter, by those favoring the view that the government should not aid or accommodate any religion or religious exercise is that the equality of treatment for all religions or belief systems envisioned by Madison could only, as a practical matter, be attained by strictly separating all religious activity from the sphere of civil authority. While, upon careful review of the historical data, the proponent of such a position would have to acknowledge that the framers, including Madison, never advocated by word or by action such a strict separation, contemporary strict separationists might seek to argue that the equality value underlying such governmental activity in the Madisonian view now requires the strict separation of church and state. However, to maintain fidelity to the Madisonian view in any form, these advocates of strict separation would have to acknowledge that Madison's primary concern was with furthering the potential for the uninhibited exercise of one's religion. With the increasingly pervasive nature of the public sector in contemporary society, it would strain credulity to assert that Madison would have prohibited the state from permitting any voluntary expressions of religious devotion in public. For Madison, the government could not legitimately inhibit the exercise of one's religion until it infringed upon another's equal right or until the interest of the state became so compelling that the very survival of the state would be manifestly endangered if the religious exercise or expression were permitted to continue.[43]

In the *Memorial,* Madison also argued that governmental determination of which religions are Christian for the purpose of selectively allocating benefits among Christian religious groups would imply that "the civil magistrate is a competent judge of truth or that he may employ religion as an engine of civil policy."[44] The first point, regarding the competence of the magistrate to judge in religious matters, has its parallel in the "entanglement" tier of the current establishment test and is indicative of Madison's fears with regard to governmental intrusion into religious matters in either a doctrinal or a discriminatory sense. His second point, regarding governmental employment of religion as an engine or means of furthering political purposes, receives further elaboration in the *Memorial.*

Madison argued that neither religion nor the civil government had benefited historically by the establishment of a particular religion by the civil authority:

> What influence, in fact, have ecclesiastical establishments had on civil society? In some instances they have been to erect a spiritual tyranny on the ruins of civil authority; in many instances they have been

---

43. Madison first used the "manifestly endangered" language in his response to Mason's proposal for dealing with religious liberty that was to be included in the Virginia Declaration of Rights. For a discussion of Madison's standard, see *supra* notes 40–42 and accompanying text.

44. 1 W. Rives, *supra* note 5, at 636.

> seen upholding the thrones of political tyranny; in no instance have
> they been seen as the guardians of the liberties of the people.[45]

Madison also noted that "rulers who wished to subvert the public liberty,
may have found an established clergy convenient auxiliaries. A just government, instituted to secure and perpetuate it, needs them not."[46] More
than any other statement in the *Memorial,* this would seem to support
the strict separationist's argument that any aid to or public accommodation of religion is detrimental both to religious and civil authority. However, such a reading of Madison's *Memorial* is unjustified, because in the
very same paragraph he concluded by once again emphasizing that the
"equal rights of all sects" should be preserved.

Perhaps there is no clearer example in Madison's *Memorial and
Remonstrance* of the fact that he contemplated some accommodation or
facilitation by the government of the religious beliefs of the American
people, and that he certainly favored public prayer in at least some form,
than the prayer with which he concluded the *Memorial.* He joined with
those who signed the *Memorial* in the following public proclamation of
a need for prayer to the Supreme Lawgiver of the Universe:

> We the subscribers, say that the General Assembly of the Common-
> wealth have no such authority to pass the Assessment Bill and in order
> that no effort may be omitted on our part against so dangerous a
> usurpation; we oppose it, *earnestly praying, as we are duty bound, that
> the Supreme Lawgiver of the Universe, by illuminating those to whom
> it is addressed, may, on the one hand, turn their councils from every
> act which would affront His holy prerogative* or violate the trust
> committed to them, *and, on the other, guide them into every measure which
> may be worthy of His blessing,* redound to their own praise, and may
> establish more firmly the liberties, the prosperity and the Happiness of
> the Commonwealth.[47]

The *Memorial and Remonstrance* did not present an argument for
the strict separation of church and state. Instead, it argued that the
Assessment Bill was beyond the authority of a just civil government
because it failed to treat all religions equally and would, therefore, inev-

---

45. *Id.* at 637.

46. *Id.* at 637–38.

47. J. Madison, *Memorial and Remonstrance* (1785), *quoted in* 1 W. Rives,
supra note 5, at 640 (emphasis added). Furthermore, Professor Cord concludes,
based on his review of the evidence, that Madison "was opposed to the Assessment Bill because it was discriminatory, and thus placed Christianity in a preferred religious position." R. Cord, SEPARATION OF CHURCH AND STATE:
HISTORICAL FACT AND CURRENT FICTION 20 (1982) (emphasis in original).

itably lead the state in the direction of having to choose which religion was to be preferred as a doctrinal matter. Such preference would, in turn, lead inexorably to the persecution of those minority religions failing to receive the doctrinal imprimatur of the state. Religion, for Madison, was a matter of individual, personal, and voluntary devotion, not a matter of majority consensus. Government could only accommodate religion when it did so evenhandedly. On the other hand, the free exercise of one's religion was to be "wholly exempt from the cognizance [of civil authority]," unless the interest of the state was in fact manifestly endangered. For Madison, there was little conflict between the right of free exercise and the prohibition against state preference for any religion. The right to the free exercise of one's religion or conviction of conscience was an inalienable right. If government preferred one religion, even nondenominational Christianity, as a theoretical or a practical matter over another, it acted in derogation of the inalienable right of free exercise.

With his proposed draft of a religious provision for the Virginia Declaration of Rights in 1776 and the drafting of the *Memorial and Remonstrance* nearly ten years later, Madison formulated a coherent philosophy regarding religious liberty. Madison maintained his allegiance to this philosophy throughout his life. He broke from the prevailing view that the Christian religion generally could be preferred, if all other sects were tolerated, and forged a new path, arguing for an inalienable right of free exercise extending to adherents of all religious views or matters of conscience. This inalienable right of free exercise was to be protected from governmental intrusion unless the very existence of the state was somehow manifestly endangered or in the event that the public exercise of the right would have derogated someone else's right of free exercise. That Madison was not alone in espousing this view is clear. It has been reported that the "table of the House of Delegates almost sunk under the weight of the accumulated copies of the memorial sent forward from the different counties."[48] The eloquence of Madison's argument along with the efforts of other petitioners had touched a responsive chord in the public and the Assessment Bill died in committee, without further action. With the death of the Assessment Bill, the proponents of religious liberty in Virginia turned to another project.

Jefferson's Bill for Establishing Freedom[49] had languished in the legislature for a number of years. Jefferson had written the bill in 1779, but it did not finally pass the Assembly until 1785, after overwhelming

---

48. 1 W. Rives, *supra* note 5, at 632.

49. Virginia Statute for Religious Freedom, 1786, *cited in* L. Pfeffer, CHURCH, STATE AND FREEDOM, at 113–14 (1967).

public support for the *Memorial* had given credence to the notion that the attitude toward religious liberty in Virginia had changed.

In his recitals to the bill, Jefferson noted that it would be improper for the "magistrate to intrude his powers into the field of opinion and to restrain the profession or propagation of principles, on the supposition of their ill-tendency [because such an intrusion] at once destroys all religious liberty."[50] The recitals also provided that it would be improper for the government to compel an individual to donate to any religion—even his own—against his will. Jefferson concluded the recitals by noting that "it is time enough for the rightful purposes of civil government for its officers to interfere when principles break out into overt acts against peace and good order."[51]

The substance of the bill, in turn, provided that:

> [N]o man shall be compelled to frequent or support any religious worship, place, or ministry whatsoever, nor shall be enforced, restrained, molested, or burdened in his body or goods, nor shall otherwise suffer, on account of his religious opinions or beliefs; but that all men shall be free to profess, and by argument to maintain their opinions in matters of religion, and that the same shall in no wise diminish, enlarge, or affect their civil capacities.[52]

When the recitals of the bill are viewed in the context of the substance of the bill itself and its contemporaneous history, it is evident that the theory of church and state relationships contemplated in the bill offers

---

50. *Id.*
51. *Id. See also,* M. Malbin, *supra* note 3, at 27–9. Malbin argues that this statement constitutes evidence of a weakening of the Madisonian position concerning the latitude given government to intrude upon matters of religious activities that the government deems to be "against peace and good order," a standard much less stringent than the Madisonian "manifestly endangered" standard. Malbin does not offer any further support from Madison's writings for his assertion that Madison compromised his more stringent position on the free-exercise issue by supporting Jefferson's bill. Without further evidence of a shift on Madison's part, Madison's silence on the issue of what standard should apply to governmental intervention in supporting Jefferson's statute generally can hardly be considered determinative, particularly in light of Madison's numerous express avowals of a standard much more stringent than that applied by Jefferson, both before and after passage of the bill.
52. Virginia Statute for Religious Freedom, 1786, *cited in* L. Pfeffer, *supra* note 49, at 113–14.

little support for the views espoused by twentieth-century advocates of strict separation.[53]

Perhaps sensing futility in placing too much emphasis on the actual history of religious liberty in Virginia prior to adoption of the First Amendment, twentieth-century strict separationists have turned to a much more dubious source to support their views, Jefferson's letter to the Danbury Baptist Association, dated 1 January 1802. In that letter, Jefferson concluded that he believed that the First Amendment, which declared that this legislature should "make no law respecting an establishment of religion, or prohibiting the free exercise thereof," thus "built a wall of separation between Church and State."[54] That Jefferson considered this reply to be significant, as a legal matter, is clear from the fact that he submitted a draft of the letter to his attorney general, Levi Lincoln, for his review. In his letter to Lincoln, Jefferson defended his reply to the Danbury Baptist Association against anticipated strong public disfavor by noting that he could not resist "the occasion...[for] sowing useful truths and principles among the people which might germinate and become rooted among their political tenets."[55] Jefferson's letter to

---

53. *See, e.g.,* W. Marnell, THE FIRST AMENDMENT 108–09 (1964). Marnell cautioned that:
> One should note, however, precisely what compromised the separation of church and state in the act. No one could be legally required to attend any church or support any ministry. No one could legally suffer any injury in his body or his goods because of his religious beliefs. All should be free to maintain their religious opinions, without benefit or loss from such profession of belief. In short, there were three factors in the equation: the church, the state, and the individual. The act protected the individual from any loss at the hands of the state because of his relationship to the church. It did not attempt to define the relations between church and state except in terms of the individual. It contained an implicit ban, of course, upon a church establishment, but beyond that it did not go. Efforts to read more into it inevitably take on the subjective case of the thought of the person who does the reading.

Id.

54. Letter from Thomas Jefferson to Messrs. Nehemiah Dodge, Ephraim Robbins, and Stephen S. Nelson, A Committee of the Danbury Baptist Association in the State of Connecticut (1 Jan. 1802), *cited in* S. Padover, THE COMPLETE JEFFERSON, at 518–19 (2d ed. 1969). *See also,* Griswold, *Absolute is in the Dark—A Discussion of the Approach of the Supreme Court to Constitutional Questions,* 8 UTAH L. REV. 167, 174 (1963).

55. Dean Griswold concludes that:
> What Jefferson wrote was a powerful way of summarizing the effect of the First Amendment. But it was clearly neither a complete statement

his attorney general not only indicated his sincerity in writing the letter, but also made it very evident that he understood that his response articulated a principle that had not yet germinated into an accepted legal or political tenet. Given Jefferson's admission that his position did not reflect then-prevailing public attitudes, the strict separationist again has to rely on subsequent development rather than upon history contemporaneous with the passage and ratification of the First Amendment to support her position.

Even assuming *arguendo* that Jefferson's metaphor of a wall of separation should be given some weight, it would still be inappropriate to read his statement as supporting an absolute or strict separation of church and state in the sense that those terms have been used in the twentieth century. For example, after an in-depth examination of Jefferson's position regarding the Establishment Clause, one author concluded that "the so-called 'wall of separation' simply meant that there shall be no official religion of State supported by public revenues, that there shall be no penalties for the peaceable and free exercise of religion, and that all religions shall enjoy equal protection and friendship of the government."[56] Furthermore, Professor Robert M. Healy noted in his book, *Jefferson on Religion in Public Education,* that while Jefferson's "'wall of separation' expresses his lifelong view of the ideal relationship [between church and state]," it is equally evident that Jefferson's "action over a period of years appeared at times to show many inconsistencies because his practices concerning this [relationship], like those concerning free government, were not doctrinaire but flexible, adapted to specific situations, reflecting his own astute resourcefulness."[57] Some of Jeffer-

___

nor a substitute for the words of the Amendment itself. Moreover, the absolute effect which some have sought to give these words is belied by Jefferson's own subsequent action and writings.

Griswold, *supra* note 54, at 174.

56. Graham, *A Restatement of the Intended Meaning of the Establishment Clause in Relation to Education and Religion,* 1981 B.Y.U. L. REV. 333, 354.

57. R. Healy, JEFFERSON ON RELIGION IN PUBLIC EDUCATION 133 (1962). Healy is not alone in this view. After an extensive review of Jefferson's actions in the church-state area, one commentator has concluded that "careful analysis of Jefferson's beliefs and actions concerning church-state relationships demonstrates that a strict separationist interpretation of his wall-of-separation metaphor is inconsistent with his intent." Comment, *Jefferson and the Church-State Wall: A Historical Examination of the Man and the Metaphor,* 1978 B.Y.U. L. REV. 645, 672–73. In another context, Professors Johnson and Haskins have noted that:

[T]he contradictions in Jefferson's thinking and character are so numerous and difficult to sort out, . . . that the reader should be alerted to

son's actions illustrate that he was not wedded to a strict-separationist view. These include his willingness to support the building of a chapel on the campus of a public university, which was to be open to use by *all* religious groups at public expense,[58] and his signing, as president, of a treaty with the Kaskaskia Indians in which the United States government annually gave one hundred dollars to support priests and three hundred dollars for the erection of a church.[59]

A final point with regard to Jefferson's views and their effect on the framers of the First Amendment should be made: Jefferson's role with regard to the adoption of the First Amendment was peripheral at best. Perhaps Jefferson himself best described his role in a letter to Dr. Joseph Priestley, dated 19 June 1802. In that letter, Jefferson responded to Priestley's assertion that Jefferson's role with regard to the adoption and ratification of the Constitution was significant as follows:

> One passage in the paper you forwarded to me, must be corrected. It is the following, "And all say it was yourself more than another individual that planned and established it," i.e., the Constitution. I was in Europe when the Constitution was planned, and never saw it until after it was established. On receiving it, I wrote strongly to Madison, arguing the want of provision for the freedom of religion, freedom of the press, trial by jury, habeas corpus, the substitution of militia for a standing army, and an express reservation to the States of all rights not specifically granted to the Union. He accordingly moved in the first Congress for these amendments, which were agreed to and ratified by the States as they now stand. This is all the hand I had—related to the Constitution.[60]

Thus, Jefferson's role was admittedly limited to the impact, particularly on Madison, of his previously articulated position. Given Madison's change of position with regard to the need for a Bill of Rights to the Constitution, which he had opposed originally but which he introduced

---

the problem yet be advised not always to take Jefferson's statements or accusations at their apparent face value. What in some other person could be labeled rank dishonesty or demogogical vituperation could, for Jefferson, be merely an expression of his political attitude, wrong-headed perhaps, yet sincere.

2 G. Haskins & H. Johnson, HISTORY OF THE SUPREME COURT OF THE UNITED STATES 9 (1981).

58. Comment, *supra* note 54, at 669–72.

59. R. Cord, *supra* note 44, at 60.

60. 9 T. Jefferson, WORKS 381 (1905).

in the First Congress,[61] Jefferson's opinon may have influenced Madison to consider adding an amendment supporting religious liberty. Nevertheless, it is Madison's role along with that of other advocates of religious liberty in the First Congress that must be examined to ascertain the intent of the framers in adopting the religion clauses of the First Amendment. However, before turning for such purposes to relevant activities in the Constitutional Convention and to the debates of the First Congress on the subject of religious liberty, a brief examination of the contemporaneous developments in states other than Virginia is warranted.

COLONIAL AND PREREVOLUTIONARY DEVELOPMENTS OUTSIDE VIRGINIA

While established churches continued to be present in a majority of states at the time of the Revolution, there was a substantial increase in religious toleration and liberty throughout the colonies. As evidently mentioned in Madison's speech in opposition to the Assessment Bill, Rhode Island, Pennsylvania, Maryland, and New York had already raised religious toleration and liberty to fairly lofty heights.[62] The influence of Roger Williams, Lord Baltimore, William Penn, and others[63] had laid a foundation for increased religious liberty, both by resisting the urge to establish or prefer a given religious sect and by creating an environment of religious toleration, first for Christian sects and ultimately for all sects.

---

61. *See* Rutland, THE BIRTH OF THE BILL OF RIGHTS: 1776-1791, 196–200 (1969).

62. The Delaware and New Jersey experience was also libertarian and has been summarized as follows:

> Both Delaware and New Jersey guaranteed that no one would be required to attend religious worship or be compelled to maintain any ministry. Both also specified, however, that "there shall be no establishment of any one religious sect...in preference to another." Delaware's second constitution, of 1792, decreed that religion be supported only by voluntary methods, but still declared that "no preference be given by law to any religious societies, denominations or modes of worship."

Curry, *supra* note 1, at 159–60. Interestingly, as will be shown in yet greater detail, the Delaware Constitution of 1792, coming as it did after the ratification of the Bill of Rights, generally summarizes one of the positions, the Madisonian, extant at the time of the framing.

63. For a discussion of the contributions of Roger Williams and William Penn, see A. Stokes & L. Pfeffer, *supra* note 4, 24–26.

As interdependence among the colonies developed, through the exigencies of war and commerce, the Middle Colonies' influence in the area of religious toleration and liberty proved to be practically, as well as philosophically, appealing. Virginia, particularly through the influence of Madison, may have led the movement to formalize this liberty in the revolutionary era, but it was the Middle Colonies and not the Southern Colonies that had set the stage.

With the growth of the evangelical movement in the second half of the eighteenth century with its emphasis on the private nature of religious experience, even New England had begun to expand its protection of religious liberty. Not only were nonestablished sects increasingly tolerated in New England, but there was also a growing understanding that the civil establishment or preference for particular sects might ultimately be detrimental to religious liberty and to public order.

Thus, while many New Englanders may have trusted in the supposed magnanimity of their own Congregational establishment, they were apprehensive that the established Anglican Church of the Southern Colonies might become the national religion. John Adams summarized the fears he had entertained at the close of the eighteenth century with regard to the establishment of an Anglican episcopacy in a letter to H. Niles in 1818. In that letter, Adams stated that

> If any gentleman supposes this controversy to be nothing to the present purpose, he is grossly mistaken. It spread an universal alarm against the authority of Parliament. It excited a general and just apprehension, that bishops, and dioceses, and churches, and priests, and tithes, were to be imposed on us by Parliament. It was known that neither king, nor ministry, nor archbishops, could appoint bishops in America, without an act of Parliament; and if Parliament could tax us, they could establish the Church of England, with all its creeds, articles, tests, ceremonies, and tithes, and prohibit all other churches, as conventicles and schism shops.[64]

Thus, while many of the states may have desired to maintain their own established religious sects, they recognized the problems attendant with any such establishment at the national level. They also generally conceded that all sects should, at a minimum, be tolerated.[65]

---

64. Letter from John Adams to H. Niles (3 Feb. 1818), *reprinted in* 10 T. Jefferson, WORKS 288.

65. Curry points out that New Englanders generally equated an "establishment" with state support for modes of worship or articles of faith. New Englanders generally believed that nonpreferential aid, of a nonfinancial nature, to

As illustrated by developments at the national level, while there was increased religious toleration and liberty throughout the colonies, there was little if any support for the principle that government should be precluded from accommodating or recognizing religious exercise in any form. For example, in the Declaration of Independence there were four references to God. Furthermore, the Northwest Ordinance, adopted by the Continental Congress in 1787, set up a government for the Northwest Territory and recognized the need to further "religion, morality and knowledge" in the Territory.[66] In 1777, the Continental Congress had imported twenty thousand Bibles.[67] In 1782, it supported "the pious and laudable undertaking" of having a printer print an American edition of the Scriptures.[68] Congress also consistently permitted invocations and other religious exercises to be performed in public facilities or buildings.[69]

Religious liberty and toleration, together with a trend toward the disestablishment of state churches and a general opposition to a national establishment of religion, were of growing concern to the states at the time of the Constitutional Convention. It should also be noted that general religion, as opposed to irreligion, held a preferred place in the public sector, although the source of that preference may simply have been the pious desire on the part of many public servants to express their own individual religious convictions publicly while permitting others of differing beliefs to do likewise. There was also clearly a growing sense that religion should receive equal treatment at the hands of the state and that the state should refrain from indulging in the excesses of the English establishment, prescribing modes of worship or articles of faith for its citizenry. This, then, was the general theoretical or philosophical setting when the framers met in Philadelphia to consider a new constitution during the summer of 1787.[70]

---

churches was acceptable, although it is clear that their theory of nonpreferential treatment often did not extend beyond Protestant Christian sects. Curry, *supra* note 1, at 165–92.

66. A. Stokes & L. Pfeffer, *supra* note 4, at 85.

67. *Id.*

68. *See Id.*

69. *See* Chief Justice Warren Burger's discussion of the historical evidence of such activity in his opinion for the Court in Marsh v. Chambers, 463 U.S. 783 (1983), holding Nebraska legislature's practice of opening each legislative day with prayer not violative of the First Amendment.

70. Curry notes that:

By emphasizing the "exclusive" favoring of "one particular sect," Americans appeared to draw a careful distinction between such an exclusive establishment and a non-exclusive establishment or favoring of several or all sects. However, during the revolutionary period, the

THE CONSTITUTIONAL CONVENTION: A TIME OF GENERAL RETICENCE IN MATTERS OF RELIGIOUS LIBERTY

During the Constitutional Convention of 1787, there was a general absence of discussion regarding religious liberty. In fact, only one clause dealing with religious matters appears in the Constitution itself, tucked neatly away in the latter portion of Article VI. That provision states that "no religious Test shall ever be required as a qualification to any Office of public Trust under the United States." Thus, while some efforts were made to recognize religious matters or liberty during the course of the Convention, the only provision that was adopted ultimately as part of the document was the bar to any religious test as a qualification for public office at the national level.

---

only serious Church-State conflicts had to do not with exclusive state preference for a single religion, but with proposals for non-preferential state support of many religious groups.... Nevertheless, when Americans discussed the relationship between religion and the new federal government, they all—including Madison—apparently ignored this crucial question, i.e., a general assessment type of support for religion, and apparently concentrated on exclusive or preferential government aid to religion—something that did not exist in America at the time and had not a public defender in the land.

Curry, *supra* note 1, at 198. While I am in general agreement with Curry, I feel that there is a sense in which he, too, has glossed over the nonpreferential-aid issue. Elsewhere in his book, Curry goes so far as to claim that, "when those connected with the passage of the Bill of Rights spoke or wrote of an establishment of religion as government imposition of one sect or articles of faith, they were not implying that government could favor all sects or sponsor religion short of imposing a creed on the populace." *Id.* at 213. There are at least two senses in which Curry's own assertion is suspect: (1) he fails to clarify the distinction between state accommodation or facilitation of free exercise and his view of the nonpreferential aid notions extant during the Revolution (i.e., while Curry may be correct that there was a general sentiment opposing even state sponsorship of all religions, he fails to distinguish between sponsorship, which presumably would not be acceptable, and accommodation of free exercise on a nonpreferential basis, which would be acceptable); and (2) he fails to distinguish between those who held the view that nondenominational Christianity of a tolerant nature did constitute the national religion and could be sponsored (for example, by purchasing, printing, and disseminating Bibles and even building churches or providing places of worship) and the views that I maintain were held by Madison and others that government could act affirmatively to facilitate religious exercise on a nonpreferential basis. *See, Id.* at 218, where Curry may face this problem or paradox by noting that the framers themselves had simply failed to recognize these finer distinctions.

Charles Pinckney and Madison proposed a national university "in which no preference or distinction should be allowed on account of religion."[71] While this proposal found support among some of the most influential delegates to the Convention, including Gouverneur Morris and James Wilson, it was nevertheless defeated.[72] There was, however, no indication that the proposal for a national university was defeated because of its reference to religion. On the contrary, it would appear that the proposal was defeated because of indifference among the delegates to the concept of a national university rather than to the inclusion of the nonpreferential religion provision in the proposal.[73]

Pinckney also advocated that a guarantee of religious freedom be included in the Constitution and proposed the addition of a provision providing that "the legislature of the United States shall pass no law on the subject of religion."[74] This provision was referred to the Committee on Detail at the Convention, where it languished and ultimately died.[75] While one would have to speculate about the reason this provision was given so little consideration during the Convention, it would be accurate to note that it never had Madison's strong support. At the time of the Convention, Madison opposed the concept of a Bill of Rights, claiming rather that the government had no legitimate right to interfere with an individual's exercise of certain inalienable rights, including the right to religious liberty. For Madison at the time of the Convention, there simply was no reason to include a specific provision in the document for the securing of religious liberty, because such rights were properly beyond the reach of legitimate governmental regulation.[76]

There were other attempts to bring religious matters before the Convention. In one of the more interesting episodes at the Constitutional Convention dealing with the matter of religion, Benjamin Franklin moved on 28 June 1787 that the Convention resort to prayer for the avowed purpose of receiving divine guidance in overcoming an impasse on certain divisive, substantive issues.[77] Recognizing that this impasse

---

71. A. Stokes & L. Pfeffer, *supra* note 4, at 62.

72. R. Morgan, THE SUPREME COURT AND RELIGION (1972). James Wilson was an interesting ally, given his view that the common law of the nation was Christian in origin.

73. *Id. See also* A. Stokes & L. Pfeffer, *supra* note 4, at 61–62.

74. A Stokes & L. Pfeffer, *supra* note 4, at 61.

75. *Id.*

76. Sky, *The Establishment Clause, The Congress and The Schools: An Historical Perspective,* 52 VA. L. REV. 1395, 1406 (1966).

77. C. Rice, THE SUPREME COURT AND PUBLIC PRAYER 36–7 (1964).

and the proliferation of bickering among the representatives of the various states threatened to undermine the purpose of the Convention to form a more stable federal union, Franklin, aided by James Wilson, who spoke for him, emphasized that:

> We have been assured, Sir, in the sacred writings, that "except the Lord build the House they labor in vain that build it." I firmly believe this; and I also believe that without His concurring aid we shall succeed in this political building no better than the Builders of Babel: We shall be divided by our little partial local interests; our projects confounded, and we ourselves shall become a reproach and bye word down to future ages. And what is worse, men may hereafter from this unfortunate instance, despair of establishing Governments by Human wisdom and leave it to chance, war and conquest....I therefore beg leave to move—that henceforth prayers imploring the assistance of Heaven, and its blessings on our deliberations be held in this Assembly every morning before we proceed to business, and that one or more of the Clergy of this City be requested to officiate in that Service.[78]

When Franklin proposed that clergy be requested to give an invocation, he took care to make it clear that "one or more of the Clergy" of Philadelphia be given the opportunity, thereby seemingly recognizing the need for at least a modicum of nonpreference among sects for such purposes. Despite what might be interpreted as an effort at impartiality and his heartfelt support for the proposal, Franklin was unable to muster sufficient support among the delegates to obtain adoption of his motion.[79]

While one might argue that the failure of Franklin's motion somehow implied an aversion among the delegates as to religious exercise in the public sector, it is generally conceded that no such antipathy was present. Stokes and Pfeffer, for example, have pointed out that such a conclusion would seem unwarranted in light of the fact that the First Congress, organized by virtue of the Constitution, followed the practice of opening each session with prayer.[80] Professor Charles E. Rice also argues against construing the failure of Franklin's motion as indicative of an "aversion of the delegates to public prayer."[81] In this regard, two different reasons for the defeat of the proposal have been cited. First, it

---

78. Cited in *Id.* at 37–8.
79. R. Morgan, *supra* note 72, at 21.
80. A. Stokes & L. Pfeffer, *supra* note 4, at 84.
81. C. Rice, THE SUPREME COURT AND PUBLIC PRAYER 39 (1964).

has been argued that Madison's report of the incident indicates that the reluctance of the delegates was probably prompted by a fear of alarming the populace through a sudden resort to prayer, which might possibly indicate that the work of the Convention had indeed reached a major impasse.[82] Second, a remark made by Hugh Williamson, a delegate from North Carolina, during the course of the proceedings seems to imply that a major reason for the defeat of the prayer proposal may simply have been that the Convention had no funds with which to pay a chaplain.[83] Congress and the framers of the First Amendment did approve and finance the development of a chaplaincy, thereby further vitiating the argument that the framers opposed public prayer. Both reasons offered for the failure of the motion are more plausible than the conclusion that the delegates opposed religious exercise in the public sector.

A final attempt to raise a religious issue at the Convention should be considered. Isaac Backus, a Baptist who had gained some notoriety for having refused to pay five dollars in taxes for the support of the Congregationalist Church in Massachusetts, presented his views before the Convention, arguing that provision should be made for the liberty of conscience and for protecting against potential taxation demands of a state church.[84] While Backus's remarks did not lead to the inclusion of a provision securing such religious liberty in the Constitution, it would, as was the case with Franklin's proposal, undoubtedly be unfair to assume that such inactivity implied opposition on the part of the delegates to the proposal. Again, they may have felt simply that it was unnecessary or that it might have political repercussions that would affect adversely the effort to have the Constitution ratified.

The preceding discussion makes it clear that religious matters were considered on a number of occasions by the delegates at the Constitutional Convention, but that only one provision, the prohibition of a religious test as a requirement for national office, was included in the Constitution. There are a number of possible reasons for the refusal of the delegates to include a provision for religious liberty in the Constitution, ranging from Alexander Hamilton's assertion that the delegates merely forgot to do so in their efforts to deal with weightier matters,[85] to the Madisonian position that such rights would be protected by the pluralistic nature of the union and by virtue of the fact that such rights were inalienable and were, therefore, beyond the reach of the government. For Madison, the silence of the Constitution would indicate that

---

82. *Id.*
83. *Id.*
84. A. Stokes & L. Pfeffer, *supra* note 4, at 43–45.
85. *See e.g.,* M. Malbin, *supra* note 3, at 3.

religious rights were reserved to the people. Between these somewhat polar positions stands another prominent position which may well have been held by a majority of the delegates: they may have believed that since the Constitution was silent as to the issue of national power regarding such matters, governmental power, if any, to regulate religious matters remained with the states. Most of the delegates were probably not opposed to state, versus national, involvement in this area, because they were familiar with current state efforts regarding religious exercise. Furthermore, there undoubtedly were delegates who feared that bringing religious matters into the Convention would have stimulated additional devisiveness and might have threatened the already fragile balance that was being struck on many sensitive issues dealing with the basic institutions of the government.

4

The Framing and Adoption
of the First Amendment

Many of the original supporters of the Constitution joined Madison in his belief that there was no need for the addition of a Bill of Rights to the Constitution, including a provision providing for religious liberty, on the ground that the federal government simply lacked authority to limit individual liberty in areas where the Constitution failed to confer express power on the government. Nevertheless, strong opposition to the ratification of the Constitution arose in a number of states on this precise issue.[1]

Many of the delegates to the state conventions were apprehensive about ratifying the Constitution without some assurance that an express Bill of Rights would be added.[2] For example, when ratifying the Constitution, the Virginia Convention of 1788 added a substantial list of proposed amendments to its Ordinance of Ratification.[3] The twentieth of

---

1. Sky, *The Establishment Clause, The Congress and The Schools: An Historical Perspective,* 52 VA. L. REV. 1395, 1406 (1966).

2. *Id.* However, Mason's proposed Bill of Rights had been unanimously rejected at the Constitutional Convention. Curry, THE FIRST FREEDOMS: CHURCH AND STATE IN AMERICA TO THE PASSAGE OF THE FIRST AMENDMENT, 197 (1986).

3. *See* Graham, *A Restatement of the Intended Meaning of the Establishment Clause in Relation to Education and Religion,* 1981 B.Y.U. L. REV. 333, 352.

those proposed amendments dealt with the issue of religious liberty and provided as follows:

> That religion, or the duty we owe to our Creator, and the manner of discharging it, can be directed only by reason and conviction, not by force or violence; and therefore all men have an equal, natural, and unalienable right to the free exercise of religion, according to the dictates of conscience, and that no particular religious sect or society ought to be favored or established, by law, in preference to others.[4]

The state of North Carolina also proposed the addition of a similar amendment dealing with the issue of religious liberty to their ratification ordinance.[5]

The Virginia and North Carolina proposals included the free-exercise language that had been used previously in the Virginia Declaration of Rights and in the Virginia Statute for Religious Freedom. Thus, as has been previously noted, the history of the free-exercise clause in Virginia is relevant for the purpose of ascertaining the meaning attributed to the language ultimately used in the First Amendment.

Other state conventions, including those held in New York and New Hampshire, also considered amendments dealing with the subject of religious liberty. The New Hampshire convention, for example, suggested the following proposal: "Congress shall make no laws touching religion or [infringing] the rights of conscience."[6] New York considered a similar amendment. These provisions indicate the sentiment prevailing in a number of states favoring addition of an amendment to secure religious liberty at the national level and also are instructive background relative to the intended meaning or purpose of the religion clauses of the First Amendment.

While James Madison originally opposed such an amendment, a number of factors caused Madison to reevaluate his position: (1) he was increasingly aware of the fact that his fellow Virginians and most Americans clearly desired an enumeration of a Bill of Rights in conjunction with the Constitution; (2) he was subsequently involved in a tight race for a seat in the House of Representatives, a race which might turn upon whether or not he was willing to support a written Bill of Rights[7]; (3) he was clearly concerned about rising opposition to the Constitution

---

4. *Cited in* M. Malbin, Religion And Politics: The Intentions Of The Authors Of The First Amendment, at 4 (1978).

5. 1 J. Elliot, The Debates In The Several State Conventions In The Adoption Of The Federal Constitution 328 (2d ed. 1836).

6. *Cited in* Malbin, *supra* note 4, at 3–4.

7. Sky, *supra* note 1, at 1406–07.

in many states, much of which seemed to be based on the fact that no Bill of Rights had been included[8]; and (4) Thomas Jefferson continued to try to persuade Madison to change his mind and come out in support of a Bill of Rights.[9] Whether persuaded or coerced, Madison eventually assured his fellow Virginians that he would personally introduce a Bill of Rights in the First Congress if elected.[10] It has been speculated that Madison primarily relented due to his realization that he might not be elected to Congress, if he did not support a Bill of Rights, and by his fear that the Constitution itself might be subjected to profound revision in a new constitutional convention.[11] It is likely that these factors were indeed a strong motivation to Madison, but it is also conceivable that he changed his mind, coming to believe sincerely that such amendments, as a practical matter, should be included in the Constitution. Despite this possible change of mind, he continued to believe such an enumeration of rights was nothing more than a reiteration of rights that could not be limited legitimately under any circumstances by the national government and that any enumeration of a Bill of Rights would almost of necessity be incomplete.

However, having once determined that a group of amendments constituting a written Bill of Rights was necessary, Madison became the leading proponent of the Bill of Rights in the First Congress. On 7 June 1789, Madison introduced a proposed set of amendments, constituting a Bill of Rights, in the House of Representatives. The Madisonian provision dealing with religious liberty provided that

> The Civil Rights of none shall be abridged on account of religious belief or worship, nor shall any national religion be established, nor shall the full and equal rights of conscience be in any manner, nor on any pretext infringed.
> No state shall violate the equal rights of conscience.[12]

It is interesting to note that the free-exercise language used in the Virginia draft and appearing in the Declaration of Rights in Virginia was

---

8. *Id.*
9. *Id. See also,* Rutland, THE BIRTH OF THE BILL OF RIGHTS: 1776-1791, 196–200 (1969). Madison had lost in his bid for election to the Senate from Virginia, largely due to his apparent opposition to the Bill of Rights, and he had come to suspect that perhaps even the Constitution was in jeopardy due to the lack of a written Bill of Rights. Political expediency, as well as the strength of Jefferson's advice and opinion regarding the need for a written Bill of Rights, no doubt helped to influence Madison to alter his earlier view.
10. *Id.*
11. *Id.*
12. 1 ANNALS 451 (J. Gales ed. 1789).

not included in Madison's initial draft. However, the draft did contain the same broad right of religious exercise that had been included in his proposed addition to the Virginia Declaration of Rights dealing with religious liberty. His language seemingly would limit the national government from performing any act that would inhibit one's right to worship or to fully and freely exercise her rights of conscience.

Arguably, this version is even broader than Madison's proposed addition to the Virginia Declaration of Rights, which would have permitted the state government to act in matters affecting religious exercise only when the interests of the state would be manifestly endangered. Whether or not one reads Madison's proposal related to religious exercise, as introduced in the First Congress, as more extensive than his 1776 proposal, it must be conceded that it goes to similar lengths in protecting free exercise. Additionally, it is clear that Madison did not advocate or envision a distinction, for the purposes of governmental regulation of such matters, between religious belief and religious worship. Both were to be broadly protected.

Madison also included the full-and-equal-rights language that characterized his abiding concern that all religious exercises or matters of conscience be treated equally and be given broad protection against governmental interference. Clearly, Madison's great concern was that religious belief or worship and the full and equal rights of conscience be protected from governmental interference.[13]

Sandwiched between these two provisions providing for the full and equal exercises of one's religious conviction and conscience was a provision prohibiting the establishment of any national religion. Madison's use of the phrase any national religion with reference to establishment is indicative of his probable intent to prohibit the establishment of a national religion, similar to those then existing in a number of states. With regard to action at the state level, however, Madison would have prohib-

---

13. Curry concludes that "at the Virginia Ratifying Convention, Madison had stated that the federal government had not the 'shadow of a right...to intermeddle with religion,' and all Americans, Federalists and Anti-Federalists, agreed with him. Apart from the literalist reading of the language used in connection with establishment, not a shred of evidence exists to verify that anyone wanted the new government to have any power in matters of religion." Curry, *supra* note 2, at 208. As has been previously noted, the government would at least be able to accommodate or facilitate free exercise, even in the public sector, as evidenced by the fact that the very first formal act of the First Congress, after adopting the First Amendment, was to pass a prayer resolution.

ited the state from violating the "equal rights of conscience," but he would have otherwise left those state establishments intact.[14].

After being introduced on 7 June 1789, Madison's proposed amendments languished in committee for a month and a half without receiving any significant attention. Finally, on 21 June 1789, the Committee of the Whole was discharged from further consideration of the amendments, and a special committee, the Committee of Eleven, was created to consider the amendments. Chaired by Representative John Vining of Delaware, with a representative from each state, including Madison who represented Virginia, the Committee of Eleven was given responsibility for reviewing the proposed amendments.[15]

After consideration of the amendments by the Committee of Eleven on 13 August 1789, a debate ensued on the floor of the House over whether the amendments ought to receive prompt consideration or be set aside pending the completion of other matters dealing with the institutional arrangements of the new government. Representative Theodore Sedgwick of Massachusetts spoke for those opposing early consideration of the amendments when he declared that he "was sorry that the motion [proposing early consideration of the amendments] was made, because he looked upon this as a very improper time to enter upon consideration of a subject which would undoubtedly consume many days; and when they had so much other and more important business requiring immediate attention."[16] Representatives William Smith of Maryland, Thomas Hartley of Pennsylvania, Elbridge Gerry of Massachusetts, and John Laurance of New York joined Representative Sedgwick in contending that "there were several matters before them of more importance [than the amendments],"[17] noting particularly that the "judicial bill was entitled to preference in point of order, and in propriety it deserved the first attention of the House."[18]

Madison, however, continued to press for early consideration of the amendments. He was concerned that the Anti-Federalists were seeking to dismantle the newly ratified Constitution, which they had opposed,

---

14. For a somewhat different view, *see* Curry, *supra* note 2, at 209, where Curry asserts that Madison meant to exclude all, not just preferential or national, aid to religion. Again, however, Curry fails to face the distinction between accommodating religious exercise and nonpreferential state sponsorship of religion.

15. *See, e.g.,* R. Morgan, THE SUPREME COURT AND RELIGION, 22 (1972); and A. Stokes and L. Pfeffer, CHURCH AND STATE IN THE UNITED STATES, 20 (1964), for a discussion of these developments.

16. 1 ANNALS 704 (J. Gales ed. 1789).

17. *Id.*

18. *Id.* at 705.

by being dilatory in considering the amendments constituting the Bill of Rights, thereby hoping to inflame popular opposition.[19] The Anti-Federalists evidently hoped to take advantage of the public's dismay over the ratification of the Constitution without a Bill of Rights. Madison, as a strong proponent of the Constitution, was therefore adamant in his effort to gain an early hearing for the amendments. Madison argued that he did not think it was an improper time to proceed in the business of considering the proposed amendments. The House had already considered subjects of a less interesting and significant nature. He added that if the judiciary bill was of such pressing importance, its consideration ought not to have been postponed in the past, while other mundane matters were considered. In this light, Madison argued that

> Already has the subject been delayed much longer than could have been wished. If after having fixed a day for taking it into consideration, we should put it off again, a spirit of jealousy may be excited, and not allayed without great inconveniences.[20]

This declaration by Madison may have been more than a skillful effort to thwart the Anti-Federalist efforts; it may have reflected his own position with regard to the amendments themselves. Instead of placing emphasis on his personal views, he merely argued for the need to recognize the desire of the people for a written Bill of Rights, thereby preserving the level of popular support which the government under the Constitution required.[21] His statement indicates that he may have retained some personal qualms regarding the necessity of the amendments, but it also indicates that he understood well the sentiment of the public on the subject. Madison prevailed, and the House agreed to consider the amendments, after a somewhat lengthy debate as to whether the amendments should be interwoven into the text of the Constitution or merely appended to it.[22] Finally, the House of Representatives as a whole initiated consideration of the amendments constituting the Bill of Rights.[23]

Since a basic premise of this book is that the intent of the framers and the ratifiers of the amendments ought to be given weight in deter-

---

19. *See, e.g.,* Sky, *supra* note 1, at 1407–08. The Anti-Federalists hoped that by engendering opposition to the Constitution, they could gain public support for a new Constitutional Convention in which they could dismantle the strong national government formed in 1787.

20. ANNALS, *supra* note 12, at 704.

21. *Id.*

22. *Id.* at 703–17.

23. *Id.*

mining issues of constitutional law, the debates in the House and the Senate will be examined in detail. While a jurist of the stature of Justice Wiley B. Rutledge has argued, in his opinion in *Everson,* that these debates are of only limited assistance in resolving issues of religious freedom because they "reveal only sparse discussion, reflecting the fact that the essential issues had been settled,"[24] it is my position that the debates are immensely helpful as a matter of constitutional interpretation.

One of the earliest amendments considered by the House was the Committee of Eleven's draft concerning religious liberty, which provided that "no religion shall be established by law, nor shall the equal rights of conscience be infringed."[25] This condensed version of Madison's original proposal immediately raised "some doubts as to the propriety of the mode of expression contained therein,"[26] on the part of Peter Sylvester, a representative from New York.

Representative Sylvester opened the debate on the subject by disclosing his fear that the amendment might be given a construction different from that envisioned by the committee that drafted it. His specific fear was that "it might be thought to have a tendency to abolish religion altogether."[27] Much of what followed in the debates constituted an effort on the part of proponents of the amendment, including Madison, to satisfy those who shared Sylvester's sentiments, by persuading them that the First Amendment accommodated rather than denigrated religious exercise.

Vining, chairman of the Committee of Eleven, which drafted the proposed amendment, was the first to speak in an effort to placate Sylvester's fears. Vining's proposal was simple and yet informative. He proposed "the propriety of transposing the two members of the sentence."[28] In other words, the phrase equal rights of conscience would be transposed so as to be prior to the establishment portion of the clause. This effort on the part of Representative Vining no doubt illustrated his view that the establishment clause should not be considered more important than the exercise of one's equal rights of conscience; rather, it was to be treated merely as a means of facilitating the free exercise of one's religious convictions.

---

24. Everson v. Board of Educ. 330 U.S. 1, 42 (1947) (Rutledge, J. Dissenting).

25. 1 Annals, *supra* note 12, at 729. For the text of the debates occurring on 15 August, *see, Id.* at 757–78. *See also,* Curry, *supra* note 2, at 200-04, for a discussion regarding these debates.

26. Annals, at 729.

27. *Id.*

28. *Id.*

Representative Gerry next asserted that the establishment clause in the proposed draft "would read better if [it provided] that no religious doctrine shall be established by law."[29] Gerry's remarks, like the remarks of Vining before him, were directed to Sylvester's complaint that the establishment language implied that the government might treat religion with disfavor by ignoring it altogether. Limiting the establishment clause to prohibiting only the establishment of particular religious doctrine would leave the government free to accommodate or facilitate voluntary religious exercise in the public sector, so long as it did not infringe upon another's right of conscience and provided that all religions received equal treatment.

Next, Representative Roger Sherman of Connecticut reiterated his belief that there was no need for the amendments, because the federal government lacked the power to act in such matters. He argued, therefore, to strike the implied power of Congress to "make religious establishments."[30] This comment is interesting for two reasons: first, it constitutes another indication that the framers did not intend to have the establishment clause limit the free exercise of one's religion or rights of conscience; and, second, given the existing governmental support for public religious exercise (e.g., opening each day's proceedings in Congress with a prayer), it implied that the propagation of a given religion or, perhaps more broadly, governmental support for specific religious doctrine (the Gerry position) constituted an establishment of religion. The prohibition of an establishment of religion did not, therefore, mandate the elimination of all religious exercise from the public sector.

Representative Daniel Carroll of Maryland was the next to speak, indicating that he supported the provision, as drafted. He stated that the provision furthered the principle that the "rights of conscience are, in their nature, of peculiar delicacy, and will bear the gentlest touch of the governmental hand."[31] Of all of the responses to Sylvester's objection, Carroll's could most easily be construed perhaps as supporting the contemporary strict-separationist view, since the gentlest-touch-of-the-governmental-hand language suggests that he might consider aid or accommodation of public religious exercise to constitute an impermissible, albeit gentle, touch of the governmental hand. Two factors seem to mitigate against this reading of the Carroll view. First, it would be in-

---

29. *Id.* at 730. *See* Curry, *supra* note 2, at 202, for the point that Gerry's suggestion was in keeping with New England tradition with regard to the establishing of modes of worship or articles of faith.

30. ANNALS, at 730.

31. *Id.*

congruous contextually given the comments immediately preceding it and in light of Madison's comments that immediately followed it. Second, Carroll argues that he was merely seeking to secure the substance of the general view of the public as a whole. It is not only clear that the strict-separationist view did not command strong support among the people at the time of the First Congress, but it is also evident that it was a view essentially foreign even to a minority.[32] The public at large divided into two basic groups, those who viewed a generalized Christianity as being the appropriate national religion and those who felt that no religion, including even a generalized Christianity, could be preferred by government. Thus, while there was support for the proposition that government could not or should not extend financial aid to all religions in an equal and nonpreferential manner, it is clear that government could and should act to accommodate individual religious exercise and to avoid religious discrimination.

Madison's comments that followed immediately after Carroll's statement further illustrate this point. Those who read (or more appropriately, misread) Madison to be an advocate of contemporary strict separation must feel some discomfort upon studying Madison's actual comments during the course of the debates. It is little wonder, then, that contemporary advocates of strict separation disparage the significance of the debates. In his very first statement regarding the issue of religious liberty, he noted that:

> he apprehended the meaning of the words to be, that Congress should not establish *a* religion, and enforce the legal observation of *it* by law, nor compel men to worship God in any manner contrary to their conscience. Whether the words are necessary or not, he did not mean to say, but they had been required by some of the State Conventions who [sic] seemed to entertain an opinion that under the clause of the Constitution, which gave Congress the power to make all laws necessary and proper to carry into execution the Constitution, and the laws under it, enabled them to *make laws of such a nature as might infringe the rights of conscience, and establish a national religion; to prevent these*

---

32. *Id.* Curry agrees, noting that: "Like many of those who had asked for an amendment protecting religious liberty, Daniel Carroll was satisfied with a statement to that effect without subjecting it to analysis. Indeed, all Americans could accept 'phraseology' protecting the 'rights of conscience' or banning the imposition of 'articles of faith' or the 'establishment of one sect in preference to another.' They disagreed, however, over the substantive meaning of such terms." Curry, *supra* note 2, at 202.

effects he presumed the amendment was intended, and he thought it was well expressed as a nature of the language would admit.[33]

What Madison opposed (and he firmly believed the intended meaning of the amendment supported his opposition) was the establishment of a national religion that would derogate individual rights of conscience. Conscience could be accommodated by government, but government could not promote religion in a manner that would compel men to worship God contrary to their conscience.

Representative Benjamin Huntington of Connecticut next addressed the subject, understanding "the amendment to mean what had been expressed by [Madison],"[34] but retaining some of Sylvester's uneasiness over how that language might be construed. He specifically noted in this regard that

> he feared, with the gentleman [Sylvester] first upon this subject, that the words might be taken in such latitude as to be extremely hurtful to the cause of religion. He understood the amendment to mean what had been expressed by the gentleman from Virginia [Madison]; but others might find it convenient to put another construction upon it. The ministers of their congregation to the Eastward were maintained by the contributions of those who belonged to this society; the expense of building meeting-houses was contributed in the same manner. These things were regulated by bylaws. If any action was brought before a Federal Circuit on any of these cases, the person who had neglected to perform his engagements could not be compelled to do it for a support of ministers, or building of places of worship might be construed into a religious establishment.... By the charter of Rhode Island, no religion could be established by law; he could give a history of the effects of such a regulation; indeed the people were now enjoying the blessed fruits of it. He hoped, therefore, the amendment would be made in such a way as to secure the rights of conscience, and a free exercise of the rights of religion, but not to patronize those who professed no religion at all.[35]

Huntington's remarks are significant for a number of reasons. To begin with, after having noted that he joined in Sylvester's fears that religion might in some unintended fashion be hindered by the establishment clause, he asserted that he agreed with Madison's interpretation

---

33. ANNALS, at 730 (emphasis added).
34. *Id.* For another view regarding Huntington's comments, *see* Curry, *supra* note 2, at 203.
35. ANNALS, at 730–31.

but was fearful that there were or might someday be those who would view the clause in a more restrictive fashion. This is important not only because it is indicative of a strong view held by Representatives Huntington and Sylvester, but also because it is intended by Huntington to be a clarification of his intentions and those of Madison. This further illustrates that Madison's colleagues did not believe that he espoused a strict-separationist view. In fact, Madison could have refuted Huntington's characterization of his position on the subject, but, rather than doing so, Madison rose, as the very next speaker, to argue for a possible amendment to the clause that would further clarify the position which he shared with Representative Huntington.

Aside from its relationship to the Madisonian position, Huntington's statement is helpful in explaining the intent of the framers with regard to the meaning of the establishment clause itself. Huntington first notes that, in his opinion, the First Amendment should not be construed as limiting the power of the government to aid congregations in collecting contributions from their members or to preclude government from otherwise assisting religion generally by helping to support ministers or by building places of worship. In this regard, Huntington may have been simply asserting that, while the federal government could not so aid religion, the state governments would and should be left free to do so under the First Amendment.

Huntington also used the history of Rhode Island to illustrate what he conceived as being the proper meaning of the establishment clause, noting that states such as Rhode Island had "secure[d] the rights of conscience, and [the] free exercise of rights of religion, but [did] not patronize those who professed no religion at all." The influence of Roger Williams in Rhode Island, therefore, is quite important. Williams, as his ship analogy illustrates, would have permitted a broad right to exercise one's religion.[36] Voluntary religious exercise was to be accommodated.[37]

---

36. *Id.* For his part, Curry seems to imply that perhaps Huntington was not enamored with the Rhode Island experience. Curry argues that "Huntington's remarks on Rhode Island could be interpreted as an assertion that the Connecticut arrangement constituted an establishment. Although he was mistaken in saying that the Rhode Island charter forbade an establishment of religion, he seemed to hold that the absence of an establishment lay at the root of what most citizens of Connecticut and elsewhere in America regarded as the irresponsibility of Rhode Island." Curry, *supra* note 2, at 203. To so read Huntington's statement one would have to assume that Huntington was being flippant when he stated

37. ANNALS, at 730–31.

This position was similar to that espoused by Huntington when he cautioned that the establishment clause must not be construed as patronizing those who believed in no religion at all. Rather, the government should permit and even accommodate individuals in their efforts to exercise their religious beliefs, in public as well as in private.

It should also be emphasized that Huntington's use of the free-exercise-of-the-rights-of-religion language was the first recorded mention in the debates of that terminology, which was to be included ultimately in the final language of the First Amendment.

Madison was the next speaker, and he rose to offer language presumably designed to allay the fears of Representatives Sylvester and Huntington. Madison thought that

> if the word national was inserted before religion, it would satisfy the minds of honorable gentlemen. *He believed that the people feared one sect might obtain a pre-eminence, or two combine together, and establish a religion to which they would compel others to conform.* He thought *if the word national was introduced, it would point the amendment directly to the object it was intended to prevent.*[38]

Clearly for Madison, the basic intent of the establishment clause was to prevent at least the national government from aiding a particular sect or group of sects in obtaining pre-eminence over other religious sects and thereby using the force of the state to compel conformity to a particular religion established by the government. Accommodation of voluntary public participation in religious exercise was not prohibited under the Madisonian position articulated in the course of the debates.

Samuel Livermore of New Hampshire next acknowledged that he "was not satisfied with the amendment; but he did not wish them to dwell long on the subject."[39] It is evident from this statement that he felt that there was no real disagreement on the subject. All of the representatives understood that the establishment clause was not intended to hinder religious exercise generally. He then made a proposal that has proven to

---

that the people of Rhode Island "were now enjoying the blessed fruits of [nonestablishment]." It seems more likely that Huntington felt that the fruit of Rhode Island's tree was, indeed, blessed, insofar as it accommodated free exercise while simultaneously prohibiting state or legal compulsion in religious matters. Particularly when one reads Huntington's statement together with Madison's prior statements, which Huntington referred to approvingly, I believe my conclusion is at least as tenable as Curry's contrary interpretation.

38. *Id.* at 731.
39. *Id.*

be misleading when read out of context and that has been relied upon inappropriately by some twentieth-century strict-separationist commentators. He suggested that "Congress too shall make no laws touching religion, or infringing the rights of conscience."[40]

Representative Gerry, an Anti-Federalist rising to speak for the second time that day, indicated his opposition to Madison's proposal to add the word national and by implication indicated his support for the proposal of Representative Livermore.[41] Two points must be raised with regard to Gerry's remarks. First, while he did not favor Madison's use of the term national, because it threatened to reopen passionate and destructive differences of recent origin between the Federalists and the Anti-Federalists over the role of the national government, it is not at all clear that Gerry opposed the substance of Madison's prior characterizations of the intended meaning of the establishment terminology. In fact, the implication that there were no real differences on the subject in the opening remarks he made during the course of his second statement, coupled with the substance of his first remarks in which he opposed only the establishment of particular doctrine, supports the conclusion that his disagreement with Madison was exclusively limited to his disfavor of the term national, on the ground that the power of the federal government should be curtailed where possible. Additionally, Gerry's apparent support for Livermore's use of the language "Congress shall make no law touching on religion" must also be viewed in light of Gerry's Anti-Federalist views and his prior comments, in which he advocated that no religious doctrine should be established. If Congress could make no law touching on religious doctrine, then the establishment issue would remain with the states, and the national government would be deprived of the power to establish any particular religious doctrine.

After Gerry's comments, and in an effort to mollify even the Anti-Federalists, Madison argued, in his final statement of the day, that his use of the term national did not imply that the government was a national one, but was rather intended merely to preclude the establishment of a national religion for all of the states.[42] After this diversion by Madison and Gerry, the House returned to the issue of Livermore's motion and passed it by a vote of thirty-one for and twenty opposed.[43]

---

40. *Id.*
41. *Id.*
42. *Id.*
43. *Id.*

While Livermore's proposal was adopted by the House of Representatives on that day, it did not form the basis of the final House version and should not be viewed as supportive of the twentieth-century view of strict separation of church and state.[44] On 20 August 1789, Representative Fisher Ames of Massachusetts suggested that the House reject the Livermore version of the religious guarantees and return to a version like that originally proposed by the Committee of Eleven. Specifically, he offered the following:

> Congress shall make no law establishing religion, or to prevent the free exercise thereof, or to infringe the rights of conscience.[45]

Ames's language incorporated Huntington's reference to the free-exercise clause, in an apparent effort to minimize Huntington's and Sylvester's uneasiness about possible antireligious interpretations of the establishment portion of the clause. It also moved away from Livermore's prohibition of "views touching religion," evidently feeling that that phrase was even more prone to ambiguity in interpretation than the committee's proposal.

Ames's proposal is itself subject to conflicting interpretations,[46] particularly in light of the fact that there was no recorded debate on the amendment; it was merely proposed and passed without comment on 24 August 1789. With only minor stylistic changes made to Ames's original proposal, it was sent to the Senate. It was Ames's language and not that of Livermore that embodied the intent of the House and that ultimately provided the basis for the First Amendment. Because of the lack of debate on the language proposed by Ames, it is subject to some variation in interpretation. However, I would assert that its quick passage suggests that it embodied the unrefuted references to intent expressed in the earlier House debates on the subject, including the substantive core common to the Sylvester, Vining, Madison, Gerry, and Huntington positions. These views provide the limits within which interpretations might differ rightfully, but it is important to note that none of the views contemplated the strict-separationist approach.[47] Even the Livermore lan-

---

44. For a fuller explanation of the dynamics of this proposal's adoption, *see, e.g.,* M. Malbin, *supra* note 4, at 10–11.

45. Annals, *supra* note 12, at 766.

46. For a discussion of these interpretations *see, e.g.,* M. Malbin, *supra* note 4, at 11–12.

47. Perhaps, therefore, it should not be surprising that strict separationists like Professor Stokes, who argue that the Livermore proposal best embodied the

guage was intended more to protect existing state religious establishments than to eliminate government aid to or accommodation of religion or religious exercise in the public sector.[48] That the states were very concerned about protecting then-existing, if failing, establishments receives strong support from the fact that Madison's original proposal, which would have made the amendment applicable to the states, was dropped by the Committee of Eleven before it reached the floor of the House for debate and was never considered again in the House, although it was proposed and defeated in the Senate on 7 September 1789.[49]

With passage of the Ames proposal, the House version was sent to the Senate, which commenced debates on the amendment on 3 September 1789. Unfortunately, the Senate debates and voting alignments on proposals were not recorded. The only information available is the language or substance of the motions or proposals themselves and a general notation of whether or not the respective motions passed.

When the Senate began debate on Ames's proposal, it was evident that many of the same misgivings present in the House debate surfaced anew in the Senate. The first proposal in the Senate provided that:

> Congress shall make no law establishing one religious sect or society in preference to others, or to infringe on the rights of conscience.[50]

While this language generally paralleled the Madisonian summary of the intent of the amendment as expressed during the House debates, it differed on a critical point. In all likelihood it would have been unacceptable to Madison, because it might not prohibit Congress from favoring a predominant group of religious sects over some minority sect or sects. It did, however, agree with the positions most often espoused in the House, in that it permitted potentially government to accommodate religious exercise, so long as it did so in a nonpreferential manner. Nevertheless, some senators would have been uneasy undoubtedly about the fact that it did not include the free-exercise language that certain members of the

---

intent of the framers, refrain from discussing the context and substance of the Ames proposal and instead emphasize their own personal reading of the ambiguous text of the Livermore proposal.

48. One commentator, after quoting Stokes's strict-separationist reading of the Livermore proposal, concludes that, based on independent research as to the Federalist position regarding religious liberty, "freedom of religion for Livermore, as to so many other Federalists, seemed to be limited to Protestants, and only to particular kinds of Protestants." Borden, *Federalists, Anti-Federalists, and Religious Freedom,* 21 J. CHURCH & ST. 469, 477–78 (1979).

49. ANNALS, *supra* note 12, at 75.

50. ANNALS, *supra* note 12, at 70.

House, such as Huntington, felt was necessary to ensure that government could accommodate or facilitate the free exercise of religion, so long as that accommodation did not inhibit another individual's exercise of her religion. Perhaps uneasiness on these points caused the Senate to vacillate on the amendment. The Senate first defeated the proposal and then, upon reconsideration, passed it.[51] Even its passage was but a prelude to further vacillation.

After rejecting a proposal advocating elimination of any amendment concerning religion from the Bill of Rights, the Senate considered and defeated two provisions similar to the first proposal that had been adopted. They first considered and rejected a provision providing that:

> Congress shall not make any law infringing the rights of conscience, or
> establishing any religious sect or society.[52]

This proposal transposed the rights-of-conscience and the establishment portions of the clause. As was the case in the House, this alteration or transposing of terms did not satisfy those in the Senate who felt that the establishment portions of the clause might jeopardize religious exercise.

The next amendment, offered and defeated, again emphasized the need for equal treatment and sought to remedy the objections of those who feared the establishment portions. It provided that:

> Congress shall make no law establishing any particular denomination
> of religion in preference to another, or prohibiting the free exercise
> thereof, nor shall the rights of conscience be infringed.[53]

This effort to add the term denomination to the original Senate proposal may have clarified what some of the senators intended the establishment language to mean, but it was still subject to the Madisonian objection that it might permit a group of denominations to band together and thereby gain preferential governmental support. It might have permitted the establishment of a generalized Christianity as the national religion, to the supposedly tolerant exclusion of other groups. It should also be noted that this version included the free-exercise language originally proposed by Huntington in the House and ultimately retained in the final version of the amendment adopted by both houses.

Finally, on 3 September, the Senate adopted a version similar to the final House version of Ames's proposal. It did, however, exclude the

---

51. *Id.*
52. *Id.*
53. *Id.*

equal-rights-of-conscience language. Whether this provision was dropped as redundant,[54] or for some other reason, remains unclear. At any rate, on 9 September 1789, the Senate eliminated that proposal altogether and again endeavored to make the establishment portion more specific by providing that

> Congress shall make no law establishing articles of faith or a mode of worship, or prohibiting the free exercise of religion.[55]

In this version, which was sent back to the House, the Senate retained the free-exercise clause, but again voiced its uneasiness over a generalized establishment clause. Like many of their counterparts in the House, the senators obviously were apprehensive that a generalized version might be used to restrain religious exercise. The House was dissatisfied with the Senate version, although there is no record of the basis of its opposition, and it requested that a conference committee be formed to seek to resolve the differences between the Senate and the House versions.[56]

---

54. Some commentators have so argued. *See, e.g.,* M. Malbin, *supra* note 4, at 13.

55. ANNALS, *supra* note 12, at 77–8.

56. One author noted that:
Congress clearly toyed with the idea of a very narrow establishment clause formulation. These attempts failed on the Senate floor. The formula which the Senate finally did adopt ("articles of faith or a mode of worship") was discarded in conference probably at the insistence of the House conferees. The flaw in these earlier versions was not that they failed to describe "establishments" which the framers desired to put beyond the reach of Congress. Their shortcoming lay in their being too specific, in barring some establishments but not others.
Sky, *supra* note 1, at 1417. Curry argues in a somewhat related view that "a concern for style, rather than a party attempt to leave room for a federal general assessment or other non-discriminatory aid to religion, better explains the different formats raised in the Senate debate." Curry, *supra* note 2, at 214. Curry adds, in summarizing the resolution of the House and Senate differences that:
[T]he debate in Congress represented not a clash between parties arguing for a "broad" or "narrow" interpretation or between those who wished to give the federal government more or less power in religious matters. It represented rather a discussion about how to state the common agreement that the new government had no authority whatsoever in religious matters.
Id. at 215. Curry, in his inclination to reduce the congressional debates to a clear-cut consensus, overgeneralizes. There was clearly some role, albeit limited, for the federal government in religious matters and the debates were over more than style, although the framers certainly realized that they were drafting for their posterity and style was, therefore, legally and practically important.

Some have speculated that the House felt the provision was not broad enough with respect to what ought to be precluded under the establishment clause.[57] Others have argued that the provision was too broad for some of the framers because it might interfere with existing state establishments.[58] Still other framers may have been concerned that it might have prevented the government from establishing a nondenominational Christian government imbued with the general trappings of Christianity. Certainly, there were many who advocated such a Christian republic and who felt it was perfectly consistent with the First Amendment as finally adopted. For them, the Senate provision may have been too broad, preventing the government from adopting even generalized modes of worship, and they may have been opposed to it on that ground. The most likely explanation is that the clause constituted an abortive effort to specify what was meant by the term establishment. In fact, the whole of the Senate and the House debate seemed to be directed to this end. However, each effort to endow the establishment clause with more specificity seemed to be inherently inadequate, carrying with it a new set of problems and misgivings.

When the House refused to adopt the Senate version, a conference committee of members of the House and Senate was formed to resolve the matter. It is likely that the members of the conference committee were under great pressure to resolve differences quickly and in a manner

---

57. *See* M. Malbin, *supra* note 4, at 15, where he concludes that:
The conference committee's language indicates that...committee members also were deeply concerned about the nation/state issue. This concern seems to have been reflected in the specific language they chose to insert, "no law *respecting* an establishment of religion."...The language the conferees chose...not only prohibits laws which "tend to" establish a religion; it also prohibits Congress from passing laws "with respect to" an establishment of religion. In other words, it prohibits Congress from passing any law that would affect the religious establishments in the states. This was designed to satisfy people from states, such as Massachusetts, that did have established churches. The conference committee's version did not go as far on this point as the proposal offered in the House by Livermore and Gerry on August 15, and that may help to explain why both men finally voted against the amendment when it was accepted by the House on September 24 by a vote of 35–14. But the conference version was a compromise between the Ames version of August 20 and the more Anti-Federalist Livermore version....[T]he final version apparently went more than halfway in a vain effort to win the support of the Anti-Federalists.
58. M. Malbin, *supra* note 4, at 14.

acceptable to members of both the Senate and House, because failure to adopt an acceptable Bill of Rights might have had the effect of forcing the dismantling of the then-fragile union formed under the Constitution. Expediency may, therefore, have mandated a degree of ambiguity, leaving specifics to future determination, and thereby avoiding the intensity of disagreement that might have been generated had Congress as a whole endeavored to draft a precise provision.

The conference committee was made up of influential members of both the Senate and the House, including a number of individuals with differing views. Madison, for example, favored limiting the states' power to infringe upon rights of conscience. Sherman argued that Congress had no authority delegated to it to make religious establishments, because the matter was reserved to the states.[59] Vining, the chairman of the Committee of Eleven, proposed the transposing of the free-exercise and establishment clauses to clarify that the committee's intent was not to "abolish religion altogether" as feared by Representative Sylvester. Senators Oliver Ellsworth of Connecticut, Charles Carroll of Maryland, and William Paterson of New Jersey were also included, and they presumably made some effort to salvage the essence of the Senate version that had been rejected by the House. This committee reported out the language that was adopted ultimately by the House on 24 September and the Senate on 25 September 1789 and that constituted the religion clauses of the First Amendment as finally ratified.[60]

While the final provision is similar to the Ames proposal, which had been adopted in the House and which provided that "Congress shall make no law establishing religion, or to prevent the free exercise thereof, or to infringe the right of conscience," there are some significant differences. To begin with, the rights-of-conscience language is not included. It will be recalled that the version of the amendment proposed by the Committee of Eleven ("no religion shall be established by law, nor shall the equal rights of conscience be infringed") included the conscience language but did not include the free-exercise language. Since there is no express indication as to why this language was deleted, one can only speculate as to why the conference committee deleted it. It might be argued that the provision was superfluous, since the free-exercise language seems to support essentially the same right. On the other hand, it could be argued with some force that the framers had specifically intended to provide special protection to the exercise of conventional religious conviction, without extending equal solicitude for rights of

---

59. *Id.* at 8.
60. *Id.* at 14.

conscience that were not religious in nature. Viewed in this light, it may have constituted an effort to satisfy those who were fearful that the amendment would unduly benefit the nonreligious. Whatever justification or justifications existed for dropping the conscience language, at a minimum it would seem likely that the framers in the conference committee desired to make the provision sufficiently innocuous to receive ready support in Congress and the states. In this sense, two conclusions can be drawn. First, it would seem that the committee clearly wanted to protect the free and equal exercise of religion but may have intentionally stopped short of extending such broad protection of general rights of conscience. Second, even advocates of a broad right of conscience, such as Madison, may have been reasonably satisfied with the provision as adopted, because it was broad enough to leave open the possibility of being elaborated into a generalized right of conscience at some time in the future.

Additionally, the establishment portion of the clause was altered. Neither the no-worship language of the Senate nor the no-law-establishing-religion language of the final House version was adopted. Rather, the language as adopted provided that "Congress shall make no law *respecting an* establishment of religion" (emphasis added). At first blush, this change may not seem significant, but on closer examination it raises two significant questions: (1) why was the term respecting added; and (2) why was the indefinite article, an, added?

One plausible reason for utilizing the term respecting may have been to protect existing state establishments.[61] The use of the term respecting, as used in the First Amendment, would preclude the national government from passing laws respecting existing state religious establishments.

The use of the indefinite rather than definite article, the, before "establishment of religion" is also significant. Since the indefinite article had not been used previously, it can be argued that it was intentionally added for the purpose of clarifying that Congress could not establish a religion but that it could accommodate religious exercise generally, provided that it did so in a nonpreferential manner. It might also be argued that the phrase "respecting an establishment" was included to restrain the national government from making any laws respecting an existing, established state religion.

Additionally, the use of the indefinite article an in the establishment clause may have constituted a compromise between the Madisonian view that Congress could not pass any laws adopting the trappings or

---

61. *Id.*

a mode of worship of any religion, including nondenominational Christianity, and what I term the Story view that Congress could not establish any specific religion but that it could adopt nondenominational Christianity as the national religion, so long as the government continued to tolerate other religions. Thus, the committee may have used the language it did in an effort to leave the dispute between what became the Story and the Madisonian views open for future determination. Such an interpretation would also be consistent with the fact that Federalists wanted to get the Bill of Rights adopted expeditiously and without undue controversy.

Despite the various and perhaps intended nuances of interpretation to which the establishment and free-exercise clauses are susceptible when viewed individually, there are some conclusions that may be drawn from the debates and congressional activity regarding the meaning of the clauses. These general conclusions, in turn, provide the basic framework within which one's analysis of a specific issue regarding religious liberty should proceed, if that analysis is to maintain interpretive fidelity to the actual history related to the adoption and ratification of the clauses.

After a review of the proposals dealing with religious liberty debated during the First Congress, one commentator indicated that if the inquiry is confined to what actually transpired during the First Congress, when the First Amendment was adopted, the following general protections were clearly intended by the framers:

> (1) To protect the individual citizens against any federal effort, direct or indirect, to compel or influence him to conform to or support religious tenets, practices, or observances in which he did not believe and to protect him against any federally inspired interference with the free exercise of his religion.
>
> (2) To protect individual denominations from disadvantage or discrimination resulting from federal favoritism toward any one sect or group of sects.
>
> (3) Probably, to protect the individual states against federal interference with existing church-state relationships in the nature of "establishments."[62]

A brief analysis and elaboration of the preceding conclusions is warranted. Beginning with Theodore Sky's third point, my only objection to his conclusion is that his use of the qualifier probably indicates equivocation. It is clear that, although some of the framers, including Madison, may have desired disestablishment of existing state establishments, they were willing to compromise on this point; the amendment

---

62. Sky, *supra* note 1, at 1427.

was intended to leave state establishments free from congressional infringement for the time being.[63]

With regard to Sky's second conclusion, it is clear that the framers intended to protect individual denominations or sects from the specter of an established religion on the national level. It is also likely that the framers intended to permit accommodation of religion generally by the national government, provided those accommodations or benefits were extended on an equal and noncoercive basis. The language and intent of the framers, however, did not foreclose the possibility of the promotion

---

63. There was a time, two days after the initial debate in the House, when it appeared that the states would be precluded from infringing on the equal rights of conscience. ANNALS, *supra* note 12, at 783–84. The debate which ensued on that date was brief:

Article 1, section 10, between the first and second paragraph, insert "no State shall infringe the equal rights of conscience, nor the freedom of speech or of the press, nor of the right of trial by jury in criminal cases."

Mr. Tucker.—This is offered, I presume, as an amendment to the constitution of the United States, but it goes only to the alteration of the constitutions of particular States. It will be much better, I apprehend, to leave the State Governments to themselves, and not to interfere with them more than we already do; and that is thought by many to be rather too much. I therefore move, sir, to strike out these words.

Mr. Madison conceived this to be the most valuable amendment in the whole list. If there was any reason to restrain the Government of the United States from infringing upon these essential rights, it was equally necessary that they should be secured against the State Governments. He thought that if they provided against the one, it was as necessary to provide against the other, and was satisfied that it would be equally grateful to the people.

Mr. Livermore had no great objection to the sentiment, but he thought it not well expressed. He wished to make it an affirmative proposition, "the equal rights of conscience, the freedom of speech or of the press, and the right of trial by jury in criminal cases, shall not be infringed by any State."

This transposition being agreed to, and Mr. Tucker's motion being rejected, the clause was adopted.

However, albeit inexplicably, the suggestion that the states would be bound by the religion clauses of the First Amendment was not revived in the First Congress and the language of the First Amendment, as adopted, clearly limited its ambit to the federal government. *See also*, Chapter 7, *infra* for a discussion of the incorporation issue.

of a generalized or nondenominational form of Christianity, provided that it could be promoted in a tolerant manner.[64]

Sky's first conclusion, which really goes to explaining the purpose of the free-exercise clause, is somewhat less evident. It is clear that the framers intended that the protection of the inalienable rights of free exercise be considered pre-eminent, with the establishment clause merely promoting that end by precluding the national government from establishing a religion.[65] It is not clear, however, how far the federal government would be permitted to go in regulating this right of free exercise. Nevertheless, the mandatory and absolutist tenor of the language ("Congress shall make no law. . .prohibiting the free exercise of religion") itself implies a very strict limitation on the government's power to regulate matters of religious exercise, either directly or indirectly.

In conclusion, while many issues are seemingly foreclosed by a close examination of the legislative history related to the adoption of the First Amendment, a number of issues were in all likelihood left open: (1) what, if anything, was the establishment clause intended to prohibit other than federal intervention with respect to established religions in the states? (2) were the establishment and free-exercise clauses intended to prohibit the federal government from adopting articles of faith, modes of worship, or other religious trappings, even when it did so in a generalized or nondenominational sense? (3) while it was conceded that the free-exercise clause should be considered pre-eminent what, if any, limits could be placed upon such exercise by the government? and (4) did the

---

64. For further discussion of the development of support for the nonde-nominational practice of Christianity, *see* Chapter 5, *infra*.

65. Professor Tribe is, therefore, correct when he concludes that:

It has become popular to see both the free exercise clause and the establishment clause as expressions of voluntarism and separatism in the Black-Rutledge sense just described. But the actual history of the establishment clause may belie this interpretation. At least some evidence exists that, for the Framers, the establishment clause was intended largely to protect state religious establishments from national displacement. It might be said that the adoption of the fourteenth amendment in 1868, and the "incorporation" of the establishment clause into the fourteenth amendment in 1947, altered this aspect of the constitutional scheme. But even if this reply is correct, it remains at best ironic and at worst perverse to appeal to the history of the establishment clause to strike at practices only remotely resembling establishment in any core sense of the concept. Whenever a free exercise claim conflicts with an absolute non-establishment theory, the support of the former would be more faithful to the consensus present at the time of the Constitutional Convention and the First Congress.

L. Tribe, AMERICAN CONSTITUTIONAL LAW 819 (1978).

framers intend to accommodate religious exercise and perhaps even permit nonpreferential aid of a financial nature to religious sects or endeavors? The answers to these questions are obviously critical to the resolution of many difficult, contemporary issues regarding religious liberty. However, the fact that explicit answers are not available from an examination of the legislative history does not render that history meaningless. Rather, it remains critically important and helpful because it sets viable limits within which any historically accurate legal analysis must proceed. It also helps to frame the issues that remain unresolved by a close examination of the legislative history, and to which the Court might appropriately have greater latitude in rendering its opinion.

This framing of the issues is also important because it provides a focus for analysis of the contemporaneous history and commentary regarding the intent of the framers. In other words, once the gaps left by an examination of the legislative history are delineated, it is helpful, if not necessary, to look at the contemporaneous history to see what the likely intent of the framers may have been regarding those issues. This intent can be determined by examining how the clauses were initially applied or construed. With this in mind, I turn next to a discussion of the contemporaneous history applicable to these open issues and then to an examination of commentary regarding those issues during the years immediately following the adoption of the amendment.

THE CONTEMPORANEOUS HISTORY

On 26 September 1789, the day after the final language of the First Amendment was adopted by Congress, and in the spirit of jubilation over passage of the Bill of Rights, the House and Senate both adopted the following resolution:

> Resolved, that a joint committee of both Houses be appointed to wait on the President of the United States, to request that he should *recommend* to the people of the United States a day of *public fasting and prayer,* to be observed, by acknowledging with grateful hearts, the *many signal favors of the Almighty God,* especially by affording them an opportunity peaceably to establish a constitution of government for their safety and happiness.[66]

This congressional act of recommending homage in the form of "public fasting and prayer" in gratitude for the "many signal favors of the

---

66. Annals, *supra* note 12, at 949 (emphasis added).

Almighty God" very shortly after passage of the First Amendment confirms that the First Congress did not intend to render all public manifestations of religious devotion unconstitutional under the establishment clause.

Upon close examination of what transpired on 26 September 1789 in Congress, this conclusion receives further support. Representative Thomas Tucker of South Carolina objected to this resolution, at the time it was considered in the House, on the ground that the practice of calling on the president to proclaim a public day of fasting and prayer constituted "a business with which Congress have nothing to do; it is a religious matter, and, as such, is proscribed to us."[67] The passage of the resolution, despite Tucker's specific raising of an establishment-type argument in opposition to it, further strengthens the conclusion that the complete or strict separation of church and state was not intended, at least insofar as accommodation or facilitation of religious activity or exercise in the public sector was concerned.

While the passage of the resolution is indicative of the intent of the First Congress to permit certain religious exercise in public, the use of the word recommend indicates a possible limit on the manner in which those religious acts could be exercised in public. Use of the word implies voluntariness and a recognition that, while public expressions of religious devotion could be permitted, they could not be required. Furthermore, the First Congress did not seek to give doctrinal content to the expression of that devotion. Congress called on the public to join in fasting and prayer, but refrained from writing the prayer or prescribing the content of the worship.

Versions of this same issue were again raised, in a related context, on a number of occasions in the years immediately following ratification of the First Amendment. Three of the first four presidents of the United States issued prayer resolutions. The first and second presidents, George Washington and John Adams, both issued broad resolutions proclaiming a day of public fasting and prayer. Evidently, neither Washington nor Adams felt inhibited by the religion clauses of the First Amendment in calling for public proclamations explicitly encouraging religious expression.[68]

Thomas Jefferson, the third president of the United States, broke with the tradition set by his predecessors. He refused to issue a proclamation or resolution calling for public fasting and prayer on the ground

---

67. *Id.* at 950.
68. For a discussion of these resolutions, *see* A. Stokes & L. Pfeffer, *supra* note 15, at 87–8.

that he considered "the *government of the United States* as interdicted by the Constitution from intermeddling with religious institutions, their doctrines, disciplines, or exercises."[69] For Jefferson, such a resolution on the part of the national government to "direct [religious] exercises"[70] was prohibited by the First Amendment. While Jefferson's view seemingly approaches the view of those contemporary scholars who advocate a strict separation between church and state, two additional points must be raised. First, it should be emphasized that Jefferson supported and even sponsored legislation appointing days of public fasting and thanksgiving in the state of Virginia.[71] Thus, Jefferson's objection seems to be based on states' rights grounds rather than on a belief in a principle of strict separation of church and state. Second, Jefferson's objection seemed to be centered upon the idea that it would be improper for the national government to direct religious exercise. Jefferson seems to be raising the argument that the national government should be precluded from intermeddling in religious matters, because it might quickly move from *permitting* voluntary exercise to *directing* that exercise. It is never-

---

69. *Id.* at 88 (emphasis added).

70. *Id.*

71. *See, e.g.,* Comment, *Jefferson and the Church-State Wall: A Historical Examination of the Man and the Metaphor,* 1978 B.Y.U. L. REV. 645. The author of that article states that:

> As President of the United States, Thomas Jefferson refused to declare a national day of fasting [and prayer], reasoning that the first amendment had created "a wall of separation between church and States." As a Virginia legislator, however, he sponsored a bill giving the Governor the power to declare days of fasting and thanksgiving. Jefferson's "wall" is a well-remembered and oft-quoted metaphor; his "Bill for Appointing Days of Public Fasting and Thanksgiving" is large [sic] forgotten. This apparent inconsistency invites further analysis. Indeed, a knowledge of how Jefferson could consistently believe that a Governor could declare a fast day which a President could not is essential to an understanding of the wall metaphor. A careful study of Jefferson's actions and utterances over the span of his life reveals that the Master of Monticello saw in religion clauses of the first amendment more than a wall of separation between church and state; to him, they constituted a study in Federalism.

Id. at 645. Thus, it is incorrect to assume that Jefferson believed that government could not accommodate or facilitate religious activity. Rather, Jefferson felt that *as a matter of federalism,* the *national* government should be limited in this area while the *state* governments should be permitted to facilitate religious exercise as they saw fit.

theless conceivable that Jefferson would have permitted individuals to fast and pray, even in public, so long as they voluntarily initiated the activity, without being directed to do so by government.

Madison's reaction to prayer resolutions is potentially far more instructive for the purposes of determining the intent of the framers of the First Amendment than is Jefferson's, particularly given Jefferson's limited role with respect to the adoption of the Bill of Rights. It is also significant because it was issued after Jefferson had refused and Adams and Washington had encouraged the adoption and implementation of public resolutions of fasting and prayer. Madison could have followed either of those precedents. However, the "author" of the First Amendment chose rather to follow a moderate course. As the fourth president, Madison cautiously joined the Washington-Adams tradition and broke with the Jeffersonian view by issuing a prayer resolution. Madison was unwilling however, to proclaim a day of public fasting and prayer, as had Washington and Adams; rather, he supported a resolution in a different form. In 1812, during the throes of a war with Great Britain, Congress passed a resolution recommending that the president proclaim a day of fasting and prayer. In response to this congressional resolution, Madison issued a permissive resolution calling upon "religious societies, so disposed, to offer at one and the same time, their common vows and adorations to Almighty God, on the solemn occasion produced by war."[72]

Thereafter, on an annual basis, commencing in 1813, Madison's prayer resolutions called upon "all who shall be piously disposed" to give thanks in the form of public fasting and prayer. His resolutions added that "if the public homage of a people can ever be worthy the favorable regard of the Holy and Omniscient Being to whom it is addressed, it must be that in which those who join in it are guided only by their free choice, by the impulse of their hearts and the dictates of their conscience."[73] Madison also asserted that only such offerings freely or

---

72. *Cited* and discussed in A. Koch, MADISON'S ADVICE TO MY COUNTRY 33 (1966) (quoting Madison's resolution).

73. *Cited in Id.* at 34. Koch, a strict separationist, goes on to argue that Madison also favored a strict separation of church and state. Koch notes a letter from Madison to Edward Everett of Harvard University that elaborated on the role of religious instruction in public education. In the letter, Madison concluded: "The settled opinion here is that religion is essentially distinct from civil government, and exempt from its cognizance; the connection between them is injurious to both." *Id.* at 36. At first blush, this comment seems to strengthen the argument that Madison advocated a strict-separationist view. However, one must remember that Madison wrote this letter when he was embroiled in a controversy

voluntarily given "can be acceptable to Him whom no hypocrisy can deceive and no forced sacrifices propitiate." Madison, therefore, was willing to issue such a resolution, but he was careful to ensure that it remain voluntary and that the formulation or drafting of the prayer be performed or initiated privately and in accordance with "the impulse of their hearts," rather than being prescribed by government.

After leaving office, however, Madison may have changed his position regarding prayer resolutions. In his *Detached Memoranda* written in 1820, Madison declared that he felt the government lacked the power to promulgate prayer proclamations or resolutions. He felt there was an inappropriate tendency "to narrow the recommendation to the standard of the predominant sect."[74] He also believed that the practice often ter-

---

with Justices Joseph Story and John Marshall over whether or not the United States could rightfully establish generalized Christianity as a national religion. Madison no doubt would be surprised to learn that subsequent scholars had converted such a statement into the proposition that the Establishment and not the Free Exercise Clause of the First Amendment should be pre-eminent in instances in which individuals sought accommodation from the government in exercising their religion or in pursuing matters of conscience. Furthermore, even if Madison may have changed his mind on this issue when he wrote this letter later in his life, the earlier view he took in adopting the prayer resolution is more significant in ascertaining the framers' intent at the time of adoption and ratification.

It is also possible to explain Madison's letter without arguing that he altered his position in his later years. One can argue that the prayer recommendation merely accommodated or facilitated voluntary free exercise in the public sector. In this regard, commentators like Koch take a step that may not be justified with regard to Madison; they are willing to permit the policy they attribute to the Establishment Clause to override the free-exercise value in some instances. Madison never intended such a result because, in his view, the Free Exercise Clause was certainly pre-eminent. Madison's view with respect to the pre-eminence of the Free Exercise Clause was in accord with the consensus of the country. *See, e.g.,* L. Tribe, AMERICAN CONSTITUTIONAL LAW 819 (1978), concluding that: "Whenever a free exercise claim conflicts with an absolute non-establishment theory, the support of the former would be more faithful to the consensus present at the time of the Constitutional Convention and of the First Congress." Therefore, Madison would permit the government to accommodate voluntary religious exercise in the public sector, as long as it did so in an equal fashion and as long as the accommodation did not manifestly endanger the state.

74. C. Rice, THE SUPREME COURT AND PUBLIC PRAYER (1964) (quoting Madison's DETACHED MEMORANDA).

minated in a "conformity to the creed of the majority and a single sect, if amounting to a majority."[75] Upon closer scrutiny, this action on the part of Madison merely appears to be a rearticulation of his lifelong opposition to the imposition of even a nondenominational Christian majority's religious views on minority religionists and of his opposition to the interposition by governmental officials of their views on the public.[76]

By 1820, it is evident that the prevailing view in the United States held that generalized, nondenominational Christianity could be promoted in a preferential, albeit tolerant, manner by the national government as well as by the states.[77] Therefore, Madison's opposition to prayer resolutions in that era may well have been based largely in his oft-articulated view that no sect or sects could be preferred by the government because to do so would inhibit or coerce others in their free exercise. In this regard, Madison may have grown increasingly skeptical about the ability of the government to act noncoercively, when it acted in a directive manner. Thus, while he continued to favor a broad role for free exercise throughout his life, Madison was vigilant in his concern that the government might adopt the trappings of a particular religion, albeit in a generalized form of religion, rather than dealing with all religions in an evenhanded manner. Madison was always offended by the

---

75. *Id.*

76. Madison referred specifically to his resolution in the closing paragraphs of his DETACHED MEMORANDA:

During the administration of Mr. Jefferson no religious proclamation was issued. It being understood that his successor [Madison] was disinclined to such *interpositions* of the Executive and by some supposed moreover that they might originate with more propriety with the Legislative Body, a resolution was passed requesting him to issue a proclamation.

It was thought not proper to refuse a compliance altogether; but a form and language were employed, which were meant to deaden as much as possible any claim of political right to enjoin religious observances by resting these expressly on the voluntary compliance of individuals, and even by limiting the recommendation to such as wished simultaneous as well as voluntary performance of a religious act on the occasion.

DETACHED MEMORANDA, as *cited in* R. Alley, JAMES MADISON ON RELIGIOUS LIBERTY, at 94 (1985). Madison's emphasis on his reluctance to interpose his views as chief executive on others is clear; it is not clear, however, that he opposed governmental accommodation of religious exercise, including prayer.

77. I label this view the Story view. The Story view predominated in the early nineteenth century. For a discussion of the view, *see* Chapter 5, *infra.*

adoption of religious trappings by government,[78] but he remained committed to the principle of the free or voluntary exercise of one's religious convictions, even in public, provided that the exercise did not infringe upon the rights of conscience of another and provided that the exercise did not manifestly endanger the existence of the state. His fidelity to this principle remained inviolate, while his espousal of the principle of equal aid to all religions may have become increasingly tempered by his fear that the national government would not treat all religions in a nonpreferential manner or that government would violate rights of conscience by declaring which forms of conscience were religious for aid purposes.

For Madison, the full and equal right of conscience required that the government refrain from adopting modes of worship, articles of faith, or anything akin to the propagation of a national religion, even if that religion constituted the union of the doctrine and beliefs of a majority of the sects in America. He believed that any such actions posed the threat of developing into a coercive, majoritarian establishment of religion that would not only limit the beneficial forces of religious pluralism but would also jeopardize the opportunity of all people to exercise freely their religious conscience in public and in private.[79]

Despite Madison's views relative to these issues, it is likely that the Washington-Adams position of unequivocal support for such public proclamations probably mirrored the general public sentiment at the time of the adoption of the First Amendment. This conclusion receives strong support from a number of sources and related events: (1) the First Congress had passed resolutions calling on the president to pro-

---

78. Sky, *supra* note 1, at 1421, observes with regard to the intent of Madison and the other framers, that:
   Indeed, in their discussion of the types of enactments which Congress might not make, the Framers were more concerned that the trappings of a national religion, rather than a full blown national religion itself, might emerge from some future congressional grist mill....The efforts to foreclose the practices that had been intimately tied into the formal establishments of the past were thus preserved in the broader version of the clause that emerged from the deliberations. Madison summed it up in his later years when he said that "the Constitution...forbids everything like an establishment of a national religion."
79. It is inconceivable that Madison, with his fidelity to free-exercise principles, would favor contemporary efforts to create an irreligious public sector in which even voluntary, self-initiated efforts to exercise one's religious beliefs cannot be facilitated or accommodated. This conclusion is buttressed by the fact that the role of the public sector, in education and otherwise, has become so pervasive today that prohibiting the voluntary exercise of one's religion in the public sector constitutes a genuine and increasingly expansive limitation on the pre-eminent right of free exercise.

claim a public day of fasting, prayer, and thanksgiving despite Tucker's protest that such governmentally proclaimed prayers violated the Establishment Clause; (2) the fact that both Jefferson and Madison felt compelled to explain their positions, which differed from the position taken by their predecessors, while members of Congress and Presidents Washington and Adams who supported such resolutions felt no similar need to justify their positions on constitutional grounds, implies that the public as a whole, which had ratified the Bill of Rights, assumed that such efforts were appropriate and desirable; and (3) other actions, including opening sessions of Congress with prayer, innumerable public professions of faith by public officials,[80] and the existence of paid chaplains in the military service, all indicate a willingness on the part of elected officials and their constituents during the founding era to recognize, accommodate, and even facilitate public religious exercise.

Nevertheless, while the position held by Washington and Adams probably constituted the prevailing public view, the Madisonian and more extreme Jeffersonian positions undoubtedly received support as well. However, even the Madisonian and Jeffersonian views were founded more on a solicitude for the rights of minorities to express their religious convictions without governmental interference, particularly at the national level, than on a belief that government should be precluded from accommodating personal or voluntary self-initiated religious exercise.[81]

In addition to the issue of fasting and prayer proclamations, there were a number of other governmental actions contemporaneous with the passage of the First Amendment that shed light on its interpretation. Public buildings were actually used for religious services. During this period, even the House of Representatives authorized the use of its hall for religious services. Even during Jefferson's presidency, the Capitol was regularly used for religious services. Additionally, at least at the state level, Jefferson specifically acknowledged his support for the principle of equal access by all religious sects to public facilities by supporting a proposal inviting sects to conduct religious exercises on the confines of the University of Virginia, provided all sects had essentially equal access to the university facilities.[82]

---

80. In his first inaugural address, George Washington liberally referred to the role of divine providence in guiding the formation of the United States. *See* Washington's First Inaugural Address, *reprinted in* 1 J. Richardson, A COMPILATION OF THE MESSAGES AND PAPERS OF THE PRESIDENTS 43 (1897).

81. As previously noted, Jefferson's views regarding religious liberty were closely tied to his notion of federalism.

82. *See* S. Padover, THE COMPLETE JEFFERSON 1110 (2d ed. 1969). Jefferson's position indicates his desire to facilitate the free and equal exercise of religious

Jefferson also exulted in the fact that in Charlottesville existing religious sects were all given equal access to or use of the local, public courthouse:

> In our village of Charlottesville, there is a good degree of religion, with a small spice of fanaticism. We have four sects, but without either church or meeting-house. The court-house is the common temple, one Sunday in the month to each. Here, Episcopalian and Presbyterian, Methodist and Baptist, meet together, join in hymning their maker, listen with attention and devotion to each others', and all mix in society with perfect harmony.[83]

Thus, even the purported father of strict separation, Thomas Jefferson, approved of the principle of equal access to public facilities for the purpose of religious exercise, particularly at the state level.[84] Furthermore,

---

exercise on public premises, although he evidently believed that this facilitation could best be accomplished at the state level. Thus, it is untenable to assume that, if he were forced to choose between the separation value he purportedly espoused at the national level and his desire to accommodate the free exercise of religious beliefs, he would consider the separation value to be pre-eminent.

One author has noted that, under the Jeffersonian proposal, "the regulations of the University 'should be so modified and accommodated' so as to give seminary students access to the university library...[and that]...Jefferson asserted finally that his plans 'would fill the chasm now existing on principles [while leaving] inviolate the constitutional freedom of religion, the most unalienable and sacred of all human rights.'" Comment, *supra* note 71, at 672 (emphasis in original).

83. Letter from Thomas Jefferson to Dr. Thomas Cooper (Nov. 2, 1822), *cited in* Comment, *supra* note 71, at 667–68.

84. In perhaps the best study of Jefferson's position regarding religious liberty, particularly as related to public education, Healy summarized Jefferson's view as follows:

> To Jefferson the elimination of whatever was inconsistent with the tenets of any particular sect did not mean the religion itself was to be outlawed in public education, any more than the interdiction of the government from meddling with religious institutions, doctrines, disciplines, or exercises meant to Jefferson that the government was without religion. This he denied. Rather, the purpose of this provision [the establishment clause] was to guarantee...religious freedom. This meant [at a minimum] that those areas of religion upon which all sects agreed were certainly to be included in the framework of public education.

R. Healy, JEFFERSON ON RELIGION IN PUBLIC EDUCATION (1962).

he never voiced a concern on his part that, if religious groups were given equal access, they would receive some economic benefit from such access.

A number of congressional actions also dealt with issues of religious liberty. The First Congress enacted the Northwest Ordinance of 1787, which provided that *"religion,* morality and knowledge" were all necessary to the good government and happiness of mankind and should be promoted or accommodated by government.[85] The ordinance provided that schools should promote religious and related values as a part of their educational function. The re-enactment of this significant ordinance by the First Congress certainly offers further support for the proposition that the First Congress felt that the accommodation and even facilitation of religious exercise in the public sector was permitted by the First Amendment and was also desirable as a matter of policy. It is also relevant to reiterate at this juncture that, in 1803, the Senate ratified and President Jefferson signed a treaty that provided for the erection by the national government of a church for the Kaskaskia Indians.[86] Thus, Congress and the executive actually promoted religious exercise in the public sector. It would, therefore, simply be inaccurate to claim that the framers intended the Establishment Clause to be interpreted as supportive of the principle of strict separation of church and state as we know it today. Even Madison and Jefferson never went that far in expressing their misgivings regarding the role of government with regard to religious exercise. Furthermore, as will be shown in the following chapter, the commentators addressing this subject during the nineteenth century uniformly agreed that the Establishment Clause did not preclude government from aiding or accommodating religion, although there was disagreement as to how that aid or accommodation could best be administered.

---

85. The Northwest Ordinance of 1787, *cited in* L. Pfeffer, CHURCH, STATE AND FREEDOM, at 85 (1967) (emphasis added).

86. W. Sweet, RELIGION IN THE DEVELOPMENT OF AMERICAN CULTURE 242 (1952), *cited in* Linden & Quinn, *One Dialogue on Constitutional Religion,* 14 CREIGHTON L. REV. 1249, 1258 (1981).

5

Religious Liberty in the Early Years of the Republic: The Rise of the Story View

From the history of the framing of the First Amendment, one can infer that the framers intended to accommodate religious exercise in the public as well as the private sector. This inference is also supported by examining the late-eighteenth- and early-nineteenth-century commentary on the subject. Since there were broad differences as to how religious exercise should be accommodated as a constitutional matter, the following analysis concentrates primarily on the differences among early commentators. The commentary delineates limits within which the framers and ratifiers may have differed in their intentions in adopting the religion clauses. If the present Court desires to remain consistent with the applicable constitutional history, it must tailor its decisions within those broad parameters. In this regard, the Supreme Court has maintained perhaps unintentionally an unsteady allegiance to one of the applicable historical positions. Therefore, the current Court needs not so much to alter precedent but rather to clarify the historical and philosophical premises behind its decisions. This should bring order to the chaos that typically characterizes church-state relations today.

Perhaps the leading commentator during the general era of the adoption, ratification, and early implementation of the First Amendment was Justice Joseph Story. In 1811, at the age of thirty-two, Story was appointed to the Supreme Court by President James Madison. Story served in that capacity until 1845 and was a major influence on the

Court. Justice Story's *Commentaries on the Constitution,* published in 1833, is generally considered to be an indispensable source for the purpose of the study of constitutional law and history. Despite the influence of the *Commentaries* regarding most constitutional issues, its extensive treatment of religious liberty has generally been disregarded or ignored by contemporary courts, although the *Commentaries* was discussed in the Court's recent decision in *Jaffree,* the meditation case.[1]

In section 1868 of his *Commentaries,* Story summarized the probable intention of the framers and ratifiers of the First Amendment with regard to religious liberty by stating that

> Probably at the time of the adoption of the constitution, and of the [first] amendment to it, now under consideration, the general, if not the universal, sentiment in America was that Christianity ought to receive encouragement from the State, so far as was not incompatible with the private rights of religious worship. *Any attempt to level all religions, and to make it a matter of state policy to hold all in utter indifference, would have created universal disapprobation, if not universal indignation.*[2]

In thus summarizing public sentiment, Justice Story made the following points: (1) the people (generally, if not universally) believed that, in adopting the First Amendment, Christianity could be encouraged by the state, provided only that such encouragement was not incompatible with rights of worship of non-Christians; and (2) any attempt "to level *all* religions, and to make it a matter of state policy to hold *all* in utter indifference" would have met with "*universal* disapprobation." The people were universally opposed to the argument for the strict separation of church and state, to which twentieth-century separationists adhere, because in their view it would possibly hinder the free exercise of religion.

In section 1870 of the *Commentaries,* Story clarified the inalienable nature of the right of conscience:

> But the duty of supporting religion, (and especially the Christian religion), is very different from the right to force the conscience of other men, or to punish them for worshipping God in the manner, which, they believe, their accountability to him requires....The rights

---

1. *See* Chapter 9, *infra,* for an in-depth discussion of the *Jaffree* case.
2. 2 J. Story, COMMENTARIES ON THE CONSTITUTION OF THE UNITED STATES (2d Ed. Boston 1851) (1st Ed. Boston 1833), hereinafter cited as COMMENTARIES, § 1874, at 593 (emphasis added).

of conscience are, indeed, beyond the just reach of any human power. They are given by God, and cannot be encroached upon by human authority.[3]

It is clear that for Story, as for Madison, the right of conscience or free exercise was the pre-eminent value of the First Amendment and was beyond the reach of government, although government could aid or accommodate but not infringe upon free exercise.

Story described the intended purpose of the Establishment Clause as follows:

> The real object of the [first] amendment was, not to countenance, much less to advance Mahometanism, or Judaism, or infidelity, by prostrating Christianity; but to exclude all rivalry among Christian sects, and to prevent any national ecclesiastical establishment, which should give to an hierarchy the exclusive patronage of the national government. It thus cut off the means of religious persecution, (the vice and pest of former ages), and of subversion of the rights of conscience in matters of religion, which had been trampled upon almost from the days of the Apostles to the present age.[4]

According to Story, therefore, the Establishment Clause merely helped to effectuate the inalienable right of free exercise or freedom of conscience by preventing any particular ecclesiastical sect or religious body from being established at the national level.

Furthermore, in a passage reflective of the federalism advocated by Thomas Jefferson, Justice Story noted that

> It was under a solemn consciousness of the dangers from ecclesiastical ambition, the bigotry of spiritual pride, and the intolerance of sects, thus exemplified in our domestic as well as foreign annals, that it was deemed advisable to exclude from national government all power to act upon the subject.... Thus the whole power over the subject of religion is left exclusively to the state governments, to be acted upon according to their own sense of justice, and the state Constitutions; and the Catholic and the Protestant, the Calvinist and the Arminian, the Jew and the Infidel, may sit down at the common table of the national councils, without any inquisition into their faith, or mode of worship.[5]

Story apparently believed that the promotion of a generalized or non-denominational Christianity, provided it did not coerce another in the

---

3. *Id.* § 1870.
4. *Id.* § 1877, at 594.
5. *Id.* § 1879, at 596–7.

exercise of her religious rights or rights of conscience, would receive its major support from within the states and not from the national government. Strict separationists might rely on this comment for the view that the national government was precluded from acting in any manner regarding public religious exercise and that the government could not, therefore, aid or even accommodate religious exercise. However, this would be reading too much into Story's comment. Story was emphasizing that the national government could not infringe upon religious exercise or pass laws respecting state religious establishments. To read Section 1879 as a complete limitation of the power of the national government to accommodate religious exercise would render the prior sections of his *Commentaries* dealing with the intent of the framers largely meaningless. Given Story's view regarding the inalienable nature of the right of conscience, the government at both the state and national levels would, it seems, at a minimum be required to accommodate public as well as private religious exercise; it could not hinder that exercise.

In describing the appropriate emphasis to be given the role of Justice Story and his *Commentaries,* it has been asserted that "Justice Story lived so near the time of the adoption of the Constitution that [the *Commentaries*] may be taken not merely as opinion formed upon a careful study of the materials of history, but as at least hearsay testimony to the fact."[6] Story's words are a major source for understanding the meaning actually attributed to the religion clauses by both the legal community and the public at the time of the ratification of the First Amendment. It is, therefore, regrettable that Story's words have largely been disregarded by contemporary courts and commentators.[7]

---

6. I. Cornelison, THE RELATION OF RELIGION TO CIVIL GOVERNMENT IN THE UNITED STATES OF AMERICA 208 (1895). Cornelison did not, however, agree with Story's conclusion that the federal government should adopt measures to promote Christianity. *Id.* at 177. In support of his position, Cornelison cited the Treaty of Tripoli of 1797, which stated that "the government of the United States of America is not, in any sense, founded in the Christian religion." *Id.* at 163. It should be remembered, however, that Story was of the view that the *states* would assume the primary role in promoting Christianity.

7. Story's COMMENTARIES were not cited in any of the opinions in the first Establishment Clause case, Everson v. Board of Education, 330 U.S.1 (1947), or in the seminal Free Exercise case of Reynolds v. United States, 98 U.S. 145 (1878) and Cantwell v. Connecticut, 310 U.S. 296 (1940). It is particularly striking that the Court disregarded Story's COMMENTARIES in the *Everson* and *Reynolds* decisions, because the justices writing those opinions purported to rely on historical material to justify their opinions.

It is evident that Story's view was not in full accordance with Madison's. It is clear that Madison did not believe that a generalized, nondenominational Christianity should be promoted at the national level. Madison's *Memorial and Remonstrance* indicated that he was also unalterably opposed to the preferential promotion of Christianity at the state level. For Madison, the First Amendment was intended to secure the equal rights of conscience for all citizens. Therefore, Story's view would have been unacceptable, because for Madison it would have constituted little more than a poorly veiled effort to maintain an established religion, while merely tolerating other sects. Despite his own adherence to the Christian faith, Madison cannot be included among those who espoused the "sentiment in America...that Christianity ought to receive [special] encouragement from the State." Rather, in Madison's view, Christianity could best flourish only when all religious groups or sects were treated equally by government. Jefferson's views with regard to state support for Christianity were more enigmatic.[8]

Madison took a strong position on free exercise and felt that the rights of conscience were inalienable and could not be abridged rightfully, except when the state was manifestly endangered. Justice Story also believed that the right of free exercise was inalienable and beyond the reach of national government; however, given his willingness to permit state-established religions, it is unclear whether he would have permitted free exercise to flourish in the states insofar as the full and free exercise of religion requires that all religions receive equal treatment at the hands of government. In this regard, Story was willing to substitute governmental toleration for nonestablished sects for Madison's more stringent equal treatment by government of all religions.

It is reasonable to conclude that Madison agreed with Justice Story's rendition of the intent of the framers on at least two matters. First, Madison joined Story in the belief, which Story deemed universal, that government should accommodate the inalienable right of conscience for all religious sects, provided it could do so without infringing upon or otherwise coercing the beliefs of others. Second, they agreed that the right of free exercise or the right of conscience was the pre-eminent right protected by the First Amendment. This right was the primary value being furthered by the adoption of the First Amendment; the Establishment Clause merely helped to effectuate it. Even on these points of agreement, however, Madison in all likelihood was more concerned with

---

8. *See* R. Healy, JEFFERSON ON RELIGION IN PUBLIC EDUCATION, at 120—22, 138—40 (1962). Healy concludes that Jefferson actually may have wanted to impose his own form of Unitarianism at the state level. *Id.* at 265.

ensuring the unfettered exercise of the rights of conscience than was Justice Story. It will be recalled that Madison would only permit governmental regulation of such rights when the exercise of those rights would manifestly endanger the state's interests, while Story may have been willing to recognize a lesser standard, particularly insofar as the states were concerned.[9]

In substance, therefore, the major disagreement between the position articulated in Story's *Commentaries* and the Madisonian position comes on the issue of whether or not government could offer preferential aid exclusively to Christian groups. An examination of the legislative history alone does not indicate unequivocally whether the Madisonian or the Story position, or some compromise position between them, was accepted by the framers. Accordingly, a further examination of other contempoary commentaries and events is warranted to elucidate further the likely intent of the framers regarding this issue.

The Treaty of Tripoli of 1797 expressly provided that the government of the United States was not founded on the Christian religion. However, this facet of the treaty, which seems to contradict Story's assertion that the Christian religion was intended to be our national religion, might be questioned on at least three bases: (1) if it represented the intent of the framers and ratifiers of the First Amendment; (2) if it merely declared that there was no national Christian religion, leaving to the state governments the privilege of determining whether they desired to establish Christianity in some form at the state level; or (3) if Christianity was considered a part of the common law that predated the founding of the United States.[10]

In determining whether the framers intended to promote a Christian republic, while merely tolerating non-Christian religions, it will be helpful to look not only at the views of Madison and Story, but also at the positions of other prominent citizens of that era.

---

9. *See, e.g.,* COMMENTARIES, *supra* note 2, §§ 1872–79, at 590–97. Story was no doubt closer to Jefferson than to Madison and would have permitted the state to regulate, at least indirectly, religious exercise in the furtherance of the public good or welfare.

10. As to Christianity's relationship to the common law, Professor Cooley observed that:

> It is frequently said that Christianity is a part of the law of the land. In a certain sense and for certain purposes this is true. The best features of the common law...if not derived from, have at least been improved and strengthened by the prevailing religion and the teachings of its sacred Book. But the law does not attempt to enforce the precepts

In 1833, Jasper Adams, then president of the College of Charleston and a proponent of the view that the government should promote Christianity, sent Madison a copy of his pamphlet entitled *The Relations of Christianity to Civil Government in the United States.* In that pamphlet, Adams argued that a general, nondenominational Christianity constituted the national religion.[11] Adams solicited Madison's comments with regard to the conclusions drawn in his pamphlet. He also sought the comments of Chief Justice John Marshall and Justice Story.[12] Madison considered the central question raised by the pamphlet to be whether or not the propagation of the Christian religion required financial aid from the government.[13]

After examining the development of religious liberty and emphasizing the developing disestablishment of churches in many of the states, Madison argued that no public funds should be used exclusively to finance the Christian religion.[14] While acknowledging that Madison's rhetoric had a separationist ring to it, it is important to note what Madison did not say. He said nothing about efforts on the part of government to assist all religions in an equal manner, financially and otherwise. He did not discuss the issue of public accommodation of the rights of conscience or free exercise of all individuals. His argument merely paralleled his earlier position, articulated in the *Memorial and Remonstrance.*

Clearly, Madison had an aversion to preferential governmental financial aid to religious establishments and, as noted previously he may

---

of Christianity on the ground of their sacred character or divine origin.... Mr. Justice *Story* has said in the Girard Will case that, although Christianity is a part of the common law of the State, it is only so in this qualified sense, *that its divine origin and truth are admitted,* and therefore it is not to be maliciously and openly reviled and blasphemed against, to the annoyance of believers or the injury of the public.

2 T. Cooley, COOLEY'S CONSTITUTIONAL LIMITATIONS, 976 (1927) (emphasis in original).

11. A. Koch, MADISON'S ADVICE TO MY COUNTRY, at 36–7 (1966). Koch notes that:

On the basis of what [Adams] called an inductive examination of colonial history, the state constitutions and...the First Amendment, Adams concluded that we do indeed have a national religion, although one that is tolerant of all Christian denominations. But he lamented that the view was gaining ground that religion and government had no connection with each other and found this view "in the highest degree pernicious in its tendency" to all our institutions, pervasively corrupting the morals of the American people.

12. *Id.*
13. *Id.* at 38.
14. *Id.* at 38–43.

have believed that as a practical matter government could best assure such equality of treatment by refraining from extending direct financial aid to any religious group or groups.[15]

Chief Justice Marshall also responded to Jasper Adams's pamphlet. He did not share any of Madison's reservations regarding the extension of collective and preferential aid to and acknowledgment of the Christian religion in America. In his response, Marshall replied that "the American population is entirely Christian, and with us, Christianity and religion are identified. It would be strange indeed, if with such a people our institutions did not presuppose Christianity."[16]

Justice Story was even more effusive in support of the position in the pamphlet. He declared that "I have read it with uncommon satisfaction. I think its tone and spirit excellent. My own private judgment has long been (and every day's experience more and more confirms me in it) that government cannot long exist without an allegiance with religion *to some extent;* and that Christianity is indispensable to the true interests and solid foundation of free government."[17]

In yet another context, James Wilson, one of the most influential delegates to the Constitutional Convention and a prominent justice on the early Supreme Court, concurred with the Marshall-Story position, asserting that Christianity was a part of the common law and that the government should not decline to recognize that fact.[18]

The contradictory positions between Madison, on the one hand, and Story, Marshall, and Wilson, on the other, bring us back to our starting point, without supplying an unequivocal depiction of the intent of the framers on this issue. Madison's response to Adams's pamphlet was not particularly clear. Additionally, Madison did not rely on the purported intent of the framers; rather, he depended upon his own general analysis of history upon the soundness of his position as a philosophical matter. Furthermore, he did not assert that public sentiment supported his view, although given support in Virginia for his *Memorial* he might well have done so. Without clarity and without invoking public support for his position, Madison's response leaves the issue open. Similarly, however, Story noted only that his "own *private* judgment" that government should ally itself to religion, not the public sentiment at the time the First Amendment was ratified, supported that position.

---

15. Curry clearly believes that Madison and most of the framers opposed even equal governmental financial assistance to all religions. *See, e.g.,* Curry, THE FIRST FREEDOMS: CHURCH AND STATE IN AMERICA TO THE PASSAGE OF THE FIRST AMENDMENT, 209 (1986).

16. A. Koch, *supra* note 11, at 43–4 (quoting Justice J. Marshall).

17. *Id.* at 45 (quoting Justice Story) (emphasis in original).

18. Wilson's view is discussed in I. Cornelison, *supra* note 6, at 126 (1895).

Thus, if either the Story or the Madisonian position was actually preferred by the First Congress in its draft of the First Amendment or by the public ratifying the amendment, it is not clear from the correspondence with Adams because both Story and Madison refrained from indicating public support for their respective views. Nevertheless, Story claimed elsewhere general, if not universal, public support for his position. However, given the nature of the difference between Story and Madison on establishment issues and despite their combined support for the amendment itself, it is more likely that the issue of support for nondenominational Christianity (Story's position) versus equal treatment (Madison's position) was intentionally left unresolved. The framers undoubtedly realized that the need to resolve the specific differences between what came to be the Story and Madison views, at the time the First Amendment was adopted, was outweighed by the likelihood that the dispute might render their overall efforts regarding both adoption of the Bill of Rights and preservation of the Constitution futile. A compromise was in order, and the only compromise that could be reached may well have been to leave this facet of the establishment issue open.[19]

Certainly the language "Congress shall make no law respecting an establishment of religion" was sufficiently ambiguous to leave this issue open for future determination. Nevertheless, based on the historical data previously discussed, it is extremely doubtful that the framers intended to permit any establishment position more extreme or absolutist, in a separationist sense, than that articulated during the debates by Madison. Madison, for his part, had sought to assuage the doubts of Benjamin Huntington, Peter Sylvester, and presumably others with regard to their apprehension that the Establishment Clause might be read as "patronize[ing] those who professed no religion at all" or as tending "to abolish religion altogether."

There are other historical facts that tend to support this conclusion. Religion clearly played a significant role in matters of education at the

---

19. If such data were available, it would not be surprising to find that the framers left this issue open to avoid the antagonism that adoption of either the Story or Madisonian position, to the exclusion of the other, would undoubtedly have engendered in the various states and among even major supporters of the Constitution itself. To endeavor to resolve those differences might have played into the hands of the Anti-Federalists who wanted to dismantle the Constitution. Additionally, since the First Amendment clearly left state establishments intact, advocates of a Christian republic had no reason to prolong the debate or otherwise jeopardize the Constitution, because the states were free to Christianize their governments.

time of the framing of the First Amendment, as well as during the early years of the Republic. Therefore, while the free-exercise right was intended to be pre-eminent, the value of the Establishment Clause was primarily intended to assure, at a minimum, that the federal government would not be permitted to infringe upon that free and equal exercise. During the early Republic, the states were free to promote and protect state religious establishments, although even Story was reluctant to provide the states with complete latitude or discretion in such matters.

An examination of later nineteenth-century religious and constitutional scholarship further illustrates that the mid-twentieth-century strict-separationist view of the Establishment Clause is a new construction and has little, if any, historical support. For example, during the early nineteenth century, Daniel Webster elaborated on the Story view and articulated what was probably the predominant position regarding the interrelationship between church and state throughout the nineteenth century:

> The massive cathedral of the Catholic; the Episcopalian Church with its lofty spire pointing heavenward; the plain temple of the Quaker; the long church of the hardy pioneer of the wilderness; the mementos and memorials around and about us; the consecrated graveyards; the tombstones and epitaphs; their silent vaults; their mouldering contents, all attest it. The dead prove it as well as the living. The generations that are gone before speak it and pronounce it from the tomb. We feel it. *All proclaim that Christianity, general tolerant Christianity, Christianity independent of sects and parties, that Christianity to which the sword and fagot are unknown, general tolerant Christianity, is the law of the land.*[20]

While some commentators on the issue of religious liberty during the nineteenth and early twentieth centuries may have disagreed with Webster's conclusion that tolerant Christianity was the law of the land, they all agreed uniformly that civil government, at both the national and state levels, could permit, if not promote, religious exercise in the public sector. In this regard, Professor Thomas Cooley, the primary constitutional commentator of the latter part of the nineteenth century, concluded that:

> By establishment of religion is meant the setting up or recognition of a state church, or at least the conferring upon one church of special favors and advantages which are denied to others. It was never intended by the Constitution that the Government should be prohibited from

---

20. WORKS OF DANIEL WEBSTER, Vol. 6, at 176, as cited in Zollman, *Religious Liberty in American Law,* 17 MICH. L. REV. 355 at 370 (1919).

recognizing religion, or that religious worship should never be provided for in cases where a proper recognition of the Divine Providence in the working of government might seem to require it, and where it can be done without drawing any invidious distinctions between religious beliefs, organizations or sects.[21]

While disputes among supporters of the First Amendment no doubt remained over its meaning or application during the nineteenth century, it was understood clearly by all factions that the First Amendment permitted governmental accommodation and perhaps even facilitation of religious exercise, so long as the government acted in a tolerant or nonpreferential manner.

The case law also reflects these conclusions drawn from the nineteenth-century commentators. The earliest Supreme Court decision was *Terrett v. Taylor*,[22] a case decided in 1815. In the opinion written by Justice Story, in *Terrett* the Supreme Court struck down an effort in Virginia under the Virginia constitution to divest the Episcopal Church of its property. The church had acquired certain property at a time when it was the established church in Virginia. During that time, the church received financial and related assistance from the colonial government. An act of the Virginia legislature in 1776 had confirmed the church's rights to its lands. Given that the church had received aid from the government, the state of Virginia contended that the grant of the lands to the church was revocable on the ground that it was inconsistent with the Virginia Declaration of Rights and state statute.

In denying the state the relief requested, in construing the Virginia constitution[23] and holding for the church, Story emphasized that:

> But, although it may be true, that "religion can be directed only by reason and conviction, not by force or violence," and that "all men are equally entitled to the free exercise of religion, according to the

---

21. T. Cooley, Principles Of Constitutional Law, 224–25 (3d Ed. 1898).
22. 13 Cranch 43 (1815).
23. Interestingly, in his opinion for the Court in *Terrett*, Justice Story's mode of constitutional analysis is informative. He appears to be taking an originalist position when he notes that:

It is asserted by the legislature of Virginia, in 1798 and 1801, that the [statute involved] was inconsistent with the bill of rights and constitution of that state, and therefore, void. Whatever weight such a declaration might properly have, as the opinion of wise and learned men, as a declaration of what the law has been or is, it can have no decisive authority. It is, however, encountered by the opinion successively given by former legislatures, from the earliest existence of the constitution itself, which were composed of men of the very first rank for talents

dictates of conscience," as the Bill of Rights of Virginia declares, yet it is difficult to perceive how it follows as a consequence, that the legislature may not enact laws more effectively to enable all sects to accomplish the great objects of religion, by giving them corporate rights for the management of their property, and the regulation of their temporal as well as spiritual concerns. Consistent with the constitution of Virginia, the legislature could not create or continue a religious establishment which should have exclusive rights and prerogatives, or compel the citizens to worship under a stipulated form of discipline, or to pay taxes to those whose creed they could not conscientiously believe. But the free exercise of religion cannot be justly deemed to be restrained by aiding with equal attention the votaries of every sect to perform their own religious duties, or by establishing funds for the support of ministers, for public charities, for the endowment of churches, or for the sepulcher of the dead.[24]

The *Terrett* case is highly instructive for the purpose of clarifying the intended meaning of the clauses securing religious liberty at the state level in Virginia. It should be recalled that the history of Virginia's commitment to religious liberty provides pertinent background for what ensued during the adoption and ratification of the First Amendment. Given the role of Madison and Jefferson in the Virginia experience and the reliance of contemporary strict separationists on their reading of the Virginia history and the thought of Jefferson and, to some extent, Madison, Story's interpretation of the law of religious liberty in Virginia at the time the Declaration of Rights was framed is strong evidence of the meaning of the Free Exercise and Establishment clauses in the First Amendment, as well. It is, therefore, unfortunate that the Supreme Court has been remiss in referring to the *Terrett* case in the First Amendment area.

There are a number of specific points that should be made with regard to Story's opinion in *Terrett*. Justice Story believed that tolerant, nondenominational Christianity could be established as the national religion but he makes no reference to this fact in *Terrett*. Instead, in interpreting Virginia law, he seemed to opt for a position much more akin to the Madisonian position, which held that: (1) "the legislature could not

---

and learning. And this opinion, too, is not only a contemporaneous exposition of the Constitution, but has the additional weight, that it was promulgated or acquiesced in by a great majority, if not the whole, of the very framers of the Constitution.
Id. at 50.
24. *Id.* at 47–8.

create or continue a religious establishment which should have exclusive rights or prerogatives"; (2) no stipulated form of religious discipline or mode of worship could be adopted; and (3) that the free exercise of religion could be facilitated by "aiding with equal attention the votaries of every sect to perform their own duties." Story may have refrained from espousing his personal interpretation of the Establishment Clause of the First Amendment in *Terrett* on the ground that he recognized that Virginia had specifically rejected his view when the Assessment Bill, which would have aided Christian sects generally, was defeated on the ground that it was improper to aid even generalized Christianity. Therefore, even recognizing the relationship between the Virginia experience and the national experience, it is conceivable that he and many others believed that the Virginia effort at disestablishment went further than required by the Establishment Clause language of the First Amendment. Since the First Amendment was not binding upon the states, Story limited his analysis in *Terrett* to Virginia law. Nevertheless, his interpretation of the Virginia experience is helpful in setting the limits of the likely meaning of the Establishment and Free Exercise clauses of the First Amendment.

Some scholars[25] have contended that the Story view should simply be dismissed as aberrational. Such a flippant dismissal of Justice Story's thought constitutes an indulgence in "law office history," in which a legal advocate merely ignores contrary data in building an argument more suitable to her own policy preferences. At a minimum, the Story view must be examined or analyzed in light of the pertinent history that purportedly renders it aberrational. A close reading or examination of the history, however, reveals that Justice Story's articulation in his *Commentaries* of the tolerant, nondenominational Christian view constitutes one of the primary views likely to have been held by the framers, while his opinion in *Terrett,* relying as it does on Virginia law, essentially recognizes a position similar to the one espoused by Madison. Either one or some hybrid combination of these views (the Story and Madisonian views) continued to predominate in American law until the mid-twentieth century. As an historical matter, therefore, if there is an aberrational view, it is the view espoused by such contemporary strict-separationist commentators.

In 1845, the Supreme Court decided *Permoli v. First Municipality,*[26] in which Father Permoli, a Catholic priest, contended that an ordinance

---

25. *See, e.g.,* R. Morgan, THE SUPREME COURT AND RELIGION at 36–40 (1972).

26. 44 U.S. (3 How.) 589 (1845).

of the municipality of New Orleans prohibiting the exposing of a corpse in any of the Catholic churches of the municipality infringed on his right to exercise his religion freely. The Court, however, in *Barron v. Baltimore,* had held that "the Constitution makes no provision for protecting the citizens of the respective states in their religious liberties; this is left to the state constitutions and laws: nor is there any inhibition imposed by the Constitution of the United States in this respect on the states."[27] Thus, with its decisions in *Barron v. Baltimore*[28] and *Permoli,* the Court had foreclosed the possibility of bringing an action based on an alleged violation of one's religious freedom under the First Amendment of the United States Constitution.

Since most issues involving religious liberty arise typically at the state level, and given that the decision in *Permoli* clearly limited the applicability of the First Amendment to national as opposed to state activity, the Supreme Court did not decide any religious-liberty issues until their decisions in the Mormon polygamy cases, beginning with *Reynolds v. United States.*[29] The *Reynolds* case, decided in 1878, was heard because it dealt with the constitutionality of a *federal* (territorial) as opposed to state statute.

---

27. *Id.* at 609.
28. 32 U.S. 242, 7 Pet. 243 (1833). *See* Chapter 7 for a discussion of what has been termed the incorporation issue, the issue of whether the states are bound by the strictures of the Bill of Rights, including the First Amendment.
29. 98 U.S. 145 (1878).

6

Getting off on the Wrong Foot: The Reynolds and Everson Decisions

THE FREE EXERCISE CLAUSE: THE REYNOLDS CASE AND ITS PROGENY

In 1878, in its first significant case dealing with the Free Exercise Clause, the Supreme Court decided *Reynolds v. United States.*[1] In the *Reynolds* case, George Reynolds, a resident of the Utah Territory and an active member of the Church of Jesus Christ of Latter-Day Saints (Mormon), was convicted of violating a statute that made the practice of polygamy a crime. As a defense, Reynolds argued that, since Mormon doctrine imposed a duty on male members to practice polygamy when circumstances permitted, the statute under which he was convicted was unconstitutional as applied to him because it violated his right of free exercise.

The Supreme Court refused to overturn the conviction on free-exercise grounds. In writing for the Court, Chief Justice Morrison Waite opted for what he characterized as the Jeffersonian view. Under this view, Waite argued that government could regulate beliefs when they broke out "into overt acts against peace and good order." Elaborating on this principle, the chief justice asserted that, by virtue of the First Amendment, "Congress was deprived of all legislative power over mere opinion, but was left free to reach actions which were in violation of

---

1. 98 U.S. 145 (1878).

social duties or subversive of good order."[2] This distinction between religious beliefs, which were essentially beyond the reach of government, and actions, which could be regulated in the interests of good order, has been labeled the belief/action dichotomy. It seems quite incredible that such a distinction could be drawn when it is clear that most religious beliefs mandate some action. The protection offered to beliefs by the *Reynolds* Court is tenuous at best.

Waite's view in *Reynolds,* relative to the scope of the right of free exercise, was far more restrictive of individual rights than the Madisonian standard that would have required that a religious activity be manifestly injurious to the interests of the state before it could be regulated properly by government. For James Madison and to a lesser extent Justice Joseph Story, as well, the free exercise of one's religious convictions or conscience constituted an inalienable right that could not be abridged without substantial justification; for the Court in *Reynolds,* and the two other subsequent related cases dealing with the practice of polygamy as then espoused by the Church of Jesus Christ of Latter-Day Saints (Mormon),[3] the right of free exercise was more in the nature of a privilege that could be withheld by the government or majority in the interests of good order. Given its adoption of this less stringent standard, the Waite Court had no difficulty holding that, even though the practice of polygamy involved in the *Reynolds* case was clearly of religious origin, it was offensive to public morals and could, therefore, be regulated.[4]

Subsequently, in *Mormon Church v. United States,*[5] the Waite Court took its position in *Reynolds* to an extreme by holding that Congress had the power to revoke the corporate charter of the Mormon Church and also had the power to seize and hold the church's property and use it for public purposes if the church refused to yield in its support of the religious practice of polygamy. Without its property and with many of its leaders in prison, the Mormon Church relented under the ecclesiastical administration of President Wilford Woodruff. In the Mormon view, a view they felt was inspired by God, the loss of a single doctrine was preferable to the loss of the entire mission of the church.

It is surprising that the *Mormon Church* case has not received more attention than it has. With the Court's willingness to permit state seizure

---

2. *Id.* at 161.

3. Mormon Church v. United States, 136 U.S. 1 (1890) (act of incorporation by Mormon Church repealed by Congress); Davis v. Beason, 133 U.S. 333 (1890) (polygamist not allowed to register to vote).

4. *Reynolds,* 98 U.S. at 164–65.

5. 136 U.S. 1 (1890).

and disposition of church property in an effort to enforce the state's conception of morality, despite a First Amendment defense on the part of members of the church, the *Mormon Church* case stands as a particularly egregious precedent. With the *Reynolds* precedent, the Court legitimized imprisonment of church leaders for practicing their religious beliefs when those beliefs were offensive to general public sensibilities, and with the *Mormon Church* decision, the Court legitimated the seizure of church property. There are, it seems, two possible explanations for the relative obscurity of the *Mormon Church* decision: (1) many religionists may not feel threatened when a minority and oft-persecuted religious group is treated as was the Church of Jesus Christ of Latter-Day Saints in the *Mormon Church* case, believing that their religious orthodoxy would protect them against such onslaughts, although strong support lately by many religious groups for the Reverend Sun Myung Moon may indicate that many religionists recognize that their rights are threatened when any group, no matter how unpopular, is persecuted; and (2) since the *Mormon Church* case is in some senses a low point in the Supreme Court's jurisprudence, opponents of the decision may feel that obscurity serves as a fitting, if not ignominious, burial.

It is clear that in relying on what it characterized as the Jeffersonian standard of free exercise, in *Reynolds* and its progeny, the Court ignored the libertarian Madisonian and tolerant Story standards, even though at best Jefferson's role in the adoption and ratification of the First Amendment was peripheral and ambivalent. Furthermore, it is not clear that even Thomas Jefferson, who was himself in many respects an advocate of a broad right of religious liberty, would have applied his peace-and-good-order standard (the standard included in the Virginia Statute for Religious Freedom) in the same manner in which the *Reynolds* Court did.

The Supreme Court's rationale in *Reynolds* is hardly defensible as an historical matter, although it is certainly conceivable that there were framers who may have espoused such a view. For example, it will be recalled that George Mason favored a somewhat similar standard in his original proposal for the Virginia Declaration of Rights.[6] The standard selected by the Court in *Reynolds* may, therefore, retain some legitimacy as a matter of constitutional interpretation because some of the framers may have adhered to a similar standard, permitting the government fairly broad regulatory latitude of religious exercise. Nevertheless, such a standard certainly is not as acceptable as a libertarian policy matter for

---

6. For a discussion of Mason's proposal, Madison's counterproposal, and the adopted version, see *supra* Chapter 3.

free-exercise purposes as the Madisonian manifestly endangered view. Furthermore, the Court's decision in *Reynolds* may not have even been consistent with the Jeffersonian peace-and-good-order standard, because the Court offered little evidence of any disruption of peace and good order by the Mormons as a result of their practice of polygamy. Even the Court acknowledged that its concern was primarily moral, based on their conception of Western morality.[7] In that light, it is doubtful that even Jefferson or Mason would have permitted the regulation of the practice of polygamy as a part of one's religion because such regulation was founded on a subjective moral view rather than on the basis that the practice of polygamy violated public peace and good order.

Fortunately, the current Court has evidently departed from the belief/action dichotomy and public good-order test articulated by the *Reynolds* Court, although they have yet to expressly overrule *Reynolds*. The Supreme Court has replaced the good-order test with a test that provides that the state can only regulate matters of religious exercise when there is a compelling state interest that justifies such regulation. Furthermore, even when the state establishes a compelling state interest, it also must show the act is closely fitted to the interest it serves.[8] This test is much more consistent with the Madisonian manifestly endangered standard,[9] and is preferable as a matter of policy. It also has greater historical support than does the peace-and-good-order standard. In my view, the Supreme Court certainly should maintain its allegiance to the more libertarian compelling-interest standard. The Court should also be encouraged to infuse the standard with meaning based on the applicable constitutional history in general and the Madisonian free-exercise view in specific.

---

7. For a recent philosophical critique of the *Reynolds* decision, *see* Miller, *A Critique of the Reynolds Decision,* 11 W. St. U. L. Rev. 165 (1984). Professor Miller concludes that *"Reynolds* was decided on a gut aversion to polygamy and the Mormons." *Id.* at 196. *See also,* Linford, The Mormons And The Law: The Polygamy Cases, 9 Utah L. Rev. 308, 543 (1964–65).

8. In a recent decision, the Supreme Court held that a state cannot regulate matters of religious exercise unless it proves that its regulation is "justified by a compelling governmental interest," and the governmental regulation of the act "is closely fitted to further the interest it allegedly serves." Larson v. Valente, 456 U.S. 228, 246–47 (1982).

9. For a discussion of the Madisonian test, *see* Chapter 3, *supra.* Clearly, the compelling-governmental-interest and closely fitted (or least restrictive means) elements track the Madisonian standard much more closely than does the peace-and-good-order test of *Reynolds.*

THE ESTABLISHMENT CLAUSE: THE EVERSON ERROR

When the Supreme Court first applied the Establishment Clause, it did not analyze history any better than it had in the *Reynolds* free-exercise case. The Court did not render a major Establishment Clause decision until the middle of the twentieth century, with its decision in *Everson v. Board of Education.*[10] In *Everson,* the Court sustained the right of a New Jersey municipality to provide bus transportation for children attending parochial schools despite an Establishment Clause challenge to the use of public funds for religious purposes. In its decision, the Court upheld public funding of transportation for parochial school pupils when such funding was

---

10. 330 U.S. 1 (1947). Actually, *Everson* was not the first Establishment Clause decision. In Terrett v. Taylor, 13 U.S. (9 Cranch) 43, 49 (1815), the Court struck down Virginia's attempt to divest the Episcopal Church of certain property. In the opinion, Justice Story noted:

Consistent with the constitution of Virginia [and its establishment clause], the legislature could not create or continue a religious establishment which should have exclusive rights and prerogatives, or compel the citizens to worship under a stipulated form of discipline, or to pay taxes to those whose creed they could not conscientiously believe. But the free exercise of religion cannot be justly deemed to be restrained by aiding with equal attention the votaries of every sect to perform their own religious duties, or by establishing funds for the support of ministers, for public charities, for the endowment of churches, or for the sepulcher of the dead.

Id. Terrett was based on the provisions in the Virginia Declaration of Rights rather than the Establishment Clause of the First Amendment. Nevertheless, it is strange that the Everson Court ignored the case completely, particularly given that the Everson Court purported to rely on Virginia history in ascertaining the intended meaning of the Establishment Clause.

There were also a couple of minor Establishment Clause decisions that predated *Everson.* In Arver v. United States, 245 U.S. 366 (1917), the Court held, in a one-paragraph aside, that the legislative exemption of certain ministers or theology students from draft law did not constitute an establishment of religion. *Id.* at 389–901. *See also* Cochran v. Louisiana State Bd. of Educ., 281 U.S. 370 (1930) (use of state money derived from taxation to supply books to private as well as public schools does not violate the Fourteenth Amendment); Quick Bear v. Teupp, 210 U.S. 50 (1908) (Indian treaty and trust fund expenditures to sectarian schools are not an appropriation of public moneys to sectarian schools in violation of the religion clauses of the Constitution); Bradfield v. Roberts, 175 U.S. 291 (1899) (appropriation of money by Congress for sectarian hospital does not constitute an appropriation to a religious society in violation of the Establishment Clause). Each of these cases only implicitly raised the establishment issue in upholding the payment of funds for religiously based educational services. Nevertheless, they do illustrate the manner in which the Court approached Establishment Clause issues in the early twentieth century.

included in a larger package under which pupils attending nonreligious schools also received similar assistance.[11]

The result in *Everson* was generally consistent with the principles set forth in both the Madisonian and the Story views of religious liberty. Under the Story view, such aid would be permitted because it supported Christianity in a nondenominational sense and was tolerant of other religious expression. For Madison, such aid would be allowed for at least two reasons. First, to single out religion and hold that government could not aid it, while extending aid to other similarly situated nonreligious groups, would constitute discrimination against religion. Madison opposed emphatically such discrimination. Second, Madison likely would have permitted such aid because all religious and nonreligious groups had equal access to the funding (i.e., no religious sect or group of sects was being preferred over other groups) and the state was not promoting any particular mode of worship. It should be noted, however, that Madison might have opposed such aid had it become evident as a practical matter that the government could not or would not permit all religious and similarly situated nonreligious groups access to that funding.

Unfortunately, neither the majority nor the minority in *Everson* properly applied the applicable constitutional history in reaching their respective decisions. In terms of historical analysis, there is little that separates Justice Hugo L. Black's majority opinion from Justice Wiley B. Rutledge's dissenting opinion in *Everson*. Both Black and Rutledge argued that strict or absolute separation of church and state was mandated historically by the Establishment Clause. Justice Black, writing for the majority, turned to the history of religious liberty in Virginia and asserted that the Virginia experience was the "great stimulus" for the inclusion of the Establishment Clause in the First Amendment. While Black noted that it would be improper for government to hinder religion, he nevertheless concluded that

> The people [in Virginia], as elsewhere, reached the conviction that individual religious liberty could be achieved best under a government which was stripped of all power to tax, to support, or otherwise to assist any or all religions, or to interfere with the beliefs of any religious individual or group.[12]

Thus, in Black's view, constitutional history precluded the government from directly assisting or interfering with any or *all* religions.

---

11. 330 U.S. at 18.
12. 330 U.S. at 11.

In dissent, Justice Rutledge, joined by Justices Felix Frankfurter, Robert H. Jackson, and Harold H. Burton, purportedly relied upon Madison's *Memorial and Remonstrance* as "the most accurate statement of views of the First Amendment's author concerning what is 'an establishment of religion,'"[13] and concluded that

> The Amendment's purpose was not to strike merely at the official establishment of a single sect, creed or religion, outlawing only a formal relation such as had prevailed in England and some of the colonies. . . . It was to create a complete and permanent separation of the spheres of religious activity and civil authority by comprehensively forbidding every form of public aid or support for religion.[14]

Thus, for Black and Rutledge the history was clear—the framers intended an absolute separation of church and state. Frankfurter voiced this same basic sentiment when he wrote in his diary in 1948 that the "public schools are [must, as a constitutional matter, be] inherently irreligious."[15]

It is not surprising that Rutledge favored the complete separation of church and state, thereby effectively rendering the public sector irreligious, given his prior opinion in the *Prince* case. In *Prince,* he followed the lead of the *Reynolds* Court and placed only minimal significance on the right of free exercise.[16]

---

13. *Id.* at 37 (Rutledge, J., Dissenting).

14. *Id.* at 31–2 (Rutledge, J., Dissenting).

15. J. Lash, FROM THE DIARIES OF FELIX FRANKFURTER 334 (1974).

16. In his opinion for the Court in Prince v. Massachusetts, 321 U.S. 158 (1944), Justice Rutledge placed minimal significance on the individual right of free exercise and indicated his willingness to find that an alleged governmental interest overrode that right. In referring to the *Prince* decision, Professor Tribe noted that:

> Thus, in *Prince v. Massachusetts,* the government's purpose— protecting children from burdensome and exploitative labor—could not be achieved if adults were permitted to enlist the young as street proselytizers for their faith. To be sure, Justice Murphy argued in dissent that the child in question was not demonstrably injured, but the Court permitted government to deal with focused, serious harms in categorical ways, protecting victims from such harms without fully individualized findings that each person within the protected class would in fact become a victim if such protection were withheld in order to facilitate someone's religiously motivated activity.

Tribe, AMERICAN CONSTITUTIONAL LAW 850 (1978).

Justice Black's opinion for the Court in *Everson,* however, is more enigmatic. In his dissent, Jackson criticized Black for the seeming discrepancy between the principles articulated in Black's strict-separationist historical analysis and his ultimate decision that permitted indirect aid to sectarian schools. Jackson mused that Black's opinion had its literary analogue by noting that "the case which irresistibly comes to mind is that of Julia who, according to Byron's reports, 'whispering "I will ne'er consent,"—consented.'"[17]

Justice Black's opinion is subject to criticism because he failed to maintain logical consistency between his historical analysis and his ultimate legal conclusion and because he could so easily have found historical support for sustaining the act of the New Jersey township without accepting the strict-separationist argument. As has been shown throughout the preceding chapters, there is much history that would support the principle that the accommodation of all religions was historically acceptable in the form of nonpreferential aid to sectarian or public students. Even if such aid would be unacceptable if given only to religious institutions, it is clear that the framers would have opposed the discriminatory notion that aid could be given to private nonreligious institutions but not to sectarian ones. When read closely, even Madison's *Memorial and Remonstrance* did not preclude aid to all religions, and the debates of the First Congress, together with other related historical data, support the proposition that governmental distribution of nondiscriminatory aid to or accommodation of religious groups or individuals was acceptable.

Justice Black failed to refer to the debates or other pertinent, contemporaneous First Amendment history in his opinion. Instead, he turned to other incomplete sources. Of particular interest is his reliance on Jefferson's letter to the Danbury Baptist Association in 1803 (it will be recalled that 1803 was the same year President Thomas Jefferson supported direct national financial aid to the Kaskaskia Indians to assist them in constructing a church). Even Black's use of more pertinent sources such as the *Memorial and Remonstrance* was unsatisfactory because he refused to recognize that those sources did not prohibit expressly the government from aiding all religions in an equal fashion. Justice Black's failure to utilize the wealth of historical materials actually supporting his and the Court's position in *Everson* is certainly regrettable. Black's lack of adequate historical analysis has contributed to the confusion and ambivalence found in many subsequent decisions.

The best indication of legislative intent would be the debates themselves. Contemporaneous eighteenth- and early nineteenth-century events

---

17. *Everson,* 330 U.S. at 19 (Jackson, J., Dissenting).

and legal activity regarding issues of religious liberty would also constitute a helpful source. However, Justice Black totally ignored the debates, contenting himself with an incomplete analysis of the *Memorial and Remonstrance,* while disregarding other significant secondary sources, including Justice Story's analysis of the meaning and proposed application of the Establishment Clause, nationally and in Virginia, as noted in the *Terrett* case and in his *Commentaries.*[18]

Were it not for Black's allegiance to the principle of strict separation, highlighted by his invocation of the "wall of separation" lifted out of Jefferson's letter to the Danbury Baptist Association, it might be possible to make some sense out of his opinion. If one could disregard Black's advocacy, in dicta, of the strict-separationist position, it would be possible to read his opinion in a manner consistent with the weight of the historical data. Justice Black's concern that government should refrain from discriminating against religion, coupled with his opposition to extending aid to any particular religion or group of religions, could be construed as being consistent with Madison's views. Unfortunately, however, at least in his articulation of the purposes of the Establishment Clause, Black went too far in the direction of supporting a strict separation of church and state.

Speculation as to the reason for Justice Black's weak historical analysis is of little help. What is important, however, is that Black's deficiency on this point, coupled with the able advocacy of Justice Rutledge in his dissent, set the tone for much of the debate over the analysis of the Establishment Clause during the past four decades. Of late, however, many of the justices on the Supreme Court seem increasingly inclined to recognize that they have become mired in an apparent conflict between the free-exercise right and the Establishment Clause. However, they have not yet acknowledged or become aware that they could extricate themselves from this *Everson*-imposed morass by accurately rearticulating the historical meaning of, or the intent behind, the religion clauses.

Justice Rutledge's selective use of the history in his dissent in *Everson* is perhaps understandable. His historical analysis was designed, in an adversarial sense, to comport with the principle of strict separation of church and state that is central to his dissent. The weak historical analysis of Black's majority opinion in *Everson* permitted Rutledge to ignore vast amounts of historical data and to dwell almost exclusively upon selected parts of Madison's *Memorial and Remonstrance.* Thus, without opposition from fellow members of the Court, Rutlege was given the opportunity in his historical analysis to further his personal position on religious liberty.

Nevertheless, Justice Rutledge deviated briefly from his charted course to note that the legislative history was sparse and to conclude that

18. 330 U.S. at 12.

the "essential issues had been settled."[19] Rutledge simply assumed that the issue had been settled in favor of his twentieth-century form of strict separation. In this regard he even stated that "if the present statute and its application were shown to apply equally to all religious schools of whatever faith, yet in light of our tradition it could not stand."[20] However, Rutledge did not offer substantive support for his view that tradition supported his strict-separationist position. In fact, given the vast amount of historical data available that would have contradicted Rutledge's conclusions, it seems clear that he was more concerned with law office history than with examining the past dispassionately. He ignored contrary historical evidence that was readily available. As the wall of separation that he labored to construct has proven to be largely unserviceable during the past four decades, the time has come to formulate a more viable and less historically suspect set of principles to guide the Court in First Amendment cases.

Justice Rutledge did recognize apparently that following his reasoning could work a hardship upon those desiring to exercise their religion. He understood that application of the strict-separationist view ultimately might force children to withdraw from private, religious schools and attend public schools that were required in his view to be irreligious.[21] For Rutledge, who in *Prince* had supported a broad right on the part of the state to regulate matters of religious exercise in the interest of the general welfare or public good, a view reminiscent of the *Reynolds* standard, it is not surprising that he gave this possible hardship little weight. He simply did not place much value on the right of free exercise protected by the religion clauses of the First Amendment.

While Justice Rutledge was willing to limit the free exercise of religion on the basis of the elusive and largely deferential general-welfare interest of the state in *Prince,* evidently he was not willing, in a reciprocal sense, to permit the state to aid all religions on similar grounds.[22] Given his limited allegiance to individual rights of free exercise, it is not surprising that Rutledge saw no great harm in the conflict between the Free Exercise and Establishment clauses. For him, the strict-separationist value of the Establishment Clause rather than the right of free exercise was pre-eminent.

---

19. *Everson,* 330 U.S. at 42 (Rutledge, J., Dissenting).

20. *Id.* at 59–60 (Rutledge, J., Dissenting).

21. *Id.* at 58–9 (Rutledge, J., Dissenting).

22. Justice White has posited a reciprocal position. Apparently, he would permit the state to aid religion incidentally under a general-welfare standard, while also permitting it to burden religious exercise incidentally under that same standard. Widmar v. Vincent, 454 U.S. 263, 282 (1981) (White, J., Dissenting).

Evidently, he was among those who feared what religion could do to the state more than he valued the rights of individuals to practice their religious convictions. As has been shown in this book, however, his conclusions were contrary to the weight of evidence about the historical intent of the framers and ratifiers of the First Amendment.

Fortunately, the Supreme Court has acknowledged in its later Establishment Clause opinions that the strict-separationist position is indefensible as a practical matter. The Court has proven increasingly willing to adhere to the Court's ultimate position in *Everson,* permitting some aid, while at least implicitly repudiating the extreme applications of the strict-separationist rationale articulated in Justice Black's majority opinion.[23] One way it has done so is by looking at specific historical data in holding that some aid to or accommodation of religion is inevitable and desirable when extended in a nondiscriminatory manner.[24] The Court should take a further step in that direction by rearticulating the principles that can be derived from a close reading of applicable constitutional history to support its future decisions concerning religious liberty. Not only would such an effort add clarity to what the Court has been doing in the area of the First Amendment, but it would also add legitimacy to its decisions. Thus, a principled historical exegesis on the part of the Court would help ultimately to limit the adverse effects of the apparent conflict between the Free Exercise and Establishment clauses, while simultaneously lending support to the general notion that the judiciary should judge rather than legislate.

In the following chapters, I will examine the Court's decisions regarding public prayer. I will discuss how the prayer cases can be legitimized by

---

23. *See, e.g.,* the Court's opinion in Larson v. Valente, 456 U.S. 228 (1982), where it stated: "Since Everson v. Board of Education, 330 U.S. 1 (1947), this Court has adhered to the principle, clearly manifested in the history and logic of the Establishment Clause, that no state can 'pass laws which aid *one* religion' or that 'prefer one religion over another.'" (Emphasis added) *Id.* at 246 (quoting *Everson,* 330 U.S. at 15). This standard is certainly consistent with the Madisonian rationale and does not contemplate a strict separation of church and state.

24. In Marsh v. Chambers, 463 U.S. 783 (1983), the Court upheld the Nebraska legislature's practice of opening each day with a prayer by a chaplain paid by the state. The Court relied heavily on the fact that these activities were permitted historically and therefore were compatible with the framers' intent. *Id.* at 786–90. *See also* Lynch v. Donnelly, 465 U.S. 668 (1984) in which the Court held that the Establishment Clause does not prohibit a municipality from including a Nativity scene in its annual Christmas display and again emphasized historical practice. Unfortunately, in looking at history on a piecemeal basis, as it did in *Marsh,* the Court failed to articulate principles that would be helpful in resolving First Amendment issues that are not part of a specific historical tradition.

applying pertinent historical principles, and I will also make some recommendations with regard to issues that are yet undecided. In doing so, I will show how the history can be used to extricate the Court from the tangled web created in large part by the faulty reasoning in the *Reynolds* and *Everson* cases. While I believe the Court has been doing implicitly what I advocate explicitly, I am strongly of the opinion that a dose of judicial candor would be particularly beneficial at this time when the Court's legitimacy is being challenged from all sides.

7

The Incorporation Debate: Are the Religion Clauses of the First Amendment Applicable Against the States?

From the very founding of our Republic, there has been a continuing debate over the issue of whether or not the first eight amendments to the Constitution constitute a limitation on state action. The question has often been raised as to whether or not the religion clauses of the First Amendment may be invoked by litigants as a limitation on state authority. The argument that the clauses are not applicable against state action receives substantial support from the wording of the clauses: "*Congress* shall make no law respecting an establishment of religion or prohibiting the free exercise thereof." This language indicates that the amendment was intended as a limit only on congressional action. The courts followed this construction of the First Amendment, rendering it applicable only against federal and not state action, for nearly one hundred years.

In 1845, the Supreme Court held that the Free Exercise Clause of the First Amendment was inapplicable to the states, in *Permoli v. First Municipality.*[1] *Permoli,* in turn, was not overruled until 1940, when the Court held in *Cantwell v. Connecticut*[2] that the Free Exercise Clause was incorporated in and made applicable to state action through the

---

1. 44 U.S. (3 How.) 589 (1845).
2. 310 U.S. 296 (1940).

Due Process Clause of the Fourteenth Amendment, which had been adopted in 1868. In 1947, in *Everson v. Board of Education,*[3] the Court took the incorporation argument a step further and held that the Establishment Clause also was incorporated through the Fourteenth Amendment and, therefore, constituted a limitation on state action.

The incorporation doctrine as applied in the First Amendment context has been strengthened by a steady stream of decisions affirming the applicability of the religion clauses against state action. However, this effort has not been free from controversy.

For example, in recently addressing this very issue, Attorney General Edwin Meese III has argued that "since [the movement to incorporate the limitations in the Bill of Rights and make them applicable to state action began in 1925] a good portion of constitutional adjudication has been aimed at extending the scope of the doctrine of incorporation. But the most that can be done is to expand the scope; nothing can be done to shore up the intellectually shaky foundation upon which the doctrine rests. And nowhere else has the principle of federalism been dealt so politically violent and constitutionally suspect a blow as by the theory of incorporation."[4] Reacting specifically to applications of the incorporation doctrine in the First Amendment context, the attorney general, quoting from a statement made by Justice William Rehnquist in another context, noted that "it is impossible...to build sound constitutional doctrine upon a mistaken understanding of constitutional theory."[5]

Judge Brevard Hand was even more blunt in his recent opinion at the trial level in *Jaffree v. Board of School Com'rs. of Mobile County.*[6] In that opinion, Judge Hand challenged the incorporation theory utilized by the Court generally and the incorporation of the religion clauses specifically. After summarizing his analysis of pertinent history supporting the Court's incorporation doctrine, particularly as applied in regard to the Establishment Clause, Judge Hand concluded, "This court's review

---

3. 330 U.S. 1 (1947).

4. Meese, *Address of the Honorable Edwin Meese III, Attorney General of the United States,* before the American Bar Association, 9 July 1985, at 13–4.

5. *Id.* at 14.

6. 554 F. Supp. 1104 (S.D. Ala. 1983). Judge Hand's views were criticized by the appellate court, which reversed the decision of the trial court. Jaffree v. Wallace, 705 F.2d 1526 (11th Cir. 1983). The Supreme Court affirmed the Eleventh Circuit Court's reversal of Judge Hand's trial court decision. 105 S.Ct. 2479 (1985). *See* Chapter 9, *infra,* for a full discussion of the Supreme Court's decision in that case.

of the relevant legislative history surrounding the adoption of both the First Amendment and of the Fourteenth Amendment, together with the plain language of those amendments, leaves no doubt that those amendments were not intended to forbid religious prayers in the schools which the states and their political subdivisions mandate."[7]

Judge Hand's argument, as well as that of Attorney General Meese, really proceeds on two separate but related fronts: that of the First Amendment (they both contend that the Establishment Clause was not intended to forbid state-mandated or composed prayers) and that of the Fourteenth Amendment (they both argue that the Fourteenth Amendment did not incorporate the Establishment Clause of the First Amendment, and, therefore, states should not be bound by the Establishment Clause).

While most courts have taken the position that the incorporation issue is settled by well-established precedent,[8] as an originalist, I cannot do so. I am, as are Meese and Hand, bound by the determination of the intent of the framers and ratifiers of the Fourteenth Amendment and would have to support efforts to overrule or set aside Court decisions to the contrary. The issue, therefore, of whether the framers and ratifiers of the Constitution or the Fourteenth Amendment intended to make the religion clauses of the First Amendment applicable against the states is of major significance.

A response to Judge Hand and Attorney General Meese is, therefore, in order. Judge Hand specifically concluded that

---

7. 554 F. Supp. 1104 at 1128.

8. For example, even the Eleventh Circuit, in reversing Judge Hand, perfunctorily dismissed Judge Hand's analysis by noting:
   The interplay between the First and Fourteenth Amendments engages scholars in endless debate. We are urged to remain mindful of the uses of history. History provides enlightenment; it appraises courts of the subtleties and complexities of problems before them. [citation omitted] The important point is: *the Supreme Court has considered and decided the historical implications surrounding the establishment clause.*
705 F.2d 1526 at 1532 (emphasis in original). In further chiding Judge Hand, the Court added, "Under our form of government and long established law and custom, the Supreme Court is the ultimate authority on the interpretation of our Constitution and laws; its interpretations may not be disregarded." *Id.*

In his stay of Judge Hand's decision, Justice Lewis F. Powell noted that "unless and until [the Supreme Court] reconsiders the foregoing decisions [the prayer decisions: *Engel, Schempp,* etc.], they appear to control this case. In my view, the District Court was obligated to follow them." Jaffree v. Board of School Com'rs. of Mobile County, 459 U.S. 1314, 1316 (1983).

The historical record clearly establishes that when the Fourteenth Amendment was ratified in 1868 that its ratification did not incorporate the First Amendment against the states. The debates in Congress at the time the Fourteenth Amendment was being drafted, the re-election speeches of the various members of Congress shortly after the passage by Congress of the Fourteenth Amendment, the contemporaneous newspaper stories reporting the effect and substance of the Fourteenth Amendment, and the legislative debates in the various state legislatures when they considered ratification of the Fourteenth Amendment indicate that the amendment was not intended to apply the Establishment Clause against the states because the Fourteenth Amendment was not intended to incorporate the federal Bill of Rights (the first eight amendments) against the states.[9]

In assessing Judge Hand's conclusions, I am willing to accept his framework and will examine: (1) the debates in Congress at the time the Fourteenth Amendment was drafted; (2) campaign speeches of members of the Thirty-ninth Congress; (3) contemporaneous newspaper accounts; (4) debates in the state legislatures ratifying the Fourteenth Amendment; and (5) subsequent court decisions. I will also analyze Judge Hand's argument to the effect that the Blaine Amendment proposed in Congress in 1875 constitutes a "conclusive argument against the incorporation theory, at least as respects the religious provisions of the First Amendment."[10] However, before examining each of these six arguments, it will be helpful to examine the issue of whether the Privileges and Immunities Clause of Article IV, Section 2, of the Constitution may have been intended to incorporate all or part of the Bill of Rights. That clause provides that "the citizens of each state shall be entitled to all privileges and immunities of citizens in the several states."[11] This exegesis will be helpful not just to determine, as a matter of original intent, whether the Privileges and Immunities Clause of Article IV was intended to make rights like those included in the Bill of Rights applicable to the states, but also as a means of illuminating the context in which the Privileges or Immunities Clause of the Fourteenth Amendment was adopted.

---

9. 554 F. Supp. 1104 at 1119.
10. *Id.* at 1125. Recently Michael Kent Curtis, a major proincorporationist scholar and attorney, wrote a fairly thorough article criticizing Judge Hand's historical analysis in the *Jaffree* case. *See* Curtis, *Judge Hand's History: An Analysis of History and Method in Jaffree v. Board of School Commissioners of Mobile County,* 86 W.Va. L. Rev. 109 (1983).
11. U.S. Const., Art. IV, § 2.

ARTICLE IV, SECTION 2: THE PRIVILEGES AND IMMUNITIES
CLAUSE OF THE CONSTITUTION

Some commentators, perhaps most notably Professor William Crosskey, have argued that the Privileges and Immunities Clause of the Constitution was intended to incorporate some or all of the Bill of Rights, making them applicable as a limitation against state action.[12]

For example, after tracing such privileges and immunities back to Sir William Blackstone, Michael Kent Curtis recently concluded that

> Blackstone wrote that there are absolute rights of Englishmen and that their fundamental articles from time to time have been asserted in Parliament. He then runs down some of the great acts of Parliament that were precursors to the American Bill of Rights and that represent the declaration of rights and liberties of Englishmen. These he says consist of "immunities" and "privileges." These various immunities and privileges can be reduced to three primary articles: personal security, personal liberty, and the right to private property—because an infringement of any of the important rights set out in any of the great acts of Parliament could not be accomplished without some invasion of one of the three fundamental rights. For Blackstone the absolute rights

---

12. Professor Crosskey has argued that, "with the exception of the First Amendment and the Appeals Clause of the Seventh, those amendments [the first eight amendments to the Constitution] had all been drawn to apply as well to the governments of the states as to that of the nation." Crosskey, *Charles Fairman, "Legislative History," and the Constitutional Limitations on State Authority,* 22 U.CHI. L. REV. 1 at 119 (1954). *See Id.* at 119–43, for an elaboration of this view. It is notable for our purposes that Professor Crosskey did not include the First Amendment in his list of the rights incorporated. He refused to do so because the First Amendment was "in the form of a series of 'restrictive clauses' relating only to the power of Congress to make...Laws." *Id.* at 124. However, the argument has been made that while, by its terms, the First Amendment may expressly limit congressional power "respecting an establishment of religion," the right of free exercise should not be so limited. *See, e.g.,* argument of Mr. Read for the plaintiff in error in Permoli v. First Municipality, 44 U.S. (3 How.) 589, 594–600 (1845). It must be acknowledged, however, that much of Read's argument was based on an argument that Louisiana was bound by the First Amendment's guarantees regarding religious liberty because Louisiana was a territory before becoming a state, and, as a territory, it had been bound by the First Amendment and could not avoid its pre-existing responsibility under that amendment by becoming a state. Note, however, that even Mr. Barton, counsel for the First Municipality of New Orleans, referred to the religious "rights or privileges of the Catholic citizens of New Orleans." *Id.* at 602.

of Englishmen encompass all their liberties. Rather than excluding the liberties in the Bill of Rights, Blackstone's three primary articles include the Bill of Rights and may include far more.[13]

Analyzing this issue from a slightly different angle in another recent article, Arnold Guminski indicated that the Privileges and Immunities Clause had an independent ancestral line for Fourteenth Amendment (as opposed to Article IV, Section 2) purposes and concluded that "the privileges of American citizens, within the meaning of the Privileges or Immunities Clause, are their constitutional freedoms—including but not limited to those specified in the First Amendment.... The immunities of American citizens, within the meaning of the Privileges or Immunities Clause, are their constitutional equalities—including, but not limited to, their right to be free from racial discrimination. No right specified in the Bill of Rights other than the First Amendment is incorporated by the Privileges or Immunities Clause."[14]

While Guminski seeks to limit his evaluation of the privileges-and-immunities language to the context of the Fourteenth Amendment, his evaluation could apply as well to Article IV, Section 2, because he relies on historical data generally contemporaneous with the adoption and ratification of the Privileges and Immunities Clause of Article IV.[15] For example, after examining three uses of the privileges-and-immunities terminology prior to the ratification of the Constitution in support of his thesis, Guminski turned to the use of the same language in conjunction with the Louisiana Purchase in 1803. Of particular interest for our purposes, Guminski cites Article III of the treaty for the purchase of Louisiana, which stated that "the inhabitants of the ceded territory shall be incorporated in the Union of the United States, and admitted as soon as possible, according to the principles of the federal Constitution, to the enjoyment of all the rights, advantages and immunities of citizens of the United States; and in the meantime they shall be maintained and protected in the free enjoyment of their liberty, property, and the religion

---

13. Curtis, *Still Further Adventures of the Nine-Lived Cat: A Rebuttal to Raoul Berger's Reply on Application of the Bill of Rights to the States,* 62 N.C. L. REV. 517, 521 (1984).

14. Guminski, *The Rights, Privileges, and Immunities of the American People: A Disjunctive Theory of Selective Incorporation of the Bill of Rights,* 7 WHITTIER L. REV. 765, 766 (1985).

15. *Id.* at 781–83. He refers to use of similar language in *The Declaration of Rights and Grievances* of 1765, *The Address to the Inhabitants of Canada* of 26 October 1774, and *Virginia's Citizenship Act* of 3 May 1779.

which they profess."[16] In conjunction with his discussion of Article III, Guminski also quoted from a letter written by Thomas Jefferson to James Madison regarding the treaty:

> It is that the inhabitants shall be admitted as soon as possible, according to the principles of our Constn., to the enjoyment of all the rights of citizens, and, in the mean time, en attendant, shall be maintained in their liberty, property, and religion. That is that they shall continue under the protection of the treaty, until the principles of our Constitution can be extended to them, when the protection of the treaty is to cease, and that of our own principles to take its place.[17]

In that statement, Jefferson seems to imply, in interpreting the treaty, that the religion of the residents of Louisiana would be protected by the treaty until such time as the residents were permitted to benefit from the protection afforded by similar principles in the Constitution.

John Randolph's views on the same subject seem to confirm just such a conclusion. Randolph stated that

> A stipulation to incorporate the ceded country does not imply that we are bound ever to admit them to the unqualified enjoyment of the privileges of citizenship. It is a covenant to incorporate them into our Union—not on the footing of the original states, or of the states created under the Constitution—but to extend to them, according to the principles of the Constitution, those rights and immunities of citizens, being those rights and immunities of jury trial, liberty of conscience, etc., which every citizen may challenge, whether he be a citizen of an individual state, or of a territory subordinate to and dependent on those states in their corporate capacity.[18]

Read together, these statements, along with the language of the treaty itself, seem to imply, as Guminski argues that they do, that the language used in the treaty of 1803 "was understood to mean, *inter alia,* the rights specified in the Bill of Rights."[19]

As Professor Crosskey also points out, a reading of contemporary commentary and case law in the early years of the Republic offers additional, albeit hardly conclusive, support for the view that Article IV, Section 2, was intended to afford protection to citizens of the respective

---

16. *Treaty Between the United States of America and the French Republic,* 30 April 1803, 8 Stat. 200, at 202, as cited in Guminski, *supra* note 14, at 783.

17. Cited in Guminski, *supra* note 14, at 784.

18. Cited in *Id.* at 784–85.

19. *Id.* at 785.

states relative to state infringements of the liberties of the type set forth in the Bill of Rights.[20] In addition to cases that indirectly or implicitly applied strictures of the Bill of Rights to the states, at both the federal and the state levels, even Justice Bushrod Washington's opinion in *Corfield v. Coryell*,[21] in which he expressly dealt with the Privileges and Immunities Clause, contains expansive dicta that would seem to indicate that the clause could be read broadly enough to include the Bill of Rights and possibly more. For example, Justice Washington emphasized that the privileges and immunities protected by the Constitution are those "which are, in their nature, fundamental; which belong, of right, to the citizens of all free governments."[22] After going through a specific litany of some of those rights, Washington added that "these, and many others which might be mentioned, are, strictly speaking, privileges and immunities."[23] The *Corfield* case can be read broadly in the natural-law tradition of that era just as easily as it can be read restrictively, as it has been read by commentators like Professor Raoul Berger.[24]

However, in *Barron v. Baltimore*,[25] the first case in which the Supreme Court dealt directly with the meaning of the Privileges and Im-

---

20. *See* Crosskey, *supra* note 12, at 125–43. Crosskey, for example, relies upon the writings of two legal commentators during the formative years of our Republic, William Rawle and Joseph K. Angell, and notes that his reliance on those commentators was not criticized by Professor Fairman, who disagrees with Professor Crosskey's views. *Id.* at 125. He also relied on a number of cases, e.g., People v. Goodwin, 18 Johns. (N.Y.) 187, 201 (1820), in which the court noted in dicta (in enforcing the double-jeopardy principle of the Fifth Amendment) that "these general and comprehensive expressions extend the provisions of the Constitution of the U.S. to every article which is not confined, by the subject matter, to the national government and is equally applicable to the states." Columbia v. Okely, 17 U.S. (4 Wheat.) 235, 242–44 (1819), in which Justice Johnson held that the strictures of the Seventh Amendment were applicable in Maryland; and Houston v. Moore, 18 U.S. 1, 15–6, 5 Wheat. 1, 32–4 (1820), in which Justice Johnson discussed the applicability of the double-jeopardy provision of the Fifth Amendment. While the Supreme Court justices never stated expressly that they were making the Bill of Rights applicable to the states through the Privileges and Immunities Clause of Article IV, it is clear that a number of judges believed that some or all of the strictures set forth in the Bill of Rights were applicable as against the states.
21. 6 F. Case 546 (C.C.E.D. Pa. 1823) (No. 3230).
22. *Id.* at 551.
23. *Id.* at 552. *See also* Curtis, *A Bill of Rights as a Limitation on State Authority: A Reply to Professor Berger,* 16 WAKE FOREST L. REV. 45, 86–8 (1980), for a proincorporation analysis of the *Corfield* case.
24. *See, e.g.,* R. Berger, GOVERNMENT BY JUDICIARY at 22 (1977).
25. 32 U.S. (7 Pet.) 242 (1833).

munities Clause of Article IV, Chief Justice John Marshall wrote an opinion for the Court that rejected expressly the incorporation theory, despite the fact that an incorporationist argument had been vigorously pressed by counsel. In rejecting counsel's argument, Marshall opined that

> Had the framers of these amendments intended them to be limita-
> tions on the powers of the state governments, they would have imitated
> the framers of the original Constitution, and have expressed that inten-
> tion. Had Congress engaged in the extraordinary occupation of im-
> proving the constitutions of the several states, by affording the people
> additional protection from the exercise of power by their own gov-
> ernments, in matters which concerned themselves alone, they would
> have declared this purpose in plain and intelligible language.[26]

It is not surprising that many commentators have taken the plain-and-intelligible-language argument made by Marshall to be dispositive of the issue of intent of the framers of the Privileges and Immunities Clause in Article IV. To buttress this argument, its proponents emphasize that Marshall was an activist judge, a judge inclined to give the Constitution a broad reading so as to strengthen the role of the Supreme Court. They add that Marshall's reluctance to open a further door to activism in *Barron* effectively constituted an admission against interest, an ac-knowledgment based on his recollection of the history that only the restrictive view was tenable.

Placed in the historical context of the case, however, this argument is somewhat suspect. In 1833, when *Barron* was decided, the Marshall Court was in precarious circumstances.[27] It had recently been shaken by

---

26. *Id.* at 249.

27. *See* Haines, THE ROLE OF THE SUPREME COURT IN AMERICAN GOVERNMENT AND POLITICS: 1789-1835 at 579–613 (1944). Perhaps Professor Haines best depicts this era in a section of Chapter XVI, *The Trend of the Supreme Court Decisions from 1828 to 1835,* entitled *Changes in the Decisions of Chief Justice Marshall,* in which he notes that:

Before...1826...the Supreme Court had reached the peak of its authority and prestige under the regime of Chief Justice Marshall. The decline in the position and power of the Court was gradual for a few years, when even the chief justice gave indications of a recognition in his decisions of the changes in public opinion. It was apparent before the election of Andrew Jackson to the presidency that the Court was giving some consideration to what Mr. Dooley called "election returns." But the decline in the Court's authority and effectiveness, which began in the middle of the decade from 1820 to 1830, grew more marked after the election of President Jackson, and the last five years of Mar-shall's chief justiceship was marked by such serious conflicts that both

the strong and threatening response of the Jackson administration to its decisions in the Cherokee Indian cases, and the Court's activist consensus was shaky at best.[28] Had the Court held that the Bill of Rights was applicable to the states, it could have expected a strong backlash from the states. Whether the Court chose to avoid a broad reading of the Privileges and Immunities Clause to consolidate the gains that had been made in a more activist era or because it truly felt that no other interpretation was tenable remains an open question. Nevertheless, its action has been taken at face value, and the Privileges and Immunities Clause of Article IV has been relegated to a rather quiescent status. It is now read to ensure to a citizen of State A who ventures into State B the same privileges which the citizens of State B enjoy.[29]

However, even if the Court in *Barron* had found that the Bill of Rights was generally applicable to the states, it is not at all clear that the religion clauses would be included, because the First Amendment, unlike Amendments II–VIII, contains restrictive language. The amendment arguably limits its applicability to federal action because it expressly provides that *"Congress* shall make no law." Under such reasoning, only Congress, and not the states, is limited by the amendment.

Such a view receives some support in the record of the framing of the First Amendment. As introduced originally by Madison, the First Amendment was submitted in the form of two separate amendments. The first provided that "the civil rights of none shall be abridged on account of religious belief or worship, nor shall any national religion be

---

Marshall and Story believed that the Supreme Court would be shorn by judicial construction, congressional legislation, and executive domination of the essential powers which were necessary to its functioning as an effective federal tribunal. The story of the uncertain and hesitant years forms a marked contrast with that of the decade from 1815 to 1825 when, with something in the nature of a pontifical air, the Court was expounding and applying the principles of Hamiltonian Nationalism.

Id. at 579–80.

28. *See* Swindler, THE CONSTITUTION AND CHIEF JUSTICE MARSHALL 21 (1978), where Professor Swindler notes that:

Signs of the ending of the Marshall Court's activism, either through the aggressiveness of the Jacksonian administration as in the Cherokee cases or the breaking up of the old judicial consensus with Justice Thompson, were clear to see in the 1830's. . . . Most significant of all was the last constitutional opinion of 1833—*Barron v. Baltimore*—which found the Chief Justice declining to take an initiative eloquently offered by counsel, to extend the Bill of Rights provisions to the states.

29. Toomes v. Witsell, 334 U.S. 385, 395 (1948).

established, nor shall the full and equal rights of conscience be in any manner, nor on any pretext infringed."[30] The second amendment provided that "no state shall violate the equal rights of conscience or the freedom of the press, or the trial by jury in criminal cases."[31] Although the limitation on the power of the state governments to restrict the right of conscience was initially passed, it soon drifted into obscurity and was not included in the Bill of Rights as finally adopted. It is not clear why this was the case, but certainly if one applies Marshall's plain-and-intelligible-language test, the lack of such a provision could be determinative of the issue of whether or not the First Amendment would be applicable against the states.

Such a conclusion may be questionable in light of case law, commentary, and statements contemporaneous with the framing and ratification of the Constitution, in which religious rights were often listed with other rights, privileges, and immunities. It is even arguable that the language of the First Amendment merely limits the federal government from making laws respecting state establishments of religion (an act expressly limiting the national government vis-à-vis the states themselves) and from making laws prohibiting the free exercise of religion (referring to acts limiting individual, as opposed to state, action). As such, it might be argued that states would be secure from congressional action respecting their established religions, but that the right of conscience or free exercise, a privilege and immunity of citizens of the United States, could not be abridged by either the national or the state governments. In this sense, the First Amendment may be viewed as a consolidation of the first two amendments originally introduced by Madison. This view receives some support from the fact that the House initially passed the provision restricting the power of the state to limit rights of conscience without significant debate.[32]

Nevertheless, given that this interpretation strains the language of the First Amendment somewhat and given Justice Joseph Story's statement in his *Commentaries on the Constitution* to the effect that "the whole power over the subject of religion is left exclusively to the state governments, to be acted upon according to their own sense of justice,

---

30. 1 ANNALS OF CONGRESS 434 (Gales and Seaton ed. 1834) (8 June 1789), as cited in Malbin, *Religion and Politics: The Intentions of the Authors of the First Amendment,* American Enterprise Institute, Studies in Legal Policy at 4 (1978).

31. 1 ANNALS OF CONGRESS 435, cited in *Id.*

32. *Id.* at 783–84. *See also* Curry, THE FIRST FREEDOMS: CHURCH AND STATE IN AMERICA TO THE PASSAGE OF THE FIRST AMENDMENT, 204–05 (1986).

and the state constitutions,"[33] I believe that more historical evidence must be amassed before it can be asserted persuasively that the framers and ratifiers of the Constitution intended to limit the power of the states relative to rights of conscience.

Absent the accumulation of such evidence, if the First Amendment is to be made applicable to the states, support must be found in the Fourteenth Amendment incorporation theory. In that light, we must deal with each of the objections raised by Judge Hand.

THE FOURTEENTH AMENDMENT: WAS IT INTENDED TO INCORPORATE THE FIRST AMENDMENT OF THE BILL OF RIGHTS?

Since the Supreme Court's decision in *Adamson v. California,*[34] in which Justice Hugo Black wrote a stinging dissent arguing that he would follow what he believed "was the original purpose of the Fourteenth Amendment—to extend to all the people of the nation the complete protection of the Bill of Rights,"[35] the controversy over the incorporation theory has grown more heated. To support his view, Black attached an appendix summarizing his view of the history of the Fourteenth Amendment to his dissent in *Adamson.* Justice Black's opinion, with its discussion of the applicable history, engendered a debate in academic circles that persists to the present.[36] At issue in this debate is the question of whether the Privileges or Immunities Clause ("No state shall make or enforce any law which shall abridge the privileges or immunities of citizens of the United States")[37] or the Due Process Clause ("nor shall any state deprive any person of life, liberty, or property, without due process

---

33. 2 J. Story, COMMENTARIES ON THE CONSTITUTION OF THE UNITED STATES § 1879 at 597 (2d. ed. Boston 1851) (1st ed. Boston 1833).

34. 332 U.S. 46 (1947).

35. *Id.* at 89.

36. Professor Fairman disagreed with Justice Black's reading of the history of the framing and ratification of the Fourteenth Amendment. *See* Fairman, *Does the Fourteenth Amendment Incorporate the Bill of Rights? The Original Understanding,* 2 STAN. L. REV. 5 (1949). Professor Crosskey countered by supporting Black's view. Crosskey, *supra* note 12. The debate was under way. Today, the primary disputants in academic circles are Professor Raoul Berger, carrying the flag of the nonincorporationists, and Michael Kent Curtis, representing the incorporationists. Others have entered the fray on both sides, and the battle rages.

37. U.S. Const., Amend. XIV, § 1.

of law")[38] of the Fourteenth Amendment was intended to incorporate all or a part of the first eight amendments to the Constitution, and make them applicable to the states. In his opinion for the District Court in *Jaffree,* Judge Hand entered the debate, arguing that the Supreme Court had erred in incorporating the religion clauses of the First Amendment, regardless of whether it did so on the basis of the Privileges or Immunities Clause or the Due Process Clause of the Fourteenth Amendment.[39] In doing so, he looked first at the debates in Congress at the time the Fourteenth Amendment was adopted.

The Debates

Judge Hand argued that "the paramount consideration in defining the scope of any constitutional provision or legislative enactment is to ascertain the intent of the legislature. The intention of the legislature may be evidenced by statements of the leading proponents. If statements of the leading proponents are found, those statements are to be regarded as good as if they were written into the enactment."[40]

As even Hand acknowledges, an examination of the debates reveals statements made by Representative John A. Bingham of Ohio,[41] sponsor of the Fourteenth Amendment as originally introduced, and Senator Jacob M. Howard of Michigan, the floor leader for the Fourteenth Amendment in the Senate,[42] supportive of the proposition that

---

38. *Id.*

39. It is clear to me that Justice Black erred in arguing that the Bill of Rights were incorporated through the Due Process Clause. There is little evidence that the framers of the Fourteenth Amendment intended to incorporate the Bill of Rights through the clause. There is, however, substantial evidence that the framers intended to incorporate the Bill of Rights through the Privileges or Immunities Clause. In *Adamson,* however, Justice Black may have felt constrained by the fact that precedent existed that viewed the Privileges or Immunities Clause restrictively. Similarly, the Due Process Clause had been read broadly in the past and was perhaps more readily susceptible in terms of Court politics to the broad reading given it by Justice Black in support of his incorporationist argument. Nevertheless, as an originalist, I would argue that the Court should clarify that incorporation is available through the history of the framing of the Privileges or Immunities Clause and not the Due Process Clause.

40. 554 F. Supp. at 1119.

41. Bingham authored the Fourteenth Amendment and repeatedly argued that it incorporated the Bill of Rights. *See* Curtis, *supra* note 10. Curtis also points out that statements of Bingham are strengthened by reading them in the context of Republican opposition to the nonincorporationist decision by Chief Justice Marshall in *Barron.*

42. Senator Howard became spokesperson for the joint committee on the floor of the Senate when the chair of that committee, Senator William Pitt Fessenden of Maine, suddenly became ill. Judge Hand, however, sought to

the Privileges or Immunities Clause of the Fourteenth Amendment was intended to incorporate the Bill of Rights. As has been shown by Professor Crosskey[43] and Michael Curtis,[44] Bingham believed that state officers were already bound by their oath of office to uphold the Constitution of the United States and to abide by the Bill of Rights. In that light, Bingham noted during the course of the debates over the amendment in the House that:

> The proposed amendment does not impose upon any state of the Union, or any citizen of any state of the Union any obligation which is not enjoined upon them by the letter of the Constitution....And, sir, it is equally clear by every construction of the Constitution, its contemporaneous construction, its continued construction, legislative, executive, and judicial, that these great provisions of the Constitution, this immortal Bill of Rights embodied in the Constitution rested for its execution and enforcement hitherto upon the fidelity of the states.[45]

Bingham thereafter referred to the nexus between the Bill of Rights and the Fourteenth Amendment on a number of other occasions during the debates.[46] During the course of congressional debates on another matter in 1871, Bingham clarified anew his intent in drafting the Privileges or Immunities Clause of the Fourteenth Amendment:

> Mr. Speaker, that the scope and meaning of the limitations imposed by the first section, Fourteenth Amendment of the Constitution,

---

demean the significance of the role of Senator Howard further by stating that "Professor Raoul Berger notes with some sarcasm that it is odd that a radical such as Senator Howard should be taken as speaking authoritatively for a committee in which the conservatives outnumbered the radicals and where there was a strong difference of opinion between the radicals and the conservatives." 554 F. Supp. 1104, 1121. It is understandable, given the tenor of Senator Howard's remarks, that both Judge Hand and Professor Berger would want to limit the significance of his role. However, it should be noted that Senator Howard expressly claimed that he was speaking on behalf of the committee and none of the conservatives on the committee contradicted explicitly Howard in this regard. Furthermore, Curtis notes, "If Howard's statement was wrong why did not Senator Fessenden, who was president *[sic]*, or any other member of the committee correct it?" Curtis, *supra* note 10, at 117–18.

43. Crosskey, *supra* note 12, at 40–1.

44. Curtis, *supra* note 23, at 67–8.

45. CONG. GLOBE, 39th Cong., 1st Sess. 1034 (1866), as cited in Curtis, *supra* note 23, at 67–8.

46. *See, e.g.,* statements cited in Curtis, *supra* note 23, at 71, 81, 84, 90. Bingham reiterated these statements in other contexts, and his position was never explicitly contradicted.

may be more fully understood, permit me to say that the privileges and immunities of citizens of the United States, as contradistinguished from the citizens of a State [Art. IV, Section 2] are chiefly defined in the first eight amendments to the Constitution of the United States. These eight amendments are as follows. [Bingham proceeded to quote each of the first eight amendments to the Constitution.][47]

Howard, who spoke on behalf of the joint committee and managed the amendment in the Senate because the chairman of the committee was ill, began his lengthy presentation in the Senate by noting that he could "only promise to present to the Senate, in a very succinct way, the views and motives which influenced [the joint committee], so far as I understand those views and motives, in presenting the report which is now before us for consideration, and the ends it aims to accomplish."[48] Having discussed generally the notion of citizenship under the amendment and having read from *Corfield v. Coryell,* regarding the Privileges and Immunities Clause of Article IV, Senator Howard continued by defining the Privileges or Immunities Clause included in the Fourteenth Amendment:

Such is the character of the privileges and immunities spoken of in the second section of the fourth article of the Constitution. To these privileges and immunities, whatever they may be—for they are not and cannot be fully defined in their entire extent and precise nature—to these should be added the personal rights guarantied [*sic*] and secured by the first eight amendments of the Constitution; such as the freedom of speech and press; the right of the people peaceably to assemble and petition the government for a redress of grievances, a right appertaining to each and all the people; the right to keep and to bear arms; the right to be exempted for the quartering of soldiers in a house without the consent of the owner; the right to be exempt from unreasonable searches and seizures, and from any search or seizure except by virtue of a warrant issued upon a formal oath or affidavit; the right of an accused person to be informed of the nature of the accusation against

47. CONG. GLOBE, 42d Cong., 1st Sess. app. 84 (1871), as cited in Curtis, *supra* note 23, at 85. It is interesting to note, when one reads the text of the whole of Bingham's speech (I have not included the preceding four paragraphs), that Bingham felt his use of language constituted a direct response to *Barron* and clearly expressed his intent to incorporate the Bill of Rights. Berger and Hand contend that this statement by Bingham in 1871 was essentially irrelevant and self-serving. However, it would seem to constitute much stronger evidence of the intent of the framer of the Fourteenth Amendment than much of the evidence marshalled by Hand and Berger to support their view to the contrary.
48. CONG. GLOBE, 39th Cong., 1st Sess. 2765 (1866), as cited in Curtis, *supra* note 23, at 93.

him, and his right to be tried by an impartial jury of the vicinage; and also the right to be secure against excessive bail and against cruel and unusual punishment.

Now, sir, here is a mass of privileges, immunities, and rights, some of them secured by the second section of the fourth article of the Constitution, which I have recited, some by the first eight amendments of the Constitution; and it is a fact well worthy of attention that the course of decision of our courts and the present settled doctrine is, that all these immunities, privileges, rights, thus guarantied [*sic*] by the Constitution or recognized by it, are secured to the citizen solely as a citizen of the United States and as a party in their courts. They do not operate in the slightest degree as a restraint or prohibition upon state legislation. States are not affected by them, and it has been repeatedly held that the restriction contained in the Constitution against the taking of private property for public use without just compensation is not a restriction upon state legislation, but applied only to the legislation of Congress referring, no doubt, to the *Barron* decision.

Now, sir, there is no power given in the Constitution to enforce and to carry out any of these guarantees. They are not powers granted by the Constitution to Congress, and of course do not come within the sweeping clause of the Constitution authorizing Congress to pass all laws necessary and proper for carrying out the foregoing or granted powers, but they stand simply as a bill of rights in the Constitution, without power on the part of Congress to give them full effect; while at the same time the states are not restrained from violating the principles embraced in them except by their own local constitutions, which may be altered from year to year. *The great object of the first section of this amendment is, therefore, to restrain the power of the states and compel them at all times to respect these great fundamental guarantees. . . .* Here is a direct affirmative delegation of power to Congress to carry out all the principles of all these guarantees, a power not found in the Constitution.[49]

These statements by Bingham and Howard serve as strong evidence of intent for the proposition that the framers of the Fourteenth Amendment intended to incorporate the Bill of Rights.[50] However, while claiming that "Congressman Bingham had no clear concept of what exactly would be accomplished by the passage of the Fourteenth Amend-

---

49. CONG. GLOBE, *supra* note 48, at 2765–66 (emphasis added), as cited in Curtis, *supra* note 23, at 94–6.

50. *See also* Curtis, *supra* note 10, at 112–13, 115–21, for a further discussion of the debates and the support therein for the incorporationist position.

ment,"[51] and agreeing with Professor Berger that "Howard...was 'one of the most...reckless of the radicals,' who had 'served consistently in the vanguard of the extreme Negrophiles,'"[52] Judge Hand dismissed the views of Bingham and Howard. He noted that "only [Bingham and Howard] said anything which could be construed as suggesting the result reached by Justice Black and the modern Supreme Court decisions."[53] He then concluded his evaluation of the debates as follows:

> The scholarly analyses of Professors Fairman and Berger persua-
> sively show that Mr. Justice Black misread the congressional debate
> surrounding the passage of the Fourteenth Amendment when he con-
> cluded that Congress intended to incorporate the federal Bill of Rights
> against the states. [citation omitted] So far as Congress was concerned,
> after the passage of the Fourteenth Amendment the states were free to
> establish one Christian religion over another in the exercise of their
> prerogative to control the establishment of religions.[54]

Hand's conclusion and his perfunctory dismissal of the views of Senator Howard and Representative Bingham are suspect on a number of grounds. First, there were comments made during the course of the debates on the Fourteenth Amendment and the Civil Rights Bill of 1866 by other members of Congress that support the notion that the Privileges or Immunities Clause of the Fourteenth Amendment was intended to be a vehicle for the incorporation of the Bill of Rights. For example, during the course of the debates over the Civil Rights Bill, James F. Wilson of Iowa, chairman of the House Judiciary Committee, refused to accept Bingham's argument that Congress lacked power to pass the Civil Rights Bill and referred directly to the Fourteenth Amendment, which had been introduced by Bingham:

> He [Bingham] says we cannot interpose in this way for the protection
> of rights. Can we not?...I find in the Bill of Rights which this gentle-
> man desires to have enforced by an amendment to the Constitution
> that "no person shall be deprived of life, liberty, or property without
> due process of law." I understand that these constitute the civil rights
> belonging to citizens in connection with those which are necessary for
> the protection and maintenance and perfect enjoyment of the rights
> specifically named and these are the rights to which this bill relates.[55]

---

51. *Jaffree,* 554 F. Supp. 1104 at 1120.
52. *Id.* at 1121.
53. *Id.* at 1120.
54. *Id.* at 1122.
55. CONG. GLOBE, 39th Cong., 1st Sess. 1294 (1866), as cited in Curtis, *supra* note 23, at 78.

Wilson was among those who had argued in previous Congresses that the southern slave states had been wantonly disregarding the supreme law of the land. Indeed, in 1864, Wilson had argued that First Amendment rights were among the privileges and immunities of Article IV, despite the Court's decision in *Barron*. At one point, he argued on the floor of the House that *"Freedom of religious opinion,* freedom of speech and press, and the right of assemblage for the purpose of petition belong to every American citizen, high or low, rich or poor, wherever he may be within the jurisdiction of the United States. With these rights no state may interfere without breach of the bond which holds the Union together."[56] Wilson joined clearly in the sentiment held by various Republicans of that era that the Supreme Court's decisions in *Barron* and *Dred Scott* were themselves improper and were not legitimate declarations of the law of the land.[57]

Other members of Congress acknowledged that the Privileges or Immunities Clause included in the Fourteenth Amendment was intended by at least some of its proponents to incorporate all or a part of the Bill of Rights.[58] This becomes strikingly clear when the debates are read in their context. A number of commentators have sought to place the debates over the Fourteenth Amendment in its historical context and, in doing so, have concluded that we have forgotten the idealism of the antislavery movement and the influence that such idealism, which was grounded firmly on the egalitarian view regarding fundamental rights,[59] had during the era in which the Fourteenth Amendment was adopted and ratified.

However, while it is clear that leading proponents of the Fourteenth Amendment favored a reading or interpretation of the Privileges or Immunities Clause of the Fourteenth Amendment that would facilitate the incorporation of the Bill of Rights, not all members of Congress held that view. Thus, even Michael Kent Curtis, who argues that the clear congressional intent was to incorporate the Bill of Rights, acknowledges that "several Congressmen observed that the amendment would eliminate any question about the power of Congress to pass the Civil Rights Bill. Others considered the amendment a reiteration of the

---

56. CONG. GLOBE, 38th Cong., 2nd Sess. 1202 (1864), as cited in Curtis, *supra* note 23, at 61.

57. *See, e.g.,* Curtis, *The Fourteenth Amendment and the Bill of Rights,* 14 CONN. L. REV. 237, 246–56 (1982), for a discussion of Republican views regarding *Barron* and *Dred Scott*.

58. *See id.* at 258–81, for an in-depth look at views extant in the 39th Congress.

59. *See, e.g.,* Cottrol, *Static History and Brittle Jurisprudence: Raoul Berger and the Problem of Constitutional Methodology,* 26 B.C. L. REV. 353, 365–75 (1985).

Civil Rights Bill. Several others suggested that the Constitution already effectively contained the provisions of the amendment."[60] This rather candid observation by a strong proponent of incorporation is indicative of a fact that neither side in the current disagreement between the non-incorporationists and the incorporationists is willing to admit that the debates simply are not reducible to a clear-cut consensus.[61] The language used was somewhat ambiguous and the intent itself is obscure. I agree with Timothy Bishop that an analysis of the debates and related materials reveals that "the Republican majority in Congress was in disarray as to the proper scope of the protection afforded to rights by the Privileges or Immunities Clause. Republicans variously thought that the clause merely constitutionalized the Civil Rights Act, incorporated also the Bill of Rights, or incorporated some conception of natural rights."[62]

Just as Justice Black, Michael Curtis, Professor Crosskey, and others have no doubt overstated the case for the incorporationist view when they assert that it is clearly reflective of the intent of Congress, Judge Hand overstated the case for the contrary, nonincorporationist view. Indeed, the debates, particularly if one focuses primarily on leading proponents as suggested by Judge Hand, seem to offer more support for the incorporationist view than for the nonincorporationist view, but neither view can be deemed to be supported conclusively by the record. We are left, rather, with bounds, just as we were in the case of the intended meaning of the religion clauses of the First Amendment, within which legitimate originalist review should proceed.

However, there are sources from which original intent can be gleaned other than the congressional debates. In this regard, after seeking to justify his nonincorporationist view based on the history of the framing of the Fourteenth Amendment, Hand turned to an evaluation of the popular understanding in an effort to lend further support to his position.

Popular Understanding

Judge Hand next argued that "an examination of popular sentiment across the country reveals that the nation as a whole did not understand the adoption of the Fourteenth Amendment to incorporate the federal

---

60. Curtis, *supra* note 57, at 276.

61. *See, e.g.,* Comment, *The Privileges or Immunities Clause of the Fourteenth Amendment: The Original Intent,* 79 N.W. L. REV. 142, 178, where the commentator concludes after analysis of the congressional debates that "the only test for intention that discovers what is demonstrably a 'congressional intent'— the majority model as a mathematically strict test—cannot operate to determine the intent behind the Privileges or Immunities Clause."

62. *Id.* at 174.

Bill of Rights against the states. Inferentially, that is to say that the people understood that each state was free to continue to support one Christian religion over another as the people of that state saw fit to do."[63] Aside from the fact that his inference is suspect as a non sequitur, Hand's basic assertion regarding public sentiment has some potential force. If the people did not support or contemplate a reading of the Fourteenth Amendment that would permit the strictures of the religion clauses of the First Amendment to be made applicable to the states, such a broad construction of the amendment might well be questioned.

Hand concluded specifically that "the Court takes the historical record to conclusively show that the general understanding of the nation at large, as illustrated by contemporaneous newspaper reports, demonstrates that the people of this country did not understand the Fourteenth Amendment to incorporate the Establishment Clause of the First Amendment against the states."[64] As was the case with the congressional debates, a review of what has been written regarding contemporaneous newspaper accounts reveals that Hand again overstated his case.

In reaching his conclusion, Judge Hand relied upon materials in a book by Horace Flack and Professor Fairman's article in the *Stanford Law Review*. Professor Crosskey criticized Professor Fairman's argument regarding the public sentiment, arguing that "Mr. Fairman, percentagewise, made a pretty good case against himself. Of the five newspapers he mentions, two, the *New York Herald* and the *New York Times,* 'quote[d] in full,' he says, 'the passage [from Senator Howard's speech] where it was said that the personal rights guaranteed by the first eight amendments were among the new privileges and immunities.'"[65] Crosskey then added that in a third of the five papers, the *Boston Daily Advertiser,* Senator Howard's statement was summarized as follows:

> The Senate having taken up the amendment, Mr. Howard explained it, section by section. The first clause of the first section was intended to secure to the citizens of all the states the privileges which are in their nature fundamental, and which belong of right to all persons in a free government. There was now no power in the Constitution to enforce its guarantees of those rights. They stood simply as declarations, and the states were not restricted from violating them, except by their own local constitutions and laws. The great object of the first section, fortified by the fifth, was to compel the states to observe these guarantees.[66]

---

63. 554 F. Supp. 1104 at 1122.
64. *Id.* at 1123.
65. Crosskey, *supra* note 12, at 102.
66. *Id.*

Evidence regarding general public sentiment on the meaning of the Privileges or Immunities Clause of the Fourteenth Amendment is inconclusive.[67] Absent more extensive research on this subject, the most that can be said is that some papers at this time did carry statements indicative of an intent to incorporate the fundamental rights included in the first eight amendments to the Constitution; others did not. Thus, Judge Hand's conclusion that a review of the papers of that era indicates that "the people of this country did not understand the Fourteenth Amendment to incorporate the Establishment Clause" is an overstatement—there was evidence to the contrary. Similarly, it would be inappropriate to assert that the newspaper accounts conclusively established that the people understood that the First Amendment was to be incorporated.

Furthermore, it would be wrong to read too much into the contemporaneous newspaper accounts even if they were more definitive, because the best sources of information regarding the intent of the ratifiers are the actual ratification debates. However, before turning to the ratification debates, Hand examined campaign speeches made by members of Congress about the Fourteenth Amendment.

Campaign Speeches

In his discussion of campaign speeches, Judge Hand agreed with Professor Fairman in concluding that *"none* of the members of Congress indicated in their campaign speeches that the Fourteenth Amendment was intended to incorporate the Bill of Rights against the states."[68]

However, as Curtis points out, Representative Bingham did speak about the amendment in Ohio after Congress adjourned. After noting that the amendment constituted a limitation on the power of the states, Bingham referred to a theme common to Republicans of the era in stressing that "hereafter the American people cannot have peace if, as in the past, states are permitted to take away freedom of speech, and to condemn men, as felons, to the penitentiary for teaching their fellow

---

67. But *see* Curtis, *supra* note 10, at 121–22, for additional support for the proposition that the people certainly should have been aware, based on newspaper and related accounts, of the framers' intent to incorporate the Bill of Rights through ratification of the Fourteenth Amendment.

68. *Id.* (emphasis added). In this regard, Judge Hand did note that he had "studied the Crosskey criticism of Professor Fairman and rejects it." 554 F. Supp. 1104, 1122 n. 31. Elsewhere, Judge Hand added that, "After reading the original articles of both Fairman and Crosskey, the rebuttal of Fairman, and many other articles on the question, the Court is persuaded that the *weight* of the disinterested scholars supports the analysis of Professor Fairman." *Id.* at 1120, n. 28.

men that there is a hereafter and a reward for those who learn to do well."[69] Curtis also pointed out that Congressman Wilson held similar views that he expressed during the campaign. Wilson noted that "we must guarantee to these boys the liberty of going into any part of the United States and causing type to speak as freely as when our army was there to back them."[70] Curtis did acknowledge, however, that "some Congressmen in campaign speeches neglected the Privileges or Immunities Clause. A few treated the amendment as a reaffirmation of the Civil Rights Bill."[71]

Again, Judge Hand's assertion that none of the Congressmen indicated that the Fourteenth Amendment was intended to incorporate the Bill of Rights against the states was an overstatement. A number of campaign speeches were in fact made in support of the incorporation of the First Amendment speech and religion clauses. Furthermore, it has been noted that almost none of the statements made in the campaign of 1866 and relied on by Professor Fairman and the *Jaffree* court are *inconsistent* with incorporation of the Bill of Rights. The general theme in the campaign of 1866 was that the amendment protected "all the rights of citizens."[72] Nevertheless, in a recent extensive reexamination of campaign speeches and related materials in which he presents substantial additional support for the incorporation theory, Curtis acknowledged that discussion was often cursory, although he added that many proponents "insisted on the need for protection of rights in the Bill of Rights, and many demanded protection of the Constitutional rights of loyalists in the South."[73]

Nevertheless, Hand's argument retains some force. The Privileges or Immunities Clause was not always a major source of controversy during the campaign. Opponents of incorporation have argued that people, particularly in the South, would have been more vocal in their opposition to the Fourteenth Amendment had they understood that it was intended to incorporate the Bill of Rights and make the states subject to the limitations on state power contained in those amendments. But there were such comments. For example, the editor of the *Raleigh Sentinel* emphasized that "the first and fifth sections [of the Fourteenth Amendment]. . . contain the germ of consolidation and destruction of

---

69. *Cincinnati Commercial,* 27 August 1866, at 1, cols. 2–3, as cited in Curtis, *supra* note 23, at 84.

70. *Cited in* Curtis, *supra* note 23, at 306.

71. *Id.*

72. Curtis, *supra* note 10, at 121 (emphasis in original).

73. Curtis, *The Fourteenth Amendment and the Bill of Rights,* 14 CONN. L. REV. 237, 292. Curtis analyzes campaign materials at pages 281–92 of the article.

the...state governments."[74] In the *Wadesboro Argus,* concern was expressed that Section 1 of the amendment might be used as a "pretext for extending the jurisdiction of the federal courts into the most minute and trivial occurrences."[75] Finally, fear was expressed in the *Wilmington Dispatch* on 13 September 1866 that the amendment would "revolutionize the whole character of government."[76]

Professor James Bond has argued that proponents of the amendment downplayed these fears. He cited statements from newspapers in which proponents argued that Congress merely wanted to ensure "the civil rights of persons."[77] Bond concluded that this meant that proponents felt the Civil Rights Bill and the Fourteenth Amendment were coextensive.[78] However, while it is fairly clear that proponents felt that the amendment only protected civil and not political rights, one commentator recently pointed out in the context of the legislative history that

> The legislature clearly distinguished between civil rights and political rights, and a careful reading of the legislative history of the Civil Rights Act and the Privileges and Immunities Clause leaves no doubt that Congress intended that they not extend to political rights. An issue that raises more doubt, however, is whether Congress intended the Privileges and Immunities Clause to protect only those civil rights enumerated in the Civil Rights Act.[79]

The same author examined the debates in detail and concluded that "the Republican majority in Congress was in disarray as to the proper scope of the protection afforded to rights by the Privileges or Immunities Clause. Republicans variously thought that the clause merely constitutionalized the Civil Rights Act, incorporated also the Bill of Rights, or incorporated some conception of natural rights....The speeches of minority Democrats confirm that there was no substantially agreed upon congressional intent as to the scope of the clause."[80]

---

74. *Raleigh Sentinel,* 2 May 1866, at 2, col. 1, as cited in Bond, *Ratification of the Fourteenth Amendment in North Carolina,* 20 WAKE FOREST L. REV. 89, 98 (1984).

75. *Wadesboro Argus,* 11 October 1866, at 1, col. 2, *cited in* Bond, *supra* note 74, at 98, n. 48.

76. *Wilmington Daily Dispatch,* 13 September 1866, at 2, col. 4, *cited in* Bond, *supra* note 74, at 98, n. 45.

77. *Cited in* Bond, *supra* note 74, at 99.

78. *Id.* at 99, n. 51.

79. Comment, *supra* note 61, at 150–51.

80. *Id.* at 174.

Given the confusion over which civil rights were included in the Privileges or Immunities Clause during the congressional debates, it would be inappropriate to conclude, as Professor Bond and Judge Hand do, that speeches and newspaper reports confirm that the people and proponents understood that the amendment merely constitutionalized the Civil Rights Act. There were those who felt the term civil rights included much more. Furthermore, even those who asserted that the amendment merely constitutionalized the Civil Rights Act may have read the intent of the Civil Rights Act too restrictively. On this point, Curtis recently concluded his analysis of the legislative history of the Civil Rights Act by stressing that

> Scholars who argue that the Fourteenth Amendment was not intended to make the Bill of Rights a limit on the states have relied on statements made by some Congressmen that the amendment incorporated the substantial protections of the Civil Rights Bill—such as rights to contract and to testify at trials, and to full and equal benefit of all laws for security of person and property. They assume these rights exclude those in the Bill of Rights. The problem with this analysis is that provisions of the Bill of Rights are, by ordinary use of language, "laws for security of person and property."[81]

The language used in the amendment was ambiguous, and public dialogue was often equally unclear. Just as the legislative history and the popular understanding were obscure, the campaign speeches and newspaper accounts were similarly ambiguous and susceptible to various interpretations. We turn, therefore, to the related issue of the intent of the state legislatures ratifying the Fourteenth Amendment.

The State Legislative Debates

The state legislative or ratification debates and proceedings are the most significant source available to a court or commentator seeking to ascertain the original intent of the Fourteenth Amendment. Since the amendment was merely referred to the states by Congress and could not become a part of the law of the land until ratified, those ratification proceedings are critical; the intent of the ratifiers in this sense takes priority over all other expressions of intent.[82]

With regard to the ratification proceedings themselves, Judge Hand concludes that "the historical record shows without equivocation that none of the states envisioned the Fourteenth Amendment as applying

---

81. Curtis, *supra* note 73, at 267.

82. *See, e.g.,* Morrison, *Does the Fourteenth Amendment Incorporate the Bill of Rights?: The Judicial Interpretation,* 2 STAN. L. REV. 140, 154–55 (1949), for an elaboration of the importance of the ratification proceedings.

the federal Bill of Rights against them through the Fourteenth Amendment. It is sufficient for purposes of this case for the Court to recognize, and the Court does so recognize, that the Fourteenth Amendment did not incorporate the Establishment Clause."[83] If Judge Hand is correct, an originalist would have to concede that the Court has improperly incorporated the Establishment Clause.

Again, however, the evidence simply does not justify Hand's unequivocal conclusion. The records of the ratification proceedings are sparse and often unhelpful. There are few records of debates in the ratifying states, and even in those states which maintained records, debate was "often perfunctory, confused, or off-point."[84] Furthermore, the ambiguous language included in the Fourteenth Amendment was certain to engender confusion and could not be altered by the ratifying bodies. Given the lack of meaningful recorded dialogue in most ratification proceedings and the ambiguity of the terminology used in the amendment, it is virtually impossible to ascertain the intent of the ratifiers with even a modicum of certainty.[85]

Nevertheless, we must examine the available records of the ratification proceedings to determine their utility as indicia of intent. Much of the recorded debate simply seems to track arguments made previously in Congress and in other fora. Despite Judge Hand's assertion to the contrary, there were a number of indications, even on the sparse record available, of an intent to make some or all of the rights enumerated in the Bill of Rights applicable to the states. For example, state Representative John S. Mann, a Republican supporter of the amendment in Pennsylvania, argued that the amendment would help overcome "suppression of the freedom of speech" in the South.[86] On a similar note Representative Samuel M'Camant of the Pennsylvania House stressed that the amendment was "necessary to secure to us the blessings of peace and the freedom of every man, woman and child in the country—that freedom of speech and action which before the war was denied."[87] Representative M'Camant concluded his comments by calling upon his fellow

---

83. 554 F. Supp. 1104 at 1124 (emphasis added).

84. Comment, *supra* note 61, at 183.

85. Another factor contributing to the lack of dialogue, particularly in the former Confederate states, was the fact that the states were under pressure to ratify as a condition precedent to participation in Congress.

86. Pa. Leg. Rec. app. at XXXII-III (1867), cited in Curtis, *supra* note 57, at 293–94.

87. Curtis, *supra* note 57, at 295.

legislators to stand with him in protecting loyal men everywhere "in the enjoyment of their Constitutional rights" and by demanding that "the freedom of speech and of the press" be secured and that the "Union [be] reconstructed upon the principles of universal justice."[88] Representative Harrison Allen added that he supported the amendment because it would assure all men "the rights which the Constitution provides for men—all the rights which this amendment indicates—in full."[89] Similar statements were made in Ohio and Massachusetts.[90]

Curtis concludes his summary of the ratification materials by discussing the majority report of the committee of the Massachusetts State House in its legislative context. That report responded to questions raised regarding the nature and extent of rights conferred under the amendment, and after citing the *First,* Second, Sixth, and Seventh Amendments and the Due Process Clause:

> Nearly every one of the amendments to the Constitution grew out of a jealousy for the rights of the people, and is in the direction, more or less direct, of a guarantee of human rights.
>
> It seems difficult to conceive how the provisions above quoted, taken in connection with the whole tenor of the instrument, could have been put into clearer language; and, upon any fair rule of interpretation, these provisions cover the whole ground of section first of the proposed amendment.[91]

As evidenced by these brief citations to the historical record of the ratification proceedings, Judge Hand is incorrect when he asserts that "the historical record shows without equivocation that none of the states envisioned the Fourteenth Amendment as applying the federal Bill of Rights against them." Similarly, however, it would be incorrect to assert that the record unequivocally establishes that the legislators understood

---

88. *Id.*

89. *Id.* at XCIX.

90. Curtis, *supra* note 57, at 292–98.

91. H.R. Doc. No. 149, Mass. Gen. Ct., at 2 (1867), as cited in Curtis, *id.* at 297. It is interesting, however, that those writing this report remained steadfast in their allegiance to a reading of the Privileges and Immunities Clause of Article IV that had been rejected by the Court in *Barron.* The report, in this regard, concluded:

We are brought to the conclusion, therefore, that this first section [of the Amendment] is, at best, mere surplusage; and that it is mischievous, inasmuch as it is an admission, either that the same guarantees do not exist in the present Constitution, or that if they are there, they have been disregarded, and by long usage or acquiescence, this disregard has hardened into constitutional right; and no security can be given that similar guarantees will not be disregarded hereafter.

Cited in Curtis, *supra* note 57, at 297.

that they were ratifying an amendment that would by its terms make the Bill of Rights enforceable against the states. An examination of the history simply does not support conclusively either the conclusions propounded by the nonincorporationists (e.g., Fairman, Berger, and Hand) or by the incorporationists (e.g., Black, Crosskey, and Curtis). Instead, the record is susceptible to various readings, none of which yields a version of the intent that could be deemed definitive with even a modicum of mathematical certainty. The ratification records, which are the most legitimate source of intent for the purposes of originalist analysis, are sparse and ambiguous. They are, however, sufficiently clear to aid in eliminating some interpretations of the original intent, particularly when they are examined in conjunction with other indicia of intent, such as the congressional proceedings. Thus, while the content of the civil rights intended is susceptible to much judicial gloss or discretionary construction, it would be inappropriate in an originalist sense for a court to read political rights like suffrage into the amendment.[92]

In support of his unequivocal conclusions regarding the intent of the ratifying legislature, Hand cites a New Hampshire case decided in 1868, just five months after ratification of the amendment. A discussion of contemporaneous cases, including those of the Supreme Court, however, really fits more appropriately in Judge Hand's next category, that of court decisions as indicia of intent.

The Federal and State Cases

Judge Hand asserts that "decisions by the United States Supreme Court rendered contemporaneously with the ratification of the Fourteenth Amendment indicate that the Court did not perceive the Fourteenth Amendment to incorporate the federal Bill of Rights against the

---

92. I am, therefore, inclined to agree with Timothy Bishop who has acknowledged that:

within these bounds, the judge often will have to make a choice. Her options, however, lie between interpretations that are all reasonably based in the intentions of the framers. Whatever choice is made among intentions that are considered equally likely to have been those of the framers, due consideration having been given to the large margin of error within which the interpreter works, is ultimately sanctioned by the people, and is therefore consistent with democratic principles.... The choice made between constructions equally likely to have been the intent of Congress [and, I would add, the state ratifying legislature] does not depend on the intentions of the framers at all; that the choice exists is evidence that analysis of historical materials has provided all the help to interpretation that it can and that the analysis has to some extent been inconclusive.

Comment, *supra* note 61, at 188–89.

states."[93] Judge Hand's reference to a case decided in the New Hampshire state courts in 1868 supports his conclusion that matters related to the establishment of religion in the states were "left exclusively to the state governments."[94] In the case, the Supreme Court of New Hampshire had cited Justice Story's *Commentaries* approvingly for the proposition that "the whole power over the subject of religion is left exclusively to the state governments to be acted upon according to their own sense of justice and the state constitutions,"[95] in holding that the legislature could "authorize towns, parishes, and religious societies to make adequate provision...for the support and maintenance of public Protestant teachers of piety, religion, and morality."[96]

In terms of original-intent analysis, these early cases are important primarily because they may reflect the contemporaneous public understanding about the meaning of the Fourteenth Amendment. They are not particularly significant, as a matter of precedent, because if they have clearly misinterpreted the intent, they should be overruled. This is a matter in which I am in full agreement with Judge Hand.

It should be pointed out, however, that contemporaneous court cases are not nearly as helpful as actual expressions of legislative intent made during the adoption and ratification of the amendment. Contemporaneous court cases are themselves secondary sources, because they are interpretations rather than expressions of intent. Furthermore, given existing distrust on the part of Radical and perhaps even moderate Republicans in Congress (and out of Congress, as illustrated by the majority report in the Massachusetts ratification proceedings) of the Supreme Court, it is evident that the Court may have had ample reason, as a political matter, to limit, if not disregard, the intent of the legislature with regard to the ambit of the Fourteenth Amendment. Furthermore, the idealism of many Republicans in Congress in the immediate postwar years had begun to give way to a more pragmatic sentiment in the 1870s and 1880s, and this pragmatism may have caused the Court to engage in some retrenchment from the earlier idealism of the Radicals. Powers assumed by the federal government during the Civil War had begun to be resumed by the states, and the notion of incorporating the Bill of Rights, with all that such incorporation would portend for federal-state relations, may have been relegated into quiescence. All of these possible factors, plus the very ambiguity of the language and the legislative record, may

---

93. 554 F. Supp. 1104 at 1124.
94. *Id.*
95. As cited in *id.* at 1124.
96. As cited in *id.* at 1123.

have contributed to a judicial willingness to opt for the more restrictive view of the Fourteenth Amendment. As a related matter, state courts could generally be expected to interpret restrictively or ignore the Constitution and its Bill of Rights in areas where a broader reading would intrude on the state's prerogative.

In the *Slaughter House Cases* in 1873, in a 5-4 decision written by Justice Samuel F. Miller, the Supreme Court read the Privileges or Immunities Clause restrictively, holding that the clause was limited to rights of national as opposed to state citizenship. The Court refused to accept the incorporationist argument urged by counsel. Nevertheless, despite the movement in postwar years back to a strengthening of state power and the fact that both the state and federal courts in the latter part of the nineteenth century had ample reason to read the Fourteenth Amendment restrictively, there is evidence in the pre-*Slaughter House Cases* era supporting a broad reading of the Fourteenth Amendment.

In *United States v. Hall*,[97] an early case in Judge Hand's own backyard, the southern district of Alabama, Judge William B. Woods, who was subsequently appointed to the United States Supreme Court, held that an Alabama statute depriving citizens of their First Amendment freedoms of speech and association was unconstitutional. After referring to the Privileges or Immunities Clause of the Fourteenth Amendment, Woods concluded that "we think, therefore, that the right of freedom of speech, and the other rights enumerated in the first eight articles of amendment to the Constitution of the United States, are the privileges and immunities of the United States."[98] Justice Joseph P. Bradley, who then sat on the United States Supreme Court, wrote Judge Woods a congratulatory letter in which he indicated his personal agreement with Woods's opinion.[99] And, Justices Stephen J. Field, John Marshall Harlan, and David J. Brewer all voiced essentially similar views during their tenures in the Supreme Court.[100] Thus, while the views of Judge Woods and Justices Bradley, Field, Harlan, and Brewer may never have commanded a majority at any one time on the Court, they did express those views. By doing so, they evidenced that such views were held by important jurists during the early years of the amendment's existence.

With Justice Miller's lengthy opinion for the Supreme Court in the *Slaughter House Cases*,[101] which was based on his recollection of the

---

97. 26 F. Case 79 (C.C.S.D. Ala. 1871) (No. 15, 282).
98. *Id.* at 82, as cited in Curtis, *supra* note 23, at 99.
99. As cited in Curtis, *supra* note 23, at 99, n. 407.
100. *Id.* at 99.
101. 83 U.S. (16 Wall.) 36 (1872).

history of the framing of the Fourteenth Amendment, the likelihood of expressions of the broader view that the Fourteenth Amendment incorporated all or significant parts of the Bill of Rights diminished. This does not prove that such a broader reading of the intent was unwarranted. It proved only that the Supreme Court, in its 5-4 decision in the *Slaughter House Cases,* had set a precedent that could not be overturned easily. As Judge Hand notes, albeit in a slightly different context, the impact of precedent is pervasive, often relegating any decision to the contrary to little "more than a voice crying in the wilderness."[102] Indeed, the strong negative reaction to Judge Hand's opinion illustrates the problems attendant with efforts, particularly at the lower court level, to shed new light on seemingly settled issues, even if the new light is based on a more accurate reading of pertinent historical materials.

Efforts to resurrect a broader view of the Fourteenth Amendment did occur periodically after the Court affirmation of the restrictive view in the *Slaughter House Cases.* The respective dissenting views of Justices Field, Harlan, and Brewer in *O'Neil v. Vermont*[103] serve as illustrative judicial examples. Additionally, lawyers raised similar objections on a number of occasions,[104] even though they were generally unsuccessful in doing so, thereby illustrating that such views were considered tenable in the legal world.

Public as well as judicial support for the broader incorporationist position persisted. Senator George S. Boutwell of Massachusetts, for example, wrote in response to the *Slaughter House Cases* that the Supreme Court had "erred in holding that there were two classes of rights, national and state,"[105] and Senator George F. Edmunds of Vermont added that "there is no word in [the Fourteenth Amendment] that did not undergo the completest scrutiny. There is no word in it that was not scanned, and intended to mean the full and beneficial thing it seems to mean. There was no discussion omitted; there was no conceivable posture of affairs to the people who had it in hand which was not considered. And yet it was found upon the first time to enforce its first clause . . . that the court, by a division of five to four, radically differed in respect both to the intention of the framers and the construction of the language used by them."[106] Turning from the legislative reaction to *Slaughter*

---

102. *Jaffree,* 554 F. Supp. 1104 at 1128.

103. 144 U.S. 323 (1892).

104. *See, e.g.,* Crosskey, *supra* note 12, at 112–14.

105. As cited in J. Marke, Vignettes Of Legal History, at 185–86 (1965), in which Professor Marke engages in an interesting examination of the *Slaughter House Cases* as one of his vignettes.

106. *Id.*

House to the reaction in the newspapers (a source that nonincorporationists find instructive for other purposes, but which they largely ignore with regard to *Slaughter House*), Professor Julius J. Marke quotes from an editorial in the *Cincinnati Enquirer* exclaiming that "we are astonished by this opinion of the Court.... It gives a legal sanction to the consummation of an outrage on individual rights that is almost unparalleled."[107] In a similar vein, after a review of the pertinent history and the use of that history by the *Slaughter House* Court, a contemporary commentator has concluded that "even interpreting the Privileges or Immunities Clause in accordance with its determinable scope under the majority or agency models results in a broader application of the provision than that held appropriate by the majority in the Slaughter House Cases."[108]

Cases prior to the *Slaughter House Cases* that sought to enshrine the proposition that the states were bound only in a very limited sense by the strictures of the Privileges or Immunities Clause indicate that the broader incorporationist view was also considered legitimate. Furthermore, legislative and, to a lesser extent, civil responses to the restrictive reading of the Court in its decision in the *Slaughter House Cases* were often characterized by a sense of surprise—surprise that the Court had refused to read the clause in a broader fashion. Hand, therefore, is simply wrong when he asserts that early court decisions, and responses to those decisions, indicate that the incorporationist position was perceived to be untenable or unacceptable.

The Blaine Amendment

Judge Hand finally declared that "the Blaine Amendment, which failed in its passage, is stark testimony to the fact that the adoptors of the Fourteenth Amendment never intended to incorporate the Establishment Clause of the First Amendment against the states."[109] Elsewhere in his opinion, Hand noted that "at the behest of President Grant, James Blaine of Maine introduced a resolution in the Senate in 1885 which read: 'No *state* shall make any law respecting an establishment of religion or prohibiting the free exercise thereof,'"[110] and, after pointing out that twenty-three members of the Thirty-Ninth Congress, the Congress which passed the Fourteenth Amendment, were members of the Congress which considered the Blaine Amendment, concluded by quoting from *Justice Reed and the First Amendment* by F. William O'Brien:

---

107. *Id.*
108. Comment, *supra* note 61, at 184, n. 258.
109. 554 F. Supp. 1104 at 1126.
110. Cited in *id.* at 1125 (emphasis in original).

Not one of the several representatives and senators who spoke on the proposal even suggested that its provisions were implicit in the amendment ratified just seven years earlier. Congressman Banks, a member of the Thirty-ninth Congress, observed: "If the Constitution is amended so as to secure the object embraced in the principle part of this proposed amendment, it prohibits the states from exercising a power they now exercise." Senator Frelinghuysen of New Jersey urged the passage of the "House Article," which "prohibits the states for the first time, from the establishment of religion, from prohibiting its free exercise." Senator Stevenson, in opposing the proposed amendment, referred to *Thomas Jefferson: "Friend as he* [Jefferson] *was of religious freedom, he would never have consented that the states...should be degraded and that the government of the United States, a government of limited authority, a mere agent of the states with prescribed powers, should undertake to take possession of their schools and of their religion."* Remarks of Randolph, Christiancy, Kernan, Whyte, Bogy, Easton, and Morton give confirmation to the belief that none of the legislators in 1875 thought the Fourteenth Amendment incorporated the religious provisions of the First.[111]

At first blush, this appears to be one of Judge Hand's stronger arguments with regard to the religion clauses. The response of the Court of Appeals failed to address the substance of this argument, preferring simply to note that the Supreme Court had rejected it in the past.[112] The circuit court's perfunctory rejection of Judge Hand's argument is understandable given that the appellate court had rejected Judge Hand's original-intent methodology. For that court, history provided enlightenment[113] and nothing more; historical intent only enlightened, it did not bind.

As an originalist, I must deal directly with Hand's argument. Hand's argument is deficient for a number of reasons. First, it is inappropriate to read too much into the legislature's reaction or lack of reaction to the Blaine Amendment, which was proposed after the Supreme Court had opted for a restrictive reading of the Fourteenth Amendment as an incorporating device in *Slaughter House*.[114] Indeed, both the language and the history behind the Blaine Amendment may be read much differently than Hand is wont to read it, particularly when the Blaine Amendment is placed in its historical context.

---

111. O'Brien, Justice Reed And The First Amendment: The Religion Clauses 116–17 (emphasis added [by Judge Hand]), *cited in* 554 F. Supp. 1104 at 1125–26.

112. Jaffree v. Wallace, 705 F.2d 1526, 1531 (11th Cir. 1983).

113. *Id.* at 1532.

114. *See* Curtis, *supra* note 10, at 122–23.

By the time the Blaine Amendment was proposed, nondenominational Protestantism had gained a foothold in the nascent public-school system. Catholics had responded to this by seeking equal treatment in the form of financial assistance. Largely in response to this Catholic effort to obtain government assistance for their schools, Representative James G. Blaine acted upon President Ulysses S. Grant's suggestion and introduced his proposed amendment, which provided that

> No state shall make any law respecting an establishment of religion or prohibiting the free exercise thereof; and, no money raised by taxation in any state for the support of public schools, or derived from any public fund therefore, nor any public lands devoted thereto, shall ever be under the control of any religious sect, nor shall any money so raised or lands so devoted be divided between religious sects or denominations.[115]

The primary purpose behind the Blaine Amendment appears to have been twofold: (1) to solidify Protestant control of the American school system at the expense of Catholics; and (2) to enshrine the strict-separationist views of Grant and others regarding financial assistance to religious educational institutions.

In both senses, Judge Hand's failure to so much as cite the latter portions of the Blaine Amendment is fatal, both as a matter of historical accuracy and as a means of understanding the amendment, and, thus, he misinforms the reader. Had the Blaine Amendment merely included the language cited by Judge Hand, Hand's ultimate argument, that the introduction of the Blaine Amendment supported his conclusion that the First Amendment was not incorporated through the Fourteenth Amendment, would be strengthened. Unfortunately for him, the actual language of the amendment belies an intent to do something more or at least something quite different from what Hand implies in his opinion.

However, before yielding to the urge to dispense entirely with Hand's position on the ground that it contains internal flaws, I must acknowledge that it does receive additional support from another source. Professor Jonathan Lurie, in examining a number of civil liberties cases in the state courts between 1870 and 1890, concluded that "in terms of the incorporation argument concerning the First Amendment, within the area of religion and the public schools there is absolutely no evidence to indicate any such linkage at all."[116] Even though I also find internal

---

115. As cited in Fairbauch, SCHOOL PRAYER, 30–3.

116. Lurie, *The Fourteenth Amendment: Use and Application in Selected State Court Civil Liberties Cases, 1870–1890—A Preliminary Assessment,* 28 AM. J. LEGAL HISTORY 295, 312.

problems with Lurie's observations (e.g., he cites only one state opinion in the religious-liberty area that was decided prior to the Supreme Court's decision in *Slaughter House)*, those cases together with the congressional debate regarding the Blaine Amendment cited by Judge Hand, do present difficulties for the incorporationist argument. They do lend support to the proposition that many people believed that the First Amendment, particularly the Establishment Clause, was not to be made applicable to the states through the Fourteenth Amendment.

The nonincorporationist position of Judge Hand seemingly receives additional support from yet another quarter, that of the language used in the Fourteenth Amendment, as compared to the restrictive language of the First Amendment's religion clauses. The vehicle for incorporating the religion clauses of the First Amendment through the Fourteenth Amendment, as a matter of original intent, is the Privileges or Immunities Clause of the Fourteenth Amendment. The clause is general in its prescription ("no state shall make or enforce any law which shall abridge the privileges or immunities of citizens of the United States") while the First Amendment is more specific ("Congress shall make no law respecting an establishment of religion or prohibiting the free exercise thereof"). An argument supportive of the Hand position can therefore be made based on the language of the respective amendments. In *Barron v. Baltimore,*[117] Chief Justice Marshall developed the plain-and-intelligible-language test for determining the intent of the Privileges and Immunities Clause. The application of such a plain-and-intelligible-language test to the Fourteenth Amendment, as a vehicle for incorporating the religion clauses of the First Amendment, which are by their very terms limitations only on the national government, makes it evident that more specific language should have been used.

Nevertheless, even though Judge Hand's final argument based on the Blaine Amendment, and buttressed by a couple of related arguments, is significant, it is not in and of itself dispositive. As I have noted throughout this chapter, there are other indicia of intent that support the incorporationist argument. Indeed, much of that evidence of intent is more direct than the argument Hand raises based on the Blaine Amendment and other post-*Slaughter House* activity.

On any number of occasions, the First Amendment, including the religion clauses, was mentioned as being among the privileges or immunities of citizens protected by the Fourteenth Amendment. Even Pro-

---

117. Barron v. Baltimore, 32 U.S. 242, 249, 7 Pet. 243, 250 (1833).

fessor Charles Fairman, a leading proponent of the nonincorporationist argument and Judge Hand's primary scholarly source, conceded that the freedom of speech may have been intended to be included in those rights secured against the states through the Fourteenth Amendment.[118] In addition, Arnold Guminski, who analyzed the origin of the privileges-and-immunities language, concluded that

> Only the First Amendment in the Bill of Rights contains provisions which expressly impose sweeping limitations upon the lawmaking power of Congress. The freedoms of the First Amendment are not just secured against abridgments. Similarly, the Privileges or Immunities Clause expressly imposes sweeping limitations upon the lawmaking power of the states. Such structural similarities between the First Amendment and the Privileges or Immunities Clause constitute persuasive evidence that First Amendment freedoms are among the rights denoted by the descriptive term of the Privileges or Immunities Clause. Such similarities suggest that no right specified in the Bill of Rights other than First Amendment freedoms are denoted by the descriptive term of the Privileges or Immunities Clause, unless that right is also a freedom.[119]

It will be recalled that Guminski also made a strong case for the proposition that religion was considered to be a privilege or immunity.[120] Similarly, even Senator Lyman Trumball of Illinois, the leading proponent of the Civil Rights Bill, which Professor Berger believes to be coextensive with the Privileges or Immunities Clause of Section 1 of the Fourteenth Amendment, argued that his bill protected the right to preach.[121]

Judge Hand's argument based on the language of the Fourteenth Amendment, even buttressed as it has been, may prove too much. The language used in the amendment may have been crafted to deal precisely with the problem raised in *Barron*. Indeed, this may well have been what Representative Bingham was referring to when he said, "that the scope and meaning of the limitations imposed by the first section, Fourteenth Amendment of the Constitution, may be more fully understood, permit me to say that the privileges and immunities of citizens of the United States, as contradistinguished from the citizens of a state [Art. IV, Section 2], are chiefly defined in the first eight amendments to the

---

118. Fairman, *supra* note 36, at 139.
119. Guminski, *supra* note 14, at 809.
120. *See supra* note 14 and related text.
121. CONG. GLOBE, 39th Cong., 1st Sess. 475 (1866), as cited in Curtis, *supra* note 13, at 529.

Constitution of the United States."[122] The Blaine Amendment, read in its post-*Slaughter House* context, even when read in conjunction with cases from that same era, does little to undermine the historical data of a direct nature previously discussed in conjunction with an analysis of the framing and ratification of the Fourteenth Amendment. Even applying Chief Justice Marshall's plain-and-intelligible-language test does little to supplement the Hand view, because the differences between the language used in Article IV ("citizens of each state shall be entitled to all privileges and immunities of citizens in the several states") and that used in the Fourteenth Amendment ("no state shall make or enforce any law which shall abridge the privileges or immunities of citizens of the United States") are significant and are susceptible to differing interpretations.

Again, therefore, while Judge Hand's argument regarding the Blaine Amendment is perhaps stronger than his prior arguments, it is at best inconclusive and peripheral. While Hand's argument may be tenable as a matter of interpretation, because some of the proponents of the Fourteenth Amendment doubtlessly espoused similar views, it is hardly dispositive.

Conclusion

One must wonder why Judge Hand was so adamant in his opinion for the lower court in *Jaffree,* in refusing to acknowledge a solid line of precedent recognizing the incorporation of the religion clauses of the First Amendment, particularly in light of an abundance of historical material supporting those incorporationist decisions. Perhaps, however, Hand answered this question when he revealed his own bias in favor of federalism or states' rights in the course of his opinion. By supplying his own emphasis to the quotation about Jefferson's view contained in O'Brien's *Justice Reed and the First Amendment,* Hand implied that his opinion was but another result-oriented opinion. Raoul Berger revealed

---

122. Cited *supra* at note 47. In this regard, Professor Cottrol has noted that:

> Bingham incidentally appears to have been less confused about the applicability of the Bill of Rights to the states than Berger indicates. Bingham was aware of the Court's decision in Barron v. Baltimore [citation omitted] that held that the fifth amendment did not apply to the states. He realized the state of the law and he disagreed with it. While Bingham argued that, in his view, the Court had misinterpreted the intent of the framers with respect to the Bill of Rights and its applicability to the states, he argued that the fourteenth amendment would correct that decision.

Cottrol, *supra* note 59, at 374, n. 215.

a similar bias in a recent article when he responded to criticism of his restrictive reading of the history of the Fourteenth Amendment by complaining that "a generation grown accustomed to *judicial rape of federalism* needs to be reminded that 'inscrutable' words [of the Privileges or Immunities Clause of the Fourteenth Amendment] cannot constitute a waiver of power reserved to the states by the tenth amendment."[123]

The language of the Fourteenth Amendment is inscrutable, and the intent of the framers and ratifiers is ambiguous as well, despite protestations to the contrary by incorporationists and nonincorporationists alike. Where, then, does that leave us? It leaves us, I believe, in the position of having to acknowledge that, while a close reading of applicable history of the sort considered by originalists eliminates some possible interpretations, it leaves the Court with fairly broad discretion. As Timothy Bishop recently noted, a principled intentionalist analysis of the Privileges or Immunities Clause "leaves a court with the task of giving it content with a choice between three possible interpretations of the original intent. The choice lies between holding that the clause was intended to protect rights listed in the Civil Rights Act of 1866, or protect also the rights that were constitutionalized in the first eight amendments, or protect all 'natural' or 'fundamental' rights identified by reference to extraconstitutional concepts."[124]

Thus, while the nonincorporationist view held by Judge Hand, Attorney General Meese, and others is not the only tenable view of the history, it may with minor modification be a legitimate view in an originalist sense. However, other viewpoints are equally legitimate. How, then, should the Court select between these available interpretations?

No doubt, Meese, Berger, Hand, and other nonincorporationists would argue that the Tenth Amendment and notions of federalism ought to prevail. Incorporationists on the other hand argue that, provided that the history does not mandate a different decision, the Court should defer to well-established, albeit largely contemporary, precedent. Indeed, since the history can be read in accord with existing Supreme Court precedent, Judge Hand was bound to follow that precedent as a lower court judge. They could add that their view is further warranted on the ground that it uniformly protects the rights of citizens from state abridgments of the fundamental rights contained in the Bill of Rights.

---

123. Berger, *Incorporation of the Bill of Rights in the Fourteenth Amendment: A Nine-Lived Cat,* 42 OHIO ST. L. J. 435, 465 (1981).

124. Comment, *supra* note 61, at 190.

For my part, I must admit that the federalism of Judge Hand and Attorney General Meese may be justified on originalist grounds with only minor modification or clarification. I would also emphasize that in my view the incorporationist view has at least as much and probably more support in the historical records than does the nonincorporationist precedent, although courts ought to clarify that such incorporation is under the aegis of the Privileges or Immunities Clause and not the Due Process Clause of the Fourteenth Amendment. Given the wealth of precedent that has developed favoring the incorporationist position during the twentieth century and the dire implications of the nonincorporationist position for the uniform protection of the individual liberties contained in the Bill of Rights, a return to the nonincorporationist states'-rights position advocated by Judge Hand and others would not only create legal chaos but would also have grave implications for human rights. The debate over the history of the intended meaning of the Privileges or Immunities Clause of the Fourteenth Amendment is interminable largely because the evidence is susceptible to at least two or three different readings. As such, I feel confident in asserting that, in a purely originalist sense, the Court would be justified in reaching the nonincorporationist result desired by Judge Hand and others, although it would have to overrule a bulk of precedent to do so. Using the same methodology, the Court also could reach the result desired by Justice Black and others. That, I acknowledge, leaves me a bit unsettled. I wish that only my preferred view, the incorporationist position, was defensible in an originalist sense, but that is not the case. However, the incorporationist view is sufficiently defensible that the remainder of this book ought to have meaning at both the state and the federal levels.

8

State-Composed Prayer and Bible Reading in the Public Schools: The Engel and Schempp Cases

The practice of prayer in the public schools, where desired, remained largely unfettered by legal precedent, until the early 1960s when the Supreme Court rendered its decision in *Engel v. Vitale.*[1] In *Engel,* the New York Board of Regents had commissioned the preparation of a short, essentially nondenominational prayer for use in the public schools of the state, directing that the prayer be recited orally each day by students. The prayer read as follows: "Almighty God, we acknowledge our dependence upon Thee, and we beg Thy blessings upon us, our parents, our teachers, and our country." The board also permitted students, who desired to refrain from praying, to leave the room during the recitation of the prayer.

The Court granted certiorari in the *Engel* case on 4 December 1961, with all of the justices other than Justice Potter Stewart and Justice Charles E. Whittaker agreeing to grant review of the lower court's determination that the practice was constitutional. The case was argued on 3 April 1962, and, on 6 April 1962, the Court met privately in conference to discuss the case. Justice Hugo L. Black led those justices opposing the prayer practice and was assigned the job of writing the majority opinion for the Court, holding the Regents' voluntary school prayer

---

1. 370 U.S. 421 (1962).

practice unconstitutional. When Justice Black delivered the opinion of the Court on 25 June 1962, only Justice Stewart dissented.[2]

In his opinion for the Court, Black distinguished the purpose of the Establishment Clause from that of the Free Exercise Clause, emphasizing that

> Although these two clauses may in certain instances overlap, they forbid two quite different kinds of governmental encroachment upon religious freedom. The Establishment Clause, unlike the Free Exercise Clause, does not depend upon any showing of direct governmental compulsion and is violated by the enactment of laws which establish an official religion whether those laws operate to directly coerce non-observing individuals or not. This is not to say, of course, that laws officially prescribing a particular form of religious worship do not involve coercion of such individuals. When the power, prestige, and financial support of government is placed behind a particular religious belief, the indirect coercive pressure upon religious minorities to conform to the prevailing officially approved religion is plain. But the purposes underlying the Establishment Clause go much further than that. Its first and most immediate purpose rested on the belief that a union of government and religion tends to destroy government and degrade religion.[3]

Thus, for Justice Black, the purposes of the Establishment Clause continued to be heavily imbued with the strict-separationist rationale first articulated in *Everson*.

Having thus articulated the purposes of the Free Exercise and Establishment clauses, Justice Black went on to hold, on behalf of the Court, that the prayer recitation practice was unconstitutional, because

> the constitutional prohibition against laws respecting an establishment of religion must at least mean that in this country *it is not part of the business of government to compose official prayers* for any group of the American people to recite as a part of a religious program carried on by government.[4]

In support of the proposition that the state could not compose a prayer for recitation in the public schools, Black examined aspects of our colonial history. In particular, he emphasized the early development of opposition in the colonies to the Anglican Book of Common Prayer.

---

2. *See* B. Schwartz, SUPER CHIEF at 440–42 (1983), for a discussion regarding the Court's internal treatment of the *Engel* case.

3. *Engel,* 370 U.S. at 430–31.

4. *Id.* at 425 (emphasis added).

Justice Black's opinion was at best a piecemeal glance at a series of sometimes tenuously related historical events, as opposed to being a concerted effort to discover, in a principled sense, the intent of the framers of the First Amendment.

Justice Stewart was the sole dissenter in *Engel.* He could not understand how an official religion would be established by simply permitting those students who wanted to recite a prayer to do so. Therefore, he felt that the Court's invalidation of the New York prayer practice abridged the students' rights of free exercise. He felt that to deny the wish of these school children to join in reciting the Regents' prayer was to deny them the opportunity of sharing in their nation's spiritual heritage. A matter of particular concern to Stewart was the total lack of evidence of any coercion in the administration of the New York practice. Noting what he considered to be the voluntary nature of the program, Stewart added that

> The Court does not hold, nor could it, that New York has interfered with the free exercise of anybody's religion. For the state courts have made clear that those who object to reciting the prayer must be entirely free of any compulsion to do so, including any embarrassments and pressures.[5]

Thus, in emphasizing the lower court's decision and findings of fact, Justice Stewart made it plain that, for him, the Regents' prayer practice was constitutionally permissible, provided all students remained *"entirely free of any compulsion. . . including embarrassments and pressures."* Given that no evidence whatsoever of compulsion or coercion was presented to the lower court, Stewart felt compelled to recognize the rights of those students who desired to pray, by permitting the New York practice. The majority, on the other hand, felt there was no need to prove actual compulsion or coercion to prohibit the students who desired to recite the requested prayer from doing so, because in the majority's view, as a matter of law, the recitation of a state-composed prayer violated the Establishment Clause of the First Amendment.

Justice Stewart also disagreed with the majority's historical analysis. He felt the Court skirted evidence related to the historical acceptance of other governmentally recognized prayers in the United States, from our nation's founding until the time of the *Engel* decision.[6] He felt that the

---

5. *Id.* at 445 (Stewart, J., dissenting). Cf. *West Virginia State Board of Education v. Barnette,* 319 U.S. 624 (1943) (compelling children to salute the flag violates First and Fourteenth Amendments).

6. *Engel,* 370 U.S. at 446–50.

majority ignored utterly our nation's largely tolerant, yet religious, heritage. He argued further that Justice Black's analogy between the Book of Common Prayer and the Regents' prayer was inappropriate, because the Regents' prayer was nondenominational, whereas the Book of Common Prayer was clearly denominational in matters of doctrine. Stewart was also particularly disturbed by Black's invocation of Jefferson's wall metaphor, which Justice Stewart felt inaccurately implied simplistic answers to complex problems, particularly where free-exercise rights and Establishment Clause values are in conflict.

With his dissent, Justice Stewart helped to frame the issues that have been of recurring concern in the area of public prayer. Additionally, and perhaps unwittingly, the Black and Stewart opinions rekindled implicitly the debate between Joseph Story and James Madison.

It is clear, based on historical analysis, that Madison would have joined with the majority, although his opinion would have been based on different reasoning, while Story would have joined with Stewart in dissent. For Madison, the recitation of the Regents' prayer would be unacceptable, because it would have constituted an adoption by the state of a particular mode of worship. The fact that the prayer was largely nondenominational would not have saved it. Madison would, therefore, have joined wholeheartedly in Black's conclusion that the state had no business composing a particular prayer for recitation by public-school children, because the state in Madison's view should not specifically promote even essentially nondenominational religious doctrine.[7]

However, it is equally likely that Madison would not have joined in much of the language utilized by Justice Black in his opinion. He would not have agreed with Black's treatment of the free-exercise issue. Madison felt that the primary purpose of the religion clauses was to accommodate the voluntary exercise of an individual's religious conscience or convictions. He would have disputed the underlying flavor of the Black opinion to the effect that the public sector must even remain free from religious activity. For Madison, such a strict-separationist rationale would effectively preclude an individual from expressing her religious convictions in the public sector. Given the increasingly pervasive nature of our contemporary public sector, Madison would have been even more concerned undoubtedly with the need to accommodate individual and voluntary religious exercise, in public as well as in private.

There is a second issue framed by the interplay between Justice Black's opinion and Justice Stewart's dissent: are free-exercise rights, as well as Establishment Clause problems, implicated in such a case? The

---

7. *Id.* at 428, 431 n. 13–14, 436.

coercion issue discussed by Stewart in *Engel* was raised somewhat more succinctly one year later in the *Schempp* case. It makes sense, therefore, as a chronological matter, to reserve discussion of the coercion issue until it is raised in conjunction with a discussion of the Court's analysis in the *Schempp* case, in which the Court invalidated devotional Bible reading in public schools.[8] However, it should be noted that the coercion issue, whether explicit or implicit governmental coercion violates the Free Exercise or Establishment clauses of the First Amendment, was a source of disagreement between the majority and Justice Stewart in *Engel*.

Public furor which was without equal in any prior case before the Supreme Court arose after the *Engel* decision was announced. This furor, fueled in some measure by public ignorance about what was really decided in *Engel*, has continued since that decision was rendered. Criticism of the *Engel* decision became so intense that Justice Tom C. Clark felt it necessary to deviate from the custom of judicial silence on substantive matters and explain that decision to the public. In a newspaper report in the *Miami Herald*, Justice Clark referred to the *Engel* decision, noting that

> [*Engel* involved] a state-written prayer circulated by state-employed teachers with instructions to have their pupils recite it in unison at the beginning of each school day....The Constitution says that government shall take no part in the establishment of religion. No means no.... As soon as the people learned that this was all the Court decided...they understood the basis on which the Court acted.

Clark sought to emphasize three factors in supporting the Court's decision in *Engel*: (1) the prayer was written by the state; (2) state-employed teachers were required to be present during the recitation; and (3) the prayer was to be recited by the students in unison rather than individually. The first two factors have commonly been addressed in such cases and the third factor seems to question the utility or importance of the practice involved in the *Engel* case in terms of accommodating *individual* religious exercise. It also seems to imply that coercion is necessarily entailed in the group nature of the practice at issue in *Engel*. While the Clark explanation, and other similar efforts to explain and in some instances to limit *Engel*, may have diffused some criticism of the Court's decision, it certainly did not eliminate all opposition. That core of opposition has persisted and perhaps has even proliferated in the 1980s. Even in the early 1960s, opposition to the *Engel* decision provoked an effort

---

8. Abington School Dist. v. Schempp, 374 U.S. 203 (1963).

to amend the Constitution to provide for voluntary prayers like the one involved in *Engel.* Today, President Ronald Reagan continues to support such efforts.[9]

Not surprisingly, after Justice Clark's public effort to explain the *Engel* decision, and given his credentials as a moderate, Chief Justice Earl Warren assigned Clark responsibility for writing the next related opinion for the Court in the case of *Abington School District v. Schempp.*[10] In *Schempp,* the Pennsylvania legislature had mandated the reading, without comment, of a minimum of ten verses from the Bible at the opening of each day in the public schools of Pennsylvania. In the Abington School District, the Bible reading was to be followed by a recitation of the Lord's Prayer. In a companion case arising in Baltimore, Maryland, the Board of School Commissioners had adopted a procedure for reading a few verses of the Bible or for reciting the Lord's Prayer in an opening exercise in its public schools. In reviewing these activities, Justice Clark held that the Establishment Clause prohibited the practices of reading from the Bible or reciting the Lord's Prayer in public schools at the commencement of each school day.[11]

Justice Clark applied the first two prongs of the prevailing Establishment Clause test that had been developed by the Court in prior cases: the secular-purpose and primary-effect prongs. Under this test, he evaluated whether the governmental activity being questioned on Establishment Clause grounds had a secular purpose and whether its primary effect was neither to advance nor inhibit religion. This test later evolved into a three-prong test, the *Lemon* test, that is often referred to in Establishment Clause cases. (The third part of the test directs the Court to examine whether the governmental activity in question would entangle the Court in religious matters and whether it would lead to political divisiveness, if permitted. This three-prong test has been fraught with internal inconsistency and may very well be relegated to the function of a signpost, guiding rather than mandating decisions in Establishment Clause cases in the future.[12])

In *Schempp,* Justice Clark concluded that both the purpose and the effect of the Bible-reading and recitation of the Lord's Prayer was

---

9. The response of Congress and the Executive to the prayer issue is discussed at length in Chapter 12, *infra.*

10. 374 U.S. 203 (1963).

11. *Id., see also* Murray v. Curlett, 228 Md. 239, 179 A. 2d 698 (1962).

12. *Schempp,* 374 U.S. at 223–27; Lemon v. Kurtzman, 403 U.S. 602 (1971). *See* Chapter 9, *infra,* for a discussion of the applicability of the so-called *Lemon* test, with its three prongs.

religious. In the view of the Court, therefore, the religious purpose and effect of the Bible reading and recitation rendered the practices unconstitutional as an establishment of religion.

Justices William O. Douglas and William J. Brennan, Jr., respectively, wrote concurrences in *Schempp* but were in general agreement with the majority's conclusion that the primary purpose and effect of the practice were religious in nature. Justice Douglas wrote separately to indicate that he continued to adhere to the position he previously articulated in *Engel,* that no state resources could in any way be used to further religious activity.[13]

Justice Brennan also wrote a separate opinion. In his opinion, Brennan engaged in an historical analysis of the origin of the Establishment Clause, concluding in an air of futility that the framers of the amendment simply "gave no distinct consideration to the particular question whether the clause...forbade devotional exercises in public institutions."[14] It is noteworthy that Brennan took the history of the religion clause seriously. Evidently, after meeting in conference regarding the *Schempp* case, Brennan indicated that he intended to prepare a separate concurring opinion that would analyze the history for the avowed purpose of developing a means of distinguishing between constitutionally acceptable and unacceptable practices for First Amendment purposes.[15] Justice Brennan is to be commended for his effort to legitimize the Court's decision by invoking historical support for principles that could aid the Court in distinguishing between acceptable and unacceptable activities.

On the issue of coercion, as related to the Pennsylvania and Maryland excusal provisions, which provided that a student could be excused from participation in the Bible-reading and recitation practices, Brennan responded to Stewart's contention that there was no proof of coercion by concluding that "the answer is that the excusal procedure itself necessarily operates in such a way as to infringe the rights of free exercise of those children who wish to be excused."[16]

To all of this, Stewart responded as he had in *Engel* with a fairly lengthy dissent, concluding that a remand was in order because "the records in the two cases before [the Court were] so fundamentally

---

13. *Schempp,* 374 U.S. at 229–30.
14. *Id.* at 237–38.
15. Schwartz, *supra* note 2, at 467.
16. *Schempp,* 374 U.S. at 288.

deficient as to make impossible an informed or responsible determination of the constitutional issues presented."[17]

Justice Stewart began his dissent in *Schempp* by reiterating his view that the Court erred when it failed to acknowledge that there are many areas in which the Free Exercise and Establishment clauses overlap and that the clauses must be read as being complementary to avoid such a conflict. In this regard, he criticized the majority and the concurring justices, including Justice Brennan, for indulging in a doctrinaire reading of each clause, which Stewart argued led to an irreconcilable conflict between the purposes delineated for each clause.

Justice Stewart also felt that the Court had been remiss in its statutory analysis applicable to the specific cases before the Court. For him, evidence in the record to the effect that variations among practices were permitted by the schools involved indicated that the procedure appeared to accommodate the free exercise of the religious convictions of the students in a voluntary, noncoercive manner. As in *Engel*, without some *actual evidence* of coercion on the part of the state or its officials, Stewart was unwilling to overturn the devotional practices involved in *Schempp*.

Stewart further chided the majority for failing to account for the religious rights of participating children and their parents. He asserted that

> It might be argued here that parents who wanted their children to be exposed to religious influences in school could, under *Pierce*, send their children to private or parochial schools. But the consideration which renders this contention too facile to be determinative has already been recognized by the Court: "Freedom of speech, freedom of the press, freedom of religion are available to all, not merely to those who can pay for them."[18]

Stewart might well have added that such a policy of strict separation in the public-school context inherently discriminates against minority denominations. Religious groups and individuals lacking the financial wherewithal or who are unable to muster an adequate number of students to warrant the operation of a separate, sectarian school system have no recourse or procedure whereby they may exercise their beliefs on an equal basis with adherents of wealthier or more established reli-

17. *Id.* at 308.
18. *Id.* at 313–14.

gious groups, which are capable of maintaining separate, nonpublic educational systems.

Furthermore, in Justice Stewart's view, given the increasingly pervasive nature of compulsory public education in the United States, it was naive to say that a child should be precluded from participating voluntarily in any religious activity in the public-school setting, on the ground that the child could fully exercise his or her religion at home. In Stewart's view:

> [A] compulsory state educational system so structures a child's life that if religious exercises are held to be an impermissible activity in schools, religion is placed at an artificial and state-created disadvantage.... And a refusal to permit religious exercises thus is seen, not as a realization of state neutrality, but rather as the establishment of a religion of secularism.[19]

Thus, Stewart raised the religion-of-secularism or secular-humanism argument, arguing that the cries of strict separationists, who oppose any religious activity in the public sector, effectively promote a preference for a religion of secularism.[20]

Justice Stewart added that "the question is not whether exercises such as those at issue [Bible reading and recitation] are constitutionally compelled, but rather whether they are constitutionally invalid."[21] This statement seems to imply a right-privilege sort of distinction.[22] However, Stewart may have retreated from such a distinction when he summarized his position in *Schempp* by noting that

> What our Constitution indispensably protects is the freedom of each of us, be he Jew or Agnostic, Christian or Atheist, Buddhist or Freethinker, to believe or disbelieve, to worship or not to worship, to keep silent, according to his own conscience, uncoerced and unrestrained by government. It is conceivable that these school boards, or even all school boards, might eventually find it impossible to administer a system of religious exercise during school hours in such a way as to meet this constitutional standard—in such a way as completely to be

---

19. *Id.* at 313.
20. *Id.*
21. *Id.* at 316.
22. *See* Smith, *Justice Potter Stewart: A Contemporary Jurist's View of Religious Liberty,* 59 N. DAK. L. REV. 183, 195–96 (1983), for a discussion of this right/privilege distinction as it relates to Justice Stewart's opinion in *Schempp.*

free from any kind of official coercion of those who do not affirmatively want to participate. But I think we must not assume that school
boards so lack the qualities of inventiveness and good will as to make
impossible the achievement of that goal.[23]

Thus, Stewart may have been indicating that religious exercise is a right
as opposed to a mere privilege, even in the public-school context. He
may have been arguing that the right is peculiarly subject to regulation
based on the school's legitimate interests. I do not object to this, so long
as it is understood that the state's interests must be genuinely compelling
and must be clearly supported by evidence.

While the majority found coercion in cases like *Schempp,* as a matter of law, Stewart required proof of coercion (i.e., proof that another
party's right of free exercise was being abridged) before he would invalidate procedures designed by a local school board to facilitate the exercise
of an individual's religious convictions in the public-school context. Since
in *Schempp,* like *Engel,* it was unclear whether there was actual proof
of such coercion, Justice Stewart would have remanded the case for the
taking of further evidence on the issue of coercion.

With the emphasis on secularity in the primary-purpose and effect
tests elaborated by the majority in *Schempp,* it is generally assumed that
the Court refused to confine the *Schempp* and *Engel* decisions to prohibiting only vocal prayers or other specific devotional activities or
modes of worship prescribed or composed by the states for use in the
schools. Even given that assumption, however, it is unclear how far the
Court intended to go in the direction of prohibiting religious exercises in
the public schools. Justice Clark took care to emphasize that the
Schempp case was distinguishable from the *Zorach* decision (a case
permitting off-campus released-time programs) on the ground that: (1)
the activities in *Schempp* were curricular, as opposed to extracurricular,
activities; (2) the activities were held in school buildings; and (3) the
teacher participated in and supervised the activities. Having distinguished
the *Zorach* decision in this manner, it remains unclear how the Court
might rule in a case in which in the future one or more of these distinguishing factors are not present.

The requirement articulated by Justice Clark in *Schempp* that "to
withstand the strictures of the Establishment Clause there must be a
secular legislative purpose and a primary effect that neither advances
nor inhibits religion"[24] is sufficiently general to leave the Court much

---

23. *Id.* at 319–20.
24. *Id.* at 222 (emphasis added).

flexibility or discretion. The *Widmar* decision, which is discussed at length in Chapter 10, clearly indicates that actual religious exercises in public buildings on the campus of a public university can survive attack on Establishment Clause grounds. The Court in *Widmar* recognized that the nondiscriminatory accommodation of student expression, among college or university students, is a legitimate secular purpose. How much further the Court might go toward acknowledging that the accommodation of religious exercise on a nondiscriminatory basis constitutes a proper secular purpose remains an open question, particularly in the elementary and secondary school context.

The primary-effect test is also flexible. The Court has emphasized that the government can neither advance *nor inhibit* religion. It is unclear nevertheless how the Court will treat the conflict that will necessarily arise in cases where free-exercise rights are limited by a state's effort to keep religious activity or practices out of the public sector. Certainly, the primary-effect test is amenable to a wide-ranging interpretation, insofar as the nonpreferential accommodation of religious exercise is concerned, because it precludes the advancement of religion by government and forbids the inhibiting of religious exercise by the government. To prevent a child from praying in public may inhibit that child in the exercise of his or her religion. To permit the child to pray might, however, be said to advance religion. The test needs clarification. Without a more principled explanation of the meaning or application of the prongs of the test, it threatens to be a source of ambiguous and inconsistent, perhaps even ad hoc, decision making.

The *Engel* and *Schempp* decisions were criticized by many religious organizations on the ground that the cases purged the public schools of all religious activity, thereby discriminating against religion. One might read the wall-of-separation rationale underlying those opinions to prove that all religious activity in public should be forbidden. However, such a strict reading of the *Engel* and *Schempp* decisions may be inaccurate and is certainly not the only plausible reading. Therefore, just as it is clear that the strict-separationist view is inconsistent with the intent of the framers and ratifiers of the First Amendment, it is also true that the holdings in *Engel* and *Schempp* are susceptible to an interpretation consistent with the pertinent constitutional history.

According to the Story view, the Court should have permitted voluntary prayer in *Engel* and the Bible-reading and recitation practices in *Schempp*. The proponents of the Story view believed that the First Amendment was designed to recognize nondenominational and tolerant Christianity as our national religion. The practice of reciting the nondenominational prayer, which was at issue in the *Engel* case, would not, therefore, have offended those espousing the Story view. In *Engel* there was a united effort, promoted by the government, to draft a prayer that would be consistent with Judeo-Christian principles common to most Americans, and there was also provision made for students to excuse themselves voluntarily from the practice if they found it to be offensive. Similarly, the Bible reading and recitation in the *Schempp* case would have been acceptable in all likelihood, because, when read without doctrinal commentary, the New Testament represents a source of common accord among Christians.

There were two problems present in the cases, however, that would have concerned even proponents of the Story position. They would have been concerned with the coercion or nonvoluntariness issue raised by Justice Stewart in his dissents, and they might have been concerned with the choice of the edition of the Bible used in the school districts in the *Schempp* case.

A proponent of the Story view would have been concerned with the possibility that young children might be coerced to engage in the Bible reading and prayer. Story noted that only those practices that were tolerant of minority religions would be permitted. It might be argued that, as implemented, the voluntary excusal provisions failed to satisfy this demand. Since young and impressionable children were involved, it might be argued that peer pressure from children of majority faiths might operate to coerce minority children to go along with the practices of the majority rather than face ridicule by excusing themselves. The very fact that they would have to excuse themselves affirmatively would possibly place undue pressure on them to conform to the religious views of the majority. Such attention from teachers and their peers might very well coerce young children into engaging in a religious practice inconsistent with their religious beliefs. Young children generally want to please their teachers and their peers. Therefore, even though they could excuse themselves from engaging in such practices, they might be very reluctant to do so on the ground that they might offend their peers and teachers. Under any circumstances, the potential for such peer pressure might force the minority children to make a difficult choice between their religion and pleasing their peers and teachers.

Therefore, just as the issue of coercion concerned Justice Stewart, it might raise questions under the Story view. However, it is likely that those espousing the Story view would have agreed with Stewart and would have permitted prayer recitation. As was the case with Stewart, it is likely that they would have wanted some proof or substantive evidence of coercion. Furthermore, it is questionable whether the Storyites would oppose the practice, even if there were the potential for coercion present, because they would emphasize that concentrating on the issue of coercion might limit the majority from recognizing their basic Christianity. Absent proof of actual coercion, minorities would rarely win such a balancing test. Their rights would seldom outweigh those of the majority. It is doubtful in this second sense, therefore, that the manner in which Story used the word toleration would limit implicit coercion of the type discussed in *Engel* and *Schempp*. However, the toleration limitation might be invoked effectively where coercion was intentional or explicit and susceptible to proof. Thus, like Stewart, proponents of the Story view would, in all likelihood, require proof of actual coercion before finding the prayer and Bible reading unconstitutional.

There would also have been problems for Storyites raised by the peculiar facts of the *Schempp* case. The school districts had encouraged Bible reading and recitation, but difficulties arose over what version of the Bible should be used. Catholics prefer the Douay version, Jews reject the New Testament, and even Protestants split as to which of many translations of the Bible is preferable. Given these differences, which are themselves often rooted in doctrine, the Bible reading and recitation involved in *Schempp* raised problems of a theological nature. The Bible is not easily susceptible to nondenominational use in a Christian or a Judeo-Christian sense. Whichever version is selected, there will be potential doctrinal objections by one group or another.

It is possible that such differences would make the Bible reading unacceptable to proponents of the Story view on the ground that it was not representative of nondenominational Christianity. However, as was the case with the prayer recitation in *Engel*, it is unlikely that a Storyite would have to reach this issue under the facts in *Schempp*. First, there is little evidence of substantial disagreement over the verses being recited. Second, even if there were such disagreement, the Court, if it adhered to the Story view, would have had to write the opinion in such a way as to encourage the practice of nondenominational Bible reading. Furthermore, the Court would also need to stress the Christian nature of the Republic, although it is clear that this issue points to one of the weaknesses Madison saw in the Story position: the Storyite would continually be faced with deciding what is Christian for such purposes. In other words, in cases like *Schempp,* the Court would have to decide repeatedly the issue of which version or translation of the Bible is Christian for purposes of public recitation.

While the Story view would likely permit the Court to uphold the prayer practice in *Engel* and the Bible reading in *Schempp,* application of the Madisonian view would not. The Madisonian view would permit state accommodation or perhaps even facilitation of religious exercise in the public sector, so long as the state acted in a nonpreferential manner and provided that, in doing so, it refrained from adopting any mode of worship or doctrine as its own. Because of this restriction, both the prayer practice in *Engel* and the Bible reading and recitation in *Schempp* would be impermissible. The voluntary-prayer practice in *Engel,* whereby the students were permitted to recite a state-composed prayer, would be unacceptable for at least two reasons: (1) it would tend to prefer one religion or group of religions over another; and (2) it effectively adopted a mode of worship or a particular devotional exercise as its own.

The practice in *Engel* was preferential in that it favored traditional Judeo-Christian religions. The prayer was an effort to combine or capture (or reduce to the lowest common denominator) the essence of basic Jewish, Catholic, and Protestant beliefs. It, therefore, excluded or depreciated other less-traditional religious beliefs not represented in or susceptible to such a reduction. As Madison indicated in his *Memorial and Remonstrance,* he would not permit the state to prefer any religion or group of religions over another.

The state-composed prayer also constituted an effort on the part of the state to prescribe a mode of worship or form of devotional exercise for use in its public schools. Such an effort would have been reprehensible to Madison, who felt that, while the state could accommodate self-initiated religious activity, it could not adopt any particular mode of worship as its own. Adopting a written prayer, even a basically nondenominational one, would be offensive, because the form used, an oral prayer, and the substance attached to the form, the doctrine included in the words of the prayer, collectively constituted the adoption of a mode of worship by the state, something Madison felt that the state could not do under the Establishment Clause of the First Amendment.

It should be noted, however, that Madison would not go to the same extreme as the contemporary strict separationist, who would say that no religious exercise may be permitted in public. It is likely, therefore, that Madison would have pointed out in his reasoning in a case like *Engel* that it was the fact that the state had composed a prayer for recitation in the public schools that was improper, not the desire of the district to accommodate individual religious exercise in the public sector.

Madison similarly would have found the Bible reading and recitation in *Schempp* to be unconstitutional. It would have been improper under his view because, while the Bible is a text used by many religions, it is rejected by others. Furthermore, even among groups accepting the Bible there are substantial differences as to what version or translation is appropriate. The Bible-reading and recitation practice would be unacceptable when it was prescribed or initiated by the state. Madison would permit an individual to read the Bible or other religious texts at an appropriate time, but he would not permit the state, through its teachers or administrators, to prescribe the use of the Bible or Bible reading as a devotional exercise. Such a practice in his view would prefer religions that believe the Bible to be the Word of God. It would, therefore, constitute the implicit adoption by the state of a given mode of worship or form of devotion rooted in the Bible. Thus, while Madison would have extolled the virtue of encouraging the exercise of conscience, he certainly would have drawn the line where the state sought to further a given mode or form of worship in preference to other forms of religious exercise.

It should be clear that the Court in *Engel* and *Schempp* could have decided the cases in diametrically different ways, depending on the view espoused. The Court could decide the case under either the Madisonian or the Story view and maintain the fidelity to the history as a matter of legitimate originalist constitutional analysis. There are those who might, therefore, argue that the applicable history is meaningless and should be disregarded, because it could lead to differing dispositions of cases as important as *Engel* and *Schempp*. Such a view is naive.

To say that the Court could rely legitimately on the history and come to either one of two differing dispositions of a case does not render that history meaningless. Rather, it merely delineates the broad area or latitude within which legitimate constitutional decision making can be rendered. There are still limits to the reasoning that may be used to support a decision and the realm within which legitimate decision making may take place. For example, the Court's decision in the *Engel* case could be supported in an originalist sense by invoking the Madisonian view. However, some of Justice Black's language and reasoning in the opinon for the Court based on the so-called wall of separation could not be supported under either the Madisonian or the Story view. The framers and ratifiers of the First Amendment never espoused a view to the effect that religious exercise must be kept completely out of the public sector.

Certainly, therefore, while it is conceded that the application of the approach will often provide the Court with broad latitude in deciding whether a given practice is constitutional, that latitude is limited, both in terms of permissible reasoning and in terms of the scope of the decision itself. The thought of giving the Court such broad latitude may be disconcerting to those who want definite, black-and-white answers to every problem, because the history, which is based on a compromise between two very different views, is not amenable to a simplistic, technical application in every case. Simplicity of the type afforded by the strict-separationist rationale ignores or depreciates either the Establishment Clause value, prohibiting excessive or improper governmental activity in religious matters, or the free-exercise right to live in accordance with one's religious convictions. Values must be balanced; simplistic legal formulae often fail to be amenable to such balancing. The history of the intent of the framers and ratifiers of the First Amendment only occasionally may be clearly dispositive in a given case, but it is always helpful, both in terms of establishing appropriate limits in cases and in terms of recognizing the appropriate latitude that ought to be given to the Court in cases like *Engel* and *Schempp*.

We are left to inquire, therefore, whether the *Engel* and *Schempp* cases were decided correctly. If by correct one means legitimate in a constitutional sense, the answer is yes, because the Court's decisions were supportable under the Madisonian view, although they were in all likelihood unsupportable under the Story view. However, even though the Court's decisions in *Engel* and *Schempp* do conform to the Madisonian view, it might be argued that the Court should have deferred to the state legislature's decision in both of those cases, because the state's action in permitting the practices was also legitimate as an historical matter under the Story view. Whether the Court ought to defer to legislative judgment in that manner is both a question of policy and, in some measure, a question of whether or not the Court's decision was legitimate according to originalist analysis.

It may be argued with substantial force that the Court ought to defer to legislative determinations regarding constitutional issues at both the state and federal levels provided that those determinations are within the limits set by original-intent analysis. In other words, when the legislature has acted in a manner consistent with either the Story or the Madisonian view, the Court should exercise restraint and defer to that legislative determination. In *Engel* and *Schempp,* for example, it could be argued that the Court should have deferred to the legislative determinations regarding Bible reading and prayer recitation in public schools, provided those legislative determinations fell within the limits set by the Story and Madisonian views.

Despite the strength of this argument, I disagree. Nevertheless, as an originalist, I remain troubled by the fact that the framers intended that the judiciary would intervene and invalidate a legislative determination only when it was clear that the legislative act was unconstitutional. However, the framers and ratifiers of the Bill of Rights were equally concerned with protecting individual rights from governmental intrusion and limitation. These two principles, judicial deference and judicial protection of individual rights, can come into conflict. However, the individual-rights limitation and the judicial-deference notion can be reconciled by permitting the Court to disregard its mandate to defer to the legislature to the limited extent that it does so to further individual rights and provided further that it can do so without rendering a decision that would fall outside the limits set by originalist analysis. For example, if the Court refuses to defer when such deference would limit an individual's right of free exercise, such a refusal would be legitimate, provided that the Court's decision would also be supportable on originalist grounds. The Court would not, however, be acting in a legitimate manner if it refused to defer to the legislative determination when that determination was consistent with the framers' intent and also furthered individual rights to a degree at least equal to the extent to which the Court's nondeferential decision would further such rights. This constitutes a ratchet-like analysis—the Court need not defer when nondeference would do more to further individual rights than deference, but it must defer in instances in which deference would arguably yield as positive a result in terms of individual liberty as would nondeference.

There are two other arguments that support nondeference, at least in instances in which such nondeference would further individual liberty. First, there is need for uniformity in constitutional decision making. If the Court were to defer to differing state legislative determinations regarding constitutional issues, our Bill of Rights would become a mishmash, with the extent of fundamental rights varying according to geography. Also, the Court might be justified in refusing to defer to a state or congressional determination when that determination is contrary to existing precedent. Adherence to precedent contributes not only to uniformity but also to certainty, two matters of significant concern in ensuring that individual rights are protected. If a party is unaware of his or her rights because they are variable, the likelihood of such rights being exercised or vindicated is diminished. Additionally, it is arguable that legislative refusal to follow the Court's precedent is a legislative repudiation of their responsibility to abide by the Constitution. Of course, if existing judicial precedent is inconsistent with the limits set by originalist analysis, it is also arguable that the legislature would be justified in repudiating the Court's determination. However, even when judicial precedent appears to be inconsistent with the applicable indicia of intent, the legislature would do well to act circumspectly, just as the Court should act with the utmost care in refusing to defer to similar legislative determinations.

Third, the legislative branches of government have not always taken their constitutional obligations as seriously as they should. They have often looked first to politics and only then, if at all, to the constitutional implications of their determinations. Perhaps, given the democratic and political nature of legislative bodies, it would be unduly idealistic to expect the legislative body to do otherwise. Even if this is the case, it only serves to strengthen further the view that the Court is the institution best suited to act as the final arbiter in constitutional matters, particularly those dealing with individual rights. When rights conflict with majoritarian whim and fancy or governmental efficiency, judicial deference to legislative activity should not be mandated, even if the legislative determination falls within the limits set by original-intent analysis, provided that the Court's decision is equally supportable on originalist grounds. Determining whether or not a judicial decision is correct, therefore, is often a difficult question both as a matter of legitimacy (is the Court acting within its intended or legitimate scope of authority?) and as a matter of policy (is the Court's decision prudent?). In either instance, however, I would argue that one's analysis must begin with the original intent and then proceed with an examination of the various policy considerations within the limits set by the intent analysis. Originalist analysis may offer guidance on the institutional issue (whether the Court should defer?) and on the individual-rights issue, but it rarely resolves them in difficult cases like *Engel* and *Schempp*.

I believe that both *Engel* and *Schempp* would have been unacceptable to Madison, and I believe that Madison's view is preferable to the Story view as a policy matter. Particularly in the 1970s and 1980s, with growing recognition of many nontraditional and nonorthodox religions, the practices in *Engel* and *Schempp* would be offensive to a substantial minority in our nation. Those minority religions ought to be accorded equal treatment. Religions can be treated equally without eliminating all individual religious exercise from the public sector.

Efforts to salvage such practices under the tolerant Story view would prove difficult and unappealing. Story would require a unifying of the Christian tradition, and yet Christian traditions differ substantially. Because of this, we would be left with a least common doctrinal denominator or perhaps very little doctrine at all. Under Story's view, as a matter of practice, doctrinal differences would have to be eliminated, leaving only a common core of beliefs that would, at best, be trivial and, at worst, heretical or meaningless for many if not most religious sects. It would be much better to emphasize individual efforts to give expression fully to one's conscience or beliefs, which would be the position taken under the Madisonian view, than to try to reduce religious beliefs to a common denominator, particularly in a pluralistic world characterized by religious sects with divergent beliefs.

There is another reason to support the *Engel* and *Schempp* decisions: stare decisis. Stare decisis is the legal doctrine that requires courts to adhere to decisions laid down in prior cases unless those decisions contravene the Constitution or principles of justice. Courts do not have to abide by the reasoning of prior courts, and in our case they should not adhere to the strict-separationist reasoning that arguably underlies the *Engel* and *Schempp* decisions. However, courts ought to abide by the actual or ultimate decision in a prior case unless that decision is unconstitutional or unjust. The decisions in *Engel* and *Schempp* are constitutionally acceptable under an application of the Madisonian view. They are also in keeping with principles of justice. Both the Bible-reading and prayer practices fail to treat all religions equally. They prefer traditional or orthodox religions, while demeaning less orthodox religions. They also tend to get the state involved in promoting doctrine rather than in merely facilitating individual religious exercise.

Furthermore, since the practices in both *Engel* and *Schempp* constitute efforts to find a basis for religious agreement among differing sects, the practices, as finally permitted, tend to weaken or trivialize rather than strengthen religious exercise. Deeper doctrinal matters, on which religious groups differ, often imbue religious exercises with much of their meaning. Permitting or promoting nondenominational religious activity reduces religion to a common denominator that threatens to deprive it of much of its vitality and meaning. Rather than promoting or accommodating religious activity, implementation of such a policy might lend itself to demeaning religion by depriving it of much of the vitality inhering in its deeper doctrines, and it might also lull the government into believing it had done all that is necessary to accommodate religious activity in the public sector. It would be better to accommodate individuals in their religious exercises, rather than endeavoring to promote particular, state-initiated, nondenominational religious activity.

For these reasons, I believe that the *Engel* and *Schempp* cases were decided appropriately. It is clear, however, that the Court could have decided otherwise and still been within its legitimate constitutional authority, in an originalist sense. Furthermore, it can be argued with some force that the Court ought to defer to determinations by its democratic counterparts, Congress and the Executive, and to determinations by the states. However, I am uneasy with such a prospect, because in the area of religious liberty particularly, the democratic majority has a well-earned reputation for demeaning minority religious sects and practices or at least treating them with a lack of equanimity.[25]

Finally, if the Court were to defer to decisions by state governments in cases like *Engel* and *Schempp*, there would be little uniformity in First Amendment law. Some states would follow the Story view, permitting practices like those involved in *Engel* and *Schempp*, and other states

---

25. Therefore, in part, I agree with Michael Perry and other rights-based theorists who assert that the Court has a special role in protecting individual rights, particularly as against incursions by the majority. *See, e.g.,* M. Perry, THE CONSTITUTION, THE COURTS AND HUMAN RIGHTS (1982).

would follow the Madisonian view, permitting different sorts of religious practices in the public sector. Such a mishmash could only weaken the First Amendment. A common complaint about the current Court is that it often lacks consistency and uniformity. Deference to state decision makers in the area of the First Amendment would only increase the uncertainty involved in exercising one's rights. We would do far better to follow the Madisonian standard, which is solicitous of individual rights and duly suspicious about governmental promotion of religion.

9

Meditation and Silent Prayer in the Public Schools: The Jaffree Case

Many states have adopted statutes permitting a moment of silent meditation or a moment of silent meditation or prayer in their public schools.[1] Such statutes are a response to the sentiment of the public and state legislators that students should be permitted and perhaps even encouraged to reflect silently upon religious or other matters during the school day. Not surprisingly, given the volatile nature of the prayer issue itself, these statutes have engendered a strong response from friend and foe alike.

In *Engel v. Vitale,*[2] the Court did not expressly prohibit silent meditation or prayer in the public schools. There was no need to do so because no such issue was before the Court. In fact, formal statutes providing for moments of silence for reflection, meditation, or prayer are of recent origin.[3] However, while the Court did not have to confront the silent prayer issue in *Engel* or *Schempp,* a door was opened in the latter case when, in his concurrence, Justice William Brennan noted that, while it was generally improper for the state to use religious means to promote secular ends, the state could not be prohibited from permitting "daily recitation of the Pledge of Allegiance (with its reference to God),

---

1. *See* L. Pfeffer, RELIGION, STATE AND THE BURGER COURT, 107 (1984); Note, *Daily Moments of Silence in Public Schools: A Constitutional Analysis,* 58 N.Y.U. L. REV. 364 (1983).
2. 370 U.S. 421 (1962).
3. *See* Note, *supra* note 1, at 407–08 app. (partial listing of such statutes).

or even the observance of a moment of reverent silence."[4] Thus, while after *Engel* and *Schempp,* state legislators were on notice that they and other government officials were precluded from composing prayers for recitation in the public schools, they were also led to believe that the moments of silent meditation (and, possibly even prayer) were permissible. It is not surprising, therefore, that in the twenty years after *Engel* and *Schempp,* nearly half of the state legislatures passed legislation permitting a moment of silence in their public-school systems.[5] These statutes varied in a number of particulars. Some statutes expressly provided for a moment of silent meditation, while others provided for a moment of silent meditation or prayer. Additionally, most statutes were not mandatory; they did not require that school districts have a moment of silence each day. Rather, they permitted school districts to decide, as a matter of their own discretion, whether or not they wanted to include a moment of silent meditation in their daily schedule.

Initially, those statutes were looked upon largely as harmless and sometimes trivial efforts to accommodate some public religious activity. However, as the strict-separationist rationale articulated in dicta in *Everson, Engel,* and *Schempp* became entrenched more solidly, attention turned to the issues of the moment of silent meditation and equal access. Opponents of public religious exercise turned their attention to the statutes allowing silent meditation or prayer, and the Supreme Court agreed ultimately to hear a case dealing with this issue in 1984, when it granted certiorari in the case of *Wallace v. Jaffree.*[6]

Court watchers concerned with the prayer issue awaited eagerly the *Jaffree* decision as the summer of 1985 approached. Finally, on 4 June 1985, the opinion was announced. The majority in *Jaffree* held that the Alabama statute authorizing a one-minute period of silence in public schools "for meditation or voluntary prayer" was unconstitutional because it violated the Establishment Clause of the First Amendment. In his opinion for the majority, Justice John Paul Stevens emphasized that the legislative purpose in passing the statute was improper, because it constituted an effort to endorse religion. Four justices joined in Stevens's opinion, although one of those justices, Justice Lewis F. Powell, Jr., wrote a separate opinion. Justice Sandra D. O'Connor, who voted with the majority, did not join in Stevens's opinion and concurred only in the judgment, and each of the three dissenters wrote separate opinions denouncing the majority's decision and reasoning.

---

4. Abington School Dist. v. Schempp, 374 U.S. 203, 281 (Brennan, J., concurring).

5. Note, *supra* note 1, at 407–08 app.

6. 105 S. Ct. 2479 (1985), *cert. granted,* 104 S. Ct. 1704 (1984).

After a close look at the *Jaffree* decision, one is struck by the fact that it closed only a few doors. Since Alabama's statute was laden with its own peculiar and rather egregious set of facts, the Court in *Jaffree* refused to reach very far even in its dicta. Many issues were left open. For example, the issue of whether a moment of silent meditation or perhaps even a moment of silent meditation or prayer might be constitutional, in a case presenting less offensive facts, remains unsettled. A close reading of *Jaffree* is in order, therefore, to determine the extent of its impact on the public-prayer issue in general and the meditation-or-prayer issue in particular.

In the remainder of this chapter I will: (1) examine the factual development of the *Jaffree* case, tracing its development in the lower courts; (2) examine the opinions of the justices of the Supreme Court in the case; (3) examine how *Jaffree* would have been decided under the Story and Madisonian views; and (4) articulate some of the policy considerations arising in regard to the meditation or prayer issue, in considering how such cases ought to be decided.

THE FACTUAL DEVELOPMENT OF THE JAFFREE CASE

In 1978, the State of Alabama passed a statute, § 16–1–20, that provided that

> At the commencement of the first class each day in the first through the sixth grades in all public schools, the teacher in charge of the room in which such class is held shall announce that a period of silence, not to exceed one minute in duration, shall be observed for meditation, and during any such period silence shall be maintained and no activities engaged in.[7]

Thereafter, in 1981, the legislature added § 16–1–20.1 that provided that

> At the commencement of the first class of each day in all grades in all public schools, the teacher in charge of the room in which each such class is held may announce that a period of silence not to exceed one minute in duration shall be observed for meditation or voluntary prayer, and during any such period no other activities shall be engaged in.[8]

The second statute added the language "or prayer" to the silent-meditation language of § 16–1–20, and also provided that the teacher may, as opposed to shall, announce the period, thereby permitting the teacher to act in her discretion.

---

7. ALABAMA CODE, § 16–1–20 (1978).
8. ALABAMA CODE, § 16–1–20.1 (1981).

Throughout this time, it was also common practice in the public schools of Alabama for teachers to lead their students in reciting vocal prayers, including blessings on food and the recitation of the Lord's Prayer. Ultimately, it was these vocal prayer recitations that led Ishmael Jaffree to bring his action.

On 28 May 1982, Jaffree filed a complaint on behalf of his three minor children, who were attending public schools in Mobile, Alabama. The complaint alleged that the school board had violated his children's First and Fourteenth Amendment rights by permitting regularly scheduled religious services or observances, vocal prayers, to occur in those schools. In seeking to enjoin the school from engaging in those practices, Mr. Jaffree asserted that his children's rights had been violated on a daily basis, because they were being led in the recitation of prayers by their teachers despite his objections. After the suit was filed, but before it was decided by the district court, the Alabama state legislature enacted additional legislation permitting public-school teachers and professors to lead willing students in the recitation of a state-composed prayer at the beginning of each school day. This legislation provided that

> From henceforth, any teacher or professor in any public educational institution within the state of Alabama, recognizing that the Lord God is one, at the beginning of any homeroom or any class, may pray, may lead willing students in prayer, or may lead the willing students in the following prayer to God:
> Almighty God, You alone are our God. We acknowledge You as the Creator and Supreme Judge of the world. May Your justice, Your truth, and Your peace abound this day in the hearts of our countrymen, in the councils of our government, in the sanctity of our homes and in the classrooms of our schools in the name of our Lord.[9]

In enacting this legislation, Alabama confirmed by statute the existing practice of vocal prayer recitations that had come to be a common occurrence in its public schools. The statute provided for recitation of an express prayer, while implicitly recognizing existing practices. In response to this legislative action, Jaffree amended his complaint to challenge the constitutionality both of this statute and of the prayer practices at his children's school. From the outset, he noted that his major concern centered on the state-composed or teacher-led prayer recitations and not on the meditation practice.[10]

---

9. ALABAMA CODE, § 16–1–20.2 (1982).
10. *Jaffree,* 105 S. Ct. at 2483.

The district court held an evidentiary hearing on 2 August 1982, to determine whether it should grant the Jaffrees' motion for a preliminary injunction. At the hearing, the primary sponsor of the silent-meditation or prayer bill (§ 16–1–20.1) testified, noting that the bill constituted an "effort to return voluntary prayer to our public schools...it is a beginning and a step in the right direction."[11] Within a week after this hearing, the court granted the Jaffrees' motion, enjoining the state from engaging in the public-prayer practices, on the ground that the Jaffrees had established a substantial likelihood that they would prevail on the merits.[12]

A four-day trial was held in November of that same year. In its findings of fact, the district court found that the Jaffree children's teachers had repeatedly led their classes in the recitation of vocal prayers, despite objections on the part of Mr. Jaffree. Nevertheless, in his conclusions of law for the court, Judge Brevard Hand dismissed their case on the ground that "the Establishment Clause of the First Amendment to the Constitution does not prohibit the state from establishing a religion."[13] In refusing to follow Supreme Court precedent relative to the incorporation of the Establishment Clause, Judge Hand challenged the highest court of the land. Hand no doubt reasoned that, since he had taken an oath to abide by the Constitution, he was bound to follow the constitutional history as he interpreted it. However, there are a number of very strong arguments against such action: (1) under Article III of the Constitution, lower courts must follow the decisions of the Supreme Court[14]; (2) as a prudential matter, if lower courts refuse to abide by the decisions of the Supreme Court, uniformity and certainty would be sacrificed, and the Constitution would lose much of its force as a consistent and unifying document; and (3) Hand's interpretation of the history was not conclusive. Since from an originalist perspective the history regarding incorporation is susceptible to interpretation consistent with existing Supreme Court precedent, Hand's action was unacceptable. Both prudence, which dictates following precedent, and originalist constitutional theory render Judge Hand's opinion suspect.

Not surprisingly, within a matter of weeks after Judge Hand delivered his decision dismissing the Jaffrees' action, Justice Powell, serving in his capacity as circuit justice for the Eleventh Circuit, entered a stay

---

11. *Id.*

12. *Id.*

13. *See* Jaffree v. Board of School Comm'rs., 554 F. Supp. 1105, 1128 (1983).

14. Article III of the federal Constitution states in pertinent part: "The judicial power of the United States, shall be vested in one *supreme* Court, and in such *inferior* courts as the Congress may from time to time ordain and establish." U.S. Const. Art. III, § 1 (emphasis added).

which prevented the district court from dissolving the preliminary injunction that had been entered initially. In his brief opinion as circuit justice, Powell noted that the *Engel* and *Schempp* cases were controlling, and that "unless and until this Court [the Supreme Court] reconsiders [those decisions], they appear to control this case. In my view, the district court was obligated to follow them. Similarly, my own authority as circuit justice is limited by controlling decisions of the full Court."[15] Having rejected both the reasoning and the holding of Judge Hand, Powell followed precedent and gave new life to the Jaffrees' claims.

The Eleventh Circuit Court of Appeals consolidated the two related cases that had been decided by Hand at the lower-court level and heard appellate argument on the issues raised in those cases. After argument, the court of appeals formally reversed Judge Hand, rejecting his nonincorporation argument outright. At some length, the court of appeals explained why it rejected Hand's historical arguments and his misapplication of the stare decisis doctrine, which requires lower courts to follow precedent set forth by higher courts. In support of their view regarding stare decisis, the judges noted a statement from Justice William Rehnquist in another context to the effect that "unless we wish anarchy to prevail within the federal judicial system, a precedent of this [Supreme] Court must be followed by the lower federal courts no matter how misguided the judges of those courts may think it to be."[16] Having rejected Hand's reasoning, the court of appeals held that the religious activities or practices in the classroom violated the Establishment Clause of the First Amendment, as made applicable to the states through the Fourteenth Amendment. The Jaffrees had once again prevailed. The battle was not over yet, however.

Alabama's next move was to obtain a rehearing en banc, a hearing before the judges of the Eleventh Circuit Court of Appeals as a whole. The initial decision had been rendered in the customary fashion by a three-judge panel, and the state sought a hearing before a larger group of judges capable of reversing the original decision. The petition for a rehearing en banc was rejected, although there was a strong dissent by four judges, who argued that the circuit court should reconsider the panel's decision insofar as § 16–1–20.1 (the prayer-or-meditation statute) was concerned.

After losing before the first panel and after having its petition for a rehearing denied, the state filed a petition for certiorari, seeking to have

---

15. Jaffree v. Board of School Comm'rs., 459 U.S. 1314, 1316 (Powell, Circuit Justice 1983).

16. Jaffree v. Wallace, 705 F. 2d 1526, 1532 (11th Cir. 1983).

the Supreme Court hear the case. Petitions for certiorari are discretionary and are granted only, as a matter of tradition, when four justices
agree that the case merits a hearing. Thousands of certiorari petitions
are filed each term, but the Court traditionally agrees to hear only 100
to 150 of them.

In its petition, the State of Alabama sought review of the entire
decision of the court of appeals. The solicitor general of the United
States also filed a petition for certiorari on the part of the United States.
The solicitor general's petition was limited to the issue of whether
§ 16–1–20.1 was constitutional. On 2 April 1984, the Supreme Court
announced that

> In [*Jaffree*] probable jurisdiction is noted limited to Question 1 in
> the jurisdictional statements. The cases are consolidated and a total of
> one hour is allotted for oral argument. The judgment with respect to
> the other issues presented by the appeals is affirmed.[17]

Justice Stevens concurred in this grant, emphasizing his understanding
that the Court had "limited argument to the question of whether Ala.
Code § 16–1–20.1 is invalid as repugnant to the Establishment Clause,
applicable to the states under the Fourteenth Amendment."[18] In effect,
the Court agreed to hear the meditation-or-prayer issue, as requested by
the solicitor general, and rejected Alabama's effort to have the other
issues decided. Not only did the Court refuse to hear the other issues,
but it also stressed that "the [court of appeals] judgment with respect to
the other issues presented by the [Alabama] appeals is affirmed."

Mr. Jaffree had commenced his action in the desire to put an end
to recitation of prayers in the public schools in Alabama. The Court on
20 April once again effectively affirmed its decision in *Engel* relative to
prayer recitations. Jaffree had won a final victory on the issues of primary concern to him, but a final issue remained, the issue of whether
the Alabama silent-meditation-or-voluntary-prayer statute was constitutional. The stage was now set for the Court's determination of an issue
that had been thought to be trivial originally but was now at the center
of attention in the public debate.

The Supreme Court and Silent Meditation or Prayer: An Analysis of the Opinions in Jaffree

Six months after hearing argument in *Jaffree,* the Court announced
its decision. Justice Stevens wrote for the Court and Justices William

---

17. 466 U.S. 924 (1984).
18. *Id.* at 925.

Brennan, Thurgood Marshall, Harry A. Blackmun, and Lewis Powell joined in his opinion, giving it the force of a majority opinion or decision for the Court. (Had only three justices joined in the opinion it would constitute a plurality opinion and would not be entitled to the same precedential weight accorded a majority opinion.) Powell, however, wrote a separate concurring opinion, and Justice O'Connor refused to join in the reasoning employed by Justice Stevens and wrote a separate opinion concurring only in the judgment of the Court. Chief Justice Warren Burger and Justices Byron R. White and William Rehnquist all wrote separate dissenting opinions. Understanding each of these opinions helps to paint a more complete picture of what the Court actually decided, what it left for future determination, and how it will decide in all likelihood future cases of a similar or related nature.

Justice Stevens's Opinion for the Court

Before examining the opinion of the Court in *Jaffree,* it should be noted that only five of the nine justices agreed with Justice Stevens's reasoning and that one of those justices, Lewis Powell, wrote a concurring opinion to clarify his views. Nevertheless, even if changes occur in the makeup of the Court or the slim majority in *Jaffree* otherwise begins to deteriorate, Stevens's opinion for the Court will be necessarily the starting point for any future departures from or clarifications of the basic direction outlined in that opinion.

The most significant part of Justice Stevens's opinion is the holding or decision itself, because future Courts theoretically are bound only by the decision and not by the language (dicta) or reasoning used to support that decision. In his opinion, Stevens held § 16–1–20.1 to be unconstitutional on the ground that it violated the Establishment Clause. It will be recalled that § 16–1–20.1 authorized a one-minute period of silence in the public schools "for meditation or voluntary silent prayer." Stevens concluded that the statute as adopted was "intended to convey a message of state-*approval* of prayer activities in the public schools."[19]

Justice Stevens examined the intent of the drafters of the Alabama statutes and the findings of the lower court in some depth in holding that the provision was unconstitutional. He noted that the only purpose articulated in support of the legislation in the record was Senator Donald G. Holmes's statement that the legislation was an "effort to return voluntary prayer" to the public schools. Indeed, Stevens emphasized that the state "did not present evidence of *any* secular purpose" for the statute,

---

19. Wallace v. Jaffree, 105 S. Ct. 2479, 2493 (1985) (emphasis added).

as it was required to do under the secular-purpose prong of the *Lemon* test applicable in cases raising Establishment Clause issues.[20] This first prong requires that state legislation that supports or accommodates religion or religious exercises must have a secular purpose. Stevens concluded that the statute was either enacted for no purpose at all (a contention that he dismissed) or for the sole purpose of "convey(ing) a message of state endorsement and promotion of prayer."[21]

Also of significance to Justice Stevens was the fact that, in 1978, Alabama had passed a statute, § 16–1–20, which provided for a period of silent meditation at the beginning of each school day. The only material addition in § 16–1–20.1, which was before the Court, was the language "or voluntary prayer." This fact, coupled with the testimony and findings below, led Stevens to conclude that the latter statute constituted an effort to demonstrate "state-approval of prayer activities."[22] For Stevens, and those justices joining with him, the Establishment Clause precluded such state sponsorship or endorsement of religious activity.

---

20. Lemon v. Kurtzman, 403 U.S. 602 (1971). In *Lemon,* a case dealing with the issue of aid to parochial schools, the Court set forth a three-part test: "First, the statute must have a secular legislative purpose; second, its principal or primary effect must be one that neither advances nor inhibits religion...; finally, the statute must not foster 'an excessive government entanglement with religion.'" *Id.* at 612–13. *See also* Chapter 11 *infra* for additional discussion regarding the status of the *Lemon* test. However, with regard to the secular-purpose prong, in Mueller v. Allen, 463 U.S. 388 (1983), a case in which the Court upheld state income tax deductions to parents of children attending sectarian and nonsectarian schools, the Court noted that:

> Under our prior decisions, governmental assistance programs have consistently survived this [secular purpose] inquiry even when they have run afoul of other aspects of the *Lemon* framework. This reflects, at least in part, our reluctance to attribute unconstitutional motives to the states, particularly when *a plausible secular purpose* for the state's program may be discerned from the face of the statute.

Id. at 394 (emphasis added). *See also* Grand Rapids School Dist. v. Ball, 105 S. Ct. 3216 (1985); and Aguilar v. Felton, 105 S. Ct. 3232 (1985), two recent aid cases decided by the Court. In each of those cases, the Court refused to hold that the statutes in question, which provided substantial aid to sectarian schools, violated the secular-purpose prong of the *Lemon* test. However, in both cases, the Court did hold that the aid programs were unconstitutional because they failed to satisfy the second, primary effect, portion of the *Lemon* test. Thus, while the secular-purpose prong can be satisfied typically with the showing of a plausible secular purpose, a litigant would also have to prove that the primary effect of the statute neither "advanced *nor* inhibited" religion.

21. *Jaffree,* 105 S. Ct. at 2491.

22. *Id.* at 2493.

Justice Stevens's emphasis on the peculiar facts of the *Jaffree* case serves to limit the force of the decision as precedent in subsequent cases dealing with similar statutes passed under different circumstances. The decision does not preclude a school district from adopting a meditation practice, like that envisioned under § 16–1–20, when prayer is not specifically noted or mentioned. In fact, a majority of the Court implied that such meditation practices are constitutional. Additionally, even some meditation-or-prayer statutes may be constitutional after *Jaffree*. Apparently, the critical issue in such a case is whether, in passing the statute, the government "intends to convey a message of endorsement or approval of [the prayer practice]."

Upon examining the facts of the *Jaffree* case, it was clear to Justice Stevens and the majority that Alabama was endorsing religion. However, it does not follow that all meditation-or-prayer statutes would constitute efforts on the part of the state to endorse religion. It is conceivable that such a statute might be passed in an effort to encourage meditation, reflection, or prayer on the part of the students, without discriminating against or favoring religious expression. For Stevens and a majority of the Court, the Alabama statute did not constitute a tolerant, nondiscriminatory effort to encourage individual meditation, reflection, or prayer on the part of the students; rather, it was a thinly veiled attempt to promote school prayer. Finally, given Justice Rehnquist's strong dissent, which relied heavily upon historical analysis, and the Court's recent decisions in *Marsh v. Chambers*[23] and *Lynch v. Donnelly*,[24] Stevens was compelled to deal with the historical data related to the framing of the religion clauses. Specifically, he had to confront Joseph Story's position, as raised in Rehnquist's dissenting opinion. Stevens noted:

> At one time it was thought that this right merely proscribed the preference of on Christian sect over another, but would not require equal respect for the conscience of the infidel, the atheist, or the adherent of a non-Christian faith such as Mohammedism or Judaism. But when the underlying principle has been examined in the crucible of litigation, the Court has unambiguously concluded that the individual freedom of conscience protected by the First Amendment embraces the right to select any religious faith or none at all. This conclusion derives support not only from the interest in respecting the individual's freedom of conscience, but also from the conviction that religious beliefs worthy of respect are the product of free and voluntary choice by the faithful, and from recognition of the fact that the political interest

---

23. Marsh v. Chambers, 463 U.S. 783 (1983) (the *Marsh* case is discussed in detail in Chapter 11, *infra).*

24. Lynch v. Donnelly, 465 U.S. 668 (1984).

in forestalling intolerance extends beyond intolerance among Christian sects—or even intolerance among "religions"—to encompass intolerance of the disbeliever and the uncertain.[25]

This brief bow to the history is inadequate. It is poor jurisprudence because Stevens fails to clarify his position relative to the appropriate weight to be given to historical data. By his statement, "at one time," and by his reference to "the crucible of [subsequent] litigation," he seems to relegate history to a secondary and insignificant position, without clearly articulating the theory of judicial review under which he is proceeding. The Court intuitively decides the case and then seeks authority, historical and otherwise, to support its decision. Such jurisprudence is inherently suspect. In footnote 38 of his opinion, Justice Stevens briefly cites Madison's *Memorial and Remonstrance* to support the proposition that the First Amendment should promote a broader right of conscience than that articulated by Justice Story in his *Commentaries*.[26] Had Stevens relied more heavily on the history, he would have discovered strong support for the broad right of conscience he seemed to advocate in his opinion. That he did not pursue the history a bit more energetically is surprising, because it would have added greater legitimacy to his decision.

Justice Powell's Concurrence

Justice Powell was the fifth member of the majority joining in the Stevens opinion. However, he felt it necessary to clarify further his views by writing a separate concurring opinion. Because Powell constituted the fifth and decisive vote in support of the majority opinion, his concurrence is particularly significant. It is important not only because it is helpful in ascertaining the kinds of arguments that might appeal to Powell in the future, but also because in a sense it becomes the least common denominator in defining the scope of the *Jaffree* opinion as precedent.

Justice Powell noted that he decided to write separately to respond to criticism of the *Lemon* test. He was afraid that criticism of the *Lemon*

---

25. *Jaffree,* 105 S. Ct. at 2488–89. Justice Stevens's reference to the interplay between the history and the role of precedent is interesting, although it is inadequately developed. He developed it a bit further in a talk he gave before the Federal Bar Association on 23 October 1985, in which he briefly discussed the *Jaffree* decision as well. *See Address* by Justice Stevens, before the Federal Bar Association, in Chicago (23 October 1985), as reprinted in 19 U.C.D. L. Rev. 15 (1985).

26. *See* Chapter 5, *supra,* for a discussion of the view expounded in Justice Story's *Commentaries.*

test "could encourage other courts to feel free to decide Establishment Clause cases on an *ad hoc* basis," because the test "is the only coherent test a majority of the Court has ever adopted."[27] For Powell, the *Lemon* test was necessary, at least until such time as a new principle or test had been accepted by a majority of the Court, to ensure consistency and uniformity in First Amendment jurisprudence and to avoid the chaos and unfairness that necessarily attend *ad hoc* decision making. However, he went a step further and outlined how the entire test applied in the case before the Court and how it might apply in the future.

He reiterated his agreement with the majority on the first prong of the *Lemon* test, the secular-purpose prong, which requires that legislation with religious implications have a secular purpose. He went a step further, though, in articulating what kinds of purposes might suffice under this first prong. In this regard, he noted that the purpose need not be exclusively secular, i.e., it might be partially religious and partially secular, and that the Court is and ought to be reluctant to attribute unconstitutional motives to a state when a plausible secular purpose may be discerned from the face of a statute. Despite these two limitations on the secular-purpose doctrine, as applied in cases like *Jaffree*, Justice Powell emphasized that "the record before us, however, makes clear that Alabama's purpose was solely religious in character."[28] There simply was no clear evidence offered as to a possible secular purpose. However, Powell did make it clear that he "would vote to uphold the Alabama statute (providing for meditation or prayer) if it also had a clear secular (as well as religious) purpose."[29]

In concluding his opinion, Justice Powell also touched on the other prongs of the *Lemon* test and declared that

> Although we do not reach the other two prongs of the *Lemon* test, I note that the "effect" of a straightforward moment-of-silence statute is unlikely to "advance or inhibit religion." [citation omitted] Nor would such a statute "foster an excessive entanglement with religion."[30]

While Justice Powell seems to imply, by a "straightforward moment-of-silence statute," that a statute that does not refer to prayer would be almost invariably acceptable, his opinion also might be read as supporting certain meditation-or-prayer statutes when they are adopted for secular as well as religious purposes. This lends support to the ar-

---

27. *Jaffree,* 105 S. Ct. at 2494 (Powell, J., concurring).
28. *Id.*
29. *Id.* at 2495.
30. *Id.* (citation omitted).

gument that the *Jaffree* decision does not, as a matter of precedent, preclude the possibility that either meditation or meditation-or-prayer statutes may be held to be constitutional in a future case, where such statutes are adopted for the purpose of accommodating meditation or reflection on matters of conscience, including, but not limited to, religious meditation or prayer.

Without dwelling at any length on historical material pertaining to the framing and ratification of the First Amendment, Justice Powell did reiterate his support for *Lynch* (the crèche case, in which the Court upheld the display of a crèche on public property, based on historical acceptance of that practice) and *Marsh* (the paid chaplain case, which was supported by similar historical practice) decisions, both of which were based almost entirely on historical analyses.

Justice O'Connor's Concurrence in the Judgment

While Justice O'Connor agreed with the majority that the Alabama meditation-or-voluntary-prayer statute was unconstitutional, she refused to join in the majority opinion written by Justice Stevens. Rather, she concurred in the judgment. In her opinion, O'Connor developed separate reasoning to support her conclusion that the Alabama meditation statute was unconstitutional.[31] Her opinion is significant for a couple of reasons. First, since she also voted to hold the Alabama statute unconstitutional, her position is important because she constitutes a possible fifth vote in a case in which the majority either breaks down or splits. Second, her opinion constitutes a candid and thoughtful effort to deal with the conflict between the values or purposes of the Free Exercise and Establishment clauses and may receive additional attention in the future.

Justice O'Connor asserts at the outset that application of the *Lemon* test has proven problematic, and she concludes that the test needs to be refined. She agrees with Justice Powell that a guiding principle is necessary in cases presenting a conflict between the Free Exercise and Establishment clauses to avoid the threat of *ad hoc* decision making. Nevertheless, she rejects the *Lemon* test as applied. She substitutes a principle or test of her own, in ascertaining whether the statute's purpose is valid. She inquires "whether the government's purpose is to endorse religion and whether the statute actually conveys a message of endorsement."[32] While this test does not appear on its face to differ substantially from the test

---

31. *Jaffree,* 105 S. Ct. at 2496 (O'Connor, J., concurring).
32. *Id.* at 2497.

applied by Stevens, it is worthwhile to examine the test to ascertain why O'Connor refused to join the majority opinion.

Despite her view that the Alabama statute did constitute an unlawful endorsement of religion under her test, Justice O'Connor noted that

> By mandating a moment of silence, a state does not necessarily endorse any activity that might occur during the period. [citation omitted] Even if a statute specifies that a student may choose to pray privately during a quiet moment, the state has not thereby encouraged prayer over other specified alternatives....The crucial question is whether the state has conveyed or attempted to convey the message that children should use the moment of silence for prayer.[33]

Specifically, Justice O'Connor concluded that "the Court holds only that Alabama has intentionally crossed the line between creating a quiet moment during which those so inclined may pray, and affirmatively endorsing the particular religious practice of prayer."[34] For O'Connor, this was a fine yet distinct line, discernible by application of her "endorsement" test.

It seems clear, upon a close reading of her opinion, that Justice O'Connor rejected the majority's test because she felt that it was potentially too restrictive of the right of free exercise. For her, the majority might be too quick to nullify the right of conscience, to be exercised in the public sector, where there was no actual evidence of endorsement by the state of a particular religious doctrine or practice.

In responding to the historical analysis in Justice Rehnquist's dissent, Justice O'Connor observed that historical precedent, particularly as it applied to religious activity in the public schools, simply did not exist when the framers drafted the First Amendment. She added, however, that

> This uncertainty as to the intent of the framers of the Bill of Rights does not mean we should ignore history for guidance on the role of religion in public education. The Court has not done so. [citation omitted] When the intent of the framers is unclear, I believe we must employ both history and reason in our analysis. The primary issue raised by Justice Rehnquist's dissent is whether the historical fact that our presidents have long called for public prayers of thanks should be dispositive on the constitutionality of prayer in public schools. I think not....Although history provides a touchstone for constitutional problems, the Establishment Clause concern for religious liberty is dispositive here.[35]

---

33. *Id.* at 2499 (citation omitted).
34. *Id.* at 2505.
35. *Id.* at 2503.

The primary difficulty with Justice O'Connor's historical approach is that she seems to imply that in engaging in originalist analysis the Court must determine whether a particular practice was, in fact, acceptable to the framers. While there is a sense in which this is what the Court has done in cases like *Marsh* (the legislative chaplaincy case discussed in Chapter 11), there is much more substance to originalist analysis of the sort used in this book and invoked by Justice Rehnquist in his dissent. Such an analysis provides a means of determining which principles imbue a given clause with its intended meaning. As such, an examination of pertinent historical data offers much more than examples of particular activities that were appropriate; it often discloses principles that stretch well beyond particular activities to define the kinds or classes of activities that are acceptable. Particular activities are evidence of principles; in this mode of analysis, they are generally not the goal of the investigation itself.

Chief Justice Burger's Dissent

The chief justice's dissenting opinion is brief. Nevertheless, Chief Justice Burger does raise a couple of points that deserve mention.

Burger, like Justice White, reads the majority opinion and Justice O'Connor's opinion as permitting a meditation statute but prohibiting a meditation-or-prayer statute.[36] This is not necessarily the case. Both the majority opinion and the concurrences are susceptible to a reading that would permit meditation-or-prayer statutes in instances when they are not accompanied by a tainted purpose, a purpose that is solely religious or endorsing specific religious practices.

Chief Justice Burger's point regarding the secular-purpose issue is a bit more telling, however. After noting that there is not a shred of evidence that the legislature as a whole shared the tainted motive of the sponsor, Mr. Holmes, in passing the statute, Burger noted that even Holmes offered a secular purpose for the legislation when he testified that, in introducing the statute, he wanted to clear up a widespread misunderstanding to the effect that children are prohibited from engaging in silent prayer during the meditation period. Furthermore, the chief justice added that "the Court cannot know whether, if this case had been tried, those state officials would have offered evidence to contravene appellees' allegations concerning legislative purpose."[37]

Chief Justice Burger is correct in asserting that none of the other justices adequately dealt with evidence that the legislation was introduced

---

36. *Id.* at 2507 (Burger, C.J., dissenting).
37. *Id.* at 2506–07.

in part to avoid perpetuation of the belief that students were prohibited from praying silently during this period. However, the district court, the finder of fact, found that the intent was tainted, and there is no indication that the state objected to these findings. In its zeal to have its vocal prayers validated, the state may have failed to give proper attention to the purpose issue. They could have objected to the court's findings, but presumably they did not. Furthermore, it is fairly clear on the record that the legislature intended to endorse or return voluntary prayer to the public schools of Alabama. Given this evidence and the failure of the state and legislators to clarify the intent issue, the Court would seem bound to support the lower court's findings regarding the purpose issue. Given Alabama's track record on prayer in public schools (prayer activities had consistently occurred in the schools), it is highly unlikely that students felt they could not pray during a moment of silence.

Finally, the chief justice disclosed his view of the intended meaning of the religion clauses when he noted that it is the Court's duty "to determine whether the statute or practice at issue is a step toward establishing a state religion."[38] This view is quite accommodating in terms of permitting public religious exercise, and is somewhat suspect in light of the history disclosed in the early chapters of this book. It also may be criticized on the ground that it is so broad or ambiguous that it would permit a substantial degree of *ad hoc* decision making on the part of governmental officials in this delicate area. Without more restraint, governmental officials might feel relatively unencumbered in their efforts to promote their religious beliefs in public schools and throughout the public sector. However, as the chief justice notes, the *Lemon* test has proven difficult of application and often serves poorly as a means of resolving difficult cases.

Justice White's Dissenting Opinion

Justice White's opinion is very brief, and in many senses merely reflects his uneasiness with the Court's test regarding Establishment Clause issues. Essentially, Justice White seems to agree with Chief Justice Burger that all of the justices voting to reject the Alabama statute would permit meditation statutes, while invalidating meditation-or-prayer statutes in all instances. This may be an ill-founded reading of the opinions of the justices in the majority in *Jaffree*, although it is conceivable that White was privy to statements by the other justices which were not clearly expressed in their opinions.

---

38. *Id.* at 2507.

Interestingly, Justice White articulates his view that "the First Amendment does not proscribe either (1) statutes authorizing or requiring in so many words a moment of silence before classes begin or (2) a statute that provides, when it is *initially* passed, for a moment of silence for meditation or prayer."[39] White's use of the term initially to modify his view regarding statutes providing for a moment of silence for prayer or meditation is puzzling. It seems that he may be drawing a distinction, as I have, between statutes that are initially drafted to provide for meditation or prayer and statutes like the Alabama statute that initially are drafted as meditation statutes and are subsequently changed to provide for meditation or prayer, as a means of promoting prayer in the public sector. Unfortunately, White offers little indication as to why he included the adverb initially, since it is clear that Alabama did not initially adopt a meditation-or-prayer statute.

Justice Rehnquist's Dissent

While Justice Rehnquist's dissent is merely the opinion of a single justice, it is of some importance for the purposes of this book and for the purpose of understanding First Amendment cases. It constitutes a significant effort to marshal applicable history to ascertain, as a matter of principle, what views or values the framers were seeking to establish when the religion clauses of the First Amendment were penned.

Justice Rehnquist begins by challenging the use of Jefferson's wall-of-separation metaphor. In doing so, he challenges the use of history in *Everson*, which laid the foundation for the Establishment Clause cases that followed. Because of this, Rehnquist's opinion constitutes a breath of fresh air; it is a major effort on the part of a justice to determine what the framers intended when the First Amendment was framed, adopted, and ratified. Prior efforts to examine the historical data, including the efforts of Justices Hugo L. Black and Wiley B. Rutledge in *Everson,* were so brief and inexhaustive that they led to the creation of First Amendment jurisprudence based on unfounded generalizations drawn from Jefferson's metaphor.

Justice Rehnquist is correct in his assertion that the wall metaphor is misleading and lacking in historical support. He is correct, as well, in his assertion that it has proved to be unworkable as a practical matter. However, while I agree with Rehnquist's conclusions that "it is impossible to build sound constitutional doctrine upon a mistaken understanding of constitutional history, [the wall metaphor],"[40] his analysis of the views

---

39. *Jaffree,* 105 S. Ct. at 2508 (White, J., dissenting) (emphasis added).
40. *Jaffree,* 105 S. Ct. at 2509 (Rehnquist, J., dissenting).

of both Thomas Jefferson and James Madison are but mere sketches, although it must be conceded that they are better sketches than those previously rendered by members of the Court in past opinions.

Rehnquist concludes that

> It seems indisputable from these glimpses of Madison's thinking, as reflected by actions on the floor of the House in 1789, that he saw the amendment as designed to prohibit the establishment of a national religion, and perhaps to prevent discrimination among sects. He did not see it as requiring neutrality on the part of government between religion and irreligion.[41]

The justice acknowledges that his conclusions are based on little more than glimpses at the history. Even a glimpse is preferable to a furtive nod. Rehnquist's summary of the Madisonian view is helpful, but it could be more complete.

In debunking the wall metaphor and the *Lemon* test, which he asserts "has no more grounding in the history of the First Amendment than does the wall theory upon which it rests," Justice Rehnquist examined the views in the constitutional treatises of Joseph Story and Thomas Cooley and noted a number of instances during the early Republic in which the federal government accommodated and, in some instances, even promoted religion. He then argued that the history supports his conclusion that

> The framers intended the Establishment Clause to prohibit the designation of any church as a "national" one. The clause was also designed to stop the federal government from asserting a preference for one religious denomination or sect over others. Given the "incorporation" of the Establishment Clause as against the states via the Fourteenth Amendment in *Everson*, states are prohibited as well from establishing a religion or discriminating between sects. As its history abundantly shows, however, nothing in the Establishment Clause requires government to be strictly neutral between religion and irreligion, nor does that clause prohibit Congress or the states from pursuing legitimate secular ends through nondiscriminatory means.[42]

In this summary, Rehnquist comes close to summarizing the Madisonian view, although some of the examples he uses are more consistent with the Story view. He is able actually to develop a surprisingly accurate

---

41. *Id.* at 2512.
42. *Id.* at 2520.

picture from a few glimpses at the history. That he is able to do so indicates how very susceptible the history is to being reduced to viable principles.

While Justice Rehnquist's analysis is brief, perhaps necessarily so given the time constraints facing a justice, it has the virtue of raising coherently some of the pertinent historical data. For example, Rehnquist praised Story's *Commentaries* and related them to events that transpired during the founding era. This historical data evidently compelled Justice Stevens to reply, and may ultimately cause the Court either to revamp its Establishment Clause tests or doctrine, as suggested by Justice O'Connor, in light of the pertinent data or to articulate a theory of judicial review in the First Amendment area that justifies the Court's repudiation of the applicable history, as a decisive factor in their analysis.

While there is much of value in Justice Rehnquist's opinion, a few minor problems remain. The fact that Justice Rehnquist fails to assess adequately the relationship between the Madisonian and Story positions is of major significance. Rather than recognizing that each of these positions provides a limit beyond which legitimate decision making ought not to proceed, he tries to condense them into a single, dispositive view. The Story and Madisonian views are in some respects contradictory and, therefore, should not be consolidated. Nonetheless, any effort to decide a case in light of a condensed, collective version of those views would arguably be legitimate in an originalist sense, because such a decision would fall within the bounds set by those views.

Justice Rehnquist's contention that the debates in Congress were not particularly illuminating[43] is also faulty. As indicated in the analysis of the debates in Chapter 4, those debates are quite helpful and actually serve as an additional indication that Rehnquist's ultimate conclusions regarding the likely intent of the framers are generally accurate.

Summary of Opinions in Jaffree

The opinions in the *Jaffree* case must be examined closely to ascertain what was, as well as what was not, decided by the Court. While the Court rejected the Alabama meditation-or-voluntary-prayer statute, it did not entirely dispose of the meditation issue as a matter of precedent. The Court clearly acknowledged that meditation statutes may be constitutional. Additionally, none of the opinions expressly rejects the possibility that meditation-or-prayer statutes might also be constitutional where:

---

43. *Id.* at 2510.

(1) they are adopted in an atmosphere less charged with religious zeal than that found in *Jaffree*; (2) the meditation-or-prayer statute at issue is the initial legislation (unlike the Alabama case in which a meditation-or-prayer statute followed on the heels of a meditation statute); (3) the meditation-or-prayer statute was adopted for secular as well as religious purposes; or (4) the meditation-or-prayer statute was adopted to accommodate expressions of conscience on the part of students.

In the preceding analysis, the historical approaches followed by some of the justices were discussed. The attention given to the historical data by those justices serves as a further indication that the Court takes pertinent constitutional history seriously. It might, nevertheless, be argued that members of the Court merely resort to the history as a means of legitimizing their decisions. Even so, opinions like Justice Rehnquist's, which conscientiously examine the historical data, will require other justices either to articulate a theory of judicial review that warrants minimizing the role of the historical data or to counter with pertinent historical data that support their respective positions. Justice Stevens apparently had to respond to the historical data raised by Justice Rehnquist. One of the attributes of our judicial process is that well-formulated, principled arguments do not generally remain unanswered. The utility of law office history, using snippets of history to support one's policy preferences, lessens in direct proportion to the conscientious use of actual, contradictory historical data. History is often susceptible to differing interpretations, but that is not to say that it is susceptible to any interpretation or that some interpretations are not better or more accurate reflections of historical data than others.

APPLYING THE HISTORY: RESOLVING JAFFREE UNDER THE
MADISONIAN AND STORY VIEWS

The Court is approaching a recognition of the important role of the positions articulated by Story and Madison. Application of those views will show that the Court does, indeed, continue to maintain a fragile, perhaps intuitive, fidelity to those positions.

Proponents of the Story view believe that the First Amendment was designed for the purpose of acknowledging that tolerant, nondenominational Christianity should be the national religion in the United States. Under such a view, nondenominational Christianity could be fostered or endorsed by the national government, so long as other religious groups were treated tolerantly.

It is likely that the entire prayer practice adopted in Alabama, vocal as well as silent prayers and meditation, would be permitted under the Story view. Story likely would have supported the practice of the meditation-or-prayer statute, even if its major purpose was to encourage voluntary prayer. For Story, such a practice would be similar to the prayer resolutions adopted by Presidents George Washington and John Adams, two early adherents of what I have labelled the Story view. The resolutions adopted by Washington and Adams proclaimed a national day of fasting and prayer. They endorsed, if you will, the practice of prayer. Alabama certainly would be permitted to do as much.

The arguments against endorsing prayer in the school context, even among small children, would carry little weight with proponents of the Story view. It will be recalled that the same Congress that adopted the First Amendment also supported the promotion of religion and morality in the schools in the Northwest Territories. The promotion of religion and the practice of prayer, a practice central to the Christian religion as practiced at the time of the framers, would have been encouraged as a practice, particularly among young children.

There is one sense, however, in which I might question the preceding application of the Story view to the facts of the *Jaffree* case. On 19 June 1985, on behalf of the National Council of Churches of Christ, the Rev. Dean M. Kelly testified before the Subcommittee on the Constitution of the Committee on the Judiciary of the United States Senate. In his testimony, Kelly opposed the practice of silent meditation or prayer, contending in part that "the National Council of Churches cannot overlook the fact that Christians are admonished by the Lord Jesus Christ in the Sermon on the Mount not to make a show of prayer in public places."[44] In his testimony, Kelly indicated that many Christians would have an aversion to a structured moment of silent meditation or prayer in public-school classrooms. It could be argued under the Story view, therefore, that the meditation-or-voluntary-prayer practice in the *Jaffree* case constituted a practice not accepted by all Christian sects. As such, it would not be considered appropriate as a governmental act supporting nondenominational Christianity.

Many and perhaps even most Christians would disagree, contending rather that the practice was and is common among Christian groups. That is precisely the point—Christians often do not agree on such matters. For his part, Madison warned that applying what was to become

---

44. *See Voluntary Silent Prayer Constitutional Amendment: Hearings on S.J. Res. 2 and S.J. Res. 212 before the Subcomm. on the Constitution of the Senate Judiciary Comm.,* 99th Cong., 1st Sess. 406 (1985) (testimony of the Rev. Dean M. Kelly, Director for Religious and Civil Liberty, The National Council of Churches of Christ).

the Story view, which purported to support nondenominational Christianity, would often place the government in the position of deciding what was and what was not "Christian."

The Madisonian view also poses some difficulties when applied to the peculiar facts of the *Jaffree* case. It will be recalled that, under the Madisonian view, the state may accommodate or facilitate religious exercise in the public sector, so long as it does so in a nonpreferential manner and provided that, in doing so, it refrains from adopting any mode of worship as its own. Potential problems arise on both the nonpreference and nonadoption-of-a-mode-of-worship prongs of the Madisonian view, as applied to the facts in *Jaffree*.

If there is a dispute among religious groups about the status of silent meditation or prayer, the adoption of a statute like that in *Jaffree* might be unacceptable on the ground that it prefers the practices of certain religious groups over others. This is particularly true under the facts of the *Jaffree* case. In *Jaffree*, the legislature added "or voluntary prayer" after having adopted a simple meditation statute. The lower court found that the purpose of adding the new statute was "to bring voluntary prayer back into the schools." Such an act seemed to endorse, or prefer, the practice of silent prayer, although Chief Justice Burger did cite evidence from the record to the effect that, perhaps, the language was added to ensure that prayer received equal treatment and not for the purpose of endorsing the prayer practice. For Madison, if the Alabama statute in fact preferred one religion over another, it would be inappropriate. However, where a meditation-or-prayer statute is passed for the purpose of developing a sense on the part of the students that religion and matters of conscience are important, without preferring one form of practice over another, I have no doubt that Madison would have supported it.

Madison might also have objected to the Alabama practice on the ground that it constituted the adoption of a mode of worship, prayer, on the part of the state. For Madison, the state could accommodate individual exercise, but it had to do so without placing its imprimatur on any particular religious practice or mode of worship. Madison would have been quite concerned with the state's intentions in adding the language "or voluntary prayer" to its statutory scheme. If the state added the language as a means of promoting prayer, as a mode of worship, he would not have supported the state's action. If, on the other hand, the language was added to facilitate individual exercise, without preferring or adopting prayer as a mode of worship, Madison would have permitted the practice.

Madison's views toward public-prayer resolutions is illustrative. During his presidency, he supported prayer resolutions that called on those who were "piously disposed" to join in prayer for particular purposes. In support of his proclamations, Madison emphasized the voluntary nature of the prescribed practices, and he endeavored to avoid placing the government's stamp of approval on prayer as a religious practice. Neither Washington nor Adams, both of whom would have followed Story, were so concerned with ensuring voluntariness and nonpreference.

Later in his life, however, Madison began to question even the voluntary form of his prayer resolutions on the ground that proponents of such resolutions had the tendency to "narrow the recommendation to the standard of the predominant sect." He was concerned, therefore, not only with the language of the resolution, but also with its administration and the intent behind the terminology used. It is clear that Madison would examine the facts in the *Jaffree* case closely.

In *Jaffree,* where the lower court found that Alabama adopted its statute for the purpose of endorsing or preferring the practice of prayer, Madison likely would have opposed the practice. However, if a similar statute had been added for the purpose and had had the effect of accommodating the exercise of conscience on an individual basis (a purpose that might be furthered by legislation providing for "meditation or prayer" in some instances), he probably would have supported the practice. Like Justice O'Connor, he would have been concerned with how the practice was administered.

Thus, under both the Story and Madisonian views the decision in meditation or prayer cases, like *Jaffree,* would be close. In either instance, the ultimate decision would turn on facts such as whether silent prayer or meditation is an act supported by nondenominational Christians (under the Story view) or whether the act was intended to prefer or had the effect of preferring one religion or group of religions over another or of promoting prayer as a particular mode of worship (under the Madisonian view). Clearly, however, under either view, the *Jaffree* case presents a poor set of facts from the state's perspective, although it is likely that Story would have supported the Alabama statute. This is not surprising because the Court has failed to articulate clear principles that would enable the parties to make a record related to the issues raised under the Madisonian and Story views, and the Court has not indicated clearly when it will defer to legislative determinations of constitutional issues when those determinations comport with, or fall within, the limits defined by original-intent analysis.

A Concluding Look at Some of the Policy Arguments Related to
the Issue of Silent Meditation or Prayer

The issue of meditation or prayer is undoubtedly the most difficult problem covered in this book, in terms of applying the views of Story and Madison. It seems to fall between the vocal prayer recitations at issue in cases like *Engel* and the equal-access issue raised in cases like *Widmar* and *Bender.* Vocal prayer recitations do not present very difficult issues for the application of either view—Madison would have opposed them and Story would have supported them. Similarly, the equal-access issue, as discussed in the following chapter, does not present problems of application for the Madisonian or the Story views—both would support such practices. Meditation-or-prayer statutes, on the other hand, seem to fall between vocal-prayer-recitation and equal-access issues in terms of the nature of the involvement of government. Government is doing more to promote a particular religious practice, silent prayer, in the meditation-or-prayer cases than when it extends equal access to religious groups, and it is doing less than it did in *Engel* when it composed a prayer for recitation by its students.

Neither the Madisonian nor the Story view will serve, therefore, as a panacea to resolve the meditation issue. The issues in meditation-or-prayer cases are close enough that they could often be decided either way, particularly under the Madisonian view. Therefore, this is an area where courts will have greater discretion; they will have to engage in independent balancing of various policies, in light of the principles elucidated in the Madisonian or Story views and in relation to the peculiar facts raised by each case.

Those who argue against meditation-or-prayer statutes typically raise the following arguments: (1) a moment of meditation is unnecessary to secure the right to pray or to meditate—that right exists already in that a student may pray silently or meditate whenever she so desires; (2) a moment of meditation is at best a trivial accommodation of free-exercise rights in the public sector, which carries substantial costs to our system of church-state relations; (3) minority religions will suffer by virtue of application of a meditation-or-prayer statute; (4) such statutes reinforce the unfortunate tendency toward governmental involvement in religious matters; and (5) meditation or prayer activities tend to disrupt the school day and the learning process.

Repeatedly, opponents of meditation-or-prayer statutes have argued that students already may pray silently. To this, Professor Grover Rees, III has responded that:

This statement is both correct and trivial. One can do anything anywhere so long as one is careful to do it in such a way that nobody notices. The use of the term "right" to denote the fact that one can pray with impunity so long as one prays silently would entail a radical reappraisal of the extent to which human rights should be said to exist in totalitarian and authoritarian regimes around the world. In this sense of the word, students have the right to pray in school not only in the United States but also in the Soviet Union. Citizens of South Africa and Cambodia have the right to call for the overthrow of the government so long as they do it silently.[45]

At first blush, Professor Rees's comment appears to be telling. Closer examination, however, reveals that the comment is somewhat flawed. The right to pray is different from the right to call for the overthrow of one's government. Silent prayer is by its very nature silent; calling for the overthrow of one's government and the exercise of many other rights are not naturally silent. One can engage fully in silent prayer without the permission of one's government and without being given a time for doing so. Nevertheless, providing a period for reflection during a busy school day would serve to accommodate the individual right of free exercise. This was the sense in which Senator Orrin G. Hatch of Utah compared governmental prohibition of moments of silent reflection or prayer to the Gulag Archipelago during the debates in the Senate;[46] and it is the sense in which Rees's comment has force.[47] The question, then, is whether

---

45. Senate Comm. on the Judiciary, Voluntary Silent Prayer Constitutional Amendment, S. Rep. No. 165, 99th Cong., 1st Sess. 34–35 (1985).

46. *See Voluntary Silent Prayer Constitutional Amendment: Hearings on S.J. Res. 2 Before the Subcomm. on the Constitution of the Senate Judiciary Comm.*, 99th Cong., 1st Sess. (1985) (statement of Senator Hatch).

47. Indeed, there certainly is a sense in which both Professor Rees and Senator Hatch are correct. The desire by some to eliminate every vestige of religion from the public sector is, for me, reminiscent of Mr. Cruncher's persecution of his dutiful and religious wife who desired to pray, in Charles Dickens's A TALE OF TWO CITIES. After encouraging his son to deprecate his mother for her desire to pray, Mr. Cruncher prevented his wife from praying further. *See* Dickens, A TALE OF TWO CITIES at 63–4 (Signet Classics, 1963). Later, having succeeded in terminating his wife's vocal prayers in his presence, Mr. Cruncher went to work on her desire to meditate, reflect, or pray silently. In Dickens's own words:

[Mr. Cruncher] devoted himself during the remainder of the evening to keeping a most vigilant watch on Mrs. Cruncher, and sullenly holding her in conversation that she might be prevented from meditating any

the government should accommodate individual meditation, reflection, or prayer or whether it should leave a student to her own devices in fulfilling her desire to pray during the school day.

Opponents of the meditation-or-prayer-statutes also argue that the right is itself trivial. They note that a minute of meditation, like that provided under the Alabama statute, hardly provides the student with a meaningful opportunity to meditate, pray, or reflect on any matter of significance. Proponents reply that any time set aside for serious individual meditation, reflection, or prayer is a boon to students desirous of reflecting on matters of conscience. While proponents may concede that five minutes would be preferable to one, they assert nevertheless that even a minute serves the twin purposes of giving the students a structured moment in which to reflect and relating to the students, as an institutional matter, the fact that such moments are of value and a legitimate part of the learning and developmental process. Opponents counter that schools should not place even such a limited imprimatur on such practices, because such practices commonly have religious overtones.

Opponents also argue that such practices harm minorities who find moments of meditation or prayer to be offensive to their beliefs. To this, proponents respond that the moments are voluntary in the purest sense of the word in that the student may think or reflect on anything and need not use the time for religious or related reflection. Those who argue against such practices generally add that they find them particularly offensive in the instance of young and impressionable children. Young children, in their view, are peculiarly susceptible to institutional pressure and are less inclined than adults to be able to ignore the religious or related overtones related to such practices. Proponents must, I believe, concede that there may be problems and must caution school officials to be very careful in administering the practices.

Opponents are also concerned that such practices open the door to increasing governmental involvement in religious matters. Adherents of this view typically advocate a strict separation of church and state. For them, any limitation on the wall of separation has the potential of bring-

---

petitions to his disadvantage. With this view, he urged his son to hold her in conversation also, and led the unfortunate woman a hard life by dwelling on any causes of complaint he could bring against her, rather than he would leave her for a moment to her own reflections.

Id. at 161. Some who oppose statutes which allow meditation, reflection, or prayer do so no doubt in an effort to keep children so occupied that they will have little time and, eventually, little desire to reflect or meditate. In this sense, the analogy to the Gulag or to Mr. Cruncher is perhaps apt.

ing the wall down. Proponents counter that the proper relationship between church and state, particularly in our contemporary world that is characterized by a pervasive public sector, cannot be one of strict separation. Strict separation for these proponents intrudes unduly on the right of free exercise. They add that principles can be developed to guard against excessive governmental involvement.

Finally, Senator Charles M. Mathias of Maryland, an opponent of moments of meditation, has argued that "today, our public school classrooms are supposed to be dedicated to learning. But under S. J. Res. 2, [laws authorizing meditation or prayer practices,] they could be given over, once or twice or ten times a day, to devotional exercises."[48] This, in my view, is really a version of what I call the hocus-pocus argument. In this sense, some opponents of all religious or potentially religious activities or exercises in the public schools argue that religion or matters of conscience are and must be kept wholly separate from the educational process. For them, schools are organized to teach facts, not to dwell on religious or related nonsense. It is rare that this argument is actually raised, though it seems clear that it lurks behind some of the opposition to recognizing any role for individual religious exercise in public education, because religion is anathema to education for those who hold this view. Those who favor some role for religious exercise in the public sector rarely have to counter this argument, because while some opponents of religious exercise are at heart anti-religious, the public is not, and opponents of religious exercise recognize that such an argument is likely to increase opposition to their position. Such a view is by its very nature intolerant, and it belies an intolerance on the part of the anti-religionist that rivals the intolerance of some of the more fanatical religionists.

With the exception of the fifth argument, I believe that each of the objections to a moment of meditation or prayer raised by opponents carry some weight and deserve careful consideration. I believe that they must be weighed when one applies the principles articulated in the Madisonian view that tries to facilitate the exercise of individual conscience without preferring any form of religious expression. The Madisonian view does provide a principled basis under which most of the objections raised by opponents of meditation-or-prayer laws may be addressed. It balances the values of the Free Exercise and Establishment clauses in an

48. Senate Comm. on the Judiciary, Voluntary Silent Prayer Constitutional Amendment, S. Rep. No. 165, 99th Cong., 1st Sess. 58 (1985) (minority views of Mr. Mathias).

effective and moderating fashion. It would permit such a statute when it accommodates individual exercise. It would not support such a law when it is intended to be used or in fact is used to prefer one religion or one form of religious exercise over another.

10

Equal Access: The Widmar
and Bender Cases

On 8 December 1981, the Supreme Court decided the case of *Widmar v. Vincent*.[1] That case raised the issue of "whether a state university, which makes its facilities generally available for the activities of registered student groups, may close its facilities to a registered student group desiring to use the facilities for religious worship and religious discussion."[2] In a decision that surprised some Court watchers, the Court, with Justice John Paul Stevens concurring in the judgment, and with Justice Byron R. White casting the lone dissenting vote, held that the state university's "exclusionary policy [under which student religious groups were refused access to campus facilities on the same basis as nonreligious student groups] violate[d] the fundamental principle that a state regulation of speech should be content-neutral, and [that] the university [was] unable to justify this violation under applicable constitutional standards."[3]

In *Widmar,* the University of Missouri at Kansas City had adopted a policy encouraging the activities of student organizations and recognized over one hundred student groups under that policy. Recognized groups routinely were provided access to university facilities for their meetings. Students generally paid an activity fee to help defray the costs attendant to activities of recognized student groups.

---

1. 454 U.S. 263 (1981).
2. *Id.* at 264–65. This is the manner in which Justice Powell phrased the issue for the majority in *Widmar.*
3. *Id.* at 277.

For a number of years, a nondenominational student organization of evangelical Christians regularly sought and received permission to conduct its meetings in campus facilities. However, in 1977, the university refused to permit the group to meet in university facilities, based on a 1972 regulation prohibiting the use of university buildings or grounds "for purposes of religious worship or religious teaching."[4] Eleven students challenged this regulation in federal district court, on free-exercise, equal-protection, and free-speech grounds. On cross motions for summary judgment, the district court upheld the regulation. On appeal, the circuit court of appeals reversed, holding that the students' rights had been abridged unconstitutionally. The Supreme Court granted certiorari, heard arguments on 6 October 1981, and rendered its decision two months later.

In his opinion for the Court, Justice Lewis F. Powell, Jr. began by examining whether or not the students' First Amendment right of free speech or expression had been violated. The Court first determined that "[t]hrough its policy of accommodating their meetings, the university [had] created a forum generally open for use by student groups."[5] Having held that the university had created a limited public forum, a forum in which the general expression of ideas was encouraged, the Court concluded that "U.M.K.C. has discriminated against student groups based on their desire to use a generally open forum to engage in religious worship and discussion. These are forms of speech and association protected by the First Amendment."[6]

Having held that the university had violated the First Amendment rights of the students, it remained for the Court to determine whether the state had shown "that its regulation [was] necessary to serve a compelling state interest and [whether the regulation was] narrowly drawn to achieve that end."[7] In addressing this issue, the State of Missouri asserted that it had a compelling state interest in regulating religious expression of worship on the campus of the University of Missouri, based on the assumption that such religious expression was incompatible with the strict-separationist rationale behind the establishment clauses of the state and federal constitutions. While recognizing that protection of the Establishment Clause value by a state certainly would constitute a com-

---

4. Cited in *Id.* at 265.
5. *Id.* at 267.
6. *Id.* at 269.
7. *Id.* at 270.

pelling state interest, Justice Powell opined that permitting student religious groups and speakers on campus on the same terms as other nonreligious student groups did not offend the Establishment Clause of the
First Amendment. Justice Powell applied the three-pronged *Lemon* test,
which is often used in Establishment Clause cases, in reaching his conclusion for the Court.[8]

The secular purpose and the entanglement prongs clearly satisfied
the majority in *Widmar*. Justice Powell noted that the secular purpose
was satisfied by the secular interest in having a limited, open public
forum that did not discriminate against religious speech. He emphasized
that permitting religious speech, together with other forms of expression,
in the limited-open-forum context of a public university in no way placed
the imprimatur of the state on that religious speech; rather, it simply
furthered the secular purpose of promoting the exchange of ideas among
college-age students.[9] Powell also distinguished *McCollum* and related
prior cases,[10] because in those cases the statutes "permitted school facilities to be used for instruction by religious groups, but *not* by others."[11]

Justice Powell disposed of the entanglement prong of the test in a
single footnote that provided:

> We agree with the court of appeals that the university would risk
> greater "entanglement" by attempting to enforce its exclusion of "reli-
> gious worship" and "religious speech." [citation omitted] Initially, the
> university would need to determine which words and activities fall
> within "religious worship and religious teaching." This alone could
> prove "an impossible task in an age where many and various beliefs

---

8. Justice Powell summarized the test by quoting from Lemon v. Kurtzman,
403 U.S. 602, 612–13 (1971), as follows:
   First the [governmental policy] must have a secular legislative purpose; second, its principal or primary effect must be one that neither
   advances nor inhibits religion...; finally, the [policy] must not foster
   "an excessive government entanglement with religion."

9. In footnote 10 of Justice Powell's opinion for the Court, he noted that it
was the avowed purpose of UMKC to provide a forum in which students can
exchange ideas. The university argued that use of the forum for religious speech
would undermine that secular aim. But, in the view of the Court, by creating a
forum the university would not thereby endorse or promote any of the particular
ideas aired there. Undoubtedly, many views advocated in such a forum would
not necessarily be supported or sponsored by the university.

10. In McCollum v. Board of Educ., 333 U.S. 203 (1948), the Court held
that in-school "released-time" programs for religious instruction were unconstitutional. Four years later, in Zorach v. Clauson, 343 U.S. 306 (1952), the Court
upheld released-time programs held off campus.

11. *Widmar,* 454 U.S. at 272, n. 10.

meet the constitutional definition of religion." There would also be a continuing need to monitor group meetings to ensure compliance with the rule.[12]

Thus, the entanglement prong was satisfied because refusal by the university to permit religious expression on the part of student groups, on an equal basis with other forms of expression, would raise more entanglement problems than would permitting religious and nonreligious organizations alike nondiscriminatory access to campus facilities.

The only issue that drew much attention from the majority was the issue of whether allowing the religious groups to participate in the limited public forum would have the primary effect of advancing religion, as argued by the state. The Court held that any religious benefits from participation in the public forum would be merely incidental. Justice Powell cited two factors in support of this conclusion: (1) "an open forum in a public university does not confer any imprimatur of state approval on religious sects or practices";[13] and (2) the forum is open to a broad class of nonreligious as well as religious groups or speakers and there is an "absence of empirical evidence that religious groups [would] dominate [the university's] open forum."[14]

An examination of these factors in a subsequent case might cause the Court to reach a different decision. If, for example, a university did not create a general or limited public forum for student expression, that university would not be bound under the Free Speech Clause to permit access to a student religious group. In that event, students would have to argue that the refusal of access abridged their right of free exercise. Justice Powell recognized this when, in footnote 13, he noted that "this case is different from the cases in which religious groups claim that the denial of facilities *not* available to other groups deprives them of their rights under the Free Exercise Clause.... Here, the university's forum is already available to other groups, and respondents' claim to use that forum does not...rest solely upon rights claimed under the Free Exercise Clause. Respondents' claim also implicates First Amendment rights of speech and association."[15]

Justice Powell also noted that access could be limited for other reasons. "We have not held...that a campus must make all of its facil-

12. *Id.* at 272, n. 11.
13. 454 U.S. at 274.
14. *Id.* at 275.
15. *Id.* at 273, n. 13.

ities equally available to students and nonstudents alike, or that a university must grant free access to all of its grounds or buildings."[16] Developing on this theme, Powell added that "our holding in this case in no way undermines the capacity of the university to establish reasonable time, place, and manner regulations. Nor do we question the right of the university to make academic judgments as to how best to allocate scarce resources or 'to determine for itself on academic grounds who may teach, what may be taught, how it shall be taught, and who may be admitted to study.'"[17] Finally he reaffirmed a line of cases that "recognize a university's right to exclude even First Amendment activities that violate reasonable campus rules or substantially interfere with the opportunity of other students to obtain an education."[18]

With all of these potential limitations on student access, it is not surprising that Justice Powell concluded by emphasizing the narrowness of the Court's decision.[19] Thus, it would hardly be accurate to intimate that *Widmar* offers carte blanche to student religious groups desiring to meet on public campuses. However, despite these express limitations on access that might apply in subsequent cases, the *Widmar* case stands as strong precedent for equal treatment for religious expression.

A couple of additional matters raised in *Widmar* are also worthy of mention. First, Missouri had argued that, under the establishment clause contained in its state constitution, it was free to demand stricter separation of church and state than that required under the Establishment Clause of the First Amendment. Justice Powell dispensed with this argument, stating that "the state interest asserted here—in achieving greater separation of church and state than is already ensured under the Establishment Clause of the federal Constitution—is limited by the Free Exercise Clause and in this case by the Free Speech Clause as well. In this constitutional context, we are unable to recognize the state's interest as sufficiently 'compelling' to justify content-based discrimination against respondents' religious speech."[20] While this statement by Justice Powell is certainly limited by the sentence that follows indicating that the *Widmar* decision was based primarily on the speech and association grounds, the notion that state efforts to enforce their view of stricter separation might be unavailing even in cases involving only free exercise and not free speech is significant. If widely applied, it would prevent state courts

---

16. *Id.* at 268, n. 5.
17. *Id.* at 276.
18. *Id.* at 277.
19. *Id.*
20. *Id.* at 276.

from cutting back on efforts to accommodate religious exercise that would be acceptable under the federal Establishment Clause but unacceptable under a state court's interpretation of its state establishment clause.

Similarly, the Court's willingness to recognize religious worship ("singing, teaching, and reading [from Scripture]") is noteworthy. Given the contemporary trend to recognize wide protection for speech or expression rights, this development may well portend an increasing willingness on the part of the Court to permit religious exercise in the public sector. This development also creates a dilemma of sorts for some contemporary liberals who favor broad rights of expression, while simultaneously seeking to limit religious exercise in the public sector. Indeed, the recognition of religious exercise as expression explains in some measure why liberal justices, who might typically vote to prohibit such religious exercise in the public sector, were compelled to concur in Justice Powell's decision. In a related sense, some religious fundamentalists who favor permissiveness for religious exercise in public but who would simultaneously prefer limited rights of expression will have to live with the marriage between rights of religious expression and other forms of expression performed in *Widmar.*

One final point about the majority opinion is in order. While Powell did not refer at all to the intent of the framers and ratifiers of the First Amendment, it is clear that his decision comports with the Madisonian view. The opinion provides for "equal access" on a nonpreferential basis and is reminiscent of a portion of Madison's view of the Establishment Clause. It is unfortunate that Powell failed to refer expressly to the applicable history, but his decision is itself unimpeachable on historical, or originalist, grounds, except, perhaps, insofar as it seems to relegate the Free Exercise Clause to a secondary role, less important than speech and association rights. Needless to say, his decision would also be acceptable under the Story view that would permit even broader access for Christian groups.

Justice Stevens concurred in the judgment in *Widmar,* arguing that a public university should be permitted "to deny recognition to a student organization—or [give] it a lesser right to use school facilities than other student groups—[if it has] a valid reason for doing so."[21] However, Stevens agreed that the university had offered no valid reason for its refusal to permit students to meet and had also failed to disclose how permitting voluntary religious activity on campus would imply state

---

21. *Id.* at 280 (emphasis added).

sponsorship of the religious activities of that student organization. In his view, the state had failed to meet its burden of proof in supporting its allegation that permitting equal access to campus facilities on the part of student religious organizations would constitute an act that implied state approval of that religious activity. While he would require a lesser level of proof in this regard and would defer more readily to the decisions of academicians than would those joining in the majority opinion, he still would require that some evidence of a valid reason for excepting student religious groups be offered.

Justice Stevens's opinion fails to give adequate weight to the rights of students, particularly in the university context. Certainly, academic institutions should be given wide latitude in structuring academic programs, but when administrative personnel in public universities selectively disparage religious expression and the free-exercise rights of students, courts ought to demand proof of a compelling state interest necessitating such discrimination. Justice Stevens's valid-reasons standard is simply fraught with ambiguity and would seemingly afford much broader license to regulators than would the stricter First Amendment standards followed by the majority in *Widmar*.

Justice White, in his dissent in *Widmar*, would have permitted the state to regulate such religious activity on campus. He outlined his philosophy of deference to the states in matters of incidental aid to religion as follows:

> The Establishment Clause, however, sets limits only on what the state may do with respect to religious organizations; it does not establish what the state is *required* to do. I have long argued that Establishment Clause limits on state action which incidentally aids religion are not as strict as the Court has held. The step from the permissible to the necessary, however, is a long one. In my view, just as there is room under the religion clauses for state policies that may have some beneficial effect on religion, there is also room for state policies that may incidentally burden religion. In other words, I believe the states to be a good deal freer to formulate policies that affect religion in divergent ways than does the majority.[22]

---

22. *Id.* at 282. (Emphasis supplied by Justice White.) It should be noted, however, that Justice White's position, a position to which he has consistently adhered during his tenure on the Court, would also permit broad rights of religious exercise in the public sector in instances in which the state approved, rather than disapproved, of such activities. His position is one of deference to the states.

It should be emphasized, however, that White's deference might be tempered by a future case in which he felt that an actual and substantial burden was in fact being placed on the students' right of free exercise.[23]

Justice White also vehemently opposed the majority's determination that religious worship or services ("offering prayer[s], singing hymns, reading Scripture, and teaching biblical principles") constituted protected speech. He concluded that "were [such a view] right, the religion clause would be emptied of any independent meaning in circumstance in which religious practice took the form of speech."[24] He is wrong, however. Such speech still could be limited by the Establishment Clause value, while other forms of nonreligious speech could not. The Court in *Widmar* merely held that the state had failed to prove a violation of the Establishment Clause. Furthermore, the right of free exercise retains independent force in cases involving "exercise" outside a public forum and, perhaps, supplemental force even within such a forum. It should be reiterated, however, that even White's deference might be tempered by a future case in which he felt that an actual and substantial burden was in fact being placed on the students' right of free exercise.[25]

Before ending discussion of the *Widmar* case, it is important to note another matter discussed by the majority. In footnote 14 to his opinion, Justice Powell placed some weight on the distinction between university (college-age) and elementary or secondary school (younger) students: "University students are, of course, young adults. They are less impressionable than younger students and should be able to appreciate that the university's policy is one of neutrality toward religion."[26] Powell used this distinction to buttress his conclusion that permitting religious speech on a college campus would not constitute support on the part of the university for the religious views expressed by the student organization. Powell reasoned that college-age students were mature enough to distinguish between state accommodation of religions in a

---

23. Justice White noted in this regard that:

Respondents complain that compliance with the regulation would require them to meet "about a block and a half" from campus under conditions less comfortable than those previously available on campus. I view this burden on free exercise as minimal. Because the burden is minimal, the State need do no more than demonstrate that the regulation furthers some permissible state end.

Id. at 288–89.

24. *Id.* at 284. The majority addressed this argument. *Id.* at 269, n. 6.

25. See *supra* note 23.

26. 454 U.S. at 274, n. 14.

general sense and state promotion or endorsement of religion, whereas younger students might have difficulty distinguishing between accommodation and promotion.

In drawing upon this age or maturation distinction in *Widmar,* Justice Powell cited the case of *Tilton v. Richardson,*[27] in which the Court (at least in the plurality opinion of Chief Justice Warren Burger) had distinguished between the religious aspects of church-related institutions of higher learning and parochial or sectarian elementary and secondary schools on the ground that college-age students are less impressionable in religious matters than students in elementary and secondary schools.[28] This maturation rationale has given force to a trend permitting greater public aid for secular purposes to private sectarian higher education.[29] This maturation distinction is significant because it may be asserted to limit the free-exercise rights of students in the secondary or elementary school context in ways that it could not be asserted at the college or university level.

In *Bender v. Williamsport School District,*[30] the Supreme Court recently decided a case which seemed to raise the issue of whether the Establishment Clause requires a public high school to prevent a student-initiated, student-led group from meeting during an extracurricular activity period. It was, therefore, anticipated that the Court would finally

---

27. 403 U.S. 672, 685–86 (1971).

28. Specifically, Chief Justice Burger had noted in *Tilton* that "there are generally significant differences between the religious aspects of the church-related institutions of higher learning and parochial elementary and secondary schools. [College-age] students are less impressionable and less susceptible to religious indoctrination." *Id.* Given that distinction, the Court, in the *Tilton* case, was willing to permit public funding of the building of certain facilities on a sectarian college campus, where the buildings were to be used for secular educational purposes, despite the fact that the so-called secular assistance would undoubtedly free private funds for use in a more sectarian manner.

29. *See, e.g.,* Hunt v. McNair, 413 U.S. 734 (1973) and Roemer v. Maryland Public Works Bd., 426 U.S. 736 (1976). Both of these cases elaborated on the principles articulated in *Tilton.* The *Roemer* case was particularly interesting because, at least implicitly, it also emphasized equality of access by sectarian groups to certain public aid, in that it upheld a statutory scheme by which noncategorical grants were made available to eligible private sectarian and nonsectarian colleges alike. *See also* P. Moots and E. Gaffney, CHURCH AND CAMPUS, 101–17 (1979), for a discussion of the application of the maturation rationale and related principles to the use of publicly funded facilities by sectarian groups.

30. 106 S. Ct. 1326 (1986).

decide whether high school students would be treated like their university counterparts for the purpose of equal access, based on the *Widmar* decision.

However, in a five-to-four decision, the Court avoided this issue in rendering its decision in *Bender*. Justice Stevens delivered the opinion of the Court. Justices William Brennan, Thurgood Marshall, Harry Blackmun, and Sandra O'Connor concurred in that decision, although Justice Marshall filed a separate concurring opinion. Four members of the Court dissented, arguing that the Court should have reached the merits and should have permitted the students to meet.

The substantive facts in *Bender* are straightforward. The school district provided a thirty-minute club or activity period on Tuesdays and Thursdays for high school students to meet in groups in separate school rooms for extracurricular purposes, including discussion on any subject of their choosing. Approximately twenty-five different student groups met during these periods. A group of students formed an organization, Petros, for the purpose of meeting during the activity period to engage in religious expression. There were no objections or complaints raised by students, faculty, or parents at that time. Nevertheless, based on the advice of legal counsel for the district, the principal advised the students that they would not be permitted to meet for religious or related purposes during the activity period.

The procedural facts, the facts under which the principal's (and ultimately the school board's) decision was challenged, are a bit more complex and ultimately provided the basis for disagreement between the justices in the majority and the dissenters. In June of 1982, after having been denied access by the principal and the school board, ten students filed suit in the United States district court against the Williamsport Area School District, the nine members of the school board, and the superintendent and the principal. Although there was a general allegation in the first paragraph of the students' complaint to the effect that the action was being brought against each defendant "in their *individual* and official capacities," the specific allegation concerning each of the named members of the school board stated that they were being sued in their capacity as a member of the board. A single answer was filed on behalf of all the defendants.

After completion of discovery and the filing of cross-motions (motions by both parties) for summary judgment, the district court requested further documentation regarding the exact nature of the activity period and the type of activities or clubs that had been permitted to function during that period. After receiving this information, the district court held that:

> After carefully reviewing the facts, and after giving full considera-
> tion to all pertinent legal authority, the court concludes that because
> the defendant school district is not constitutionally required to deny
> the plaintiffs the opportunity to meet, by doing so solely on constitu-
> tional grounds it has impermissibly burdened their free speech rights.
> Accordingly, summary judgment will be granted in favor of the
> students.[31]

After the district court's decision in favor of the students, the board
voted 8-1 not to appeal and to permit the students to meet as ordered.

However, John C. Youngman, a lawyer and a member of the board
(evidently, the sole member of the board who had voted to appeal the
matter), filed individually a timely notice of appeal. Youngman's standing
was not raised at the court of appeals level, and the Court of Appeals
for the Second Circuit reversed the District Court in a two-to-one decision, holding that "the particular circumstances disclosed by this record
and present at the Williamsport Area High School lead to the inexorable
conclusion that the constitutional balance of interests tilts against permitting the Petros activity to be conducted within the school as a general
activity program."[32]

Although it had not been raised previously, it was clear at oral
argument at the Supreme Court level that the Court was concerned with
the issue of whether Youngman had standing to challenge the district
court's decision. Satisfied that Youngman should not be accorded standing, five justices voted to vacate the judgment of the court of appeals
and remanded the case "with instructions to dismiss the appeal for want
of jurisdiction," thereby reinstating the district court's decision permitting
the students to meet.[33]

The "standing" doctrine upon which the Court based its decision is
predicated on the premise that federal courts are not courts of general
jurisdiction capable of hearing any issue and that the Court should in-
dependently review the record below to ascertain whether the parties
have standing. They do so, in the words of Justice Stevens, "to ensure
that our deliberations will have the benefit of adversary presentation
and a full development of the relevant facts."[34] In other words, as a

---

31. 563 F. Supp. 697, 700 (M.D. Pa 1983).
32. 741 F.2d 538, 561 (2d Cir. 1984). Judge Adams dissented, arguing that,
based on the facts in the present case, the district court's opinion permitting the
students to meet should have been affirmed.
33. 106 S. Ct. at 1335.
34. *Id.* at 1331.

theoretical matter, when the Court invokes the standing doctrine to avoid deciding the underlying substantive issue (the issue of equal access for religious expression in *Bender*), it does so on the ground that one of the parties lacks standing or a sufficient interest in the case to prosecute their side of the case with sufficient ardor.[35] There are commentators, however, who argue that the standing doctrine is often invoked as a means of avoiding politically sensitive issues.[36]

In this regard, the Court concluded first that, "since the judgment against Mr. Youngman was not in his individual capacity, he had no standing to appeal in that capacity."[37] However, Youngman had also asserted at oral argument that he was the parent of a student attending the high school and that as a matter of conscience he was opposed to the practice of permitting students to meet on campus for religious purposes. Normally, where such an allegation appeared in the record, the Court would find that someone in Youngman's position, as a parent of a student, would have standing. However, Justice Stevens opined for the Court that, "since Mr. Youngman was not sued as a parent in the district court, he had no right to participate in the proceedings in that court in that capacity without first filing an appropriate motion or pleading setting forth the claim or defense that he desired to assert."[38] Because of this, Youngman lacked standing, and it was unnecessary for the Court to reach the merits.

It does not take much thought to realize that whether or not Youngman moved formally to participate in the district court proceedings in his capacity as a parent has little to do with whether or not the proceeding is adversarial. Nevertheless, Justice Stevens and the other members of the majority were inclined to apply the law formalistically, denying Youngman standing, rather than determining whether the spirit of the law, requisite adversariness, was sufficient to assure that both sides would be adequately argued. (As an aside, this presents one of the interesting facts of the Court's decision. The more liberal members of the Court who joined with Justice Stevens normally are more inclined than many of the more conservative members of the Court, who in this

---

35. Our adversary system, in turn, is based on the assumption that judges can best decide a case when each side in a controversy is significantly involved and well represented.

36. *See, e.g.,* A. Bickel, THE LEAST DANGEROUS BRANCH, 116–27 (1962), where Professor Bickel referred to standing as a passive virtue.

37. 106 S. Ct. at 1332.

38. *Id.* at 1335.

case dissented, to follow the spirit as opposed to the letter of the law in standing cases.)[39] However, in this case, the justices who are generally considered liberal, Brennan and Marshall and to a lesser extent Stevens and Blackmun, opted to read precedent regarding the standing doctrine restrictively. Many of the more conservative members, however, and equally as paradoxically as a matter of principle, opted to invoke the spirit and not the letter of the standing doctrine.

Indeed, it was perhaps this very point that caused Justice Marshall to file a separate concurring opinion. In his opinion, Marshall endeavored to depict how very limited the scope of the *Bender* decision was. He specifically noted that "I do not contest that Mr. Youngman could pursue this dispute on appeal had he intervened in the lawsuit in his capacity as a parent. Absent such intervention, it is conceivable that Mr. Youngman might bottom his standing to raise such an argument on facts in the record setting out his status as a parent. There are, however, no such facts anywhere in the extensive record in this case. There is not one word in the *record* indicating that Mr. Youngman is a father at all. Nor did Mr. Youngman claim such status in his Notice of Appeal."[40]

The dissenters (Chief Justice Burger and Justices White, Powell, and Rehnquist) disagreed. In arguing that the standing requirement should be relaxed in this case, the chief justice asserted that, "once the jurisdiction of the district court over a particular dispute is established, it seems clear that the same dispute between the same parties will remain within the Article III powers of the courts on appeal."[41]

Having thus dispensed with the standing issue, Burger turned to the substantive issue. After noting that "it is common ground that nothing in the Establishment Clause requires the state to suppress a person's speech merely because the *content* of the speech is religious in character,"[42] he

---

39. *See, e.g.,* the alignment of the justices in Valley Forge Christian College v. Americans United for Separation of Church and State, Inc., 454 U.S. 464 (1982), a standing case in which the Court held that Americans United lacked standing to challenge a financial windfall given by the government to a religious institution. In that case the alignment on the Court was virtually reversed and seems to indicate a certain political side to the *Bender* and *Valley Forge* standing decisions.

40. 106 S. Ct. at 1336. Of course, one would be surprised to see Justice Marshall take such a formalistic or technical procedural stand in a case in which he had more sympathy with the underlying substantive claim of the party whose standing was in issue. However, the dissenters who argue for a less formalistic application of standing are just as susceptible to a claim of politics as usual on this ground.

41. *Id.* at 1336–37 (C.J. Burger, dissenting).

42. *Id.* at 1337 (emphasis in original).

concluded that *Widmar* clearly controls the resolution of this case."[43] Evidently, the chief justice was not troubled by the maturation distinction and was willing to treat high school students in the same manner as the college students involved in *Widmar*.

In support of his conclusion that "granting the student prayer group equal access to the student activity forum.... 'follows the best of our traditions,'" Burger reasoned that

> The several commands of the First Amendment require vision capable of distinguishing between *state* establishment of religion, which is prohibited by the Establishment Clause, and *individual* participation and advocacy of religion which, far from being prohibited by the Establishment Clause, is affirmatively protected by the Free Exercise and Free Speech Clauses of the First Amendment. If the latter two commands are to retain any vitality, utterly unproven, subjective impressions of some hypothetical students should not be allowed to transform *individual* expression of religious belief into *state* advancement of religion.[44]

The chief justice's emphasis on the *individual* nature of the exercise involved and on the burden of proof is significant.

In emphasizing the *individual* nature of the exercise involved in the *Bender* case, Chief Justice Burger seems to reflect the sentiment of the framers, insofar as he seeks to indicate his support for the accommodation and perhaps even facilitation of individual free exercise in the public sector. His expectation that proof be offered to establish an actual, as opposed to hypothetical, violation of the Establishment Clause, on the other hand, is reminiscent of the view espoused by Justice Potter Stewart in his dissents in *Engel* and *Schempp*.[45] While such a view may create problems in terms of the broad application of principles (i.e., the limits of legal principles are often tested hypothetically, as a means of ascertaining whether they are viable and sound), it does have the virtue of requiring some proof of establishment before one's individual right of free exercise can be limited. In a sense, therefore, it returns the right of free exercise to its preeminent status vis-à-vis the Establishment Clause.

Justice Powell also dissented. He indicated that he agreed with the chief justice's conclusion that the case was controlled by *Widmar*. After emphasizing that there were a significant number, twenty-five, of nonre-

---

43. *Id.*

44. *Id.*

45. *See* Chapter 8, *supra,* for a discussion of Justice Stewart's treatment of the burden of proof related to the coercion issue in religion cases.

ligious student organizations that had been permitted to meet, Powell articulated his view regarding the maturation issue:

> The only arguable distinction between *Widmar* and this case is that *Widmar* involved university students while the groups here [in *Bender]* are composed of high school students. We did note in *Widmar* that university students are "less impressionable than younger students and should be able to appreciate that the university's policy is one of neutrality to a religion." *Id.,* at 274, n. 14, 102 S. Ct., at 277, n. 14. Other decisions, however, have recognized that the First Amendment rights of speech and association extend also to high school students. [citations omitted] I do not believe—particularly in this age of massive media information—that the few years difference in age between high school and college students justifies departing from *Widmar.*[46]

Powell's willingness to treat high school and university students similarly for the purposes of equal access indicates some weakening of the maturation distinction that has been drawn in previous decisions. However, it would be incorrect to read too much into Powell's dissenting opinion. The distinction between the impressionability of high school and university students retains some vitality, but Powell's decision does indicate his willingness to erode the distinction somewhat.

Another point raised by Justice Powell's opinion is the increasing willingness of the Court to treat religious expression like other forms of expression or at least to assure that religious expression and association not suffer discrimination. This similarity in treatment for various forms of student expression often confounds conservatives and liberals alike. Many conservatives tend to oppose broad rights of nonreligious expression in the public schools and would like to permit school officials to exercise broad discretion with regard to nonreligious student expression (e.g., whether students may wear armbands for purposes of political expression or what books should be made available to students), while paradoxically they favor extending religious expression (e.g., prayer). Many liberals, on the other hand, want to see broad rights of political and other nonreligious forms of expression, while simultaneously endeavoring to limit all forms of religious expression on the part of students. Both of these views belie a content-based bias; the liberals want broad rights of

---

46. 106 S. Ct. at 1339. Justice Powell's view is supported in a recent article concluding that "research in the field of adolescent psychology suggests that high school students are generally independent and capable of critical inquiry." Note, *The Constitutional Dimensions of Student-Initiated Religious Activity in Public High Schools,* 92 YALE L. J. 499, 507 (1983).

nonreligious expression but do not care for religious expression, while conservatives do not care for broad rights of expression except when that expression is religious in nature. In each instance, their views are dictated by their personal preferences about expression. If the Court follows Powell's lead as it did in *Widmar*, both liberals and conservatives may have to live with a form of expression that they find unacceptable, but that has often been the cost of principled liberty.

A couple of additional points should be raised in concluding this discussion of the *Bender* case. First, given that the majority opted to avoid the underlying substantive issue by holding that Youngman lacked standing, it would be inappropriate to read too much into the decision as a substantive matter. At some time in the not too distant future, the Court will have the opportunity to decide that underlying substantive issue. Because of the passage of the Equal Access Act,[47] the Court may yet have to confront the issue of whether or not the government can permit individual religious expression in public secondary schools where other forms of expression are encouraged. Given the somewhat enigmatic position of some members of the majority who in the past have applied the standing doctrine leniently,[48] one must resist the inclination to speculate that decisions on the standing issue evidence politics over principle. Suffice it to say that parties must be careful to put facts into the record that will support standing.

Second, as a substantive matter in *Bender*, none of the justices referred to the history. That is, of course, explicable on the ground that an historical exegesis was simply unnecessary, given that the decision was decided on the basis of a lack of standing. In the future, however, when all of the justices have to turn their energy to the substantive issue of equal access, it is clear that, under either the Story or the Madisonian view, a practice like that involved in *Bender* would be constitutional. If the Court rejects both the Madisonian and the Story view in a future case by rendering a decision precluding the students from meeting for purposes of religious expression, the Court will have acted illegitimately, from an originalist point of view, because it will have substituted the views of the justices for those of the framers and ratifiers. To date, the Court has managed to refrain from doing so, and it can be anticipated, I believe,

---

47. *See* Chapter 12, *infra*, for a discussion of the Equal Access Act.
48. Of course, the position of some of the dissenters is equally enigmatic, because in the past they have applied the standing doctrine in a very strict manner.

that they will continue to resist the urge to apply an absolute or strict-separationist view. If, however, the Court does discard the history by substituting their views for the framers, the time for concerted legislative action may be at hand.[49]

---

49. *See* Chapter 12, *infra,* for a discussion as to when an amendment is appropriate.

11

Governmental Chaplains and Public Prayers Outside the School Context: The Marsh Case

In every state, legislative and related meetings often open with prayer.[1] Indeed, many state legislatures hire a chaplain to offer the prayer, as well as for counseling on an individual basis with members of the legislature. Other states follow the practice of inviting on a rotating basis clergy or other individuals to offer an invocation at the opening of their legislative sessions. Public prayers are offered frequently at the commencement of public meetings at the city and county levels as well. At the federal level, both the Senate and the House of Representatives have chaplains and begin each legislative day with the offering of a prayer or similar invocation. Even cabinet meetings in the Executive Branch have on occasion started with a word of prayer. The Supreme Court itself begins each day of argument with the statement, "God save the United States and this Honorable Court."[2]

If we were to adhere strictly to the principle of a separation of church and state for purposes of the Establishment Clause, none of these practices would be acceptable as a matter of constitutional law. However, these practices have deep historical roots. Many of the practices had their

---

1. *See, e.g.,* Marsh v. Chambers, 103 S.Ct. 3330, 3335, n. 11.
2. Indeed, Professor Lawrence Tribe drew upon this phrase in designating the title of his recent book, GOD SAVE THIS HONORABLE COURT (1985).

genesis before the founding of our country and were perpetuated without abatement after the passage of the First Amendment. Are such practices constitutional? Should they be held to be constitutional?

In 1983, in *Marsh v. Chambers,*[3] the Court agreed to hear a case dealing with public prayer in the nonschool context. The facts in the *Marsh* case were not complicated. Ernest Chambers, a taxpayer and member of the Nebraska legislature, brought an action against the state treasurer, Frank Marsh, challenging the constitutionality of the legislature's practice of opening each legislative session with a prayer given by a chaplain hired by a majority of the legislature and paid with state funds. The chaplain of the legislature was Robert E. Palmer, a Presbyterian minister, who was hired in 1965 and had been employed continuously by the legislature from that time to the time of the filing of the action. The Rev. Mr. Palmer was paid $319.75 per month for each month the legislature was in session, and at the end of each session, his prayers were collected in book form and published at public expense for distribution to members of the legislature and the general public. Palmer testified that he sought to offer essentially nonsectarian prayers. In fact, after an objection was raised by a Jewish legislator to the Christian content of Palmer's prayers, he endeavored to remove references to Christ and Christian doctrine. Ultimately, based on these facts, the question facing the Court was whether the Nebraska legislature's practice of opening each legislative day with a prayer by a chaplain paid by the state violated the Establishment Clause of the First Amendment.

In *Marsh,* the Court held, by a 6-3 margin, that the Nebraska legislature was permitted, as a constitutional matter, to hire a chaplain and to open each legislative day with a prayer. Justices Byron White, Harry Blackmun, Lewis Powell, William Rehnquist, and Sandra O'Connor joined in the majority opinion, which was written by Chief Justice Warren Burger. None of these justices felt it necessary to file separate concurring opinions, so it may be assumed that they were essentially in agreement with the content of the opinion drafted by the chief justice. There were, however, two dissenting opinions filed; Justice William Brennan filed a lengthy, substantive dissent, in which Justice Thurgood Marshall joined, and Justice John Paul Stevens filed a terse dissent.

CHIEF JUSTICE BURGER'S OPINION FOR THE COURT

In reasoning that the Nebraska chaplaincy practices were constitutional, Chief Justice Burger relied heavily on historical materials. Burger did not turn to the *Lemon* test, which has often been invoked in cases

---

3. 103 S.Ct. 3330 (1983).

raising potential Establishment Clause problems. Rather, he reasoned that historical evidence specifically supported the proposition that the framers and ratifiers of the First Amendment must have intended to permit such practices, because similar chaplaincy practices were commonly engaged in and supported by the framers themselves. The chief justice noted that

> Standing alone, historical patterns cannot justify contemporary violations of constitutional guarantees, but there is far more here than simply historical patterns. In this context, historical evidence sheds light not only on what the draftsmen intended the Establishment Clause to mean, but also on how they thought that clause applied to the practice authorized by the First Congress—their actions reveal their intent.[4]

For the majority in *Marsh,* historical evidence of acceptance of the practice of hiring a chaplain to offer legislative prayers was so strong that it not only clarified the issues raised, but it also disposed of them because it revealed the intent of the framers.

The Court accumulated a number of pieces of historical evidence to support its conclusion that the practice of opening legislative sessions with prayer was accepted by the framers of the First Amendment. Burger began by noting that Virginia consistently "followed the practice of opening legislative sessions with prayer,"[5] both before and after the adoption of the Virginia Declaration of Rights in 1776. He mentioned in addition that the Virginia Declaration of Rights has commonly been considered to be "the precursor of both the Free Exercise and Establishment Clauses."[6] Given that the Virginia Declaration of Rights is generally conceded to be a precursor to the Bill of Rights, given the role of Virginia and Virginians in promoting and formulating the language and theory of the First Amendment, and given that the practice of hiring chaplains was consistently accepted in Virginia beginning in the early eighteenth century (even the Virginia ratification convention in which the First Amendment was debated and ratified opened with a prayer offered by a paid chaplain), the majority found strong support for their conclusion that "from colonial times through the founding of the Republic and ever since, the practice of legislative prayer has coexisted with the principles of disestablishment and religious freedom."[7]

---

4. *Id.* at 3335.
5. *Id.* at 3334, n. 5.
6. *Id.* at 3333, n. 5.
7. *Id.* at 3333.

However, the chief justice was not satisfied with merely invoking the Virginia example. He relied on additional historical evidence as well. He noted that Rhode Island, which was founded by Roger Williams, began the sessions of its ratification convention and subsequent legislative sessions with prayers offered by chaplains hired by the convention or the legislature.[8] Both the Continental Congress and the First Congress, which adopted the First Amendment, selected chaplains to open each session with prayer.[9] Burger stressed that from our nation's birth both the House of Representatives and the Senate elected chaplains. Furthermore, on 22 September 1789, just three days before final agreement was reached on the Bill of Rights, a statute was adopted authorizing payment of compensation to these chaplains for their services.[10] Thus, as the chief justice emphasized, in the course of a single week, the First Congress reached agreement on the language of the Bill of Rights, with its provisions protecting religious liberty, authorized the appointment of two paid chaplains of differing denominations who would alternate between the House and Senate chambers on a weekly basis, and sent a resolution from the House to the president requesting that he designate a day of thanksgiving and prayer to acknowledge "the many signal favors of Almighty God."[11]

The Court also noted the unbroken nature of the practice of selecting and paying a chaplain to offer prayers at the opening of each legislative day at both the federal and state levels, although it did acknowledge that the practice had been challenged on occasion. There was overwhelming evidence for the Court that the framers intended to permit the hiring of legislative chaplains. Furthermore, prudence as well as history dictated that the Court leave such a long-standing practice intact.

As previously noted, the Court did recognize that there were a number of occasions when the practice of hiring a chaplain had been challenged. John Jay and John Rutledge opposed a motion to begin the first session of the Continental Congress with prayer.[12] Objections to prayer were apparently raised successfully during the ratification debates in Pennsylvania.[13] James Madison, who initially favored a form of chaplaincy legislation, wrote subsequently of his opposition to aspects of the legislative chaplaincy as it had developed by 1820.[14] A proposal offered by

---

8. *Id.* at 3334, n. 5.
9. *Id.* at 3333–34.
10. *Id.* at 3334.
11. *Id.* at 3334, n. 9.
12. *Id.* at 3336.
13. *Id.* at 3336, n. 12.
14. *Id.*

Benjamin Franklin during the Constitutional Convention relative to the hiring of a chaplain had failed.[15] In the 1850s, a number of senators engaged in an unsuccessful effort to eliminate paid chaplains on the ground that their service violated the Establishment Clause.[16] While a few of these efforts to have the legislative chaplaincy declared unconstitutional on Establishment Clause or related grounds were successful, the chief justice stressed that overwhelming historical support existed for the proposition that legislative chaplaincies were constitutionally acceptable. Indeed, he concluded that evidence of opposition merely demonstrated "that the subject was considered carefully and the action not taken thoughtlessly, by force of long tradition and without regard to the problems posed by a pluralistic society."[17]

It is not surprising that the Court, in a statement reminiscent of the Story approach, concluded its analysis of the history by stating that

> In light of the unambiguous and unbroken history of more than 200 years, there can be no doubt that the practice of opening legislative sessions with prayer has become part of the fabric of our society. To invoke Divine guidance on a public body entrusted with making the laws is not, in these circumstances, an "establishment" of religion or a step toward establishment; it is simply a tolerable acknowledgment of beliefs widely held among the people of this country.[18]

However, even having found that the history supported the constitutionality of hiring chaplains as a general matter, the Court had to determine whether aspects of the Nebraska practice rendered it unconstitutional.

The first specific problem was whether the Nebraska practice was unconstitutional because a clergyman of only one denomination had continuously been selected as the legislative chaplain over a sixteen-year period. The court of appeals had noted that this lengthy tenure had the effect of giving a preference to a single religious denomination. The Supreme Court, however, rejected the conclusion of the court of appeals that choosing a clergyman of one church necessarily advances the beliefs of that church. Burger noted that, "absent proof that the chaplain's reappointment stemmed from an impermissible motive, we conclude that his long tenure does not in itself conflict with the Establishment Clause."[19] This leaves open the issue of motive in subsequent cases, but proving an evil motive is never easy.

---

15. *Id.* at 3334, n. 6.
16. *Id.* at 3334–35, n. 10.
17. *Id.* at 3335.
18. *Id.* at 3336.
19. *Id.* at 3337.

A second problem peculiar to the facts of the case centered on the issue of compensation for the chaplain. Referring briefly to the history, which supported the notion that it was appropriate to pay a chaplain with state funds, and noting that many states continue to compensate their chaplains, the Court concluded that the payment of compensation did not render the Nebraska practice unconstitutional. The Court was able to avoid a more difficult and somewhat unique problem attributable to the Nebraska practice. Nebraska not only compensated its chaplains, but it also collected the prayers into a book, which was published and distributed at state expense. In a sense, the government was publishing religious material under its imprimatur. The Court, however, was able to avoid facing this problem on technical grounds, because "the state did not appeal the district court order enjoining further publications."[20]

Finally, the Court had to deal with the issue of whether the theological content of the prayers rendered the Nebraska practice unconstitutional. The Court, again, simply avoided this by concluding that "the content of the prayer is not of concern to judges where, as here, there is no indication that the prayer opportunity has been exploited to proselytize or advance any one, or to disparage any other, faith or belief."[21] In support of this conclusion, the Court had cited previously a dialogue between Samuel Adams and John Jay and John Rutledge that the Court felt emphasized that delegates to the Continental Congress "did not consider opening prayers as a proselytizing activity or as symbolically placing the government's 'official seal of approval on one religious view.' ...Rather, the Founding Fathers looked at invocations as 'conduct whose...effect...harmonize[d] with the tenets of some or all religions.'"[22] The Court also emphasized that legislators, unlike school children, are adults, "presumably not readily susceptible to 'religious indoctrination.'"[23]

It seems clear on the facts, as characterized by the majority, that the decision of the Court is consistent with the Story position and is inconsistent with the Madisonian view. Joseph Story thought that most framers and ratifiers believed that the First Amendment was drafted to ensure that, while no single church was to be recognized as the national church, nondenominational Christianity, of a tolerant (albeit sometimes anti-Catholic) variety, was to be accepted as the national religion.

For Story, therefore, the employment of a chaplain to give nonsectarian, Christian prayers would be in keeping with the intent of the

20. *Id.* at 3337, n. 15.
21. *Id.* at 3337–38.
22. *Id.* at 3336.
23. *Id.*

framers and ratifiers of the First Amendment. The Story view predominated during the nineteenth century and supported the notion that religious practices of a nondenominational Christian (essentially Protestant) sort had a place in the operation of our national government. It is not surprising, therefore, that many states as well as the federal government recognized that appointing a chaplain of the Christian faith was an acceptable practice. The fact that Congress hired two chaplains of different Christian denominations who were to alternate between the Senate and the House may have constituted an effort to assure the nondenominational nature of the practice.

James Madison, however, whose views represent those of a number of supporters of the First Amendment, may have reached a different conclusion about the constitutionality of the Nebraska practice. Madison's view is a bit more difficult to delineate and apply in this area, because during the First Congress he supported a chaplaincy statute, but later wrote a memorandum indicating his opposition to a paid chaplaincy elected by members of Congress.

Undoubtedly, the most elaborate source of Madison's view on this precise issue can be found in his *Detached Memoranda*. In that document, written in the 1820's, Madison dealt with the issue of whether the appointment of chaplains to the two houses of Congress was consistent with the Constitution and the principle of religious freedom, and concluded that

> In strictness the answer on both points must be in the negative. The Constitution of the U.S. forbids everything like an establishment of a national religion. The law appointing chaplains establishes a religious worship for the national representatives, to be performed by ministers of religion, elected by a majority of them; and these are to be paid out of the national taxes. Does this not involve the principle of a national establishment, applicable to a provision for a religious worship for the constituent as well as of the representative body, approved by the majority, and conducted by ministers of religion paid by the entire nation?
>
> The establishment of the chaplainship to Congress is a palpable violation of equal rights, as well as of constitutional principles: The tenets of the chaplains elected (by the majority) shut the door of worship ag[ain]st the members whose creeds & consciences forbid a participation in that of the majority. To say nothing of other sects, this is the case with that of Roman Catholics & Quakers who have always had members in one or both of the Legislative branches. Could a Catholic clergyman ever hope to be appointed a chaplain? To say that his religious principles are obnoxious or that his sect is small, is to lift the evil at once and exhibit in its naked deformity the doctrine that religious truth is to be tested by numbers, or that the major sects have a right to govern the minor.

If Religion consist[s] in voluntary acts of individuals, singly, or voluntarily associated, and it be proper that public functionaries, as well as their constituents should discharge their religious duties, let them like their constituents, do so at their own expense. How small a contribution from each member of Cong[res]s would suffice for the purpose? How just w[oul]d it be in its principle? How noble in its exemplary sacrifice to the genius of the Constitution; and the divine right of conscience? Why should the expense of a religious worship be allowed for the Legislature, be paid by the public, more than that for the Ex[ecutive] or the Judiciary branch of the Gov[ernme]nt?[24]

I have discussed the *Detached Memoranda* in its historical context,[25] but I should reiterate that I do not believe that it is indicative of any change in the principles articulated by Madison at the time of the framing of the First Amendment.

Madison believed that the religion clauses of the First Amendment were drafted for the primary purpose of protecting the inalienable right of conscience. In particular, he felt that the First Amendment required of the government equal treatment or nonpreference in its treatment of various religious sects. In other words, while Madison believed that the government could accommodate or facilitate the right of conscience, he maintained that government had to do so evenhandedly, without showing preference for any religious sect or doctrine. In a related sense, he felt that it was inappropriate for government to adopt any particular mode of worship as its own. From the time of the debate on the Declaration of Rights in Virginia in 1776, when Madison first articulated his views regarding religious liberty, until the 1820s, when he prepared his *Detached Memoranda,* he did not deviate in any significant way from his adherence to these views. Therefore, the *Detached Memoranda* really constitutes but another piece of evidence suggesting surprising consistency in Madison's views throughout his lifetime.

At the outset in his *Detached Memoranda,* Madison notes that the Constitution prohibits "everything like an establishment of religion." The basic principles infusing Madison's objection to a paid chaplaincy are identical to those that remained throughout his lifetime. The practice should be prohibited as an establishment of religion because it constituted an effort on the part of government to mandate a mode or form of worship, the chaplain's prayer, that advanced the religious beliefs of the majority and might, therefore, result in unequal treatment for the votaries

---

24. As cited in R. Alley, JAMES MADISON ON RELIGIOUS LIBERTY, 91–92 (1985).

25. *See supra* Chapter 4.

of minority sects. This, in Madison's view, was prohibited by the Establishment Clause of the First Amendment. In Madison's own words, it constituted a "palpable violation of equal rights" and, therefore, infringed on the "divine right of conscience." The Establishment Clause prohibitions against unequal treatment and the adoption by government of a particular mode of worship, in Madison's view, were formulated to protect the right of conscience but not to render the public sector irreligious.

The *Detached Memoranda* clearly delineates Madison's opposition to a paid chaplaincy like that at issue in *Marsh*. However, the majority in *Marsh* was quick to note that Madison originally supported a statute providing for a paid chaplaincy for Congress. This seems to indicate that Madison may have changed his mind later in life and that his original intent, in introducing the First Amendment, would not have opposed the practice of hiring a chaplain. Since views extant at the time of the adoption and ratification of the First Amendment are critical for the purpose of interpreting the meaning of the religion clauses, it follows that Madison's initial support for the chaplaincy statute constitutes significant evidence of his intent, as well as that of other members of the First Congress, on the issue of a paid chaplaincy.

To this, Justice William Brennan, in his dissent, responded that "Madison's later views may not have represented so much a change of *mind* as a change of *role,* from a member of Congress engaged in the hurly-burly of legislative activity to a detached observer engaged in unpressured reflection. Since the latter role is precisely the one with which this Court is charged, I am not at all sure that Madison's later writings should be any less influential in our deliberations than his earlier vote."[26] Brennan is at least partially correct, although for the originalist Madison's role as a legislator would be critical. Madison was very interested in obtaining quick passage of the Bill of Rights during the same time period when the chaplaincy statute was passed. He felt quick passage was necessary to avoid Anti-Federalist efforts to dismantle the newly established constitutional government. Therefore, the political pressures of the moment may have contributed to Madison's willingness to favor the chaplaincy statute without necessarily changing his views and without acknowledging that his views were less acceptable as a matter of principled constitutional interpretation.

Justice Brennan's explanation of Madison's apparent shift on the chaplaincy issue is incomplete. Certainly, Madison was an astute politician and may have been engaging in a bit of logrolling; however, there is also a sense in which his behavior on the chaplaincy issue may be consistent

---

26. 103 S.Ct. at 3348.

with his views on religious liberty. As originally constituted, the congressional chaplaincy provided for two chaplains of different denominations to alternate between the Senate and the House. In a sense, therefore, the original procedure provided for at least a modicum of equality and non-preference regarding religious exercises. This may have constituted an effort on the part of those adhering to the Madisonian view to obtain some equality of treatment, without opposing the chaplaincy itself as a matter of principle. Additionally, Madison may have been exhibiting faith in his fellow legislators, who adhered to the view later articulated by Justice Story, believing that they would assure that Congress acted in a tolerant manner. He may, therefore, have been willing to go along with those who favored the chaplaincy as a means of ensuring at least a measure of tolerance and equality, without jeopardizing his position on other issues. However, by 1820, Madison's faith in the tolerance and possible equanimity of proponents of the Story view had largely dissipated. Those favoring the Story view during the early 1800s were well on the way to consolidating their position by limiting the equal-treatment views of Madison and others. The rising acceptance of the Story view in the early nineteenth century, with a concomitant de-emphasis on tolerance, must have been unsettling to Madison. Because of this, he undoubtedly felt compelled to clarify his views with precision in the *Detached Memoranda*.

It is evident that Madison opposed a chaplaincy system, like that existing in Nebraska, in his *Detached Memoranda*. It is also clear that such a system would be unacceptable under the equal-treatment and mode-of-worship analyses favored, as a matter of principle, by Madison at the time the First Amendment was adopted. His vote in favor of the congressional chaplaincy, therefore, remains in part an enigma. While I believe my explanation of his behavior on the issue is more than plausible, I must concede that it is not dispositive. Chief Justice Burger and the majority may be correct in asserting that Madison's action in the First Congress supported their holding. However, such a conclusion is based on piecemeal jurisprudence searching for evidence of acceptance for specific historical practices to determine the constitutionality of similar practices in the future rather than principled jurisprudence, which involves examining the history to determine the principle that ought to be applied in a given area. As one who favors principled as opposed to piecemeal jurisprudence, I recognize that principled review gives the Court greater latitude in cases like *Marsh*. I do not find such discretion to be *malum in se;* rather, it becomes an evil when Courts exceed the bounds set by discernible principles and begin to fashion principles of their own as a means of facilitating their own policy choices. Furthermore, principles have the added virtue of providing guidance in cases where evidence of previous practices is not available. A practice is strong evidence of the principle or principles that were accepted, but it should not be used as a panacea without examining how a given practice fits within the bounds set by broader principles.

It is worthwhile to examine the majority's methodological use of history in its analysis. The chief justice stated, "Standing alone, historical patterns cannot justify contemporary violations of constitutional guarantees, but there is far more here than simply historical patterns. In this context, historical evidence sheds light not only on what the draftsmen intended the Establishment Clause to mean, but also on how they thought that clause applied to the practice authorized by the First Congress—their actions reveal their intent."[27] In turn, the majority concluded that the framers' intent ought to be controlling. The framers, particularly men like Madison, were in some measure "natural lawyers": they believed in, or at least made reference to, natural law principles and inalienable rights, although it is clear that they had doubts about the possibility of replicating natural law principles in the positive law of their day.[28] As such, the framers would no doubt find the Court's piecemeal mode of adjudication foreign and perhaps even disingenuous. Therefore, while I would applaud the Court's willingness to look to the history, I would have been happier had they searched for or derived principles from the practices, rather than merely invoking the existence of similar practices as a device for disposing of a sensitive case. The Court could, and probably should, have held the Nebraska chaplaincy practice to be constitutional under a principled mode of analysis. In doing so, however, it could have articulated lucid principles that would offer guidance in future cases. Otherwise, I fear that we may be left with a strange two-tiered analytical approach under which the Court looks first to historical practices and then, if and when it cannot conjure up a similar practice to use as precedent, it turns to its tests (e.g., the *Lemon* test), which are often not rooted in principles derivable from the history. Such two-tiered analyses will no doubt result in a crazy quilt of legal precedent, adding confusion to an area of the law that is already plagued with uncertainty and inconsistency.

JUSTICE BRENNAN'S DISSENTING OPINION

Justice Brennan's dissent, which was joined by Justice Marshall, constitutes a fairly significant and scholarly effort to deal with the *Marsh* issue in light of applicable constitutional history and doctrine. As such, the opinion is interesting not only for its content but also for its approach.

---

27. *Id.* at 3335.
28. *See, e.g.,* discussion regarding natural law and the framers in Ely, DEMOCRACY AND DISTRUST, 39, 48–54 (1980).

Justice Brennan shrewdly begins his opinion by noting, "The Court today has written a narrow and, on the whole, careful opinion. In effect, the Court holds that officially sponsored legislative prayer, primarily on account of its 'unique history,'... is generally exempted from the First Amendment's prohibition against 'an establishment of religion.' The Court's opinion is consistent with dictum in at least one of our prior decisions, and its limited rationale should pose little threat to the overall fate of the Establishment Clause."[29] In so limiting the impact of the majority opinion, Brennan opts for a somewhat conservative course. Oftentimes, dissenting opinions in cases like *Marsh* will go to pains to point out the dramatic consequences accompanying extension of the doctrines enunciated in the majority opinion. In *Marsh,* Brennan refused to yield to the allure of such an approach. Instead, he sought to limit the ambit of the decision by characterizing it as anomalous. He was inclined to treat it as a bit of piecemeal jurisprudence, limited to its particular facts, rather than indulging in playing with its principles. If he had characterized the majority's decision as a broad one, he might have played into the hands of those who would like to undermine the Court and, in Brennan's view, the salutary benefits of existing doctrine.

After limiting the majority's opinion, Justice Brennan nevertheless elucidated the reasons for his dissent. He began by noting that he opposed the Court's implicit rejection of the *Lemon* test, although he acknowledged that the failure of the Court to subject the facts of the Nebraska chaplaincy issue to the *Lemon* test was in a sense a good thing, because instead of molding the *Lemon* test or doctrine to fit the facts, the Court merely carved out "an exception to the Establishment Clause rather than reshaping Establishment Clause doctrine to accommodate legislative prayer."[30]

Justice Brennan then applied the *Lemon* test and concluded that he had no doubt that if "any group of law students were asked to apply the principles of *Lemon* to the question of legislative prayer, they would nearly unanimously find the practice to be unconstitutional."[31] He also noted that the decision did not comport with other tests or analytical approaches that have been used in resolving Establishment Clause issues.[32]

After his brief examination of existing tests, Justice Brennan proceeded to examine the case in light of the "underlying function of the Establishment Clause, and the forces that have shaped its doctrine."[33]

---

29. *Id.* at 3338.
30. *Id.*
31. *Id.* at 3341.
32. *Id.* at 3341. n. 11.
33. *Id.* at 3341.

According to Brennan, the Establishment Clause should be invoked to support the principles of separation and neutrality. Unfortunately, he purports to derive these principles from the *Everson* and *Reynolds* decisions.[34] However, with his enunciation of the purposes served by these principles and the exceptions to them, Brennan does much to disavow the impact of the *Everson* and *Reynolds* decisions.[35]

After citing the separation and neutrality principles, Justice Brennan enumerated the purposes served by those principles: (1) "to guarantee the individual right of conscience (against indirect as well as direct coercion)";[36] (2) "to keep the state from interfering in the essential autonomy of religious life, either by taking upon itself the decision of religious issues, or by unduly involving itself in the supervision of religious institutions or officials";[37] (3) "to prevent the trivialization and degradation of religion by too close an attachment to the organs of government";[38] and (4) to "assure that essentially religious issues, precisely because of their importance and sensitivity, not become the occasion for battle in the political arena."[39]

Justice Brennan then concluded that

> Legislative prayer clearly violates the principles of neutrality and separation that are embedded within the Establishment Clause. It is contrary to the fundamental message of *Engel* and *Schempp*. It intrudes on the right to conscience by forcing some legislators either to participate in a "prayer opportunity,"... with which they are in basic disagreement, or to make their disagreement a matter of public comment by declining to participate. It forces all residents of the state to support a religious exercise that may be contrary to their own beliefs. It requires the state to commit itself on fundamental theological issues. It has the potential for degrading religion by allowing a religious call to worship to be intermeshed with a secular call to order. And it injects religion into the political sphere by creating the potential that each and every selection of a chaplain, or consideration of a particular prayer, or even reconsideration of the practice itself, will provoke a political battle along religious lines and ultimately alienate some religiously identified group of citizens.[40]

---

34. *Id.* at 3342.
35. *Id.*
36. *Id.*
37. *Id.*
38. *Id.*
39. *Id.*
40. *Id.* at 3344–45.

Each of these faults would also be objectionable under the Madisonian view that prohibits inequality in the treatment of religions and precludes the government from adopting a particular mode of worship or religious doctrine as its own. Madison's view, however, unlike that espoused by Justice Brennan, has the virtue of being more straightforward, of being rooted in the actual history of the framing and ratification of the First Amendment, and of not being based on the faulty reasoning and historical analyses contained in the *Everson* and *Reynolds* opinions.

In endeavoring to place his reasoning in its precedential framework, Justice Brennan had to take another step that convoluted his reasoning even further; he had to recognize that, given the tension between the Free Exercise right and Establishment Clause value, some exceptions to a strict application of the separation and neutrality principles have been developed. He noted five such exceptions: (1) "religious practices may, in certain contexts, receive the benefit of government programs and policies generally available, on the basis of some secular criterion, to a wide class of similarly situated nonreligious beneficiaries";[41] (2) "religion can encompass a broad, if not total, spectrum of concerns, overlapping considerably with the range of secular concerns, and that not every governmental act which coincides with or conflicts with a particular religious belief is for that reason an establishment of religion";[42] (3) "government cannot, without adopting a decidedly *anti*-religious point of view, be forbidden to recognize the religious beliefs and practices of the American people as an aspect of our history and culture";[43] (4) "the purposes of the Establishment Clause can sometimes conflict";[44] and (5) "under the Free Exercise Clause religiously motivated claims of conscience may give rise to constitutional rights that other strongly held beliefs do not. ...Moreover, even when the government is not compelled to do so by the Free Exercise Clause it may to some extent act to *facilitate* the opportunities of individuals to practice their religion."[45]

Justice Brennan then concluded that, just as the Nebraska practice failed to satisfy the four purposes of the separation and neutrality principles, it could not be redeemed under any of the existing exceptions to those principles.

---

41. *Id.* at 3345.
42. *Id.*
43. *Id.* at 3346.
44. *Id.*
45. *Id.* (emphasis added).

Brennan's opinion certainly constituted a yeoman effort to unite the various precedents and their reasoning in the First Amendment area. However, the opinion leaves one a bit unsettled. Not only does it constitute an after-the-fact effort to consolidate the reasoning employed in the prior cases, but it also leaves one bewildered as to the original source of the consolidating principles. How much better it would be to combine the decisions under the rubric of principles derived from an examination of the history of the framing and ratification of the First Amendment. This Justice Brennan could have done by invoking the Madisonian view. Brennan's machinations add nothing, in a policy sense, to the Madisonian view, and they clearly serve as an example of how difficult it is to pull the material together without some prior, principled basis for doing so.

While Justice Brennan's search for a unified mode of analysis is commendable, his use of the history is suspect methodologically. He begins the historical portion of his opinion by noting that he "agree[s] that historical practice is 'of considerable import in the interpretation of abstract constitutional language.'"[46] He goes on to note, however, that there are "at least three reasons why specific historical practice should not in this case override [the] clear constitutional imperative [found in prior cases]."[47]

First, he argues that "the Court's historical argument does not rely on the legislative history of the Establishment Clause itself."[48] He concludes that the history is "profoundly unilluminating"[49] and concedes that, therefore, the majority's use of historical practice as opposed to legislative history is understandable. Ultimately, however, he finds the majority's use of historical practice to be regrettable and unsupportable because "legislators, influenced by the passions and exigencies of the moment, the pressure of constituents and colleagues, and the press of business, do not always pass sober constitutional judgment on every piece of legislation they enact, and this must be assumed to be as true of the members of the First Congress as any other."[50]

Justice Brennan's conclusions are flawed in at least two senses. First, the legislative history is much more illuminating than he is willing to recognize. It is unfortunate that since the time of *Everson*, members of

---

46. *Id.* at 3347.
47. *Id.*
48. *Id.*
49. *Id.*
50. *Id.* at 3348.

the Court have as a general matter blithely concluded that the legislative history is not helpful, without so much as examining that history to illustrate its nonutility. Second, Brennan also errs when he concludes that politicians at the time of the founding were inclined just as their political counterparts are today to neglect constitutional principles in the rush and pressure of daily congressional activity. While I am much less willing than Brennan to concede that Congress today is often so consumed in the exigencies of political activity that they neglect weightier and deeper constitutional issues,[51] I will accept that proposition for the moment for the sake of argument. It is not equally clear that representatives in the First Congress were by their nature inclined to ignore the constitutional impact of issues raised on a daily basis. It will be recalled that Representative Thomas Tudor Tucker of South Carolina challenged a "prayer resolution" on establishment grounds during the First Congress.[52] It should also be emphasized that the members of the First Congress actually debated, drafted, and adopted the First Amendment. It was their handiwork, and it is, therefore, much less likely that they would ignore it during the press of the legislative agenda. Indeed, as the majority noted, it was just three days after Congress authorized the appointment of paid chaplains that final agreement was reached on the language of the Bill of Rights. Given this and their belief in the importance of natural law principles of the sort included in the Bill of Rights and in their obligations to render public service of a selfless nature,[53] it is not at all clear that members of the First Congress would ignore principled consti-

---

51. *See* Chapter 12, *infra,* for an analysis of the legislative role in constitutional decision making.

52. *See* Chapter 4, *supra.*

53. For example, speaking of the Republicanism of John Adams, Forrest McDonald recently wrote that

The public passion, he emphasized, "must be Superiour to all private Passions. Men must be happy to sacrifice...their private Friendships and dearest Connections, when they stand in Competition with the Rights of Society." To his wife Abigail, Adams wrote that their children might suppose that he should have labored more for their benefit, but "I will not bear the Reproaches of my Children. I will tell them that I studied and laboured to procure a free Constitution of Government for them to solace themselves under, and if they do not prefer this to ample Fortune, to Ease and Elegance, they are not my Children, and I care not what becomes of them." His sons must "revere nothing but Religion, Morality, and Liberty"—the liberty to be good republicans.

F. McDonald, Novus Ordo Seclorum: The Intellectual Origins Of The Constitution, 72 (1985).

tutional limitations. Furthermore, at this time, prior to Chief Justice Marshall's decision in *Marbury v. Madison*,[54] upholding the Court's power of judicial review, it is certainly arguable that many members believed they had a special role in safeguarding constitutional principles.

Second, Justice Brennan asserts that the majority's

> analysis treats the First Amendment simply as an Act of Congress, as to whose meaning the intent of Congress is the single touchstone. Both the Constitution and its amendments, however, became supreme law only by virtue of their ratification by the states, and the understanding of the states should be as relevant to our analysis as the understanding of Congress.[55]

This objection is more telling. Intent analysis is indeed incomplete without resort to what transpired in the ratification debates. As Hamilton noted in *Federalist No. 78*, the Court engages in judicial review precisely because the will of the people is superior to the will of their agents, the legislators. The Court, therefore, ought to look beyond the acts of the legislators and even the views held by delegates to a ratifying convention to the will of the people, as manifested in the ratification debates.[56] In this sense, Justice Brennan notes that "as a practical matter, 'we know practically nothing about what went on in the state legislatures' during the process of ratifying the Bill of Rights."[57] Justice Brennan, however, does little to enlighten us further about the ratification debates and rather seems content to chide the majority for refusing to look to that primary source. Nevertheless, absent the availability of extensive data from the ratification debates, it is clear that evidence of the congressional debates, which reflected as well as affected public discourse in the state ratifying conventions and elsewhere, together with actions and contemporaneous commentary are helpful in determining what the intended meaning of a given provision must have been. Thus, while it is clear that research regarding the ratification debates should be utilized where possible, there is a mass of other helpful, contemporaneous material available that should not be discounted unduly. Given Brennan's failure to do further research of his own on the ratification debates and given the sparse attention he paid to

---

54. 5 U.S. 137 (1803).

55. Marsh v. Chambers, 103 S.Ct. 3330 at 3348.

56. Unfortunately, as has been noted, the ratification debates are themselves often sketchy at best, given the weakness of reporting at the state level.

57. 103 S.Ct. at 3348, n. 32.

other, readily available historical material, it seems that his criticism of the Court may be more of an argumentative ploy than an effort to engage in enlightened analysis.

Third, Justice Brennan places a limitation on the role of history in determining constitutional cases. He argues that

> Finally, and most importantly, the argument tendered by the Court is misguided because the Constitution is not a static document whose meaning on every detail is fixed for all time by the life experience of the framers. We have recognized in a wide variety of constitutional contexts that the practices that were in place at the time any particular guarantee was enacted into the Constitution do not necessarily fix forever the meaning of that guarantee. To be truly faithful to the framers, "our use of history of their time must limit itself to broad purposes, not specific practices." [citations omitted] Our primary task must be to translate "the majestic generalities of the Bill of Rights, conceived as part of the pattern of liberal government in the eighteenth century, into concrete restraints on officials dealing with the problems of the twentieth century."[58]

This statement, a seeming articulation of Justice Brennan's views regarding the use of constitutional history, appears schizophrenic. On the one hand, Brennan seems to be saying that since the "Constitution is not a static document," the Court is largely free to mold doctrine according to their twentieth-century views. On the other, in the sentences that immediately follow this proclamation, he either equivocates or limits this view by noting that the Court is constrained in its interpretation by the "broad purposes" or "majestic generalities" that imbue the First Amendment with its meaning. If by this he means that the Court should apply the basic principles or purposes conceived by the framers, he is advocating a view not unlike that espoused in the course of this book. However, it appears, when one looks at how Brennan applies his theory to the history, that he views the history of the framing as little more than a weak beginning point.

In this light, it is helpful to examine how Justice Brennan uses the history as a matter of methodology. He quotes from Justice Joseph Story's *Commentaries* for the proposition that the "real object" of the religion clauses of the First Amendment, as originally drafted and supported, "was, not to countenance, much less to advance Mahometanism, Judaism, or infidelity, by prostrating Christianity; but to exclude all rivalry among Christian sects."[59] In doing so, he recognized the wealth of data supporting

---

58. *Id.* at 3348–49.
59. *Id.* at 3349.

the proposition that the framers—at least some of them—believed that the First Amendment was promulgated to promote or protect a tolerant version of nondenominational Christianity as our national religion. In other words, Justice Brennan recognized the vitality of the Story view during the framing and ratification era. However, rather than seeking to fit that view into a larger picture, he rejected it outright by noting that, in our age of religious diversity, "whatever deference Adams's actions and Story's views might once have deserved in this Court, the Establishment Clause must now be read in a very different light."[60] Thus, while Brennan spoke of the need to fit snippets of history into general principles or purposes, he failed to do so when analyzing the Story view. Rather, with what amounts to little more than an ipse dixit, Justice Brennan disregarded the wealth of historical material and turned to his own personal weighing of the policies involved in the case. Even his argument to the effect that current religious diversity justifies different treatment today is suspect, because maintaining religious diversity was an issue of significant concern to the framers. Furthermore, as has been pointed out in this book and elsewhere, there is substantial evidence indicating that the framers believed that religious diversity was a virtue to be promoted in an evenhanded fashion and not to be avoided or feared under the First Amendment.[61]

Despite the apparent weaknesses in his historical analysis, Justice Brennan does conclude his opinion by raising some significant policy justifications supporting rejection of the Nebraska prayer practice that might otherwise have been helpful in indicating why the principles articulated in the Madisonian rather than the Story view ought to be applied in such a case. Interestingly, nearly all of his policy arguments are similar to arguments raised by James Madison nearly two hundred years ago.

Justice Brennan began his policy argument by noting that the Nebraska chaplaincy constituted more than a *de minimis* violation of the Establishment Clause. He noted that the Nebraska practice "can easily turn narrowly and obviously sectarian."[62] He added that "*any* practice of legislative prayer, even if it might look 'nonsectarian' to nine justices of the Supreme Court, will inevitably and continuously involve the state in one or another religious debate."[63] He concluded that it is "inconsistent with our conceptions of liberty, for the state to take upon itself the

---

60. *Id.* at 3349.
61. *See, e.g., supra,* Chapters 2–4.
62. 103 S.Ct. at 3350 (emphasis in original).
63. *Id.* (emphasis in original).

role of ecclesiastical arbiter."[64] It will be recalled that Madison raised each of these arguments on a number of occasions, most notably during the debate in Virginia over the *Memorial and Remonstrance*.[65] While Brennan is wont to rely on contemporary views in developing his arguments on these policy issues, he could have found strong, principled support for each of his points in the constitutional history related to the development of the Madisonian view.

In concluding his analysis, Justice Brennan acknowledged that "if the Court had struck down legislative prayer today, it would likely have stimulated a furious reaction."[66] Nevertheless, he stressed that "it would also...have invigorated both the 'spirit of religion' and the 'spirit of freedom.'"[67] Brennan's conclusion amply illustrates that this was a difficult and somewhat courageous opinion for him to write. His willingness to buck public opinion in support of a constitutional principle is admirable, if a bit misplaced.

Before leaving Justice Brennan's dissenting opinion, however, a couple of points should be clarified, lest my critique of the opinion be deemed too harsh. First, it is clear that Brennan's opinion in *Marsh* is significant in terms of his concern for history, as a matter both of fact and of methodology. Second, his policy analysis was not in my opinion out of line as a matter of judicial interpretation. He could have easily couched his arguments in light of the Madisonian view and, in doing so, he would have maintained a basic fidelity to one of the predominant views held by the framers. I would, therefore, reiterate that the originalist mode of analysis advocated in the course of this book often yields helpful analytical boundaries and permits the Court fairly broad discretion in weighing alternative policies. New arguments are themselves acceptable when they are used to assist the Court in deciding an issue, provided the arguments do not extend beyond the limits set by the principles articulated by the framers. In that regard, Brennan's policy arguments are acceptable because they are consistent with the Madisonian view. Indeed, the *Marsh* case is one of those cases in which the Court could decide the issue either way; it could uphold the Nebraska practice and thereby maintain fidelity to the Story view, or it could reject the practice by invoking the principles set forth in the Madisonian view.

---

64. *Id.* at 3351.
65. *See* Chapter 3, *supra.*
66. 103 S. Ct. at 3351–52.
67. *Id.* at 3352.

THE STEVENS DISSENT

Justice Stevens also wrote a brief dissent. He concluded that "it seems plain to me that the designation of a member of one religious faith to serve as the sole official chaplain of a state legislature for a period of sixteen years constitutes the preference of one faith over another in violation of the Establishment Clause of the First Amendment."[68] While Justice Stevens does not indulge in any historical analysis, he has articulated a position consistent with Madison's view and inconsistent with the Story view.

CONCLUSION

While all of the opinions in *Marsh* are deficient to some degree as a matter of historical analysis, it is clear in a policy sense that the differences between the majority and the dissenters is but a revival of the old debate between the Storyites and the Madisonians. As has been shown, the framers did not resolve this dispute; politics and perhaps even prudence dictated that they leave its resolution to posterity. These views form the limits within which legitimate decision making may occur. Therefore, it should be clear that, while I object to the use of history in the reasoning contained in all of the opinions, I do not object, on the interpretivist grounds, to either the resolution proffered by the majority or that preferred by the dissenters.

The Court in *Marsh* adheres effectively to the Story view, a view that permits the hiring of a Christian chaplain so long as that chaplain does not prefer one Christian sect over another. The Court's decison is, therefore, legitimate in terms of originalist analysis. However, it must be conceded that *Marsh* makes for a strange fit with the Court's prior decisions. For the most part, the Court's decisions have been consistent with the Madisonian and not the Story view. Therefore, the Court's ambivalence, in rejecting the Madisonian view and favoring the Story view in *Marsh,* sends a confusing message to the bar; it is unclear what view is or ought to be controlling in a given case.

Nevertheless, there is a way of placing the *Marsh* decision in a larger picture that will be helpful in offering a greater sense of certainty about which view, Madisonian or Storyite, ought to apply in a subsequent case. In *Marsh*, the majority doubtless was concerned about the ramifications

---

68. *Id.*

of rejecting a practice that had been ongoing for nearly two hundred years at both federal and state levels. Upending such a practice, particularly in the religious context, would create a significant public stir and might jeopardize the Court's authority in other related areas. Had the majority decided against the chaplaincy practice, they might have played into the hands of those who favor limiting the Court's jurisdiction or amending the Constitution. These opponents of the Court's decision in *Engel* and other cases no doubt would have once again raised a hue and cry against the Court. Mindful of how close those opponents had come previously in their efforts to meddle with the Court's jurisdiction,[69] the majority in *Marsh* well may have believed that they were protecting the prerogative of the Court, without yielding entirely to the Story view. Such a position is borne out, in some measure, in the Court's subsequent decision in the *Jaffree* case, in which the Court once again effectively opted for the Madisonian rather than the Story view.

The Court may have been signalling that practices with definite historical roots will be viewed favorably, even though they are consistent with the Story view, which is otherwise largely in disrepute in terms of the Court's contemporary case law. In other words, while the Court normally will apply tests that are essentially consistent with the Madisonian view when dealing with an issue that lacks significant historical roots, it will nevertheless permit practices with historical roots in the Story era to persist even though they are inconsistent with the Madisonian view. Additionally, the Court may be evidencing a trend toward deferring to state legislative determinations in cases like *Marsh.*

I sympathize with the Court as a prudential matter. I believe I understand what Chief Justice Burger is implying when he notes that "the unbroken practice for two centuries in the national Congress and for more than a century in Nebraska and in many other states gives abundant assurance that there is no real threat 'while this Court sits.'"[70] The chief justice seems to be implying that the more than two hundred years of history behind the chaplaincy practice not only support its perpetuation as a matter of constitutional law, but also indicate that the fears raised by the dissenters to the practices have never materialized despite the long history of the practice. If in the future, however, offensive consequences do begin to occur, the Court might intervene under its more commonly utilized standards, which are in large measure based on a rea-

---

69. *See* Chapter 12, *infra,* for a discussion as to how close Senator Helms recently came to obtaining requisite support for his legislative proposal that would have limited the jurisdiction of the Supreme Court to hear a number of constitutional issues, including prayer issues arising in the public schools.

70. *Id.* at 3338.

soning similar to that espoused by Madison. The cost of intervention in *Marsh,* on the ground that the chaplaincy practice violated the nonpreference and prohibition of prescribed modes-of-worship principles first articulated by Madison, might have been high. Such costs should not be incurred in cases where the objectionable practice has a long and relatively tolerant history. Thus, it seems that, without repudiating the Madisonian view, the Court in *Marsh* upheld the chaplaincy practice on prudential grounds. Such a decision was acceptable from an originalist perspective, because it was in keeping with the Story view, and it can be melded into existing precedent, which largely recognizes that the Madisonian view ought to prevail.

12

Legislative Proposals and Congressional Activity: A Study in Political Persistence

There have been a number of efforts to amend the First Amendment as it relates to religious liberty generally and the prayer issue specifically. The first effort to amend the Constitution occurred during the early 1870s.

The public-school movement had achieved notable success by the middle of the nineteenth century. Americans, through the efforts of Horace Mann and others, were beginning to act upon the belief that government should make available some public education for all children. As belief in accessible public education gained increasing popular support, it was clear that the issue of religion and religious exercise in the public schools would be raised. Horace Mann recognized this problem and responded by instituting a form of essentially nonsectarian religion in public schools.[1] The nonsectarian religion practiced in schools in America throughout the mid-to-latter nineteenth century basically followed the Story model, permitting the exercise of a watered-down, nonsectarian or nondenominational Protestantism. For example, he permitted reading from the King James version of the Bible and the giving of nondenominational (essentially Protestant), Christian prayers.[2]

This practice of reading the King James version of the Bible and the promotion of modes of worship of a general Protestant nature in

---

1. *See* Laubach, SCHOOL PRAYER, 26 (1969).
2. *Id.* at 26–7.

many of the public schools caused political turmoil, particularly between Catholics and mainline Protestant sects, which generally constituted the majority in most communities. This political upheaval even led to outbreaks of violence on occasion during the nineteenth century.[3]

Ultimately, Catholics responded to the nondenominational Protestantism practiced in American public schools by forming their own parochial schools. Having formed their own school system, Catholics began to seek financial support from the government for their educational efforts.

Largely in response to this movement, President Ulysses S. Grant indicated his strong support for a constitutional amendment that would prohibit the expenditure of public funds for aid to any religious sects.[4]

---

3. Thomas Askew and Peter Spellman have noted that during the nineteenth century

Some Catholic beliefs and customs in predominantly and dogmatically Protestant surroundings aroused fears in native groups. Anti-Catholicism in America was never purely religious, for social and economic factors aggravated suspicion of the stranger. Some of the recent arrivals [Catholics came to America in ever-increasing numbers during the mid-nineteenth century]...crowded the labor market.... Salacious stories, which followed a formula that has never completely died in Protestant American folklore, led to the burning of the Charlestown, Massachusetts, convent in 1836. The chartering of Saint Louis University by the State of Missouri aroused hysterical fears of Roman domination in the West. Catholic churches were burned in Philadelphia in 1844; in New York a show of armed defense by Catholic congregations frightened off would-be torchers. Opposition to Roman Catholicism gave rise to the Native American party in 1837, an organization that sought to curtail immigration.

Askew and Spellman, THE CHURCHES AND THE AMERICAN EXPERIENCE, 113 (1984).

4. Speaking on 29 September 1875, in Des Moines, Iowa, Grant stated that

Let us all labor to add all needful guarantees for the security of free thought, free speech, a free press, pure morals, unfettered religious sentiments, and of equal rights and privileges to all men, irrespective of nationality, color, or religion. Encourage free schools, and resolve that not one dollar unappropriated for their support shall be appropriated to the support of any sectarian schools. Resolve that neither the state nor nation, nor both combined, shall support institutions of learning other than those sufficient to afford every child growing up in the land of the opportunity of a good common-school education, unmixed with sectarian, pagan, or atheistical dogmas. Leave the matter of religion to the family altar, the church, and the private school, supported entirely

His proposed amendment would also have forbade the teaching in public schools of any "religious, atheistic, or pagan tenets."[5]

Acting upon President Grant's suggestion, Representative James G. Blaine of Maine introduced an amendment to the religion clauses of the First Amendment. As introduced in the House of Representatives, the Blaine Amendment provided that:

> No state shall make any law respecting an establishment of religion or prohibiting the free exercise thereof; and no money raised by taxation in any state for the support of public schools, or derived from any public fund therefore, nor any public lands devoted thereto, shall ever be under the control of any religious sect, nor shall any money so raised or lands so devoted be divided between religious sects or denominations.[6]

The Blaine Amendment passed the House of Representatives on 4 August 1876, by a vote of 180 to 7 with 98 not voting, but bogged down in the Senate where the Judiciary Committee sought to clarify aspects of

---

by private contributions. Keep the church and the state forever separate.
As cited in THE CATHOLIC WORLD, Vol. XXII, No. 130, January 1876, at 434–35. The CATHOLIC WORLD article is interesting in that its author agrees with President Grant's philosophy, while emphasizing that

> Now, what is it that Catholics complain of, except that the state has supported, and does support, "institutions of learning" mixed "with sectarian, pagan, and atheistical dogmas"?... There is no doubt about this fact. Protestants insist upon having the Bible read in the public schools, lest they become irreligious. Catholics maintain that the version used is garbled, and that, even if it were not, no one has a right to teach it except those who have compiled it, and are today the only responsible witnesses to its true meaning. The Jews maintain that the New Testament part of it is not true. Infidels deny it altogether. What right has any school board, or any other human institution, to decide this controversy?

Id. at 438.

5. *Id.* However, Professor Morgan agreed with the author of the *Catholic World* article, in concluding, "While nineteenth-century Americans [such as President Grant] talked and generally practiced a tough separationism where specific expenditures of public funds were involved, they tended to accept a sort of low-key, watered-down Protestantism as a public religion.... Many legislators who supported state 'Blaine amendments' advocated, apparently without sense of contradiction, the perpetuation of their public religion." Morgan, THE SUPREME COURT AND RELIGION, 50 (1972).

6. This provision is cited and discussed in Laubach, *supra* note 1, at 30–1.

the House version of the amendment. One such clarification sought by the senators would have provided a limitation that "This article shall not be construed to prohibit a reading of the Bible in any school or institution; and it shall not have the effect to impair rights of property already vested."[7]

When the modified version of the Blaine Amendment reached the floor of the Senate, the vote was 28 to 16 for the amendment with 27 not voting. With such a large number of abstentions, the vote was short of the two-thirds majority required for passage. Thereafter, the Blaine Amendment or some variation on that theme was continuously reintroduced in Congress between 1870 and 1888. After repeated failures to gain necessary support for such an amendment, the legislative effort to prevent the government from aiding sectarian, private education by constitutional amendment ultimately died.

The experience related to the Blaine Amendment illustrated two points of some significance: (1) at least during the latter part of the nineteenth century, supporters of an amendment like that introduced by Representative Blaine felt that such an amendment was, at a minimum, necessary to clarify that the government was prohibited from offering financial support to religious sects; and (2) the failure of the Blaine Amendment to pass despite its auspicious beginnings is, as will be shown, reminiscent of contemporary efforts to pass prayer or related amendments—general support is initially fairly strong but begins to dissipate when specific applications or clarifications are discussed.

The Blaine Amendment died late in the nineteenth century, but the strict-separationist view purportedly inhering in the amendment was revived judicially in the mid-twentieth century with the opinions of Justices Hugo L. Black and Wiley B. Rutledge in *Everson*.[8] Since *Everson*, efforts to extend aid to parochial schools have been largely stymied. While limited educational aid, as opposed to direct aid to a religious school for religious purposes, has been deemed permissible on occasion by the Court,[9] the principle of no aid to church-related schools, which President Grant and a large majority of those voting in the House and Senate in the 1870s believed could only be enforced by amending the First

---

7. *Id.*

8. *See* Chapter 6, *supra*, for a discussion of the *Everson* case.

9. *See, e.g.,* Mueller v. Allen, 463 U.S. 388 (1983), in which the Court sustained a tax deduction for certain educational expenses, even though the great majority of the beneficiaries were parents of children attending sectarian schools, and Witters v. Washington Department of Services for the Blind, 106 S. Ct. 748 (1986), in which the Supreme Court reversed the Washington supreme court in

Amendment, has been largely decreed judicially to be a part of the First Amendment.

By the 1960s, with their decision in *Engel,* in which the Court held that the recitation of state-composed prayer in the public schools violated the Establishment Clause of the First Amendment, the Supreme Court, in dicta, extended the rationale of strict separation of church and state inhering in the decisions against aid to parochial schools, which had been accepted largely by the Protestant majority, and applied it to other school cases involving religious exercises. With its rearticulation of the strict-separationist rationale in *Everson* and its decision in *Engel,* the Court opened the door to another legislative battle. Thus, in the early 1960s, in addition to verbal threats of impeachment directed at members of the Court, the *Engel* decision provoked congressional efforts to alter the First Amendment for the ostensible aim of ensuring the continuation of prayer exercises in the public schools. However, unlike the nineteenth-century effort manifested in the Blaine Amendment, in which proponents of the amendment were trying to amend the Constitution to prohibit all aid to sectarian schools and thereby to enshrine the strict-separationist principle in the Constitution, the more recent effort to amend the Constitution has been based largely on the sentiment that an amendment was necessary to ensure that some religious activity would be permitted in the public sector. Because of *Everson* and its progeny, the Court had stimulated a 180-degree shift from the era of the Blaine Amendment.

The first legislation offered to amend the religion clauses of the First Amendment in response to the *Engel* decision was sponsored by Representative Frank J. Becker of New York. The Becker Amendment was designed to permit the practice of student recitation of a voluntary, state-composed prayer in the public schools, a practice that the Court had held to be unconstitutional in *Engel.* Opposition to the Becker Amendment centered on uneasiness over the prospect of amending the First Amendment. Even Dean Erwin N. Griswold of the Harvard Law School, who had opposed strongly the action of the Court in invalidating the prayer practice in *Engel,* joined the opposition to the Becker Amendment, fearing that the amendment was both premature and ambiguous. Given growing uneasiness with the language of the Becker

---

holding that there was no constitutional barrier that would preclude the State of Washington from extending assistance under a state vocational rehabilitation assistance program to a blind person studying at a sectarian college and seeking to become a pastor, missionary, or youth director. However, *see* Grand Rapids School District v. Ball, 105 S.Ct. 3248 (1985), for another recent case in which the Court refused to uphold aid to sectarian institutions.

proposal, and despite strong initial public support, the amendment failed to garner the votes necessary in Congress for its adoption and submission to the states for their ratification.[10]

Congressional efforts to amend the Constitution to promote school prayer were just beginning, however. On 14 July 1964, in its National Convention, the Republican party adopted a resolution in its platform that supported "a Constitutional amendment permitting those individuals and groups who choose to do so to exercise their religion freely in public places, provided religious exercises are not prepared or prescribed by the state or political subdivision thereof and no person's participation therein is coerced, thus preserving the traditional separation of church and state."[11] The Democrats did not address the prayer issue in their platform in 1964. It is interesting to note that the Republican proposal addressed a number of the objections to the Becker Amendment by precluding the government from composing a prayer and by otherwise including more specific language.

Thereafter, in the Eighty-ninth Congress, Senator Everett Dirksen of Illinois introduced a resolution supporting an amendment that would provide for or permit "the voluntary participation by students or others in prayers."[12] The Supreme Court had just refused to grant certiorari in *Stein v. Oshinsky,*[13] a case in which the Second Circuit Court of Appeals had held that public-school officials were not required to set aside a part of the school day to permit recitation of a prayer by a voluntary student group. Much of the debate in Congress over the Dirksen Amendment focused upon whether the prayer issue had been finally resolved in the Court, based on its denial of certiorari in the *Stein* decision and over the meaning of the general language used in the Dirksen resolution. Since the Court had merely refused to grant certiorari in *Stein,* an act that is traditionally considered to have no precedential weight, it was conceded that many variations of the prayer issue remained open and undecided. There was, in this regard, a general feeling that an amendment to the Bill of Rights should not be passed until it was clear that the Court had rendered its final determination of the issue.

This sentiment has been articulated effectively by Theodore Sky, who stated that he did not

> subscribe to the notion that the Bill of Rights should never be amended. Madison may have hoped that it would be unamendable when he sug-

---

10. See Laubach, *supra* note 1, at 47–75.

11. Cited in *Id.* at 93.

12. Cited in Sky, THE ESTABLISHMENT CLAUSE, THE CONGRESS AND THE SCHOOLS: AN HISTORICAL PERSPECTIVE, 52 VA. L. REV. 1395, 1398–99 (1966).

13. 348 F.2d 999 (2d Cir. 1965), *cert. denied,* 382 U.S. 957 (1965).

gested that it would provide an "impenetrable bulwark," but the Constitution provides otherwise. I do submit that the process of constitutional amendment, at all times a matter of last resort, should be applied with even greater caution where the amendment is to qualify the reach of the Bill of Rights. At the very least, the issue which the amendment purports to resolve should be finally and fully adjudicated by the Supreme Court before the amendment is submitted. To use the amendment process as a basis for anticipating decisions or protesting interests in advance of adjudication is to take too lightly the overriding need to preserve intact the "magnificent generalities" of the Bill.[14]

Also, this sentiment has been expressed repeatedly during the course of recent debates over efforts to amend the Constitution to provide for voluntary prayer in the public schools or to provide for a moment of silent reflection or prayer.

While efforts to amend the Constitution to provide for the recitation of voluntary prayers in the public schools continued unabated throughout the latter part of the 1960s and through the 1970s, it was not until the eve of the presidential elections in 1980 that the intensity of the activity on the part of proponents of such efforts reached a high pitch once again. In 1979, for example, Senator Jesse Helms of North Carolina introduced a rider to the legislation that, if passed, would have barred the Supreme Court from reviewing any case that concerned voluntary prayers in the public schools. While unsuccessful in 1979, Senator Helms's rider was followed, nevertheless, by the introduction of additional legislation that would have limited the Supreme Court's jurisdiction on the prayer issue. Extensive hearings were held before the Subcommittee on the Constitution of the Judiciary Committee of the Senate during the First Session of the Ninety-seventh Congress on 20 and 21 May and 22 June 1981.[15]

Arguments were raised both favoring and opposing the legislation during the course of those hearings. Those arguments necessarily responded to two separate but related issues: (1) whether Article III of the Constitution permits Congress to except or otherwise limit the Court's jurisdiction over certain issues, such as prayer in the public schools; and (2) whether, if permissible, such legislation as drafted was prudent as a policy matter.

---

14. Sky, *supra* note 12, at 1463.

15. *See* Hearings Before the Subcommittee on the Constitution on the Committee of the Judiciary, United States Senate, 97th Congress, First Session, *Constitutional Restraints Upon the Judiciary* (1981).

Former Supreme Court Justice Owen Roberts evidently was convinced that Congress had the power to limit or remove the jurisdiction of the federal courts, including the Supreme Court, by virtue of the power vested in Congress by the Exceptions Clause of Article III, Section 2. His apprehension over the potential for abuse of the exceptions power by Congress caused Roberts to propose an amendment to the Constitution that would have taken the exceptions power away from Congress, vesting it solely in the Supreme Court.[16] Roberts's amendment was not adopted by Congress and Article III continues to include the exceptions language.

Those who argued for the constitutionality of such legislation relied most heavily upon the argument that the Exceptions Clause permits Congress to limit the appellate jurisdiction of the Supreme Court over specific issues such as public prayer. The pertinent part of the clause provides that:

> In all cases affecting ambassadors, other public ministers and consuls, and those in which a state shall be a party, the Supreme Court shall have original jurisdiction. In all other cases before mentioned, the Supreme Court shall have appellate jurisdiction, both as to law and fact, with such exceptions, and under such regulations as the Congress shall make.[17]

In his testimony before the Subcommittee on the Constitution, Professor Martin H. Redish referred to this language in concluding that, "if Congress truly desires, it can do almost anything it wants to the jurisdiction of the lower federal courts or to the appellate jurisdiction of the Supreme Court."[18] Professor William Van Alstyne agreed, noting that

> The [exceptions] clause does not know any interior restrictions. The emphasis is appropriately on the adjective "such." That is to say, such exceptions as Congress shall make.

---

16. Justice Roberts's proposed amendment stated, "The Supreme Court shall have appellate jurisdiction in all cases arising under the Constitution of the United States, both as to law and fact, with such exceptions and under such regulations as it shall make." Proceedings of House of Delegates of the American Bar Association, 6–9 September 1948, cited in Comment, *Restoring School Prayer by Eliminating Judicial Review: An Examination of Congressional Power to Limit Federal Court Jurisdiction*, 60 N.C. L. REV. 831, 836, n. 40 (1982).

17. U.S. Const., Art. III, § 2.

18. Prepared Statement of Prof. Martin H. Redish. Hearings on *Constitutional Restraints Upon the Judiciary, supra* note 15, at 89.

It does not, as some few clauses do, build into it explicit limitations directed to appropriate uses to which it may be put.

Like the commerce power, it may be put to promiscuous and undesirable uses, but the power is there to make those damaging uses.[19]

Professor Charles E. Rice agreed with Van Alstyne and Redish on the issue of whether or not Congress had the constitutional power to limit the jurisdiction of the Supreme Court over issues such as abortion, school prayer, and busing. Professor Rice stressed that

> If it be contended that the Exceptions Clause cannot be used to deprive the Supreme Court of appellate jurisdiction in cases involving fundamental constitutional rights, it must be replied that such a limitation can be found neither in the language of the clause nor in its explications by the Supreme Court. Indeed, the Supreme Court's conclusions, prior to 1891, that there was no general right of appeal to that Court in criminal cases surely involved the denial of the right to appeal in cases involving constitutional rights. For what constitutional right is more fundamental than the Fifth Amendment right not to be deprived of life or liberty without due process of law?[20]

Rice proceeded to argue that the "specious character of the argument that Congress cannot exercise its Exceptions Clause power in cases involving fundamental rights" is clearly shown by a close examination of the school-prayer issue.[21]

Professors Redish, Van Alstyne, and Rice, as well as other commentators who have argued that the sweep of the Exceptions Clause is broad, rely heavily upon historical documentation to support their argument.[22] Illustrative of the many statements made was one of John

---

19. Statement of William Van Alstyne, *Id.* at 99.

20. Prepared statement of Professor Charles E. Rice, *Id.* at 161.

21. *Id.* at 161–63.

22. Professor Van Alstyne summarized those historical materials in concluding that

Beginning with the Constitutional Convention in Virginia and beginning with the utterances of Governor Randolph, who was a party at the Philadelphia Convention, and statements by John Marshall at the ratifying convention, and carrying on through unqualified iterations by the third Chief Justice of the United States, Oliver Ellsworth, and identical utterances by Chief Justice Marshall and identical utterances by his successor, Roger Taney, and identical utterances by his successor, Sam Chase, a Lincoln appointee, and an identical utterance by Chief Justice White right on through the modern Court with people who disagreed within themselves as much as did Justice Rutledge and Frankfurter, 20

Marshall during the Virginia ratification debates? "What is the meaning of the term exceptions? Does it mean an alteration and diminution? Congress is empowered to make exceptions to appellate jurisdiction as to law and fact of the Supreme Court. These exceptions certainly go as far *as the legislature* may think proper for the interest and liberty of the people."[23]

Other witnesses disagreed with the Exceptions Clause analysis of Redish, Rice, and Van Alstyne. For example, echoing a theme that would be taken up by other opponents of efforts to limit the Supreme Court's jurisdiction over specific constitutional issues, Professor Leonard Ratner opened testimony before the Subcommittee on the Constitution by arguing that

> Article III of the Constitution defines the judicial power of the United States, creates the Supreme Court, and identifies the jurisdiction of the Court. The original jurisdiction of the Court (as a court of first instance) is limited to cases affecting ambassadors, public ministers, and consuls or in which a state is a party, and cannot be modified by Congress. The Court, however, is given appellate jurisdiction, both as to law and fact, over all other cases to which the judicial power of the United States extends *"with such exceptions and under such regulations as the Congress shall make"* (emphasis added). The language, though not the holdings, of some earlier Supreme Court cases suggests that the Exceptions and Regulations Clause gives Congress unlimited control over the appellate jurisdiction of the Court, but such an interpretation is not consistent with the constitutional plan, and modern judicial approval of such an interpretation is doubtful. [citations omitted][24]

Ratner concluded his statement by stressing that

> In contrast with its original jurisdiction, the Supreme Court's appellate jurisdiction under the Constitution is an extensive one, arising not only from the presence of federal questions but also from the status or citizenship of the parties, encompassing issues of both law and fact,

---

years ago, there is simply no qualification to the general position that "such exceptions as Congress shall make" means what it says, Mr. Chairman. Whatever exceptions Congress sees fit to make with regard to those cases which might otherwise be adjudicated in the Supreme Court.

Id. at 102. *But see* Clinton, *A Mandatory View of Federal Court Jurisdiction: A Guided Quest for the Original Understanding of Article III,* 132 U. PENN. L. REV. 741 (1984), for a contrary view of the history.

23. Cited in *Id.* (emphasis added).

24. *Id.* at 13.

and extending to cases which originate in state as well as federal courts. Orderly procedures for invoking that jurisdiction and a method of adjusting it to changing social needs and political attitudes are required. It is reasonable to conclude, therefore, that the convention gave Congress authority to specify such orderly procedures and to modify the jurisdiction from time to time in response to prevailing social and political requirements, within the limits imposed by the Court's essential constitutional role. It is not reasonable to conclude that the convention gave Congress the power to destroy that role. Reasonably interpreted, the clause means "with such exceptions and under such regulations as Congress may make, not inconsistent with the essential functions of the Supreme Court under this Constitution."

Congressional legislation that restricts the procedures for obtaining Supreme Court review does not transgress constitutional limitations so long as the Court remains available ultimately to resolve conflicting interpretations of federal law and conflicts between state and federal law. But legislation that precludes Supreme Court review in any case that involves a particular subject, such as school prayer or abortion, is an unconstitutional encroachment on the Court's *essential functions.*[25]

Professor Telford Taylor agreed and added that he knew of nothing in constitutional history that would

support the idea that congressional power over Court jurisdiction was intended as a means by which Congress may foreclose or nullify Supreme Court decisions construing and enforcing constitutional limitation. So applied, the power over jurisdiction would leave the legislative branch bound only by its own interpretation of its own powers, and would move this nation a long way toward the English system of parliamentary supremacy. There may be much to be said for such a system, but if so drastic and revolutionary a change is to be made, it should not be the result of a majority vote in the Congress triggered by strong feelings on particular issues, but rather by the specified and established procedures of Constitutional amendment.[26]

In articulating a similar view, Lloyd N. Cutler, a prominent attorney in Washington, D.C., argued that Article III of the Constitution itself placed a limit upon how much power Congress could exercise under the Exceptions Clause. Cutler emphasized, "Under Article III, there must be a Supreme Court. The Supreme Court, together with whatever lower courts Congress may create, must exercise the full judicial power of the

---

25. *Id.* at 19–20 (emphasis added).
26. *Id.* at 82.

United States. Congress has a large say as to which federal courts exercise this judicial power, but Congress cannot remove any part of this power from all federal courts."[27]

Mr. Cutler and Professors Ratner and Taylor, as well as most other opponents of efforts to limit the Court's jurisdiction over issues like school prayer, asserted that such limitations would render the Court less supreme, would deprive constitutional law of necessary uniformity, and would wreak havoc on our constitutional system.[28] If Congress were permitted to so limit the Court's jurisdiction, the very power or *essential function* of the Supreme Court would be usurped. Such action would constitute a step in the direction of tyranny by the majority.

While, as a prudential matter, these essential functions of the Court ought to be left intact and exercised in a judicious manner, I tend to agree with Senator Orrin G. Hatch's conclusion. Hatch suggested that

> any bill using the Exceptions Clause must be a measured and careful approach. On the other hand, I do not think that there is anything in the history or background of Founding Fathers' statements on precedents that would negate the right of Congress to use that approach, particularly with regard to the lower courts and probably, as most witnesses have indicated, even with regard to the Supreme Court.
>
> Whether, under certain circumstances, it would be wise to do so or to exercise that power is a matter for debate.[29]

However, even if Hatch is wrong about the difficult issue of whether or not Congress has the power under the Exceptions Clause to limit the jurisdiction of the Supreme Court over specific issues, all commentators—opponents and proponents of such measures alike—must concede that the existence of such congressional power is plausible given the language of Article III. The ambiguous nature of the exceptions language in its context in Article III, together with available indicia of intent that might clarify such language, arguably offer sufficient latitude to permit Congress to seek to limit the jurisdiction of the Supreme Court if prudence dictates such a limitation. It is necessary, therefore, to examine whether or not such a limitation is presently warranted as a matter of public policy, in the case of school prayer.

Most commentators, including many who agreed reluctantly that Congress did have the power to limit the Court's jurisdiction, agreed in the 1981 hearings that it would be imprudent for Congress to exercise that power. Professor Paul Bator's reaction was typical:

---

27. *Id.* at 140.

28. *See, e.g.,* 28 May 1981, letter of Professor Ratner to Senator Hatch, *Id.* at 21–6, for a further elaboration of these arguments.

29. *Id.* at 225.

[R]esort to the power to make exceptions to the appellate jurisdiction of the United States Supreme Court by making the state courts the courts of last resort in one or more important categories of constitutional litigation is a dubious expedient. The validity of such a measure would be surrounded by serious doubts. Such a measure would in any event be criticized as flying in the face of the spirit of the Constitution; its legitimacy would therefore be extremely vulnerable, as was the proposal of President Roosevelt to "pack" the Supreme Court. And, finally, such a measure would create a host of serious and perhaps intolerable problems in the fair and rational administration of the laws.[30]

In his concluding comments, Professor Van Alstyne aptly summarized the various prudential arguments against existing efforts to limit the Court's jurisdiction:

[V]irtually never, however, has Congress sought to preclude all recourse to the Supreme Court for the purpose of leaving finality of *constitutional* interpretations irreconcilably to the unreviewable determinations of inferior federal courts or to the numerous state supreme courts. The last enacted attempt by Congress to do so, for the purpose of preventing the Supreme Court from adjudicating a case challenging an act of Congress on constitutional grounds, was in 1868. Technically, the attempt failed—because Congress had overlooked an obscure alternative procedure which remained available contrary to Congress's misunderstanding. See, *Ex parte McCardle,* 74 U.S. (7 Wall.) 506 (1869) and compare *Ex parte Yerger,* 75 U.S. (8 Wall.) 85 (1869).

Since that time, no similar attempt has yet found favor with Congress itself. I would, respectfully, urge the Congress not to break with this record of the past one hundred years. I do so, not so much for "the Court's sake," nor even especially for "the nation's sake," but rather, also for the sake of Congress. This Congress is not in the general business of "approving" decisions of the Supreme Court. Least of all do people generally seek to hold *Congress* accountable for the *Court's* interpretations of the Constitution. But an act of Congress effectively disabling the Court from adjudicating any one kind of state (or federal) law, on no better basis than that Congress believes that in respect to that kind of law the Court is "incorrect," virtually declares that such laws Congress does not remove from Supreme Court appellate jurisdiction it must believe to be dealt with "correctly" by the Court. If you are excused in the one instance for diminishing the Supreme Court as a co-equal department because you are of the opinion it has abused

---

30. *Id.* at 567.

"the judicial power," you are not to be excused if, then, you fail in every other instance of alleged "abuse" from acting likewise.

It is not, moreover, merely because such state (or federal) laws that you might seek to insulate from appropriate challenge in the Supreme Court will ironically convey the unmistakable message that this Congress actually *doubts* (rather than believes in) the constitutionality of such laws, that I would urge this committee to support no legislation of this kind. Nor is it merely because, in withdrawing such possibilities of constitutional challenge only from the Supreme Court (or from the inferior federal courts as well), that a chaos of constitutional uncertainty must then be the general result (with eleven federal courts of appeal reaching diverse outcomes on the *identical* constitutional issue raised by *identical* laws, or fifty state supreme courts holding, in identical cases, that in State #1, the Fourteenth Amendment is violated, in State #3 it is not violated, in State #27 it is violated, though of course it is all the same Fourteenth Amendment to the same national Constitution). Without doubt it is true that selective uses of the Exceptions Clause may belittle the Constitution by yielding nonuniform and irreconcilable "interpretations" which, like bus transfers, change color as one crosses a state line. And without doubt there are immense practical reasons (considerations with respect to the *interpretation* of federal statutes quite apart from their constitutionality that are virtually insurmountable) for not proceeding in this fashion. But the best reason here, in Congress, is that this Congress ought itself not welcome a fragmented Constitution of the United States of no national supremacy at all, but merely a ludicrous document of vagrant "meanings" unreviewably determined by state courts, many of which are subject to political control and possessed of no particular institutional independence. When, therefore, decisions by the Supreme Court have been popularly perceived as so far "wrong" or intolerable that the constitutional constructions they have represented would not be tolerated (even as in the *Dred Scott* [the slavery] case), Congress had sought their correction by the means contemplated properly by the Constitution itself—by an amendment which, ratified, then yields a single and uniform constitutional rule for the nation, just as the constitutional rule it replaced. And at the margin, this Congress (with the president) significantly also influences the interpretations reached by the Supreme Court through its participation in the appointment process where, to be sure, the "interpretative" predilections of nominees are fair game for your votes. But here, too, the change in the subsequent interpretation of the Constitution by the Supreme Court itself, reflecting the influence of the appointment process itself, is one of a uniform Constitution as thus construed.[31]

_____

31. *Id.* at 133–34.

As Professor Van Alstyne's comments aptly illustrate, the prudential arguments against limiting the Court's jurisdiction are significant.[32] Nevertheless, it must be conceded that the Court should, where possible, also do its part to avoid creating or promoting such crises. If the Court enters into the political fray—ignoring the intent of the framers—it may anticipate rough treatment at the hands of a Congress armed with the

---

32. For his part, Professor Rice did not believe that limiting the Court's jurisdiction in the area of school prayer "would be such a terrible thing." While he acknowledged that some state courts "would strictly follow [existing Supreme Court decisions]," he added that at least there "would be no opportunity for further extensions of its errors by the Court," and concluded that

it may be expected, however, that some state courts would openly disregard the Supreme Court precedents and would decide in favor of school prayer once the prospect of being reversed by the Supreme Court has been removed. But that result would not be such a terrible thing. It must be remembered that we are talking about Supreme Court decisions which, in the judgment of the elected representatives of the people and the president (or of two-thirds of the Congress overriding his veto), would appear so erroneous as to be virtually usurpations. It would be a healthful corrective of those decisions for the people to trust for a time in the state courts upon which the framers of the Constitution primarily relied and to be protected against further excesses in that area on the part of the Court. In the process, the Court might learn a salutary lesson so that future excursions by the Court beyond its proper bounds would be avoided. Finally, because a statute rather than a constitutional amendment is involved, the Court's jurisdiction could readily be restored should the need for it become apparent.

Id. at 163.

While Professor Rice makes some strong arguments, I believe his basic premise—that the Court has strayed inexorably from the framers' intent, regarding the framing and the application of the First Amendment—is ill-founded. As has been shown throughout this book, while the Court has seemingly repudiated the Story view in most instances, it has effectively left the Madisonian view intact in its opinions. Because of this, the Court has continued to render decisions within the limits set by the framers' intent. Clearly, however, if the Court deviates from its present course and commences to decide cases without maintaining fidelity to the framers' intent, Congress would be justified in taking dramatic action, although, like Van Alstyne, I would prefer that the Court use the amendment, as opposed to the more questionable jurisdiction-limiting process. A principled amendment would maintain much needed uniformity and could be drafted along the lines of the Madisonian view, thereby affording matters of individual conscience protection against the tyranny of the majority of the sort that historically existed when the states retained the power to act legislatively in the area of religious liberty without being subject to uniform constitutional restraints.

Exceptions Clause of Article III. Indeed, Senator Helms almost succeeded in his effort in the Senate to eliminate the Court's appellate jurisdiction in the area of school prayer. Helms's court-stripping bill, which was attached as a rider to a debt-ceiling bill, would have limited the jurisdiction of the federal courts on the school-prayer issue and would have effectively permitted state courts, which would be so inclined, to ignore or overrule the Supreme Court's decision in *Engel v. Vitale.*

Senator Helms's proposed rider, together with antiabortion legislation, was resisted by filibuster on the part of a group of senators for over a month.[33] Cloture failed, fifty-three to forty-five, falling seven votes short of the sixty votes needed to end debate. Despite being able to garner a majority of votes in the Senate, Senator Helms's effort was defeated. The closeness of the vote should be a source of concern, if not trepidation, for those who assert that Congress would never be so brash as to limit the Court's jurisdiction. Furthermore, it is clear that similar attempts will occur in the future,[34] and it is conceivable that, if public antipathy toward Supreme Court decisions increases, such an act may become law, thereby creating the very crisis many commentators have refused to believe could ever come to pass.

Having failed to obtain the necessary sixty votes for cloture on the Helms rider, the forces advocating school prayer in the Senate turned their energy to the president's voluntary-prayer amendment. As proposed, President Ronald Reagan's prayer amendment provided that:

> Nothing in this Constitution shall be construed to prohibit individual or group prayer in public schools or other public institutions. No person shall be required by the United States or by any state to participate in prayer.[35]

---

33. *See Washington Post,* "Senate Kills School Prayer for Session," 24 September 1982, at 1, for a short article summarizing congressional activity on Senator Helms's court-stripping rider.

34. *See, e.g.,* S.47, as introduced on 3 January 1985, by Senator Helms. In Helms's own words, his bill would take "advantage of the congressional authority, given explicitly in Article III of the Constitution, to regulate the general jurisdiction of the inferior federal courts and the appellate jurisdiction of the Supreme Court. The bill [S.47] curtails such jurisdiction so that federal courts no longer have the power to hear cases involving voluntary prayer, Bible reading, and religious meetings in the public schools." *Congressional Record,* 99th Cong., 1st Sess., 1985, Vol. 131, No. 1, S.20. In introducing S.47, on 3 January 1985, Senator Helms also stressed his belief that there was strong continuing support in Congress for his effort.

35. Cited in George Will, "Opposing Prefab Prayer," NEWSWEEK, 7 June 1982, Vol. 99, No. 23. at 84.

The president's prayer amendment was introduced in the First Session of the Ninety-eighth Congress, without modifications, on 24 March (legislative day, 21 March) 1983 as S.J. Res. 73, by Senator Strom Thurmond of South Carolina, chairman of the Senate Judiciary Committee, for himself, and Senators Orrin G. Hatch of Utah, Lawton Chiles of Florida, James Abdnor of South Dakota, Don Nickles of Oklahoma, and Helms. While the effect of the proposed amendment was to amend the First Amendment and overrule the *Engel* case, the president's proposal did not do so expressly. The effort, which was clearly intended to skirt a direct confrontation with the First Amendment by merely declaring that nothing in the Constitution "prohibits individual or group prayer in public schools or other public institutions" raises a number of disturbing issues.

If only voluntary prayer is permitted as a constitutional matter and the Court otherwise may interpret the First Amendment in accordance with prior case law, the law becomes part principle and part patchwork. The Court may interpret the Constitution in accordance with whatever principles it might develop (e.g., it could apply the strict-separationist principle) except in a single instance, that of school prayer. Soon, proponents of the prayer amendment might have to seek amendments in other areas, and the Bill of Rights might soon become little more than a miscellany of amendments rather than a repository of principles.

Additionally, unlike the resolution in the 1964 Republican platform, S.J. Res. 73 would have permitted the recitation of governmentally composed prayers, a practice specifically invalidated in the *Engel* decision. State officials would be free to fashion prayers of a strongly denominational nature, and intense political maneuvering would likely ensue as religious groups jockeyed to have their prayers endorsed by the state and recited in the public schools.[36] This facet of S.J. Res. 73, as introduced, prompted Senator John Danforth of Missouri to suggest clarifying the definition of the term voluntary prayer:

> The term voluntary prayer shall not include any prayer composed, prescribed, directed, supervised, or organized by an official or employee of a state or local governmental agency, including public school principals and teachers.[37]

---

36. Dean Paul Bender raised these points in arguing against the president's prayer amendment. *See Voluntary School Prayer Constitutional Amendment: Hearings on S.J. Res. 73 and S.J. Res. 212 Before the Subcommittee on the Constitution of the Senate Committee on the Judiciary,* 98th Cong., 1st Sess. 379 (1983) (Statement of Professor Paul Bender).

37. Cited in NEWSWEEK, *supra* note 35.

Generally, the Danforth distinction seemingly would have constituted an effort to bring the president's proposal into conformity with the principle articulated in the 1964 Republican party platform resolution prohibiting governmentally composed prayers. Also, this arguably would have brought the amendment into conformity with the *Engel* and *Schempp* decisions but would have limited expansion of the strict-separationist rationale to the facts of those cases.

In a further effort to clarify matters, the Danforth proposal also would have prohibited prayers supervised by a teacher or other state employee. This would follow the Court's holding in those cases that have recognized that the role of the teacher in such activities should be limited expressly. The Danforth proposal, therefore, would have supported voluntary, student-initiated prayers (e.g., providing equal access for student religious groups) without lending support to the *Engel* practice of reciting governmentally composed prayers. President Reagan's proposal, however, remained ambiguous. What would constitute a prayer? What would constitute being "required...to participate in prayer"? Would governmental entities be required to permit all "individual or group" requests for prayer? Questions about who would make such decisions and the latitude permitted decisionmakers would be critical.[38] These questions, which are not intended to constitute a complete list of potential problems, merely illustrate that using general language to promote a specific practice of religious exercise raises substantial problems of interpretation. Therefore, even if the amendment passed, problems of interpretation would linger and would have to be resolved by the judiciary.[39]

Finally, on 20 March 1984, the full Senate voted on the president's prayer amendment, with fifty-six senators voting in favor of the amendment and forty-four voting against it. The vote fell eleven votes

---

38. In Professor Walter Dellinger's testimony, he emphasized this problem, noting that "once you remove the only barrier in the Constitution that prevents a prayer from being drafted by government officials—once you remove that by completely carving out of the Constitution all issues relating to prayer in public schools and other public institutions, then whoever is in charge of the premises, whatever level of government has ultimate authority to make determinations about that public institution or public school, then has a constitutional carte blanche to draft and determine whatever the prayer will be." Hearings, *supra* note 36, at 59.

39. *See, e.g., Id.* at 275–83 (THE PRAYER AMENDMENT, Report of the Association of the Bar of the City of New York) for a discussion of the undesirability of the possible interpretations of S.J. Res. 73.

short of the two-thirds majority necessary to send the amendment on to the House and, if passed in the House, to the states for their ratification. However, it should be noted that the amendment only came to the floor after Senator Howard H. Baker of Tennessee, the majority leader of the Senate and a leading supporter of the amendment, and Senator Lowell P. Weicker of Connecticut, a leading opponent of the amendment who had threatened to filibuster, agreed to "permit a vote on [the president's prayer] amendment—and only that one." Despite objections by Senator Alan J. Dixon of Illinois and others who sought to propose amendments to S.J. Res. 73, Senator Baker hoped that senators who were undecided would opt for the president's prayer amendment rather than risk having Congress fail to act affirmatively on the prayer issue before the 1984 elections. Senator Weicker felt he had the votes necessary to defeat the president's amendment, although he may have doubted that he had the votes to defeat an equal-access or silent-reflection proposal. As it turned out, Senator Baker's strategy did not succeed; he was unable to obtain the requisite two-thirds vote for passage of the president's amendment.[40]

While the prayer amendment was criticized largely on the ground that it was ambiguous and might lead to coercive, state-endorsed, religious practice in our public schools, there is a sense in which the president should be commended for his efforts. In supporting the amendment, he invited dialogue and ultimately may have done much to sensitize members of Congress to the many nuances of the prayer issue. As the efforts of many representatives illustrated, support in Congress for legislation favoring equal access for religious groups and moments of silent reflection or prayer may have increased as the debates ensued over the president's amendment. Indeed, President Reagan reacted to the defeat of the prayer amendment by stressing that

> This has been an important debate, revealing the extent to which the freedom of religious speech has been abridged in our nation's public schools. The issue of free religious speech is not dead as a result of this vote. We have suffered a setback, but we have not been defeated. Our struggle will go on. . . I urge the Congress to consider the equal access legislation before both houses so that voluntary student religious groups can meet on public school property on the same terms as other student groups.[41]

---

40. *Senator Dixon Bars Vote on Prayer, Washington Post,* 15 March 1984, at A3.

41. Cited in *Senate Defeats Amendment for Prayer in School, Washington Post,* 15 March 1984, at A1.

The president's suggestion was followed quickly. While future attempts probably will be made to obtain support for a prayer amendment like that proposed by President Reagan, activity on equal-access legislation increased, and the possibility of having a vote prior to recess for elections in the fall of 1984 became a reality. Equal-access legislation now was at the forefront, and its proponents were determined to capitalize on the mood in Congress supporting passage of legislation permitting some religious activity in the public schools.

Congress had been considering equal-access legislation since 17 September 1982, when Senator Mark O. Hatfield of Oregon introduced S.2928, which would have required public secondary schools receiving federal aid to permit equal access to school facilities by students meeting voluntarily for the purpose of religious expression if those schools had a policy of permitting other extracurricular clubs or groups to meet during noninstructional periods. Senator Hatfield's legislation failed to come to the floor for a vote in the Ninety-seventh Congress, in part because it had been introduced late in the session, but further activity took place during the Ninety-eighth Congress.

On 3 February 1983, Senator Jeremiah Denton of Alabama, a member of the Senate Judiciary Committee, introduced S.1059, an equal-access bill that differed slightly from the Hatfield version.[42] After holding hearings on S.1059 on 15 September 1983, the Judiciary Committee reported the legislation out of committee with a favorable vote. Twelve senators voted for the legislation (Senators Strom Thurmond, Paul Laxalt, Orrin G. Hatch, Robert J. Dole, Alan K. Simpson, Charles E. Grassley, Jeremiah Denton, Arlen Specter, Joseph R. Biden, Dennis DeConcini, Howell Heflin, and John P. East) and four voted against it (Senators Charles McC. Mathias, Edward M. Kennedy, Howard M. Metzenbaum, and Max Baucus). Opponents of S.1059 raised a number of objections during the hearings, and two minority views were included in the committee's report.

While the Senate was acting on S.1059, the House of Representatives was also considering H.R. 4996, the Equal Access Act, which had been introduced by Representative Don Bonker of Washington on 1 March 1984. On 28 March 1984, the Subcommittee on Elementary, Secondary, and Vocational Education held a hearing on H.R. 4996. Thereafter, on 4 April 1984, after a mark-up session on the bill, Representative Bonker, Chairman Carl D. Perkins of the House Committee on Education and Labor, Representative William F. Goodling, and

---

42. *See Senate Comm. on the Judiciary, Equal Access Act,* S. Rep. No. 357, 98th Cong., 2d Sess. 1–3 (1984), for the text of Senator Denton's bill.

Representative Rodney Chandler introduced a clean bill, H.R. 5345, which was voted favorably out of the full committee on 5 April 1984, without further amendment, by a vote of thirty to three.

Both bills encountered significant opposition on the floor, although they both were supported by a substantial majority of the members of the Senate and the House. Ultimately, on 15 May 1984, the House rejected H.R. 5345. The House voted 270 to 151 in favor of H.R. 5345, but that proved to be 11 votes short, because the measure was brought up under a short-cut procedural rule that required a two-thirds majority for passage.[43]

Later during the same session of Congress, a modified version of equal-access legislation was passed as a rider to H.R. 1310, the 1984 Math-Science Bill. That legislation, which did not contain some of the more objectionable parts of H.R. 5345 (most notably the requirements that federal education funding would be cut off if schools failed to comply and that schools would have to permit such access during the school day) passed overwhelmingly in the House by a vote of 337 to 77, on 25 July 1984. The Senate had passed the same measure on 27 June 1984, by a vote of 88 to 11. When, on 11 August 1984, President Reagan signed the act into law as Title VIII of Public Law 98–337, "equal access," albeit in a modified form, was written into law.

To understand the version of the Equal Access Act that ultimately was written into law and to anticipate possible challenges to that act in the future, it will be helpful to examine objections raised in the Senate and the House to S.1059 and H.R. 5345.

Of major concern in both the Senate and the House was the maturation issue, the question raised as to the impressionability of school children. For example, in his Minority View to Senate Report analyzing S.1059, Senator Mathias made the following statement:

> One of the major problems with S.1059 is that instead of redrawing the [maturation] line, it would erase it altogether. Six-year-old first-graders and eighteen-year-old high school seniors would be guaranteed an identical right "to engage in voluntary extracurricular activities that include prayer or religious speech." The fallacy of this across-the-board approach is obvious to any parent. Few elementary school students would be able to discern that permission for a particular religious activity in the school differs from official approval of that

---

43. Cited in, *"Bill Mandating 'Equal Access' Defeated in House," Washington Post,* Wed., 16 May 1984, at A5. The article notes that Representatives Bonker and Perkins sought to bring the bill to the floor under rules that prohibit amendment but that also require a two-thirds majority for passage, because the measure might otherwise have been "amended to death." *Id.*

activity. It is likely that any legislation which applies the same standard to kindergarteners and collegians will impermissibly entangle the state with religion.[44]

In his dissenting view to the committee report, Senator Metzenbaum agreed, emphasizing that "the impressionability of high school students and their elementary school counterparts may lead to the perception of school, and consequently state, sponsorship of student religious activity."[45] S.1059 would have applied to public elementary or secondary schools. A significant source of the opposition on grounds of immaturity was satisfied when the Equal Access Act, as finally adopted, was limited to secondary schools. The maturation issue will no doubt be raised on occasion in the courts because the Supreme Court has emphasized its importance, and it does seem to retain vitality.[46]

Other objections were raised in the Senate. Questions were raised regarding the role of the Judiciary and the attorney general in enforcement of the act if passed. For example, Senator Metzenbaum noted that, with or without a statute, the courts will have to decide numerous issues (e.g., what constitutes a voluntary extracurricular activity), and he added that "religious activities in state-run schools would enjoy the protection of the United States attorney general, and it is not hard to conclude that the existence of such a strong power might provoke misjudgment by school officials where close questions have to be decided."[47] While the Court will have to engage in some interpretation of the act, objections regarding the role of the attorney general were resolved in the Equal Access Act, when the entire section dealing with "action by the attorney general" was deleted.

In a related sense, opponents argued that passage of the Equal Access Act was premature because the Court had only begun "to chart the frontier between associational rights and the establishment prohibition," adding that "unless there is a compelling reason for immediate congressional action we should stay our hand to give the courts more of an opportunity to articulate the guiding principles and to apply them to particular cases."[48] While I have argued elsewhere that such concerns over the premature nature of legislation in the form of an amendment

---

44. Committee Report, *supra* note 42, at 43.
45. *Id.* at 48.
46. *See, e.g.,* the discussion of this issue as developed in the *Widmar* and *Bender* cases discussed in Chapter 10. In particular, however, *see* Justice Powell's dissent, in which he indicates that the distinction between high school and college-age students should not be too dramatic.
47. Cited in Committee Report, *supra* note 42, at 45.
48. *Id.* at 43–4.

are critical,[49] in the case of simple legislation (as opposed to efforts to amend the Constitution), Congress should take an active role in this area. Congress and other legislative bodies, through their hearings process, can take testimony regarding issues such as psychological maturity and the role of public education in accommodating religious exercise (two issues that are often central to school-prayer cases), and should be willing to enter the fray. When Congress does so, it should be concerned with issues raised relative to the constitutionality of their acts, as the hearings on the various prayer or religious exercise issues indicate they are. That concern should not, however, always translate into inactivity. Indeed, given the high costs associated with litigating a case in the judicial system[50] and the difficulty of finding the right case to raise, Congress should act. To fail to act often translates into deference to those who espouse a strict-separationist viewpoint. In this light, it is not surprising that opponents of equal access in the Senate and House alike concluded, "It is unconstitutional and simply inappropriate to allow religious practices to *invade* the public classroom. There are various appropriate places for supervised religious expression, including the home, the church, the synagogue, the mosque and the temple; but the public school is not one of them."[51]

---

49. *See infra* at 288, for a discussion of S.J. Res. 2, the proposed amendment to provide for a moment of silent reflection or prayer in the public schools.

50. In his dissenting view, Senator Metzenbaum argued that "a fundamental flaw of S.1059 is that it seeks to provide a sweeping legislative solution to a problem which has been successfully handled by the courts on a case-by-case basis." Committee Report, *supra* note 42, at 46. Such a view simply fails to take into account the high transaction costs involved in bringing a lawsuit, particularly in areas where the Court engages in case-by-case or *ad hoc* analysis. Every lawsuit of this nature requires the expenditure of vast sums of money—on the part of the parties and on the part of the public which must fund the operation of the court system—and energy. Considering the high cost of litigation, deciding such issues on a case-by-case basis makes it very difficult for individuals to vindicate their rights. In effect, therefore, Metzenbaum's argument may be but another veiled effort to further his strict-separationist bias by making religious exercise in the public sector a costly commodity.

51. *House Comm. on Education and Labor Equal Access Act,* H.R. Rep. No. 710, 98th Cong., 2d Sess. 13 (1984) (dissenting views of Congressman Gary Ackerman, Congresswoman Sala Burton, Congressman William Ford, and Congressman Paul Simon on H.R. 5345) (emphasis added). *See also* Senator Metzenbaum's dissenting view, *supra* note 42, at 47.

Indeed, when reduced to their essence, objections in the Senate turned on the strict-separationist views of opponents. Opponents to equal access raised ancillary objections in the Senate and House, but their basic premise in opposing the notion of permitting any organized religious activity in the public schools was that it would violate strict-separationist principles. Perhaps the dissenters to H.R. 5345 in the House Committee on Education and Labor said it best when they stressed, "Under the Constitution which has carefully guided our Nation for nearly two centuries, there has been a careful delineation between the role of our schoolroom and the purpose of our religious institutions. Schools provide the environment for intellectual pursuits, while religious institutions provide for spiritual awakening."[52] Aside from obvious questions regarding whether or not the intellectual and spiritual dimensions can be so deftly separated, this statement of the House dissenters belies some prejudice against religious exercise or matters of conscience. The second prong of the *Lemon* test, which is generally applied in cases to help determine whether or not the Establishment Clause has been violated, provides that governmental action with regard to religion or religious exercise should neither advance nor inhibit religion. The dissenters' attitude (that religious exercise must be purged from the secular, "intellectual" world) certainly inhibits individual religious exercise, particularly given the expanding and consequently pervasive nature of the public sector. That attitude also conveys a message to impressionable students—the message that schools, the repository of learning and education, must not be fettered by religion or matters of conscience. The Madisonian view, with its accommodation of religious exercise and opposition to state endorsement or preference for particular modes of worship, takes a balanced approach, a very viable approach, and maximizes religious liberty. The dissenters' strict-separationist view does not.

Even though their basic premise may have been questionable, the dissenters in the House did raise some helpful arguments. During subcommittee mark-up of the bill, Ackerman unsuccessfully offered an amendment that would have prohibited "discrimination against a religious group based on the number of individuals who belonged to the group."[53] Fortunately, by the time the Equal Access Act passed, Section 802(d) (5) had been added, providing, "Nothing in this title shall be construed to authorize the United States or any state or political subdi-

---

52. House Report, *supra* note 51, at 13.
53. *Id.* at 16–17. Representative Ackerman's amendment was defeated by a vote of eight for and ten against.

vision thereof to limit the rights of groups of students which are not of a specified numerical size." Minority groups and individuals were thereby protected, as suggested by the House dissenters.

Representative Ackerman also offered an amendment that would have denied "leaders and agents of religious organizations access to school facilities for religious activities."[54] Again, while this amendment was defeated in the House committee, it was subsequently incorporated in § 802(c) (5) that provides, "Schools may be deemed to offer a fair opportunity to students who wish to conduct a meeting within its limited open forum if such school uniformly provides that nonschool persons may not direct, conduct, control, or regularly attend activities of student groups."

The House dissenters also objected to the nature of the remedy provided in H.R. 5345. They noted that

> Any group that asserts that it represents a religious sect may claim the privileges extended by this act. To deny admittance to any—even for good cause in the best judgment of the school principal—would subject the entire school district to a cut-off of federal education dollars. Additionally, the entire school district would suffer the penalty even if only one school was in technical violation of the law.[55]

Again, as finally adopted, the Equal Access Act addressed this problem. The remedy was changed. Section 802(e) of the act, as finally adopted, was added. It provides that, "notwithstanding the availability of any other remedy under the Constitution or the laws of the United States, nothing in this title shall be construed to authorize the United States to deny or withhold federal financial assistance to any school." Thus, while aggrieved students, who are not afforded equal access, may sue under the First and Fourteenth Amendments or under 42 U.S.C. § 1983 for a violation of their free-exercise rights, they may not seek relief in the form of a withholding of federal financial assistance.

Despite all of the efforts to accommodate the specific concerns of the dissenters, many of them clung tenaciously to their opposition, revealing that their primary opposition had little to do with specific problems with the act. Rather, as pointed out previously, they simply opposed any accommodation of religious exercise in the public sector, believing as they did that, when a conflict arises between the Free Exercise Clause and the Establishment Clause, the Establishment Clause always should predominate. As has been shown in the opening chapters of this book,

---

54. *Id.* at 14.
55. *Id.* at 16.

such a view is largely a twentieth-century construct propagated in part to limit the religious rights and to separate the secular and spiritual spheres.

While some of the dissenters should be chided for their restrictive views regarding the importance of matters of conscience, they ought to be commended for the constructive suggestions they made during the course of the debates in committee and on the floor. The Equal Access Act, as ultimately adopted, was a better act in many respects due to the contributions of the dissenters.

Some issues have already arisen regarding the application of the Equal Access Act.[56] For example, shortly after the act was passed, a dispute arose in Boulder, Colorado. One high school student requested classroom space for a student religious group. While the principal was considering that student's request, another student came forward to protest the idea, complaining about potential evangelizing on campus. Students on both sides began to circulate petitions supporting their respective positions, and the dispute overflowed into the public at large when the issue was placed on the school board's agenda. The result was chronicled in the *Washington Post:*

> The board unanimously adopted a policy that classrooms will not be available for any student group unless it is "curriculum-related, school-sponsored."
>
> The key phrase, "curriculum-related," was left undefined. But lawyer Caplan said it probably would mean that the Spanish Club gets a classroom and the Ski Club does not. No religious or political student group will be curriculum-related, he said, so all will be banned.
>
> In essence, Boulder turned the equal access law into an equal non-access policy. Caplan said there was really not much choice.
>
> "It is a very, very broad law," he told board members. "You either let everybody in, or you keep everybody out."[57]

In a similar view, some "final thoughts" relative to the impact of the Equal Access Act were offered in an article appearing in *School Board News:*

> School Boards should look at the Equal Access Act as a requirement of fair treatment of all students with no discrimination against

---

56. *See, e.g.,* Remes, *"Equal Access Act, 'Humanism' Ban Extend an Invitation to Litigation,"* NAT'L. L. J., 24 June 1985, at 16.

57. *Boulder's Equal-Access Split, Washington Post,* 19 December 1984, at A3.

any group of students on the basis of the content of the speech at their meetings.

Controversial student groups might seek the right to hold meetings on school property. Local boards are well advised to inform parents *now* of their equal access policies and of the fact that the authorization of the use of school property does not indicate that the board approves of or advocates the matters which are discussed at the meetings.

While the genuinely equal nature of the act may cause isolated problems in application on occasion, problems of application should hardly be considered to be intractable. Numerous publications have dealt with potential difficulties in a straightforward manner.[58]

Philosophical as opposed to practical problems will no doubt linger for a period of time. Indeed, the problem in Boulder is one of philosophy, not one of practicality. Rather than permit students desiring to express themselves in a religious manner on an equal basis with students desiring to express themselves otherwise, the school board opted to permit no expression. While this result is regrettable, it should be recalled that parties have often been slow to adjust to efforts to equalize access in society. The strict separationists, who have long had their way in precluding essentially all religious expression in the schools, will now have to either tolerate it on an equal basis or give up their preferred forms of expression. Similarly, mainline Protestant groups, which once were able to proclaim that their religion was the national religion and could be preferred on that basis, must now afford other groups equal access. Despite the reaction in Boulder, it can be anticipated that in the future the moderate, libertarian nature of equal access will be accepted as fears dissipate.

Nevertheless, there is one sense in which the Boulder dispute depicts a potential problem of significant magnitude. Will some religious groups use their new-found freedom to coerce or pressure those who do not belong to their group? I am reminded of an incident that occurred when I shared the podium with a minister at a rally for religious liberty. Before the rally, I was talking with him and took the opportunity to extol the virtues of the Madisonian view of nonpreference. He responded that he felt that he, as a member of the religious right, saw a future in which he, or his group, would hold the reins of power, and he would then permit secular humanists to believe whatever they wanted to believe; however,

---

58. *See, e.g., The Equal Access Act: Implications for Secondary School Policies*, a pamphlet prepared by the Christian Legal Society in Oak Park, Illinois, for an effective response to the most commonly asked questions relative to the application of the Equal Access Act.

he would prohibit them from acting on those beliefs. In my opinion, his position is as reprehensible as the position held by many proponents of strict separation who have decided as a personal matter that religious exercise is meaningless (and perhaps even an evil) and have sought to use their power to purge the public sector of everything religious. Both the minister and the strict separationists are wrong, for precisely the unhealthy reason that the Equal Access Act seeks to cure—they want their views to be preferred or endorsed by the powers of the state.

Furthermore, it is clear that the constitutional remedy expressed in the Equal Access Act is available to protect against excesses on both sides by mandating equality and nonpreference. The First and Fourteenth Amendments, as well as 20 U.S.C. § 1983, remain viable as means to remedy excesses, and the use of them ought to be encouraged to assure that equality of access is maintained once access is granted.

After the Equal Access Act passed into law, support in Congress for an amendment to permit silent reflection or prayer in the public schools grew. This support was strengthened when the Supreme Court found an Alabama statute providing for a voluntary moment of silent meditation or prayer to be unconstitutional in the *Jaffree* case.[59]

On 3 January 1985, Senator Hatch (for himself and Senator DeConcini) introduced S.J. Res. 2, a joint resolution proposing an amendment to the Constitution of the United States permitting voluntary silent prayer or reflection. S.J. Res. 2 provided in pertinent part as follows:

> Nothing in this Constitution shall be construed to prohibit individual or group silent prayer or reflection in public schools. Neither the United States nor any state shall require any person to participate in such prayer or reflection, nor shall they encourage any particular form of prayer or reflection.[60]

---

59. *See* Chapter 9, *supra,* for a lengthy discussion of the *Jaffree* case.

60. S.J. Res. 2, 99th Cong., 1st Sess. (1985). S.J. Res. 2 is the successor to S.J. Res. 212, as introduced in the Second Session of the Ninety-eighth Congress. Indeed, there was only a single variation in substantive language between S.J. Res. 2 and S.J. Res. 212. S.J. Res. 212 provided, "Nothing in this Constitution shall be construed to prohibit individual or group silent prayer or *meditation* in public schools" (emphasis added); whereas, S.J. Res. 2 stated, "Nothing in this Constitution shall be construed to prohibit individual or group silent prayer or *reflection* in public schools" (emphasis added). S.J. Res. 2 merely substituted the word reflection for meditation. In all other substantive respects the resolutions were identical. The change from meditation to reflection was of some signifi-

While S.J. Res. 2 was introduced in January of 1985, meaningful hearings were not held on the resolution until after the Supreme Court's decision in *Jaffree* that was rendered on 4 June 1985. The Senate Judiciary Committee proceeded to consider S.J. Res. 2 on 19 September 1985, although there was some disagreement among senators on the committee as to whether or not there was an agreement on their part to vote on the resolution at that time. Ultimately, the hearings continued without a vote on the nineteenth, but not until the senators had agreed to vote "after reasonable debate next time."[61] The committee met again on 3 October 1985, and after considerable debate, passed S.J. Res. 2 by a vote of twelve to six.[62]

As I noted earlier,[63] in dealing with the *Jaffree* case, most of the justices clearly refrained from holding that legislation providing for a moment of silent reflection, meditation, or prayer would be unconstitutional. Rather, the opinions were limited carefully to the facts of the case, particularly in light of the legislative history of the Alabama statute.[64] A carefully drafted statute providing for such practices probably would be constitutional. Therefore, a constitutional amendment is unnecessary. Until the Court has an opportunity to hold otherwise, an amendment like S.J. Res. 2 is premature.

---

cance, however, because reflection is arguably broader than meditation and, therefore, effectively provides a wider ambit for the expression of matters of conscience. It also clearly includes nonreligious reflection, while a statute providing only for meditation or prayer is arguably limited to two religious forms of reflection. Extensive hearings were held before the Subcommittee on the Constitution of the Committee on the Judiciary of the United States Senate on S.J. Res. 212. *See* Hearings on S.J. Res. 73 (the president's prayer amendment) and S.J. Res. 212, *supra* note 36.

61. *See* transcript of Proceedings, United States Senate, Committee on the Judiciary, Washington, D.C., 19 September 1985, at 69.

62. Manuscript of Proceedings, United States Senate, Committee on the Judiciary, Washington, D.C., 3 October 1985, at 50.

63. *See* Chapter 9, *supra,* for a discussion of the policy arguments favoring such a practice.

64. None of the opinions precluded the possibility of finding legislation permitting a moment of silent reflection or prayer (or meditation or prayer) to be constitutional, if it has a secular legislative purpose. Despite the chief justice's argument to the contrary in his dissent, the majority in *Jaffree* held that there was no secular purpose whatsoever offered for the Alabama statute.

S.J. Res. 2 should have been put in the standard legislative form of a simple bill. Such legislation likely would receive as much support in the Senate and House as an amendment like S.J. Res. 2 and would not require a two-thirds majority vote in Congress and ratification by three-fourths of the state legislatures as would an amendment. Absent procedural machinations, simple legislation would require only a majority vote in both houses.

One cannot help but wonder why S.J. Res. 2 was proposed as an amendment given the comparative ease with which standard legislation could have been adopted. Moreover, the strong possibility that well-crafted legislation[65] would pass muster under *Jaffree's* secular-purpose test makes the amendment form even more questionable. Furthermore, even if it is ultimately established that the Court has misconstrued the general principles that ought to infuse the First Amendment with its meaning, opponents of the Court's decisions would do well to offer a general, principled articulation of what they consider to be the appropriate First Amendment values or principles, rather than seeking to amend the Constitution on a piecemeal basis.[66]

Despite their error in selecting the amendment form rather than the preferable simple legislative form, proponents of S.J. Res. 2 generally

---

65. In this context, well-crafted legislation refers to legislation that is drafted carefully and is supported in the record as a means of accommodating reflection or individual silent expressions of conscience, including but not limited to prayer. In the words of Senator Denton, such legislation could be crafted to "permit the freedom of thought" or conscience, as opposed to being promulgated for the sole purpose of endorsing or promoting specified religious activity. *See* Senate Comm. on the Judiciary, 99th Cong., 1st Sess., *Transcript of the Proceeding on S.J. Res. 2,* 39 (Comm. Print. 1985) (statement of Senator Denton) (hereinafter cited as *Transcript on S.J. Res. 2).*

66. Amending the Constitution is a difficult enterprise, particularly given the climate of judicial activism extant in many courts today. Professor William Van Alstyne made such an argument when he noted:

My own sense of the ill-fated Equal Rights Amendment, for instance, is that it became a casualty to the apprehensions of persons who frankly feared not what it said, but how it might be judicially construed. My best impression of efforts in England to secure an equivalent, enforceable Bill of Rights in that country is that the task has been made much more difficult, rather than more likely, because of our experience. I also think a great deal of this is due to the judiciary's own excessive ingenuity and to the misplaced wisdom that has urged upon the Supreme Court a variety of utterly remarkable views respecting the interpretation (and "noninterpretation") of the Constitution.

Van Alstyne, *Interpreting This Constitution: The Unhelpful Contributions of Special Theories of Judicial Review,* 35 U. FLA. L. REV. 209, 212 (1983).

created the type of legislative history that would allow the Court to uphold such legislation against constitutional attacks. Thus, S.J. Res. 2 easily could be changed from its present amendment form to a statute without the necessity of engineering a completely new legislative history, although proponents could certainly buttress existing history with additional hearings designed to focus on the right of conscience, not only as a right but as an important facet of education. With minor exceptions, the current legislative history would support a secular purpose.

During the debates, some proponents of S.J. Res. 2 appeared to be trying to get prayer back in the schools, or otherwise to endorse a particular religious exercise or mode of worship.[67] Although proponents attempted to avoid such appearances,[68] some danger remains that the legislation may be interpreted as preferring prayer over other forms of reflection. A tainted legislative record would be unfortunate, because S.J. Res. 2 merely provides students with an organized moment of silence and reflection for whatever purposes the students may select. However, while there is some evidence on the record of a tainted purpose (e.g., Senator Thurmond's statement), there is substantial evidence of a contrary secular purpose, the promotion of conscience and reflection, on the record. The purpose need not be solely secular to pass constitutional muster.

The proponents of such legislation should strengthen the record for the purpose of establishing clearly a secular purpose for the legislation. The proponents could make such a record by drawing on psychological and educational sources as well as religious or related sources supporting the secular as well as the sectarian value of moments of reflection or prayer. Such a record would acknowledge the important role that matters of conscience should play in the education and lives of young people. Evidence of a separate, secular purpose for promoting matters of conscience in the public schools would show that the legislation is intended to promote freedom of thought or conscience[69] without discriminating

---

67. See, e.g., Chairman Thurmond's statement, Transcript on S.J. Res. 2, supra note 65, at 40–2, in which he refers to the amendment as "a step in the right direction," to get the "right to pray" back in the Constitution. The chairman's purpose for supporting S.J. Res. 2 was clearly religious.

68. See, e.g., discussion between Senators Metzenbaum and Simon, opponents of the resolution, and various proponents (Senators Biden, Denton, DeConcini, and Hatch), in which the proponents clearly sought to clarify that the resolution was not intended to endorse religion or religious exercise. Id. at 55–66.

69. Id., at 39 (statement of Senator Denton).

against religious reflection. With such a record, it is likely that the Court will defer to the legislative findings and conclusions regarding the presence of a secular purpose. Such a record would also help to defray arguments that the primary effect of the legislation was to promote or endorse religion.

S.J. Res. 2, therefore, is premature as an amendment: the best way to promote silent reflection or prayer at this time is to pass simple legislation supported by a strong record. The Supreme Court has shown some willingness recently to expand rights of free exercise of a devotional nature in the public context with its decisions in *Marsh v. Chambers*[70] and *Widmar v. Vincent*.[71] Recently, in *Bender,* on grounds of standing, the Court refused to decide whether high school students should also be afforded equal access, despite the fact that four justices would have reached the merits and would have held that the students should be afforded equal access.[72] Until the Court repudiates this trend toward accommodating individual, voluntary religious exercise in the public sector, a constitutional amendment of the sort contemplated by S.J. Res. 2 is imprudent and premature.

Such an amendment may provoke an unnecessary constitutional confrontation between the Court and Congress. The proposed amendment assumes that the Court opposes the accommodation of rights of exercise in the public sector and may contribute, thereby, to a public perception of judicial antipathy to religious exercise, when recent case law is indicative of a trend otherwise. In fact, of the recent cases, only *Jaffree* is at all susceptible to the interpretation that the Court desires to maintain a strict separation of church and state, and such a reading of *Jaffree* is clearly unjustified. The debate in the Senate over S.J. Res. 2, with repeated efforts by its proponents to provide a secular purpose for the resolution, indicates that the senators and the Court do not differ substantially over matters of principle.[73]

---

70. 463 U.S. 783 (1983). *See* Chapter 11, *supra,* for an analysis of the *Marsh* decision.

71. 454 U.S. 263 (1981). *See* Chapter 10, *supra,* for an analysis of the *Widmar* decision.

72. Bender v. Williamsport Area School Dist., 106 S.Ct. 1326 (1986). It is worthy of note that the Court's decision effectively reinstated the district court decision that permitted the student religious group to meet on campus during the club period. *See* Chapter 10, *supra,* for an analysis of the *Bender* decision.

73. *See* Staff of Senate Comm. on the Judiciary, 99th Cong., 1st Sess., Report on Voluntary Silent Prayer Constitutional Amendment (Comm. Print. 1985).

Nevertheless, if at some future time the Court actually refuses to accommodate in a nonpreferential manner individual, voluntary free exercise of religious expression in the public sector, an amendment may be in order. At that time, however, a general amendment would be preferable to the piecemeal approach contemplated by S.J. Res. 2 with its focus on a single, specific practice. A general, principled amendment could be fashioned, for example, after the Madisonian approach, which would permit an individual to exercise his or her religion in the public sector so long as the government (1) refrains from showing preference for one religion over another; and (2) refuses to endorse or otherwise adopt any mode of worship. Such an amendment would enshrine once again the principled view of the author of the First Amendment. Also, it would be preferable as a matter of policy because it would provide a way to accommodate religious exercise in an increasingly expanding public sector, without placing the imprimatur of the state on any particular religion or religious practice.

Because I have discussed previously the policy arguments favoring and opposing such a reflection or prayer resolution and have applied the Madison and Story positions to such a practice to ascertain its acceptability from the originalist perspective,[74] only a few concluding points are in order. In a general sense, it should be noted that a properly drafted and administered reflection, meditation, or prayer statute, similar substantively but differing in form from S.J. Res. 2, can serve a very salutary purpose. It can provide young children with an organized opportunity to engage in reflection, meditation, or prayer. Moreover, it can help children to understand that matters of *individual* conscience are important and that reflection about individual matters of conscience should be encouraged by the state in a nonpreferential fashion. Care must be taken, however, to ensure that such practices emphasize the importance of individual, inner-directed reflection about moral, ethical, and even religious matters, without trying to direct the content of that reflection. When used properly, such moments can enhance the likelihood that a young person will become an expressive individual.

Silent reflection, meditation, or prayer legislation may also serve an effective educational function, particularly as students are beginning to be exposed to the tools of expression. In a world in which the medium may be the message, the time has come to permit our children to be taught anew that reflection, meditation, or even prayer (for the religiously inclined) is a worthwhile endeavor. Care must be taken in accommodating individual meditation, reflection, or prayer (when the

---

74. *See* Chapter 9, *supra.*

student is religiously inclined) in the public schools. In that regard, application of the Madisonian standard would accommodate free exercise without lending the imprimatur of the state to the practice.

A few points should be re-emphasized in conclusion. First, contemporary efforts to amend the Constitution are generally imprudent (they tend to lend state support to specific religious beliefs and practices) and premature from a policy point of view (they are unnecessary and tend to disparage rather than build upon recent judicial efforts to accommodate individual exercise of rights of conscience). Second, efforts to limit the Court's jurisdiction at a time when the Court is doing much to accommodate religious exercise in an evenhanded way would seem to be highly inappropriate because such efforts are unduly confrontational and because they likely would beget a system lacking in uniformity and consistency, thereby ultimately demeaning rather than fostering individual rights. Finally, even though many contemporary legislative efforts are either premature or imprudent as a matter of policy, congressional activity in the area of religious liberty can have, and to some extent has had, the salutary effect of enhancing individual rights of free exercise without placing the state's imprimatur on particular religions or religious practices. The framers anticipated that Congress would take an active role in the constitutional process. It should do so by refusing to defer to the Judiciary on all issues. Congress is particularly well suited to hold hearings and make assessments regarding issues dealing with the maturity of children and educational policy. In those and related areas, Congress should be active. Furthermore, Congress can and should engage in its own originalist analysis, in assessing whether proposed legislation comports with the original intent of the framers and ratifiers.

Index